The Second Wave

Economy and Society in the Modern South

The Second Wave

Southern Industrialization
from the 1940s to the 1970s

PHILIP SCRANTON, EDITOR

The University of Georgia Press   *Athens & London*

© 2001 by the University of Georgia Press
Athens, Georgia 30602
www.ugapress.org
All rights reserved
Designed by Walton Harris
Set in 10/13 Ehrhardt by G&S Typesetters, Inc.

Most University of Georgia Press titles are
available from popular e-book vendors.

Printed digitally

Library of Congress Cataloging-in-Publication Data

The second wave : southern industrialization from the
1940s to the 1970s / Philip Scranton, editor.
xiv, 310 p. : ill. ; 24 cm.
Includes bibliographical references and index.

1. Industrialization—Southern States—20th century.
2. Industries—Southern States—20th century.
3. Southern States—Economic conditions—20th century.
I. Scranton, Philip. II. Series.

HC107.A13 S43 2001
338.0975'09045—dc21   00-054492

ISBN-13: 978-0-8203-5714-0

British Library Cataloging-in-Publication Data available

Contents

Introduction PHILIP SCRANTON ix

Winning World War II in an Atlanta Suburb: Local Boosters and the Recruitment of Bell Bomber THOMAS A. SCOTT 1

Aircraft Manufacturing in Georgia: A Case Study of Federal Industrial Investment RICHARD S. COMBES 24

The Politics of Exclusion: Wartime Industrialization, Civil Rights Mobilization, and Black Politics in Atlanta, 1942–1946 KAREN FERGUSON 43

Regional Advantage in the New South: The Creation of North Georgia's Carpet Industry, 1945–1970 RANDALL PATTON 81

Dismantling the South's Cotton Mill Village System TOBY MOORE 114

Texas v. the Petrochemical Industry: Contesting Pollution in an Era of Industrial Growth CRAIG E. COLTEN 146

The Forest Is the Future? Industrial Forestry and the Southern Pulp and Paper Complex WILLIAM BOYD 168

Greenfields in the Heart of Dixie: How the American Auto Industry Discovered the South KARSTEN HÜLSEMANN 219

Guns and Butter, North and South: The Federal Contribution to Manufacturing Growth, 1940–1990 GREGORY HOOKS 255

Afterword GAVIN WRIGHT 286

The Contributors 301

Index 303

Introduction

Looking out across Atlanta's current-day skyscraper parks, extensive ex–urban industrial and service sector concentrations, and Los Angeles–style traffic lockups and pollution overloads, it takes a measure of effort to recollect an earlier era in which such assets and liabilities were simply unimaginable. Before the Second World War, Charlotte's financial and commercial engines, the Research Triangle's innovations, the redolent but powerful Gulf Coast petrochemical crescent, and the mass of defense-related or tourist-magnet complexes, which now make the region a force and a destination, existed largely in the fevered imaginations of pre–air conditioning southern boosters. Perhaps not even there, for most advocates' images of southern growth involved fast-forwarding what had already been accomplished: drawing regional and national capital investment toward low-wage, low-value-added production by means of "inducements"—tractable non-union labor, thin taxation, and immunization against social and political change.

By the late 1930s, the South continued to struggle with a deeply troubled industrial economy whose travails hardly had begun with the 1929 Crash. After the mid-1920s, for example, textile production's profitability swooned. A decade later, New Deal initiatives did bring an early version of minimum wage conditions to manufacturing, though enforcement was problematic, along with the legitimation of union organizing. Southern labor's successes, however, remained few, in stark contrast to both CIO and AFL gains in the North's concentrated industrial centers. The Tennessee Valley Authority certainly represented one of the nation's most ambitious public works efforts, yet its hotly contested achievements spurred construction employment (using materials and electrical technologies chiefly produced in other regions) far more than they created manufacturing jobs, at least until the Second World War.

With the depression decade drawing to a close, the South's share of industrial work was roughly half its proportion of America's population, whereas its agricultural sector stood half again as large as the national mean. As is well documented, southern farmers, cash tenants, and sharecroppers had experienced few cheering seasons in the twenty years since the commodity price collapse after World War I. New Deal efforts to reduce farm production, which had overreached conceivable demand and yielded crushing price collapses, proved successful in the long run, but brutal in the short term. The congressional significance of a deeply conservative southern political oligarchy assured state-level implementation of agricultural and other "reforms," which then chiefly benefited politically dominant landowners (and their millmen allies), whilst further impoverishing (and displacing) tenants and croppers, black and white. Driven from rural places to towns, cities, and the North and West, such refugees packed labor markets, kept industrial wages slack, and like far too many even today, endured the contempt of the better-fixed.[1]

Meanwhile, though the cigarette-making giants posted profits, hard times hammered many of the region's textile firms, its mines and lumber camps, and its few steel and metal trades clusters. Workers' resistance against wage cuts and the intensification of labor, though often fierce, proved sporadic and doomed. Moreover, in Albert Hirschman's terms, black southerners often chose exit, extending the Great Migration, for white supremacy denied voice or made it hazardous, while loyalty was demeaning, though "required." Denied the vote, barred from all but menial nonfarm jobs, and expected to be silent and invisible, southern African Americans relied on family, faith, and fortitude to manage their way through this miserable maze.[2]

What, in this dispiriting complex of economy, culture, and politics, did World War II and its aftermath change? More specifically, what shifts in the region's industrial system took shape in the decades after 1940, thus gradually erecting the bridges to its present-day vitality? These questions, given the context sketched above, animated planning for the June 1998 Georgia Institute of Technology conference, sponsored by Tech's Center for the Study of Southern Industrialization (CSSI), at which the essays presented here originated. Although a cluster of economic and policy history studies had outlined what we termed the "Second Wave" transition in southern industrialization, they had chiefly examined aggregate indicators and political initiatives, taking the wide and long view. Given current understandings, for example, that durably reelected congressmen heaped federal investment dollars onto southern terrains or that new-style aggressive boosters broke ranks with the low-wage cadre, securing branch plants of corporations from industries long underrepresented in the South, we sought in-depth case studies of specific districts and sectors during and after World War II that might supplement or modify these judgments.

A literature search suggested that research on southern industrialization was rich and extensive from the antebellum through the 1930s and that numerous policy and planning studies had surfaced in recent years. The era in between, roughly the 1940s through the 1970s, had drawn much less attention, though the cluster of published work, interestingly, arose from inquiries by historians, sociologists, geographers, and others in fields from environmental studies to cultural resource management. The cross-disciplinary response to the conference call satisfyingly yielded proposals that reflected each of these diverse approaches. Authors of the twelve papers selected came to Atlanta from near (four Georgia scholars) and far (California, Washington, British Columbia, Germany) and included four doctoral candidates and a public historian. CSSI director Douglas Flamming and the editor selected nine essays for publication, after revisions in light of their own and commentators' suggestions.

Three of these studies provide contrasting yet complementary views of the Atlanta region's Bell, later Lockheed, aircraft plant whose wartime erection laid the foundations for Cobb County's explosive development. Five others focus on industrial sectors, old and new: cotton textiles, timber and pulp, carpeting, oil refining/petrochemicals, and automobiles. The last, using aggregate data, many of them newly available, reopens the question of the South's perceived advantage in reaping a disproportionate share of federal investment during the war and over the ensuing decades. In addition to the perspectives they offer on the sectoral, technological, managerial, and spatial transitions of the Second Wave, taken together they reinforce the salience of several common themes in understanding these regional dynamics.

Though readers may discern others, consider the following:

the site-specific significance and localized impact of federal wartime investments and postwar private and public development, which bypassed vast areas of the rural South;

the labor market and training dilemmas posed by introducing relatively sophisticated production technologies in the context of a regionally limited skills pool;

issues of corporate cost consciousness and long-term/short-term planning in relation to the environmental impacts of both new and older sectors;

political tensions within the South which the Second Wave of industrialization triggered, including racial exclusions/openings, uneasy partnerships and recurrent controversies among local, state, and federal governments, and state-enterprise alliances and tangles;

the intersection of fresh industrial initiatives with continuing rural out-migration and the transformation or decay of country districts' economies;

the enduring challenge of growing the South's own entrepreneurial class versus seducing investment from outside, increasingly from multinational corporations;

Introduction

the complex problem of generating a regional/local nexus of supplier and service enterprises for final product manufacturers;

and beyond the usual realms of business and politics, the diverse challenges to southern culture and southern ways that the Second Wave brought in its train.

Though, of course, not all these themes are evident in every essay, readers will encounter each of them at multiple points.

Commencing the three-sided historians' review of aircraft production's arrival in Marietta, Georgia, Thomas A. Scott reconstructs the intersection of local "old boy" networks, regional booster institutions, and national policy priorities that yielded construction of the world's hugest bomber plant in sleepy Cobb County, a dozen or so miles from downtown Atlanta. Richard S. Combes follows with an analysis of policy formation and technology management, which carries us from the 1945 shutdown through a Korean War era reopening that transformed the Marietta facility into a permanent defense industry production center. Karen Ferguson then brings the focus back to World War II, probing the conflicts and intracommunity tensions sparked by efforts by elite African Americans to secure black Atlantans' access to production (rather than janitorial or cafeteria) jobs, along with training and unhindered use of public transit.

In tracing the postwar initiation of carpet production at Dalton, Georgia, and that district's rise to national dominance in the industry, regional historian Randall Patton reflects on the emergence of local entrepreneurs, regionally based technological innovation, and the unexpected consequences of a rare union organizing victory. If Patton's story delineates a growth process, geographer Toby Moore explicates an early form of restructuring, as veteran textile firms commenced liquidating the mill village housing stocks that had long distinguished southern factory culture. In so doing, companies added modest to sizable sums to their capital stocks and adjusted to automobility and the dispersion of employees' residences, while instituting a new tool for worker control: the home mortgage.

As in Marietta, the war reshaped Texas's Gulf Coast oil districts, bringing vast investments in expanded refining capacities, pipeline construction, and the first substantial set of petrochemical facilities. Geographer Craig E. Colten's contribution relates a small, underfunded state agency's episodic efforts (cyclically linked to rainfall/streamflow levels) to combat the ensuing water pollution in the late 1940s and 1950s. Here popular views of small business's virtue and big business's perfidy are reversed in intriguing ways. Perverse incentives, the centrality of long-term planning, and the salience of equally long-term biological research are some of the key elements in William Boyd's analysis of the southern timber industry's reorientation toward pulp and paper production, a process that continues to unfold into the 1990s. From a policy specialist's perspective, Boyd explores the means through which aspiring forest managers, public and corporate, reversed environmentally damaging public policies and rural customs, helping to transform cut-over districts into vast ranges of renewable resources, though not without some disquieting implications. Karsten Hülsemann offers the final sectoral study, a sociologist's review of the South's late and halting entry into the global networks of automobile production, assessing the shift from initial metropolitan area branch assembly plants (Ford, GM) to a series of "greenfield" investments that non-U.S. makers initiated in and after the 1970s. The competitive bidding by states and communities for these plants reminds us that the "selling of the South," though perhaps more sophisticated than half a century or more ago, remains significant in the rhetoric and practice of economic development activists.[3]

Bringing the full toolbox of quantitative social science's techniques for data analysis to bear on statistics reflecting federal investments, c. 1940–1990, Gregory Hooks reassesses the presumed political advantages the South held in reaping government largesse. Disaggregating the nation to the county level and measuring the extent and impacts of federal defense, production, and research spending in the South versus the North and West, he presents a set of conclusions that, in part, should encourage scholars to reconsider their assumptions on this issue. A methodological appendix is provided for reference by the statistically adept reader.

Gavin Wright's afterword closes the work at hand with a set of reflections on the nine essays and the implications for future study that flow from digesting their diverse themes, concepts, methods, and underlying theoretical commitments. As Wright's pathbreaking studies of the southern economy in fair measure created the context for research projects such as these, we appreciate his willingness to join this discussion.[4]

Others also merit more words of thanks than can be offered in this space. The University System of Georgia's Teaching and Learning Grants program provided core funding for the Second Wave conference, supplemented by allocations from the Georgia Tech Provost's Office and the Frank N. Magill Lectureship in the Humanities, administered through Tech's School of History, Technology, and Society. Steven Vallas and Nancy Green Leigh of the Georgia Tech faculty, Bryant Simon from the University of Georgia, and Merl Reed of Georgia State University delivered commentaries on the conference sessions that both stimulated discussion and aided our authors in revisions. Tech graduate students David Ezell and Phil Unger, along with HTS staff members Rudy Paratchek and Denise Marshall, assisted in conference management and editorial efforts. Malcolm Call, at the University of Georgia Press, lent his support to the project of sharing research on the Second Wave of southern industrialization with a larger public than could join our June 1998 meeting.

Conference evaluator James Cobb (University of Georgia) observed in his assessment that the Second Wave sessions offered not just a multidisciplinary, but a truly interdisciplinary perspective on crucial issues in the South's recent history. If we have succeeded in reshaping conference presentations into the essays that follow, the spirit of speaking and listening across disciplinary boundaries and thereby enriching our understanding will be conveyed here as well.

NOTES

1. See Bruce Schulman, *From Cotton Belt to Sunbelt* (Durham, N.C.: Duke University Press, 1994), chapter 1; Bryant Simon, *A Fabric of Defeat* (Chapel Hill: University of North Carolina Press, 1998).

2. Albert Hirschman, *Exit, Voice, and Loyalty* (Cambridge: Harvard University Press, 1970).

3. James C. Cobb, *The Selling of the South: The Southern Crusade for Industrial Development, 1936–1990*, 2d ed. (Urbana: University of Illinois Press, 1993).

4. Gavin Wright, *The Political Economy of the Cotton South* (New York: W. W. Norton, 1978); *Old South, New South: Revolutions in the Southern Economy since the Civil War* (New York: Basic Books, 1986).

The Second Wave

Winning World War II in an Atlanta Suburb

Local Boosters and the Recruitment of Bell Bomber

THOMAS A. SCOTT

During World War II the Bell Aircraft Corporation opened a huge manufacturing plant just north of Atlanta in little Marietta, Georgia, the commercial hub of rural Cobb County. Today this prosperous suburban county contains well over a half million residents; but in 1940 it held only 38,300, most living on modest farms. Wartime industrialization transformed overnight a sleepy society with traditional values into a place of rapid growth and change.[1] This essay examines how such a site was able to recruit and build one of the largest manufacturing plants in the South and how that industry reshaped the area. In particular, it will explore the crucial roles of a northerner, Lawrence D. Bell, and three prominent Cobb countians, Lucius D. Clay, Leon M. (Rip) Blair, and James V. Carmichael. The local leaders came from distinguished families, active in law, politics, and trade but with little prior involvement in industry.

These Marietta boosters shared with counterparts throughout the South a philosophy described by Bruce Schulman as the new "Whiggery."[2] Like nineteenth-century Whigs, the emerging Dixie industrialists championed an activist government dedicated to economic development. The old Whigs favored direct aid to private railroads, because they deemed it in the national interest to develop a first-rate transportation system. Twentieth-century southern Whigs championed federal contracts to companies promoting the national interest by building ships and airplanes. With their Chamber of Commerce mentality, they were progrowth but not necessarily liberal. Most of them had no desire to help labor unions or end segregation, yet they were quite happy if their efforts created high-paying jobs, at least for those prepared to take advantage of the new opportunities. These regional leaders saw a role for government in building the infrastructure and creating an educational system that produced talented workers for the modern economy. They were essentially southern-style, probusiness progressives.

This chapter attempts to show that Blair, Clay, and Carmichael were on the progressive end of the southern political spectrum, supporting New Deal relief programs, championing a governmental role in stimulating economic development, battling against the anti-Roosevelt Talmadge faction in Georgia politics, and favoring the growth of a competitive, two-party system. While they had little use for labor organizers or civil rights advocates, they were spokesmen for a more industrialized, more enlightened, more affluent South. Along with a large supporting cast from Marietta, Atlanta, Buffalo, New York, and elsewhere, they reshaped the history of a North Georgia county, transforming its stagnant economy and turning it into an Atlanta suburb with a bright future.

BACKGROUND

Since its incorporation as a village in 1834, Marietta has served as the government seat of Cobb County, one of ten Georgia counties carved from the old Cherokee nation. Early on, the town was blessed with a major railroad when, in 1836, the state approved the construction of the Western & Atlantic from the future site of Atlanta to Chattanooga. In 1845, when the Western & Atlantic began regular traffic between Atlanta and Marietta, the latter developed as a popular resort for aristocrats from coastal Georgia and South Carolina. With an elevation of over one thousand feet and spring waters containing a high concentration of minerals, Cobb County seemed an ideal summer place for planters escaping the malaria and yellow fever epidemics that raged through their low-country rice fields, swamps, and marshes.[3]

In June 1864 a major battle occurred just outside Marietta at Kennesaw Mountain. As General William T. Sherman advanced to Atlanta and then to the sea, the Marietta business district was put to the torch. The courthouse, all but one building on the town square, and at least twenty private homes were destroyed.[4] After the war the economy recovered slowly, but by the early 1900s Marietta could boast of small paper, chair, marble, and cotton mills and an iron foundry that manufactured several hundred locomotives for private companies around the world. Wages, however, remained low. Until the New Deal of Franklin Roosevelt, factory workers, male and female, rarely made over ten cents an hour.[5]

Before World War II, farming was Cobb County's largest occupation. Lying in the Upper Piedmont, Cobb contained pockets of fertile soil but was north of Georgia's most productive sections. Small farmers, working their fields with little outside help, dominated the region. In the antebellum era slaves made up only 27 percent of the population, compared to 44 percent statewide. Following the Civil War, an agricultural depression struck everywhere, as overproduction and declining market prices drove many landowners into tenancy or off the soil altogether. By 1900 fewer than half of Cobb's farm operators owned their land. The overwhelming majority of tenants paid their rent with a share of the crop, typically a third of the corn and a fourth of the cotton. In that year the average farm size in the county had fallen to a mere seventy-two acres.[6]

Like most Georgia small towns, Marietta was not without wealthy citizens. A few lawyers, doctors, bankers, and businessmen did well enough to live in beautiful Greek Revival or Victorian mansions lining the main arteries into downtown. The children of the elite graduated from Marietta High School and often went on to Georgia colleges. For the rest of society, however, opportunity was severely limited. Future state legislator and Marietta mayor, Joe Mack Wilson, completed high school in the midst of the Great Depression. His father's jewelry business barely stayed open during the hard times. Wilson recalled:

> Christmas Eve was the biggest day in the jewelry business. One Christmas Eve, I remember my father buying little cotton-filled boxes and things that you would deliver gifts in. He spent, oh, maybe $100 on merchandise and on boxes and so forth. That Christmas Eve, at the height of the Depression, he took in 75 cents. Not enough to have Christmas dinner. . . .
>
> When I graduated in 1936, I could not find a job in Marietta, Georgia, not even on the WPA. I had to go to South Carolina, and got a job digging ditches for $15 a week, forty hours for $15. . . . There was a lot of politics in WPA jobs. I couldn't get one, because I wasn't inside the clique. That's the reason I had to go to South Carolina. . . .[7]

Local attorney Fred Bentley Sr. gives a vivid account of the talent drain from the area in the years before World War II. Born in 1926 to the manager of a local hardware store, Bentley came from an old, but not especially wealthy, Cobb County family. He remembers:

> The old Mariettans were afraid of growth. As a matter of fact, for years the older manufacturing plants fought to keep other manufacturers out of here. This was because of what they perceived to be competition for the labor. . . .
> I always felt that when I grew up, the only job I could ever aspire to was the manager of the Holeproof Hosiery Company; and, I had to wait till everybody died off before I could possibly achieve that. . . .
>
> All of your young men at that time, who were halfway bright, planned to move away, and your brighter people *were* moving away. I had made up my mind that I was going to move to Milwaukee, Wisconsin.[8]

If the future seemed bleak to ordinary whites, it was bleaker for African Americans. Despite a flourishing black business district and a few prosperous farm owners, blacks earned far less than Caucasians. In 1900, when African Americans made up 30 percent of Cobb's population, almost three-fourths of their family heads earned their living as tenants, farm hands, servants, or common laborers. Only 5 percent of all black families owned a farm, compared to 25 percent of white families. Over the next fifty years African Americans left the area in large numbers, participating in the Great Migration from the rural South to the northern cities. By 1950 the black population was smaller than it had been at the beginning of the century and only 10 percent of the county total. At that time the typical African American family earned just 53 percent of the county average income.[9]

POLITICS AND PREPAREDNESS

In the Depression year of 1938 Leon M. (Rip) Blair took office as mayor of Marietta. He had graduated from Marietta High School in 1912, two years ahead of Lucius D. Clay. Their fathers were once law partners, and Alexander Stephens Clay, a progressive Democrat, was a U.S. Senator from 1897 until his death in 1910. Rip became a lawyer and served in the army in World War I. Lucius trained as a soldier, graduating from the United States Military Academy in 1918. Along with the other cadets in the top fourth of his class, Clay was assigned to the U.S. Army Corps of Engineers.

Due to the political nature of Corps construction activities, Clay had more contact with federal bureaucrats and congressmen than did most West Point graduates. The man who, after World War II, served as military governor of Germany and directed the Berlin Airlift, spent the 1930s coordinating projects between the Corps of Engineers and the WPA. Respected by prominent New Dealers such as Harry Hopkins and Representative Sam Rayburn (D-Texas), Clay was chosen in 1939 to build the huge Denison Dam in Rayburn's district. Then, in September 1940 he returned to Washington to head FDR's emergency airport construction program. With a military rank of major, Clay also held the title of secretary of the approval board for airport construction and assistant to the administrator of the Civil Aeronautics Administration (CAA), headed by Colonel Donald H. Connolly. Consisting of the secretaries of commerce, war, and navy, the approval board never actually met. For a few months Clay submitted all plans to secretary of commerce Jesse Jones; then Jones told Clay to stop reporting and run the program as he pleased. In the fifteen months before Pearl Harbor, Clay was responsible for building 450 airports in the United States, including National Airport in Washington, D.C.[10]

Meanwhile, his old friend Blair was trying to find ways to stimulate the depressed economy of little Marietta. Turning to the federal government, the mayor persuaded the Roosevelt administration to build two large public housing projects in downtown Marietta, one for whites and one for blacks. Blair told his fellow Rotarians that government-assisted apartments had worked well for thirty-five years in Scandinavia and that the Marietta units had eliminated half the city's slums. Further, he asserted that civic leaders had a duty to pressure slumlords to add indoor plumbing and electricity.[11]

Blair also supported the National Youth Administration and the WPA and was actively involved in building parks and paving streets. A combative man, with a basic sense of social justice, the mayor often sided with the underdog. He liked to remember lending his pistol to a Syrian immigrant who had been threatened by the Ku Klux Klan. Blair was delighted that the man was harassed no more after frequently taking target practice in his front yard. When Blair believed his integrity had been compromised by a business associate who sought special considerations, the mayor publicly denounced the man as a liar and brawled with him in council chambers.[12]

In the early fall of 1940, shortly after Clay was recalled to Washington, Atlanta Chamber of Commerce officials invited Blair to a meeting. They had heard that the federal government was starting an emergency airport program. Hoping to create a series of airfields circling Atlanta, the chamber officials urged Blair to seek federal funds for Marietta. Leading an official delegation to Washington, Blair claimed he happened to see Clay's name on a door at the CAA, and it was like "'Brer Rabbit' heading for the briar patch."[13] Clay recommended that Marietta and Cobb County gain title to a tract of land large enough for an airport. He advised Mayor Blair to gain letters of endorsement from leaders in Atlanta, while Clay persuaded the CAA to fund the construction of runways.

On 28 October 1940 Blair wrote Clay that he was enclosing letters of support from Atlanta mayor William B. Hartsfield, from the Chamber of Commerce, and from a Georgia Tech professor. He also indicated that he had secured options on three suitable sites, of which the best was a tract about three and a half miles south of downtown Marietta, which was spacious enough to accommodate both commercial and military aircraft. Blair informed Clay that Marietta would settle for an airport only of a high classification. He said that a CAA inspector had toured the favored site on the previous day and had assured Marietta officials that it met all specifications for a quality airport. The mayor concluded by asking his friend to put Marietta, if possible, on the preferred list of high-priority sites, and if not, to advise him what needed to be done to be placed on the extended list for eventual consideration.[14]

The letter from Mayor Hartsfield asserted that the Atlanta airport (Candler Field) would always be the main facility for the metropolitan area, but nearby airstrips could be used for private flying and aircraft manufacturers and as landing fields if bad weather closed Candler. The letter from the Atlanta Chamber of Commerce, signed by Ivan Allen Sr., argued that Atlanta needed more than Candler Field, which was hard to reach by automobile. This argument was repeated by Montgomery Knight, director of the Daniel Guggenheim School of Aeronautics at Georgia Tech, who maintained that "heavy downtown traffic" made it difficult for North Atlanta residents to reach the southside airport. He claimed more students had accidents while traveling to the airport than in their flight training. Knight commended Marietta for planning a site that was sufficiently large for future expansion and for any potential aircraft manufacturing plant.[15]

Clay immediately forwarded the correspondence to Major A. B. McMullen, Chief of the Airport Section at the CAA. In a memo the Marietta native alluded to a recent survey, suggesting that the terrain around Candler Field would make improvement to a Class 4 airport very expensive. Arguing that the Marietta property seemed to be supported by the leaders of Atlanta, he asked that the CAA regional representative review the location and submit a recommendation as to its potential.[16] Nine days later, McMullen wrote the regional manager in Atlanta, endorsing an alternative to Candler Field and asking for a detailed survey, including cost estimates, to determine whether the CAA should fund an expansion of the Atlanta airport or a new development in Marietta. In a confidential memo Clay passed on a copy of McMullen's letter, which, he claimed, "I have had sent to our Regional Manager." CAA records make clear that Blair and Clay stayed in constant contact, with the latter advising the former on every step in maneuvering the proposal to fruition. For a little more than half a year the Marietta airport remained in doubt as CAA officials considered the various options.[17]

In the early negotiations, the City of Marietta received strong support from the county government, led by Commissioner Charles M. Head. However, on 19 April 1941, Head died suddenly of a heart attack at the age of seventy-three. A month later the voters chose George H. McMillan to finish Head's term. McMillan was a popular merchant from the little railroad town of Acworth, in Cobb County's northwest corner. He went to work immediately, gaining title to 563 acres of land at the preferred airport site.[18] Blair's law partner and county attorney, James V. Carmichael, assisted McMillan in this task. Born in October 1910, Carmichael was barely thirty years old at the time, some fifteen years younger than Blair. Nonetheless, the Emory University Law School graduate was already a veteran of four years in the Georgia legislature. His good friend, Judson C. Ward, a fellow Cobb countian and longtime Emory administrator, recalls that Carmichael quickly became a leader in the General Assembly, winning the respect and devotion of much older legislators, who sought his advice. An authority on post-Reconstruction southern history, Jake Ward remembers his friend as a man of vision whose leadership qualities shone through despite an excruciatingly painful disability. A speeding motorist struck Carmichael during his junior year of high school, when he stepped into the Dixie Highway in front of his parents' general store. Suffering from a broken back, he missed a year of school.

For a long time he used a wheelchair, although he could walk short distances with a cane.[19]

On 16 May 1941 the *Marietta Daily Journal* reported that CAA surveyors had arrived. Mayor Blair revealed that, as soon as Marietta and Cobb County had acquired the necessary acreage, the government would provide $400,000 to build the airstrip. According to Carmichael, the airport would be as large as Candler Field with three runways of concrete, each 4,000 feet in length. The project was facilitated when the state, in mid-June, began paving through Cobb County an additional five miles of Georgia's first modern four-lane highway. Thus, the airport lay between the super highway to the east and the old Dixie Highway (present Atlanta Road) to the west.

By June, Cobb had acquired three small tracts through legal condemnation and the rest through negotiation with a number of small property owners.[20] The county financed these purchases by selling $160,000 of revenue certificates at 4 percent interest, through the services of a local man in the securities business, Lex Jolley. With the acquisitions completed, the county government, headed by commissioner George McMillan, adopted a resolution accepting the CAA's offer of aid and agreeing to operate and maintain the facility. On 27 June attorney Carmichael informed the CAA Atlanta regional manager, H. Harvie Perkins, that the county now had title to all the property in question. Perkins then notified his Washington superiors that the paperwork was in order and that the district engineer could begin work.[21]

While the airstrip clearly had military potential, Cobb countians dreamed in the summer of 1941 of a commercial airport with regular passenger flights. When the president of Eastern Airlines, Eddie Rickenbacker, offered to send passenger planes into Marietta, local officials named the site Rickenbacker Field in his honor. Following a visit to Washington by Blair and Carmichael, the CAA agreed in October to give an additional $75,000 to lengthen one of the runways to 5,000 feet. The CAA assured Mariettans that a second runway would be extended to 6,000 feet, enough to accommodate the largest commercial planes, following the next congressional appropriation to the agency.[22]

LARRY BELL AND THE WAR EMERGENCY

Suddenly the Japanese bombed Pearl Harbor, and plans for the airport quickly changed. According to Jean Edward Smith, Marietta became a likely site for an airplane manufacturing establishment, in part because of Lucius Clay's power in Washington. As soon as war broke out, Clay received orders to attend a conference in which the chief of staff, General George C. Marshall, announced a reorganization of the War Department. The army divided into three branches: ground forces, air forces, and services of supply, the last group headed by Lieutenant General Brehon B. Somervell. Services of supply had two divisions under a director of supply, Brigadier General LeRoy Lutes, and a director of materiel, Brigadier General Lucius Clay. With this announcement, Clay not only received a promotion, but held one of the most important jobs in wartime Washington. With considerable influence over military contracts, Clay could easily direct attention southward. Clay later told an oral historian:

> The air force had to have a new plant—and a big plant, and they came to me to ask for a list of possible places where there was both a labor supply available and an existing airport. And I happened to remember Marietta, so I gave it to them as one of the names. It had a tremendous labor potential—both from Atlanta and from the surrounding mountain area.
>
> Larry Bell went down there. He liked the area, and so they built a plant there, the Bell bomber plant. And I think Larry Bell was always very happy with it.... they brought labor out of those hills that had never had an opportunity to work before, and they did remarkably well.

Asked whether he aided in putting Bell Bomber in Marietta, the general replied, "I helped them in every way I could. It was my hometown. I had no financial interest of any shape, form, or fashion, and none of my relatives did either. But I did have an interest in the town."[23]

Lawrence D. Bell was one of the remarkable pioneers of early aviation. Born in Indiana in 1894, he moved with his parents to California as a teenager. With a knack for mechanical pursuits, he and his older brother, Grover, became fascinated with airplanes. Despite Grover's death in a 1913 plane crash, young Larry continued his lifelong love for this new mode of transportation. About this time he began as a stockroom clerk for the Glenn L. Martin Company. Through hard work and great organizational skills he rose in a few years to superintendent, then vice president and general manager. Among the brilliant inventors he helped recruit for Martin was MIT graduate Donald W. Douglas. In 1925 Bell left Martin when the latter refused to make him a partner. After working at odd jobs for three years, he moved from California to Buffalo, New York, to work for another aviation pioneer, Major Reuben H. Fleet (U.S. Army, retired), who allowed Bell to purchase 2 percent of the stock in his Consolidated Aircraft Company. When Fleet decided to relocate to San Diego, Bell stayed in Buffalo, forming his own company in 1935. With the Great Depression still in full force, the early years of the Bell Aircraft Corporation were difficult. By 1941, however, the company had developed a successful Airacobra pursuit plane for the military and had just over a thousand employees.[24]

Wartime demand led to a vast expansion of the aircraft manufacturing industry. With huge military contracts and demands from Washington that companies share supplies, designs, and other secrets, all the companies experienced good times. While Larry Bell looked for a southern site, his legal counsel, William J. O'Connor, approached Ivan Allen Sr., chairman of the Industrial Bureau of the Atlanta Chamber of Commerce. Allen then called Blair. O'Connor accepted an invitation to visit Marietta, arriving in late January 1942.[25] By this point workers had almost completed the original runways and had started construction of prefab hangars and the 1,000-foot extension of the east–west runway. O'Connor was impressed with the Marietta site.

At a press conference held in Jimmie Carmichael's law office, the Bell official announced that the company stood ready to occupy 260 acres, where employees would produce a new Boeing-designed aircraft which the U.S. Army Air Corps wanted them to build. Described as one of the largest planes in the national arsenal, the bomber was identified as a B-29. Still in the testing stage, the four-motor aircraft was to be ready for production later in the year with the project financed by the Defense Plant Corporation. Bell would lease the plant from the government with an option to buy; and while the airport could be operated for other purposes, Bell would use the runways to test its planes.

Salaries would be far above the prevailing wage scale in the county, with supervisory jobs beginning at $2,600 a year and skilled and unskilled workers earning, respectively, eighty-five and seventy cents an hour (roughly $1,700 and $1,400 annually). In contrast, the nearby Glover Machine Works, an old Marietta business, paid common laborers only thirty-five cents an hour. Ultimately employing over 28,000 workers, the Bell facility would be an assembly plant, bringing in parts and motors from throughout the country. Attorney O'Connor credited the decision to build a Marietta factory to the area's "natural facilities" and the "ability to get labor" that could be trained in area vocational schools. He also noted the presence in Atlanta of the Fisher Body Company and Ford and General Motors assembly plants, currently operating on limited Depression-era schedules. These businesses could do important subcontracting for Bell.[26]

Despite this good news, Cobb countians had to overcome several large hurdles before actually winning the bomber plant. If the runways were extended, they would come too close to high voltage lines, blocking large planes trying to land and take off. The Georgia Power Company wanted Cobb County to pay to move the lines. In a 1987 interview bond broker Lex Jolley remembered serving on a Cobb grand jury that considered whether the county should assume the cost. While instructing the jurors, the judge brought up the matter of the high lines at the airport. As Jolley told the story, "We got in the jury room, and one of them was this farmer from west Cobb with a copy of the newspaper in his pocket that had the story in it about the problem. I was wondering which side he was going to be on. Before we even had a chance to elect a foreman, he pulled that paper out of his pocket and slapped it down on the table and said, 'I know the county's in good shape! Why in hell don't Cobb County go ahead and move the line so we can get it [the airport] in operation?' I just drew a long breath and relaxed." In early December Cobb County agreed to pay Georgia Power $22,350 to relocate the lines underground, some three-quarters of a mile from the runway's edge.²⁷

Competition between the army and navy posed another problem. On 18 December 1941 Blair frantically wired Clay that Lieutenant Commander D. Ward Harrigan of the Navy Reserve Aviation Base in neighboring Chamblee had contacted county officials. Harrigan wanted Rickenbacker Field as an auxiliary site for the navy training program. While Blair asserted that Marietta was "naturally anxious to cooperate" he added he wanted the field "used to best advantage." Clay wired back that Marietta may have to give the navy "exclusive rights if required for their operations," but he suggested that their need might be temporary, since the CAA was working on nearby Ellenwood Airport, which would make an excellent training field. The following day Blair shot off a letter to Clay that Rickenbacker Field was too fine a site to be used merely as an auxiliary location. Moreover, he feared that Cobb would lose the contracts it already held if the navy used the airport for only a few months until Ellenwood was completed. Reminding Clay of Cobb's huge indebtedness to build the facility, he added that "if the Navy desires the field it would be better for them to take it for the entire duration of the war rather than for a few months period."²⁸

At his press conference in Marietta in late January, Bell attorney O'Connor identified the uncertainty over the navy's plans as the only obstacle to building the Marietta plant, but warned that Bell would go outside Georgia if the navy took over the site. Writing in the *Cobb County Times,* columnist Joe Harrison reported the frustrations of local leaders in resolving this issue. For weeks Blair, Carmichael, and others sent telegrams and telephone calls all over the country. Matters would seem resolved one day, only to fall apart the next. One January day Harrison dropped by Carmichael's office for a cigarette and found everything in an uproar. "Where in the H—— is Blair," the county attorney barked at the mayor's secretary. "Tell him to get down here as fast as he can. All hell's to pay." Harrison left while the two again placed calls to Washington, Atlanta, Miami, and other sites. He said, "I can't state it accurately as a fact, but I hear tell as how even O'Connor gave up hope. But not Carmichael and Blair. They kept on fighting." Eventually, their efforts were rewarded. On Sunday, 24 January 1942, Senator Walter George announced in Washington that the navy had backed off, but, the reporter concluded, "the ground work for the action was done right here by two men."²⁹

In later years Blair had similar memories of the fight with the navy. With the support of the Atlanta newspapers, the Atlanta Chamber of Commerce, and the Georgia Power Company, Marietta and Cobb County officials lobbied hard to persuade the navy not to seek control of Rickenbacker Field. Blair credited Senator Walter George and Seventh District Congressman Malcolm Tarver with bringing political pressure on the navy. He said that while Senator Richard Russell did what he could, he had relatively limited influence due to his junior status. Others have given credit to Georgia Congressmen Carl Vinson and Robert Ramspeck, county commissioner George McMillan, and former governor James M. Cox of Ohio, the Democratic candidate for president in 1920, then owner of the *Atlanta Journal*.

Blair recalled living on "cokes and cigarettes" during this period and staying awake many nights. Beginning to despair, the mayor finally received a call from former Marietta resident Admiral John H. Towers, who said that the navy would withdraw its claim upon a direct request from the army, but would not do so for Bell. Thus, local leaders turned their attention to persuading the army. Even as the navy began condemnation proceedings, army and navy officials held a number of top level conferences in Washington. After receiving a formal statement from the War Department that Bell Aircraft needed the facility, Admiral Towers stopped the navy's takeover. At the same time, Commander Harrigan of the Naval Reserve Base announced a huge expansion of his facilities at old Camp Gordon in Chamblee.[30]

With this problem resolved, William O'Connor quickly signed the necessary contracts with local officials and left for Buffalo. Cobb leaders, however, continued to be plagued by frustrations and uncertainties, as the neighboring Fulton County Commission lobbied in Washington for a Fairburn site, south of Atlanta. Blair blamed the Southern Railway for the Fairburn scheme, while the *Cobb County Times* spoke more generally of powerful railroad executives who were unhappy "because it looked like, for once, they would not get ALL the traffic to and from the projected plant." This threat was removed in early February, when an Army Air Corps board of investigators recommended Rickenbacker Field as the preferred site and Candler Field as the second choice. Marietta's case received a further assist from Atlanta mayor Roy LeCraw, who made clear his city's opposition to placing an aircraft industry at Candler, fearing it would destroy commercial aviation at the fourth busiest airport in the country. Finally, on 19 February 1942 the War Department announced that Marietta had been chosen. The perseverance of Cobb and Atlanta leaders thus secured victory.[31]

The reaction in both locations was remarkable. Mariettans began preparing immediately for immense changes in their lifestyles. Marietta textile executive and civic leader Guy Northcutt advised that "whether we like it or not, our way of life in Marietta, Georgia will soon be gone forever." He predicted that old timers would divide into those who griped about it and those who adjusted and "cashed in" on the new opportunities.[32] The *Cobb County Times* editorialized that "our quiet, peaceful 'aristocratic' little city" was about to be altered and that it would "mean great things to many who never expected anything much out of life." The paper challenged longtime residents to make sure that the new Marietta bore a "family resemblance" to the former. *Atlanta Constitution* editor Ralph McGill was extremely pleased that Marietta had landed the bomber plant. In a column entitled "Marietta's Sir Galahads" he said that Rip Blair, Jimmie Carmichael, and George McMillan "seemed to have an aura about them, and to be as handsome and as noble as shining knights in armor." McGill concluded that "they had done one of the finest jobs, in behalf of one of the finest counties, that had ever been done in behalf of any county in Georgia. And in doing it they did a job for the whole state."[33]

In March 1942 the U.S. Corps of Engineers took over the completion of the airstrip runways. The CAA had already invested $470,000, but the corps spent two million dollars more on extensions and improvements. Unfortunately, according to Mayor Blair, "the airfield, the reason for putting Bell here in the first place, turned out to be completely unsuitable. The runways were too narrow, too thin, too short, and were pointed in the wrong direction." They had to be plowed up and new runways put in, but the replacements, completed by 1 March 1943, were some of the best in the country. In May 1943 the Army Air Corps accepted title to Rickenbacker Field strictly for military purposes.[34]

While the Corps of Engineers completed the airport, Atlanta-based Robert & Co. designed and managed the construction of the aircraft assembly plant. By 15 March 1943 the project was 86 percent finished, permitting most of Bell's 1,179 employees to move into the facility from their temporary headquarters in downtown Atlanta. L. W. Robert Jr., the architectural-engineering firm's president, described the structure as big enough to house the nation's cotton crop and large enough for sixty-three football fields, all under one roof. It had sufficient tracks for a dozen passenger trains, and the roof rose four and a half stories above the ground. Jimmie Carmichael recalled visiting the building while it was still empty, just before occupation. Its far end was so distant he found it hard to believe the company could find enough workers and parts to fill the place, yet he took pride in the fact that a relatively poor county would now have year-round employment at regionally high wages. Thirty years later Carmichael told historian B. C. Yates that "aircraft payrolls helped build the new Cobb County!"[35]

BUILDING THE B-29s

Bell began in earnest to build airplanes, with the first two delivered just after Christmas, 1943. Eventually, the Marietta facility built 663 B-29s and employed a peak labor force of 28,158 workers, about nine-tenths from the South and over a third women. Semiskilled workers trained at Marietta's Rickenbacker Aircraft

Training School and at several other vocational facilities. General manager Carmichael took great satisfaction in the bomber plant's record of employing 1,757 handicapped workers, who, he claimed, had less absenteeism, fewer work stoppages for health reasons, and a better retention rate than other workers.[36]

Situated in the segregated Deep South, the company conformed to local traditions by concentrating black laborers in menial jobs and doing little to address the numerous complaints of discrimination filed with the Fair Employment Practices Committee. After a 1945 meeting with Bell executive Jimmie Carmichael, Dr. Witherspoon Dodge, the FEPC Region VII director, concluded that the company had no intention of integrating black and white workers and that Carmichael was knowingly in violation of FDR's executive order barring racial discrimination in the defense industries. Nonetheless, by May 1945 Bell provided employment for some 1,785 nonwhite workers, many of whom earned three or four times as much as they received in the Atlanta area before the war. Former domestic servant Ernestine Slade, for example, saw her income rise from less than ten dollars a week to well over thirty. While recognizing the company's discriminatory practices, she seemed more impressed with the expanded economic opportunities that Bell provided.[37]

The first man in charge of the Georgia branch of Bell Aircraft, Captain Harry E. Collins, had excellent political skills and was ideal while the plant was under construction. In June 1943, with production underway, Larry Bell transferred Collins to the Washington, D.C., office, replacing him with a top executive from the Buffalo plant, Omer L. Woodson.[38] The latter performed admirably until the pressures of the job became too great. Telling everyone he was leaving for a nonexistent job with Howard Hughes, Woodson resigned in August 1944. Carl Cover took his place, while Jimmie Carmichael moved up from legal counsel to assistant general manager and Rip Blair became plant attorney. When Cover was killed in a plane crash in late November, Carmichael assumed the role of manager for the duration of the war.[39] In something resembling a World War II version of affirmative action, Larry Bell expressed satisfaction in finding a southerner qualified to run his factory. Previously, he had described Carmichael and Blair as "the best minds of the South." Now, in a private letter, he told his new general manager how happy he was "that there was available a southerner, and more particularly, a Marietta boy to assume command of this great enterprise."[40]

Carmichael insisted on safety, but still met production goals on time. When the four hundredth B-29 was completed in May 1945, Bell complimented his general manager on the fact that there had never been a crash in test flying or delivering the planes to the military. He called it perhaps the greatest achievement of its kind in the brief history of aviation, particularly for a new plant and an inexperienced workforce. The northern executive concluded that "the people of the South can forever be proud of that record and contribution to the war." Having followed the young businessman around the plant, staff writer M. L. St. John of the *Atlanta Constitution* concluded that Carmichael quickly picked up the technical language of his engineers. The general manager told him that he had to depend on specialists to run their departments, but "when the bombers fail to leave the factory on time, I know something is wrong. I find out where the slowdown occurred. Then, if some specialist continues to fail to produce, he is replaced by someone who can."[41]

By mid-1945 the plant was scaling back its workforce in preparation for the war's end. After the Japanese surrendered, the military canceled Bell's Marietta contracts. On 17 August 1945, less than two weeks after the bombing of Hiroshima, the company announced the sudden termination of 8,000 workers. By the end of September the workforce was down to a few thousand. Carmichael recalled that Larry Bell, fearing public reaction, came down to Marietta when the facility was closed. When the general manager called a mass assembly, the employees accepted the change calmly. As executives mingled with workers, Carmichael recollected that people "came by, spoke to us, told us that it had been good to have a part in the war effort," and that they appreciated the opportunity to be involved in the B-29 project. He added that he was never prouder of the people of Cobb County than on that day.[42]

The calmness of the ex-employees resulted in part from the fact that good jobs now seemed abundant and unemployment rates remained low. Fred Bentley had observed that during the 1930s all the intelligent young people thought of moving away. Then he came home in 1945 on leave from the navy. He remembers getting lost as he drove through Pine Forest, a large development of duplex houses on tree-lined streets, built during the war by Mayor Blair and his partners. Years later he exclaimed that "for me to get lost in Marietta, Georgia—especially here where I had grown up—was amazing. I said, 'Things are happening here.' So, I thought of Russell Conwell's great old speech, 'acres of diamonds in your own back yard.'" Bentley settled down in Marietta and became a highly successful attorney and state legislator. Many others had similar success stories. Even without Bell Aircraft, the population by 1950 reached 20,687 in the city and 61,830 in the whole county (increases of 139 percent and 62 percent, respectively, over the 1940 figures). Carmichael cited a host of new businesses (machine shops, electrical appliance manufacturers, furniture and chenille plants, etc.) as part of the explanation for the continued good times, claiming there were no empty houses in town and virtually every factory had a large backlog of orders.[43]

After the war Larry Bell presided over a much smaller company. While retrenchment was not as rapid in Buffalo as it was in Marietta, total corporate employment fell from over 50,000 to about 3,000. Despite a hostile takeover attempt in 1947 by dissident stockholders and a nasty strike at the Buffalo plant in

1949 by UAW Local 501, Bell's company gradually recovered. In 1956 its experimental X-2 airplane reached altitudes of over 126,000 feet and speeds in excess of 2,100 miles per hour. By then the company was heavily involved in building helicopters and guided missiles. Gradually employment rose to over 20,000 workers. Unfortunately, Bell's health deteriorated, and on 20 October 1956 he died of congestive heart failure at age sixty-two.

The greatest legacy of this aviation pioneer may well be the bomber plant in Georgia. Biographer Donald Norton argues that Bell became convinced, as the affluent Sunbelt emerged, that his company had started the growth. He quotes Bell that "my friends down there have repeatedly told me that the operation of Bell Aircraft probably had more influence on the rebirth of the South than anything that's ever been done." The aircraft industry, of course, was not the whole story of southern economic progress. During and after the war, the larger picture includes a vast increase of federal funds going to a host of defense industries and military installations. Wartime factories not only put more dollars in southerners' pockets, they trained a skilled workforce. Thus, many top corporations built southern offices and plants in the postwar era to take advantage of the new markets and talented labor pools in metropolitan Atlanta and other urban centers. By cooperating with the federal government in building a Georgia division, Bell justly took satisfaction in helping to initiate the southern economic revival.[44]

AFTERMATH

Of those responsible for bringing the Bell Bomber plant to Marietta, Lucius Clay became the most internationally famous. After World War II he served as military governor of Germany and was a Cold War hero for ordering and directing the Berlin Airlift of 1948–49, which kept West Berlin out of the hands of the Soviets. In 1949 he retired from the military and returned to the United States to become CEO of the Continental Can Company. To avoid conflicts of interest, he turned down important executive positions with defense contractors such as General Motors and IBM. A New Deal liberal, he became a Republican after helping persuade his close friend Dwight D. Eisenhower to run for the presidency in 1952. President-elect Eisenhower asked Clay to select his initial cabinet heads. Then, when President Eisenhower became convinced that a public works program was needed to keep the economy healthy, he chose Clay to head the committee that created the interstate highway program. While the Marietta native generally stayed out of state and local politics, in 1966 he publicly endorsed the candidacy of Howard (Bo) Callaway, the first Georgia Republican to run for governor in the twentieth century.[45] Clay continued to be a national figure in business and politics into the early 1970s. Suffering from emphysema caused by years of heavy cigarette smoking, he died in 1978, just six days shy of his eightieth birthday, and was buried at West Point with full military honors.[46]

Another New Deal Democrat, Rip Blair served five two-year terms as mayor of Marietta before being defeated for reelection in 1947. He did well for himself as owner of an aluminum furniture business and developer and manager of rental properties in Marietta. He died in 1964 at the age of sixty-nine.[47] Jimmie Carmichael ran for governor in 1946, promising to continue the progressive record of the liberal Ellis Arnall administration. Despite outpolling reactionary Gene Talmadge by almost 16,000 votes, Carmichael lost the Democratic primary due to the anachronistic county unit system, a uniquely Georgian device somewhat similar to the federal electoral college, which gave greater weight to rural than to urban votes.[48]

Returning to the business world, he headed Scripto, Inc., turning it into an international leader in the production of writing instruments. When the Korean War broke out, the air force asked Lockheed to come to Marietta to take over the vacant facilities of the old Bell Aircraft plant. The California giant persuaded Carmichael in 1951 to take a leave of absence from Scripto and start up Lockheed-Georgia. His successor as general manager, Dan Haughton, gave Carmichael principal credit for reactivating the plant to modify B-29s, construct B-47s, and begin the task of "marketing and building the C-130 Hercules." For over four decades the C-130 has been central to the success of Lockheed-Georgia and its successor, Lockheed Martin Aeronautical Systems. In 1952 Carmichael returned to the pen company, but continued to serve on the Lockheed board of directors until a few months before his death at age sixty-two on 28 November 1972.[49]

Carmichael is also remembered for his remarkable record of public service. In addition to being the first head of the Atlanta Arts Alliance, he was a trustee of Emory University and from 1965 until his death a member of the Board of Regents of the University System of Georgia. In a commencement address at Emory University in 1950, Carmichael articulated the creed that governed his life and animated the progressive business elite who led Georgia into the new era. Despite his ties to liberal Democrats, such as former governor Arnall, he demonstrated his distrust of New Deal excesses by ridiculing those who lived off Uncle Sam rather than working. In a poem which he read to the graduates, a son angers his father by asking why the parent thought it was all right to live at the public expense, when he could be contributing to society. The father concludes:

> My faith in you is shrinking, son,
> You nosey little brat,
> You do too damn much thinking, son,
> To be a Democrat.

To the Emory graduates the former Bell executive made clear that he despised not only welfare cheats but those who clung to the Confederate past. He said in his 1950 speech: "I sicken of these people who are always waving the Confederate Flag, and telling us what a glorious heritage the South has. No one denies this heritage, but too many of our people want to keep on living on who they are and where they came from. The only criteria of individual worth is what a person is doing and where he is going." He called on the graduates to live in the present and to learn how to serve the current and future needs of the region. The Emory trustee claimed that his heart ached over the section's backward economy, inferior schools, limited cultural opportunities, and "complete absence of an acceptable, nationally recognized advanced graduate school in so large an area of the South." Carmichael maintained that the region had sadly isolated itself from the rest of the country either out of false pride, a sense of inferiority, or lack of vision. However, the time had come to merge into the national mainstream, "economically, culturally and educationally." He insisted it was no longer acceptable for a school such as Emory to think of itself as the "best in the South." In the future regional leaders had to set their sights much higher.[50]

In a solidly Democratic state, Carmichael would have committed political suicide by openly joining the Republican Party, but he demonstrated a strong tendency in that direction as early as 1947. A few months after his loss to Gene Talmadge, the erstwhile gubernatorial candidate told interviewers Calvin Kytle and James A. Mackay that Georgia needed two competing parties ("Call 'em Democrats and Republicans, Democrats and Loyal Democrats, or anything you please"), so that races would be decided in the general election rather than the Democratic primary. In 1960 he again advocated a "true two-party system" while introducing Richard Nixon during the presidential candidate's Atlanta campaign appearance. Like Clay and Blair, this heir of a professional, small-business heritage found his vision not in a past of "white columned plantation homes with the fragrance of Magnolia and Wisteria in the air," but in a meritocracy where one would be honored for bringing the South to wealth, power, and cultural influence. With equal disdain, he denounced members of the lower classes who felt entitled to public support, and members of the upper classes who would stop progress to protect their privileges.[51]

In an era when Georgia politicians divided into Talmadge and anti-Talmadge camps, the Marietta businessman was consistently in the latter. Resembling the antebellum Whigs and urban, post-Civil War leaders of "New South" and Progressive campaigns, Carmichael opposed the small-government, limited-service philosophy of the Talmadge camp. Along with his friends Blair and Clay, he viewed government as a potentially positive force in bringing economic development to an impoverished region. These progrowth progressives parted company with liberals on labor and racial issues, but they favored good schools and adequate services for all Georgians and saw economic growth as favoring rich and poor, black and white. Through their experience in bringing the Bell Aircraft Corporation to Georgia, Jimmie Carmichael and his associates helped to produce a long anticipated, prosperous New Georgia.

NOTES

1. U.S. Department of Commerce, *Sixteenth Census of the United States: 1940, Population*, vol. 1, *Number of Inhabitants* (Washington, D.C.: GPO, 1942), 246.

2. Bruce J. Schulman, *From Cotton Belt to Sunbelt: Federal Policy, Economic Development, and the Transformation of the South, 1938–1980* (New York: Oxford University Press, 1991), 124; the author is grateful to Craig E. Aronoff, Distinguished Chair of Private Enterprise at Kennesaw State University, for first offering him this insight into Sun Belt development. See also Numan V. Bartley, *The New South, 1945–1980* (Baton Rouge: Louisiana State University Press, 1995), especially chapters 1 and 4.

3. Sarah Blackwell Gober Temple, *The First Hundred Years: A Short History of Cobb County, in Georgia* (Atlanta: Walter W. Brown, 1935), 35, 103, 155–57.

4. Ibid., 265–319; Louisa Warren Fletcher, *Journal of a Landlady: A Personal Account of Life in the Deep South during the Civil War Era by a Loyal Union Family*, ed. Henry Higgins and Connie Cox with Jean Cole Anderson (Chapel Hill, N.C.: Professional Press, 1995), 151.

5. Temple, 404–9; Eugene R. Huck, "Locomotives to Latin America: The Marietta Connection during World War I," *Georgia Historical Quarterly* 76 (Spring 1992): 100–114; Guy Haynes Northcutt, interview by Kathleen Sherlock Scott and Thomas A. Scott, 30 March 1973, transcript, pp. 2–4, Cobb County Oral History Series, No. 31, Bentley Rare Book Room, Sturgis Library, Kennesaw State University, Kennesaw, Georgia (hereafter cited as KSU; Leon McKenzie (Rip) Blair, untitled autobiographical sketch at request of Junior League, c. 1962, transcript, p. 14, Cobb County: Biography, Blair, Leon M., vertical files, Georgia Room, Cobb County Public Library, Marietta, Georgia.

6. The exact figures are 56 percent for farm tenancy, compared to 60 percent statewide. In Cobb County 78 percent of the tenants were sharecroppers. Average farm size had declined from 112 acres in 1880; these figures were similar to other Upper Piedmont counties, but much lower than farm size in all other areas of Georgia. Thomas Allan Scott, "Cobb County, Georgia, 1880–1900: A Socioeconomic Study of an Upper Piedmont County" (Ph.D. diss., University of Tennessee, 1978), 4, 7.

7. Joe Mack Wilson, interview by Thomas A. Scott, 1 April 1988, transcript, pp. 5, 8, 9, Cobb County Oral History Series, No. 19, Bentley Rare Book Room, KSU).

8. Fred D. Bentley Sr., interview by Thomas Allan Scott and Mary Boswell Cawley, 11 July 1987, transcript, pp. 12, 45, Cobb County Oral History Series, No. 8, Bentley Rare Book Room, KSU.

9. Comparable figures for the entire state in 1950 were the following: 31 percent of the people were nonwhite; median family income for all Georgians was $1,644, for whites $2,159 and for nonwhites $909. Scott, "Cobb County, Georgia, 1880–1900," 4, 25; U.S. Department of Commerce, *Census of Population: 1950*, Vol. II, *Characteristics of the Population*, Part 11, *Georgia* (Washington, D.C.: GPO, 1952), 35, 56, 117, 146, 155, 160.

10. *Marietta Daily Journal*, 31 May 1912, 29 May 1914 (also see "'Rip' Blair Going Strong," *Marietta Daily Journal*, 21 October 1962, 17A); Jean Edward Smith, *Lucius D. Clay: An American Life* (New York: Henry Holt and Company, 1990), 17–100; also see Jean Edward Smith, interview by Brian Lamb, 18 November 1991, C-SPAN, *Booknotes* transcript, pp. 1–9, <www.booknotes.org/transcripts/10108.htm>.

11. Clay attended the dedication in October 1941, when the segregated white facility was named in memory of his father. *Marietta Daily Journal*, 16 October 1941. For Blair's views on public housing, see the *Rotalight*, 21 January 1942, in Scrapbook 1 (2 January to 25 March 1942), Box 1, Blair Collection, Bentley Rare Book Room, KSU. Compiled by City Clerk Odene L. Johnson, the scrapbooks consist of clippings from Marietta and Atlanta newspapers, covering Blair's mayoral administration from January 1942 to January 1948 and much of the history of the Bell Bomber plant in Marietta.

12. "Memories of Marietta," summary of interview with Leon M. Blair, no author, no date, transcript, p. 15, Cobb County: Marietta, Miscellaneous I, vertical files, Georgia Room, Cobb County Public Library, Marietta, Georgia; *Marietta Daily Journal*, 11 March 1941, 8 January 1942.

13. "Memories of Marietta," 17.

14. L. M. Blair, Mayor, to Civil Aeronautics Authority, Washington, D.C., attention: Major Clay, 28 October 1940, Marietta, Georgia, folder, Box 22, Civil Aeronautics Administration Office of Airports, DLA Correspondence File, 1941–1947, Record Group 237, Federal Aviation Administration, National Archives II, College Park, Maryland (hereafter cited as Marietta folder, CAA).

15. W. B. Hartsfield to Hon. C. M. Head, Commissioner, Cobb County, 23 October 1940; Ivan Allen, Chairman, Industrial Bureau, Atlanta Chamber of Commerce, to James Carmichael, Marietta, 23 October 1940; Montgomery Knight to Honorable L. M. Blair, 23 October 1940, Marietta folder, CAA.

16. A Class 4 airport had runways that were long enough and thick enough to handle the largest commercial airplanes of the era. Blair made clear that Marietta was not interested in the smaller first- or second-class airports, but wanted only a Class 3 or Class 4 facility. Major Clay to Major McMullen, 31 October 1940; L. M. Blair to Major Clay, 28 October 1940; Marietta folder, CAA.

17. McMullen's endorsement was quite strong. He told the Atlanta regional manager that the Marietta site seemed "advantageously located" and that the cost of upgrading Candler Field seemed prohibitive. McMullen argued, "it is believed that the development of a new Class 4 airport could be constructed on a more suitable site for the same money that would be required to enlarge and improve Candler Field. In other words, two airports might be obtained with the same amount of money required to enlarge Candler Field." A. B. McMullen to Regional Manager, CAA, Atlanta, Georgia, 9 November 1940; Lucius D. Clay to Honorable L. M. Blair, 15 November 1940, Marietta folder, CAA.

18. *Marietta Daily Journal,* 22 April and 21 May 1942; L. M. Blair, "Reader Comment: McMillan Given Airport Credit," *Marietta Daily Journal,* 26 October 1962, p. 4.

19. Ibid., 7 July 1941; Judson C. Ward Jr., "Carmichael, James Vinson," in *Dictionary of Georgia Biography,* ed. Kenneth Coleman and Charles Stephen Gurr (Athens: University of Georgia Press, 1983); Dr. Judson Clements Ward Jr., interview by Thomas A. Scott, 30 September 1992, transcript, pp. 21–25, Cobb County Oral History Series, No. 23, Bentley Rare Book Room, KSU.

20. Blair recalled one couple in their nineties who refused all offers to move. When the mayor was given complete authority to make a deal, he spent a day visiting with them, finally making an "outrageous" offer and agreeing to help them relocate. "Memories of Marietta," 19–20.

21. At the time Lex Jolley was cashier for Johnson, Lane, Space & Company, the Atlanta firm selected to issue revenue bonds for the airport. *Marietta Daily Journal,* 16 May and 19 June 1941; minutes of meeting of the Commissioner of Roads and Revenues and the Advisory Board of Cobb County, 10 June 1941; Carmichael to Perkins, 12 and 27 June 1941; Perkins to Director of Airports, CAA, Washington, D.C., 28 June 1941, Marietta folder, CAA; Joe Kirby, "Unwitting Father of Dobbins Still Flying High," *Marietta Daily Journal,* 18 November 1987, 5C; Lex and LeoDelle Jolley, interview by Mary Boswell Cawley, 13 and 20 October 1987, transcript, pp. 48, 52–53, Cobb County Oral History Series, No. 4, Bentley Rare Book Room, KSU; "Memories of Marietta," 18.

22. *Marietta Daily Journal,* 4 September and 27 October 1941, 18 November 1987.

23. Smith, *Lucius D. Clay,* 98–99, 109, 155; Lucius D. Clay, interview by Jean Smith, 9 January 1971, interview #12, transcript, pp. 403–4, Dwight D. Eisenhower Library, Abilene, Kansas. The quotation comes from the published work. The wording differs slightly from the original oral history transcript, but the meaning remains identical. The oral history makes clear that Clay volunteered information on his role in bringing Bell to Marietta in response to a general question about the factors responsible for placing defense industries in particular locations.

24. Donald J. Norton, *Larry: A Biography of Lawrence D. Bell* (Chicago: Nelson-Hall, 1981), 1–103.

25. "Memories of Marietta," 18; *Atlanta Journal,* 23 January 1942.

26. The wage figure for the family-owned Glover Machine Works comes from the firsthand recollection of James Bolan Glover IV, as ascertained for the author on 14 June 1999 by Glover's son, James Bolan Glover V. Originally estimated as a $15-million project, by the end of the war the Bell plant had cost the War Department about $73 million. The first experimental XB-29 flew successfully on 14 September 1942. The Boeing plant in Wichita completed the first production model in July 1943. *Marietta Daily Journal,* 23 January 1942; *Atlanta Constitution,* 24 and 25 January 1942; *Atlanta Journal,* 23 and 24 January 1942; *Cobb County Times,* 27 September 1945; Press release, District Public Relations Officer, Southeastern District, Air Technical Service Command, "B-29 Characteristics, Performance and History," n.d., folder 3.46, Blair Collection, KSU.

27. Blair added that he and Carmichael personally backed the bonds. "Memories of Marietta," 17–18; Blair to Clay, 17 December 1941; Clay to Blair, 22 December 1941, Marietta folder, CAA; *Marietta Daily Journal,* 18 November 1987.

28. Blair to Clay, 18 December 1941; Clay to Blair, 18 December 1941; Blair to Clay, 19 December 1941, Marietta folder, CAA.

29. *Atlanta Journal*, 23 January 1942; Joe Harrison, "Everything under the Sun," column in *Cobb County Times*, 29 January 1942; in the 5 February 1942 issue Harrison added the name of County Commissioner George McMillan as one who played a key role in persuading the navy to drop its demands.

30. "Memories of Marietta," 18–19; Otis A. Brumby, "Jambalaya," *Cobb County Times*, 26 February 1942; Rufus Jarman, "Navy Surrenders Site for Big Bomber Plant," *Atlanta Journal*, 25 January 1942; *Marietta Daily Journal*, 26 January 1942; *Cobb County Times*, 5 February 1942; "Obstacles Removed, Work on Big Bomber Plant Here to Begin," *Atlanta Constitution*, 25 January 1942.

31. *Marietta Daily Journal*, 27 January and 18 February 1942; *Atlanta Journal*, 1 February 1942; *Cobb County Times*, 5 February 1942; "Memories of Marietta," 19; *Atlanta Constitution*, 9 February 1942.

32. *Rotalight*, 4 February 1942, Scrapbook 1, Box 1, Blair Collection, KSU.

33. *Cobb County Times*, 29 January and 26 February 1942; Ralph McGill, "One Word More," *Atlanta Constitution*, 25 February 1942.

34. *Marietta Daily Journal*, 15 February, 12 May, and 30 August 1943; "Memories of Marietta," 20. In 1950 the site would officially be renamed Dobbins Air Force Base, in memory of Georgia boys killed in the war, particularly Captain Charles M. Dobbins of Marietta, whose plane was shot down at sea near Sicily in July 1943.

35. *Marietta Daily Journal*, 27 February and 30 March 1942, 17 March and 15 April 1943; Bowling C. Yates, "Jimmy Carmichael Recalls 'Bell' Days," *Historic Highlights in Cobb County* (Marietta: Cobb Exchange Bank, 1973), 59; A. O. Willauer, Staff Assistant to the Manager, Bell Aircraft Corporation, Georgia Division, "Outline History of B-29 Program at Bell Bomber Plant, Dec. 22, 1941 to Dec. 31, 1943," pp. 3, 19. The original copy of the "Outline History" is in the Air Force Historical Research Agency collection, call number 208–1, Montgomery, Alabama; the author is grateful to Richard S. Combes, senior research engineer at the Georgia Tech Research Institute, for giving him a xerox copy of this unpublished manuscript.

36. Larry Bell is the source for the number of B-29s built in Marietta. *Marietta Daily Journal*, 3 November 1945. The peak employment was reached in February 1945. At that time 10,354 employees were female (37 percent of the total). "Marietta, Georgia: A Problem in Reconversion," Federal Reserve Bank of Atlanta *Monthly Review* 31 (October 1945): 109–14; also see *Marietta Daily Journal*, 22 November 1943. For Carmichael's views on disabled workers, see *Georgia Vocational Rehabilitation News*, January 1946, article by James V. Carmichael, Box 9, folder 11, Series I, subseries 2, General Correspondence, 1946, James Vinson Carmichael Papers, Special Collections, Woodruff Library, Emory University, Atlanta, Georgia (hereafter referred to as Carmichael papers, Emory).

37. Ernestine Slade, interview by Kathryn A. Kelley, 28 April and 19 May 1992, transcript, Cobb County Oral History Series, No. 28, Bentley Rare Book Room, KSU; Jennifer L. Fraire, "The Fair Employment Practices Committee in Atlanta: Southern White Reaction to Antidiscrimination Legislation during World War II, *Journal of the Georgia Association of Historians* 16 (1995): 175–88; Witherspoon Dodge to Clarence M. Mitch-

ell, Associate Director of Field Operations, 12 March 1945, Bell Aircraft Corporation folder, Administrative Files, Region VII, Records of the Committee on Fair Employment Practice, Record Group 228, National Archives–Southeast Region, East Point, Ga.

38. Willauer, "Outline History," 25–26; William G. Gisel, interview by Thomas A. Scott and Hugh M. Neeson, 25 October 1998, transcript, Cobb County Oral History Series, No. 50, Bentley Rare Book Room, KSU.

39. Norton, *Larry*, 133–41; see the *Marietta Daily Journal*, 28 and 29 November 1944 for an account of Carl Cover's death, when the twin-engine plane he was piloting struck a power line and burned while landing at Wright Field in Dayton, Ohio. The same paper on 27 December 1944 carried a story of Carmichael's elevation on 1 December 1944 to manager and on 26 December to corporate vice president.

40. Bell told Carmichael that managers of small companies needed to know the technical details of how their products were made, but that it was less important in a big organization, where department and division heads with specialized training could work under the leadership of a strong manager. He also advised that no one could succeed in his job without realizing that in a contest between quality and quantity, the former had to come first when one was making airplanes. Bell to Carmichael, 28 July 1944, folder 2, Box 4; "Larry" to "Dear Jimmy," 19 December 1944, folder 6, Box 5, Carmichael papers, Emory.

41. "Larry" to "Jimmie," 12 May 1945, folder 11, Box 7, ibid; M. L. St. John, "Marietta's Jimmy Carmichael Won't Stand for Buck-Passing," *Atlanta Constitution*, 10 June 1945, B-2.

42. *Marietta Daily Journal*, 17 August 1945; Yates, "Jimmy Carmichael Recalls 'Bell' Days," 59; Norton, *Larry*, 141.

43. Bentley interview, 13; *Census of Population: 1950, Characteristics of the Population, Georgia*, 9, 13; James V. Carmichael, handwritten manuscript (1946?), folder 20, Box 62, Carmichael papers, Emory.

44. Norton, *Larry*, 133–41, 187–253; the quotation is from p. 138. Also see David R. Goldfield, *Promised Land: The South since 1945* (Arlington Heights, Ill.: Harlan Davidson, 1987), 1–10; Kenneth Coleman, general ed., *A History of Georgia*, 2d ed. (Athens: University of Georgia Press, 1991), 339–47; and Gavin Wright, *Old South, New South: Revolutions in the Southern Economy since the Civil War* (1986; reprint, Baton Rouge: Louisiana State University Press, 1996), 239–41.

45. News release, 27 October 1966, file folder 6, Box IIA-7, Political File: Campaigns, Gubernatorial 1966, Howard H. Callaway Collection, Richard B. Russell Library, University of Georgia, Athens.

46. Smith, *Lucius D. Clay*, books 3 and 4; Smith, interview by Brian Lamb, *Booknotes*, 10–26; see also Lucius D. Clay, *Decision in Germany* (Garden City, N.Y.: Doubleday, 1950).

47. "'Rip' Blair Going Strong," *Marietta Daily Journal*, 21 October 1962, A17; biographical data, Leon McKenzie Blair, Cobb County: Biography, Blair, Leon M., vertical files, Georgia Room, Cobb County Public Library, Marietta, Ga.

48. Despite his association with Ellis Arnall, Carmichael clearly lacked the governor's appeal to organized labor. During the 1946 campaign Arnall asked U.S. Commerce secretary Henry Wallace to appeal to his CIO friends in behalf of the erstwhile Bell general

manager, whom the unionists distrusted as a "boss." Through Wallace, the governor urged Georgia CIO leaders to endorse Carmichael on faith, as a favor to Arnall, a friend of labor who had never let the working people down. Telephone conversation, Governor Arnall to Secretary Wallace, 10 May 1946, "Telephone Logs," Henry Agard Wallace Papers, Reel 66, University of Iowa Microfilm Collections. The author is grateful to colleague Randall L. Patton for alerting him to the existence of this request.

49. Coleman, *History of Georgia*, 393; Ward, "Carmichael, James Vinson"; "A Tribute to Our First General Manager," Lockheed *Southern Star*, 7 December 1972, p. 3; D. J. Haughton, corporate management memo to all members of supervision, Lockheed Aircraft Corporation, 29 November 1972 (copy in possession of author).

50. *Marietta Daily Journal*, 29 November 1972; James V. Carmichael, manuscript copy of Emory University commencement address, 1950, folder 23, Box 62, Carmichael papers, Emory. Large extracts from the commencement speech were published under the headline "James V. Carmichael's Analysis of Regional Needs: Education Called South's Key to Prosperity; Sales Tax Urged to Aid Georgia's Schools," in the *Atlanta Journal/Constitution*, 11 June 1950, F-1.

51. In their classic 1947 study, *Who Runs Georgia?*, Kytle and Mackay concluded that the state's political system ignored urban dwellers but also did little for "country folks," despite the apparent influence that the county unit system gave the latter. Real control, the authors maintained, resided with corporations such as the Georgia Power Company, whose officers and directors provided the campaign contributions necessary for electoral victory. Carmichael told the authors that "the Power Company must always maintain such a favored position that if the time ever comes when a higher tax rate is threatened on kilowatts or whenever a bill is introduced that might single it out, it can kill it through its influence with the assembly, and that failing, through its influence with the governor." During the 1946 gubernatorial election campaign, a chief executive of Georgia Power informed Carmichael that the company could not back him because he "wasn't a safe man," since he "would decide an issue on its merits and not on the basis of special interest." Calvin Kytle and James A. Mackay, *Who Runs Georgia?* (Athens: University of Georgia Press, 1998), 6–24, 256–57. The study was commissioned by a group of liberal activists in Atlanta and remained in manuscript form until its 1998 publication. The Richard Nixon introductory speech may be found in folder 29, Box 62, Carmichael papers, Emory.

Aircraft Manufacturing in Georgia

A Case Study of Federal Industrial Investment

RICHARD S. COMBES

Recent histories of southern economic development by Bruce Schulman and Dewey Grantham suggest that the role of federal investments in defense and space have been important factors in the post–World War II transformation of the region declared to be the "nation's number one economic problem" in 1938.[1] Other public policy analysts, such as Ann Markusen and David Roessner, contend that the policy model of directing federal defense and space investments to the South and West constitutes a "de facto" industrial policy that has existed in the United States since the beginning of World War II.[2] During the military buildup preceding the war, southern business leaders and legislators sought defense industry investments with enthusiasm previously reserved for recruiting branch plants to the region. Thus, when southern political backlash to New Deal programs occurred after the 1938 elections, federal development policy quickly became aligned with the patriotic conservatism of the region's leadership, and "Dr. New Deal" was replaced with "Dr. Win the War."[3]

This chapter addresses the building of Air Force Plant #6 in Marietta, Georgia, beginning in 1941, as a component of the massive federal program to manufacture the B-29 bomber. Although the plant manufactured B-29s for less than three years, its legacy of a trained workforce of 28,000, mammoth manufacturing facility, and cultural transformation of rural Georgia helped convince Lockheed Aircraft Company to establish a permanent presence in Georgia that in 1998 remained the largest manufacturing operation in the state. The initial decision to build a plant to manufacture bombers stemmed from federal investment policy influenced by southern economic development considerations, New South boosterism, and war-related urgency to mass-produce aircraft. The 7 December

1941 bombing of Pearl Harbor spurred the implementation of the military's plan and subsequent budgeting of unprecedented funding for building aircraft. In this environment, the army selected a New York–based defense contractor, the Bell Aircraft Company, to build the largest aircraft assembly facility in the world in a region that had little to offer other than unemployed workers and a "can do" spirit among local elected officials and business leaders. The effort by Bell to make the plant operational and train more than 28,000 local workers to build a total of 668 giant aircraft in just over two years demonstrated the area's ability to successfully house a large technology-based manufacturing facility.

Although local politicians had envisioned a continuation of manufacturing operations at the Bell plant after the war, manufacturing operations shut down quickly after V-J Day, and for the next five years the plant was used to warehouse surplus government equipment. In 1950, Korean War defense investments again brought the facility to life as a bomber factory. A new coalition of congressional and Pentagon strategists convinced the Lockheed Aircraft Corporation, headquartered at the time in Burbank, California, to take over and operate the plant as a permanent industrial tenant. The recently (1947) created U.S. Air Force persuaded Lockheed, a major defense contractor, to restart manufacturing at the plant with the inducement of contracts to build aircraft to fight the Korean War and the Cold War. Lockheed has operated the plant continuously for more than 50 years and has been the largest manufacturing employer in Georgia throughout that time, with a workforce ranging from 10,000 to over 32,000. In 1995, Lockheed's Aircraft Division Headquarters moved from Burbank, where the company was founded, to the Georgia plant.

THE DECISION TO BUILD AIR FORCE PLANT #6

At the 1939 outbreak of war in Europe, the Army Air Corps had convinced a reluctant Congress to appropriate funds for designing a new "superbomber" that became the B-29. The B-17, a four-engine heavy bomber, had been in production for several years (a prototype B-17 had first flown in 1936), but military planners, including Charles Lindbergh, feared that the United States would need a bomber with longer range, higher speed, and higher carrying capacity than the B-17. The army issued a request for design proposals in 1940 and subsequently gave Boeing a contract to build two prototypes of their design. Using a new cost plus fixed fee (CPFF) contracting arrangement, Boeing committed to delivery of the first operational B-29 in April 1942. The CPFF contract committed the government to covering all legitimate costs of the aircraft manufacturers, with a guarantee of 6 percent profit (i.e., the fixed percentage fee).[4] With the costs incurred by Boeing guaranteed to be covered by the army, the CPFF approach effectively made Boeing employees working on the contract government employees and subjected them to federal work rules and workplace standards.

The B-29 program was a revolutionary initiative in government-financed aircraft manufacturing that was unprecedented in scale; the program costs totaled $3 billion and represented the costliest weapons program of World War II (e.g., the Manhattan Project cost $2.5 billion).[5] In 1941 and early 1942, the army signed contracts with a number of firms to build B-29s and to supply parts and subassemblies for the bombers. In addition to agreements with Boeing to build 1,065 B-29s, Bell Aircraft Corporation of Buffalo initially signed up to build 400 planes, and General Motors was to build 200 (GM's share was later shifted to Glenn L. Martin Corporation). The Bell production plan called for manufacturing aircraft in a new government-owned factory to be built in Marietta, Georgia, by the Army Corps of Engineers. The military set up a consortium of the B-29 contractors, with Boeing responsible for providing all design specifications, tooling information, and other production support to Bell and GM, an arrangement that recognized the scale of the program was too large for Boeing alone.[6]

The new plant in Georgia was the largest of several aircraft plants built during the war. Great Britain first used the concept of the government constructing and owning aircraft manufacturing facilities in the mid-1930s as Europe moved toward war. In order to provide a large increase in national capacity to manufacture military aircraft, the British built "shadow plants" that used contract labor and management from outside the aircraft industry and were located in conjunction with other large manufacturing operations, such as auto factories.[7] With government-provided facilities instead of private capital investment, aircraft manufacturers could be assured that they would not build capacity that couldn't be used after wartime demand for planes had disappeared. As early as 1937, U.S. military planners had considered using government-owned, contractor-operated (GOCO) plants to produce aircraft; however, considerable resistance to a rapid military buildup arose from Congress's ambivalence about preparing for war.[8] Congress finally voted funds to build GOCO plants to manufacture heavy bombers in 1940, after Franklin Roosevelt had set a goal in May 1940 of having 50,000 military aircraft available for the war effort (as late as 1939 the authorized number of U.S. military aircraft was just 2,230).

Bomber plants were particularly capital intensive and the aircraft industry would be hard pressed to use these giant facilities after the war, so federal assumption of the investment risk convinced aircraft firms to participate in these massive operations. In 1940, after the National Defense Advisory Commission developed a strategy to build an additional 12,000 bombers, the War Department created a Plant Site Board that conducted extensive site selection studies focusing primarily on local labor and infrastructure availability. By the end of

1940, bomber factories were under construction in Omaha, Kansas City, Tulsa, and Fort Worth. The Omaha facility originally manufactured B-26 medium bombers, and was converted in late 1943 so that contractor Glenn L. Martin Aircraft Corporation could build the newer B-29.[9]

The announcement of Marietta as the site for a new bomber plant came on 24 January 1942 with much local fanfare. At that time, Marietta was the county seat for Cobb County (1941 population of 35,000) and an economically tethered satellite of nearby Atlanta with few prospects for rapid development. Atlanta business boosters, working through the Atlanta Chamber of Commerce, and elected officials in Marietta led the effort to bring an Army Air Corps installation to northwest Georgia. At the time, the state government offered little interest or support. Eugene Talmadge, an anti-New Dealer and ardent segregationist, had been reelected as Georgia's governor in 1940; he had no use for recruiting industry, particularly industry funded by the federal government. E. D. Rivers, who served as Georgia's governor from 1937 to 1941, had been a progressive whose "little New Deal" created the first statewide board to plan and coordinate economic development projects. However, a conservative state legislature refused to vote new taxes needed to finance new programs, and stymied Rivers's agenda for progressive action.[10] Thus, any enthusiasm for recruiting a new army plant to the state had to come from local supporters.

As an inducement to locate the B-29 plant in Marietta, the city offered the army its new municipal airport, which was under construction in 1941. The site for the airport, named Rickenbacker Field after Eddie Rickenbacker, World War I ace and then president of Eastern Airlines, had originally been surveyed in January 1940. James Vinson Carmichael, the city attorney for Marietta and an individual who had ties to the Marietta plant until his death in 1972, was responsible for purchasing land for the new airport. Carmichael and other Marietta and Cobb County officials worked closely with Atlanta business leaders in a classic example of New South boosterism to deliver the Marietta site to the army just a month after America's entry into World War II. Atlanta had supported aviation business since it had leased land at Candler Field (a former auto raceway owned by Asa Candler of Coca-Cola fame) for a municipal airport in 1925, making the facility permanent with the purchase of 297 acres at the site in 1929.[11] The Bureau of Industry of the Atlanta Chamber of Commerce had first pitched the Atlanta Municipal Airport (now Hartsfield International Airport) as the site for a major Army Air Corps Overhaul and Repair Depot, but in 1941 this facility was built at the small rural town of Wellston, Georgia.[12] In a September 1941 letter to the army's Industrial Location Section, Frank Shaw, secretary of the Bureau, proposed the new "Marietta-Atlanta Airport" as a suitable site for a new army facility. In this letter, Shaw claimed that records of the Georgia Unemployment Service showed that 25,696 persons were registered as unemployed in the metropolitan Atlanta region, suggesting a large available workforce. Just a month earlier, Shaw had written Eddie Rickenbacker and claimed that the Marietta airport was superior to the Atlanta Municipal Airport at Candler Field for army aircraft, specifically citing the suitability of the new runways for "4-engine bombers."[13]

In a letter Carmichael wrote to General Nichols of the Air Corps on 10 January 1942, just two weeks before the formal announcement of the new plant, he described the site as comprising 600 acres of land on the new highway U.S. 41, with additional land available at $125/acre.[14] A railroad and natural gas pipeline served the site, with a gasoline pipeline within three miles. Carmichael called the labor conditions at the site "ideal" and indicated that less than 2 percent of Atlanta's population and less than 0.5 percent of Cobb County's population were foreign-born. The issue of national origin ranked high as a consideration of security-conscious planners of new defense facilities, who saw foreign-born workers as potential labor agitators or sympathetic to Socialist, Communist, or Nazi causes.[15]

On 23 January 1942, Bell Aircraft Corporation officials signed agreements with the City of Marietta to turn over to the Air Corps the Rickenbacker Field site and all buildings and runways under construction at the time for a new bomber plant. Local individuals credited in the *Atlanta Constitution* for working with Bell officials included Marietta mayor L. M. "Rip" Blair, Marietta city attorney James V. Carmichael, Cobb County commissioner George McMillan, U.S. Congressman Malcolm Tarver, U.S. Senator Walter George, Atlanta Federal Reserve Bank chairman Frank H. Neely, and Ivan Allen Sr. and Frank Shaw of the Atlanta Chamber of Commerce.[16] At a "Victory Dinner" held at the Atlanta Athletic Club to celebrate the new army/Bell plant, Atlanta mayor Buck LeCraw joked that Atlanta had had to "annex herself to Cobb County, but was proud to do it" to recruit the facility.[17] The Atlanta/Marietta coalition of boosters had been well prepared to respond quickly to the opportunity to recruit a major new industry to the region by offering the Marietta airport and promising a pool of available labor.[18] The prize was a huge defense plant that eventually employed 28,000.

BUILDING AND OPERATING THE BELL BOMBER PLANT

Once the decision to locate the plant in Marietta was finalized in late February 1942, work proceeded quickly to build it. The army named Robert and Company, an Atlanta engineering firm, as the project's architect/engineering manager, and James Carmichael expedited the transfer of ownership of land and facilities to the federal government. The Army Corps of Engineers prepared the site and constructed the plant, breaking ground on 30 March 1942. The blueprint called for the total floor space of all buildings to be 3,955,800 square feet, with the main assembly building covering 3,287,000 square feet, nearly 76 acres under one roof.[19] The plant was designed as a "blackout facility" with no windows, to guard against enemy air raids that army planners thought possible in 1942. The windowless main assembly building required a huge air conditioning system, a relatively new technology in the sultry South. The Corps of Engineers turned the plant over to Bell on 15 April 1943, with buildings 93 percent complete and 50 percent of the equipment in place; by 1 January 1944 the army had invested $47 million in Marietta's bomber capacity.[20]

In December 1941, the army "drafted" the Bell Aircraft Company "for this forbidding assignment" of building B-29s in Georgia.[21] Larry Bell and his brother started the firm in Buffalo, New York, in 1935, and by 1941 Bell was successfully manufacturing the P-39 Airacobra, a much smaller aircraft than the B-29. As soon as plans for the Marietta plant were finalized, Bell started coordinating with Boeing in Seattle, the firm designated as design engineer for the B-29 airframe, parts, subassemblies, and production tooling. The B-29 production consortium of Boeing, Bell, Glenn L. Martin, and Fisher Body (a General Motors subsidiary) held regular meetings during 1942 through 1945 to coordinate and resolve design and production issues arising from the contract work of the consortium and its subcontractors. Bell engineers initially handled all layout design for the Marietta plant from the Buffalo facility and not until 14 December 1942 did a contingent of 700 Bell employees move from Buffalo to temporary offices in downtown Atlanta.[22] The Bell contract with the army called for delivery of the first Georgia-built B-29 in September 1943, and delivery of the four hundredth bomber by January 1945. The actual first flight of a Bell B-29 took place on 4 November 1943. That plane was more a hand-built model than one produced by the Marietta assembly line, due to numerous delays in plant construction and the simultaneous B-29 design changes taking place at Boeing.[23]

When it first occupied the plant, Bell had 1,179 employees in Georgia; by the end of 1943, Bell employed 17,094 employees and was adding 2,000–3,000 more per month.[24] This rapid buildup of a new southern workforce caused some problems; in June 1943, with about 8,000 workers in the plant, 500 Bell workers quit. Although the workers were represented by a new union, United Auto Workers Local 10, complaints of the Bell management style caused "considerable underground muttering," and the new union couldn't deal with the problems to the satisfaction of all workers.[25] By April 1945 the plant workforce stood at 27,000, manufacturing 60–65 planes each month (exceeding the design production rate of the plant), and Bell had instituted a number of programs aimed at improving the work environment. For example, the firm erected hundreds of small houses for workers near the plant site to create a complex not unlike a southern mill village. However, most workers commuted to the plant from their homes, and Bell and local governments facilitated commuting with construction of huge parking lots, traffic management during shift changes, and completion of a new highway from south Atlanta to the plant in late 1943. Despite local officials' earlier assurances of available workers, Bell had to recruit new employees from outlying areas and provide bus transportation between the plant and communities as far as sixty miles away. By February 1944, Bell workers were commuting from 106 Georgia communities, and traffic and driving safety warnings appeared regularly in the plant newsletter.[26] In February 1945 Marietta completed a new $195,000 recreation center for workers, and Bell promoted extensive team sports programs, with sports news regularly featured in the "Bell Aircraft News." The plant opened two cafeterias in June 1943 that were serving 24,000 meals per day by March 1945. In addition, Bell operated day care centers near the plant, instituted an employee suggestion system that gave monetary awards to workers whose suggestions were used, and held an annual family day when families of workers could visit the plant.[27] The management gave workers a Christmas bonus in December 1944 and a day off for Christmas shopping that same month, as a reward for achieving the monthly production goal.

The Bell workforce was mostly white and female, and most workers had to be trained quickly to assemble sophisticated aircraft. The task of training new workers fell to a number of organizations, including the local National Youth Administration (NYA) program, vocational training schools in Atlanta, Cobb County and Fulton County, the Georgia School of Technology in Atlanta, and an extensive in-plant program. When the plant was first announced, officials predicted that 1,000 workers per month could be trained by the NYA and county trade schools. However, a June 1943 NYA Region 7 (northwest Georgia) report indicated that during the previous *year* 969 "boys and girls from 26 northwest Georgia counties" had completed training under their War Production Training Project. Of that meager total, only 441 males and 175 females secured war production jobs.[28] It appears that the early plan for existing schools to handle the intensive training needs proved overly ambitious, and new training programs were needed.

In November 1942, the Cobb County Board of Education opened the new Rickenbacker Aircraft Training School in buildings previously used by the Civilian Conservation Corps, with a $5,000 donation from Eddie Rickenbacker.[29] After Bell occupied the plant in 1943, the company instituted extensive training programs at the manufacturing site, making scrap metal available to teach skills such as riveting, sheet metal work, and welding. B-29s built at other Boeing plants were flown to Marietta and used to give new workers on-the-job training. By September 1943, as thousands of new workers were being hired, Bell employed 25 training counselors at the plant.[30]

Manufacturing the B-29 required skills new even to experienced aircraft plant workers because the design of the plane incorporated innovations for improved aerodynamic performance, such as butt jointing sheet metal parts, as opposed to overlapped joints, and flush mounted rivet heads. Creating sheet metal parts and assembling them into complex shapes was one of the primary work requirements, and while experienced aircraft builders did this work with pride, training new, unskilled workers in these difficult tasks presented a major challenge to Bell. One approach unique to the Bell plant among the four facilities building the B-29 was the use of lofting. The lofting department produced full-scale, precision production drawings of airframe parts, and created templates from these huge drawings for use in setting up tools and manufacturing dies. The Bell engineers indicated that lofting was "now considered the backbone of Bell's aircraft manufacturing methods," and they insisted on using this approach instead of having Boeing supply templates to Marietta.[31] Lofting personnel ("loftsmen") were highly specialized draftsmen, few of whom could be found in Georgia (Bell had "borrowed" their lofting system from the shipbuilding industry, and Georgia had neither large shipyards nor aircraft manufacturing in 1943). To train these essential loftsmen, Bell sought workers who could master the drafting tasks after an intensive five-month training program at the Bell plant in Buffalo. The loftsmen hired in Georgia included a professor, a sculptor, and a patternmaker from the chenille bedspread industry.[32]

In addition to requiring workers to learn new skills, the Bell plant presented numerous cultural changes in the traditional southern workplace to Georgia residents who came to work there. The plant warranted a secret classification (e.g., a photo of a B-29 couldn't be published in the newsletter until after the first B-29 raid on Japan in mid-1944) and all workers had to use time clocks, undergo security checks, and wear ID badges. The rhythms of work in the factory included mastering the logistics of commuting by auto or bus, shift changes involving thousands of workers, eating in huge plant cafeterias, two- or three-shift workdays, and a six-day workweek (Saturday work ended after 18 June 1945). The plant newsletter preached a doctrine of tolerance for union activities and published unbiased announcements of union elections.[33] In addition to having a union shop, Bell also employed a few black workers in skilled positions, and hired blind and "deaf-mute" workers for specialized positions. The 13 August 1944 edition of "Bell Aircraft News" included a small article praising the contributions of "about 1,500 Negroes" employed at the plant and welcomed their families to that summer's Family Day. The article indicated that, while most of the black employees worked in plant custodial services, 250 held "metal fabrication" jobs; however, there was no suggestion that an integrated workplace existed.

As in all defense plants during the war, women accepted new work roles and were a major reason for the ultimate success of the B-29 operation. Frances Light took a job as a bookkeeper in the fall of 1943 and worked at the plant until it closed in late 1945. Frances's husband Ed had gone overseas to war in 1942, and she and their one-year-old daughter were living at her family home in Sandy Springs, Georgia, when Bell started its intensive recruiting efforts in 1943. Frances and two of her sisters went to work at the bomber plant, carpooling from Sandy Springs and downtown Atlanta; she rode together with four or five other workers because gasoline and tire rubber were rationed at the time. (One of her sisters had a job in the Transportation Department where Bell coordinated rides and car pools.) Although Frances was able to leave her child with her mother during her shifts, other women employees were able to use several day care centers that Bell operated near the plant site.[34]

Other new workplace institutions included drives encouraging workers to buy war bonds and donate blood, withholding of federal taxes from paychecks, and payroll deduction options for bond purchases. Perhaps the biggest change for southerners at Bell's Marietta factory was answering to "Yankee" bosses from Buffalo, New York. Bell brought almost all of the plant executives from New York to manage the startup, worker recruitment and training, and production operations that had to meet critical contract deadlines. However, the plant provided one southerner a chance to shine. James Carmichael, a Marietta native educated in the town's public schools and Emory Law School, was only 32 years old when the plant was announced. As Marietta city attorney, Carmichael had played a major role in securing the plant site for the army and Bell hired him as the plant's assistant general manager in 1944. O. L. Woodson, a top Bell executive who transferred to Georgia in 1942 from Buffalo, served as general manager of the Georgia Division of Bell Aircraft Company until July 1944. Carl Cover succeeded Woodson but died in a December 1944 plane crash, at which time Carmichael became general manager, the top Bell executive in Georgia. Under Carmichael's supervision the plant flourished; during his first month as general manager, the plant exceeded its monthly production quota for the first time (Carmichael recognized the workers' success with a Christmas bonus).[35] During his tenure as assistant and later general manager, the plant manufactured 617 bombers, or 92 percent of its total output as a B-29 plant,[36] and employed between 22,000 and 28,000 workers. This war experience launched Carmichael's career as an industrial executive; in 1947 he became president of Scripto, Inc., a large Atlanta manufacturing firm. When Lockheed moved into the plant in January 1951, it hired Carmichael as vice president and general manager, a position he held for over a year while continuing his responsibilities at Scripto.[37] Thereafter, he served as a director for Lockheed-Georgia until his death in 1972.

By August of 1945, it was clear to Bell workers that the war would end shortly and the plant would close soon thereafter. In spite of earlier assurances from Carmichael, layoffs began that same month, and by the end of 1945 the Bell workforce was completely gone. Despite efforts to find a peacetime use for the giant plant, a workforce representing an annual payroll of $60 million and a facility worth $47 million were put in a standby mode, and the army used the plant as a military surplus warehouse for the next five years.

OPERATIONS OF THE LOCKHEED-GEORGIA DIVISION

In late 1950, with the Korean conflict going badly for the United States, the air force convinced the Lockheed Aircraft Corporation to reopen Air Force Plant #6 to refurbish B-29s that had been in storage in Texas since the end of World War II. Within a year the plant employed 10,000, including a team of 275 key Lockheed engineers and managers who moved to Georgia from Burbank, California.[38] In 1952 the air force awarded Lockheed a contract to build the B-47, a new jet bomber designed by Boeing; the plant eventually manufactured 394 of them over a ten-year period. In 1953 Lockheed made a decision to build its new C-130 military transport plane at Marietta. The C-130 became one of the most versatile and durable aircraft ever built for the military and is still being manufactured in Georgia.

The contrast between the type of operation Bell managed during the war years to the one that Lockheed initiated after the 1953 introduction of the C-130 represents a transition from a temporary wartime effort to a permanent regional manufacturing presence sustained by ongoing federal contracts. The Bell B-29 plant underwent an extremely rapid buildup of manufacturing capacity under the impetus of the World War II superbomber program. Engineering and management talent required for the Bell operation was imported from the northeast United States, and assembly line workers (albeit a highly specialized assembly line) were recruited from the available southern labor pool. After the war, most Bell white-collar workers returned to Buffalo, the Georgians who had built bombers became unemployed, and the federal plant owners had no alternate production use for the huge plant. In 1950, the military reevaluated use of the plants it still owned at the time and decided to reactivate Marietta's Plant #6 for the war effort. When Lockheed reopened the plant to again work on B-29s, it hired not only James Carmichael but also many Bell-trained workers, such as Eli Cook, a northwest Georgia native who had started a dry-cleaning business in Ball Ground, Georgia, after the Bell operation shut down. Brought back as a toolmaker in 1950, Cook retired twenty years later as a manager in the Lockheed tool-making shop.[39]

Through the first two years of the Lockheed operation (the Korean War was ongoing), the plant operated as it had been designed—to assemble/modify bombers engineered outside the region. However, with the 1953 decision to move production of the C-130 to Marietta, the plant became a permanent and complete aircraft manufacturing operation. The design and engineering component added at the plant with the start of C-130 production transformed it from the branch plant model, where high value-added operations such as design, engineering, and sales were done outside the region, to a division model, with all operations resident at the production facility. This transformation changed the makeup of the plant's workforce. The ratio of hourly workers to salaried workers was about 27 to 1 at the height of the Bell B-29 operation, while it averaged 2.7 to 1 for the Lockheed operation during the period 1960–67.[40] In 1961, when production of the B-47 was being phased out, Lockheed-Georgia won the design contract for a new military jet transport, the C-141. Then in 1965, when the end of production of the C-141 was in sight, the plant won a nearly $3 billion contract to build the C-5, the largest aircraft ever built to that time.[41]

The Marietta facility led the proposal efforts for these contracts, attesting to the depth and sophistication of the plant's engineering and R&D capability developed since 1953. The Georgia plant became the exclusive design/manufacturing site for the C-130 (1,400 built by 1976 and over 2,400 to present), C-141 (284 built through 2/16/68), and the C-5 (81 built through 1973) together with other limited production aircraft.[42] In addition, the plant has received numerous contracts to modify the aircraft they built either to correct defects (e.g., wing modifications for the C-141 and C-5), or to increase the capacity/performance of the planes (e.g., stretching the fuselage of the C-130 and C-141 "stretch" models). The plant currently has an air force contract to build the F-22 stealth fighter aircraft. The Marietta plant and the former General Dynamics plant in Fort Worth, Texas, are now the only active aircraft manufacturing facilities for the Lockheed-Martin Corporation.[43]

Unlike the wartime experience of the Bell operation, Lockheed came into Georgia with the assurance that a trained workforce would be available. The 1946 shutdown of the B-29 plant resulted in the availability of 27,000 specialized workers who likely stayed in the region, and Lockheed found it could quickly hire 10,000 workers to start bomber assembly/modification operations by the end of 1951. The special training programs, such as the Rickenbacker Aircraft Training School, had disbanded after the war; however, like the earlier Bell operation, Lockheed brought established in-plant training techniques to Georgia. For example, in 1953 a full-scale wooden mockup of the C-130, weighing 100,000 pounds, was loaded on a ship in Los Angeles and routed through the Panama Canal to Savannah, Georgia, where it was trucked to Marietta. One account of the trip across Georgia explains: "Along the route, schools let out so children could watch the procession, mayors greeted the convoy with proclamations, and cotton pickers stopped in their tracks to view the whale-like monster."[44] This mockup represented "thousands of man-hours of engineering and manufacturing time" to familiarize engineers and workers with the physical aspects of the C-130 as they started the task of going into production.[45]

With the large number of engineers needed for the design and development of new aircraft, Lockheed developed a close working relationship with the Georgia Institute of Technology, located just 13 miles south of the plant in Atlanta. Georgia Tech's engineering schools, including an aeronautical engineering department established in 1930 following an award from the Guggenheim Foundation, soon set up cooperative work/study programs with Lockheed. The Southern Technical Institute, a two-year Georgia Tech extension program, also provided engineering technology students and graduates to the plant. In 1963, Southern Tech moved its campus from Chamblee (just northeast of Atlanta) to Marietta with the encouragement and support of Lockheed and other businesses needing technical workers. The City of Marietta participated by donating 120 acres of land for the new campus. In 1980 Southern Tech became independent of Georgia Tech and today, as Southern Polytechnic University, offers bachelor's and master's programs in engineering technology and maintains close ties to the nearby Lockheed plant. In 1962, Cobb County started a new vocational school in Marietta that has grown to be the Chattahoochee Technical Institute, comprising three campuses in Marietta and nearby communities.

At the time Lockheed came to Georgia, few other job opportunities existed for the technical workers and engineers who worked at the plant. Not until 1949, just two years before Lockheed's arrival, did the number of manufacturing jobs surpass agricultural jobs in Georgia. At that time, most manufacturing opportunities were low-wage, low-skill positions in textiles, food processing, and branch plants, such as automobile assembly. To develop the technically skilled workforce needed to build the C-130 and later design/build the C-141 and C-5, Lockheed transplanted hundreds of key engineers from Burbank, recruited others from around the country,[46] and started hiring new engineers from the region's engineering and technical schools. The aircraft manufacturing operation provided a large number of technology-based jobs for southerners who might otherwise have had to leave the region to work in their field. For example, Jim Hills graduated from Georgia Tech as a mechanical engineer in 1952 and joined Lockheed in Marietta. Assigned to the test group at the plant, he became involved in sophisticated metallurgical testing, for strength and performance of new metal alloys were critical to the successful design and performance of Lockheed aircraft. While still working at the plant in the early 1970s, Hills started an engineering firm in Marietta, Applied Technical Services, Inc. (ATS), that specialized in materials testing and failure analysis. When he retired from Lockheed, he worked full-time as president of ATS until his death in 1996. Today ATS, headed by Jim Hills's son, is a thriving technical services firm with annual sales of over $8 million. Lockheed also offered opportunities for southern executives such as

James Carmichael to manage a large-scale, unionized factory. Daniel Haughton, an Alabama native who transferred to Marietta from Lockheed's Burbank headquarters, became general manager of the plant after working for a year under Carmichael. Haughton, a real "shirtsleeves executive," inspired all workers to make the C-130 a success because he believed this was necessary to establish Lockheed's permanent presence in Marietta. Haughton later served for a number of years as chairman and CEO of Lockheed Corporation.[47]

What would entice a California-based firm to start a major manufacturing operation in the South in 1951? The Bell experience had demonstrated that aircraft could be successfully produced in Georgia, but unlike General Kenneth Wolfe's "drafting" of the Bell Aircraft Company to manufacture B-29s in 1941, Lockheed's continuing business in Marietta depended on winning competitions for contracts. By the time Lockheed was ready to build the C-130, the Lockheed-Georgia Division had proven its capabilities with the B-47 program and use of the air force plant presented an opportunity to avoid the substantial investment of building another aircraft plant.[48]

Another important aspect of competing successfully in building military planes was the politics of Washington; at the time Lockheed won the C-141 and C-5 contracts, the plant had powerful support in the person of Georgia Senator Richard Russell, chairman of the Senate Armed Forces Committee from 1951 to 1969. According to Russell's biographer, the senator engaged in a bit of "horse-trading" with President Johnson in 1965 to help secure the C-5 contract for Lockheed. Then in 1969, when Senator William Proxmire wanted to investigate an expected $2 billion overrun on the same contract, Russell made certain that hearings did not focus on Lockheed's performance.[49] Senator Russell, Senator Walter George (served 1922–1956), and Congressman Carl Vinson (served 1911–1962, chairman of House Armed Forces Committee 1947–1962) were powerful allies for Bell and Lockheed while they were tenants at the plant, exerting considerable political influence to see that contract work continued to go to Marietta.

The procurement process so vital to the operation of the Marietta facility has evolved and grown considerably since the then-innovative CPFF contracts were used to procure the B-29. The C-130 and C-141 were both produced under CPFF contracts from the air force, although Lockheed requested a fixed price–incentive type contract for the initial design and production of the C-141.[50] The initial C-141 contract, signed in April 1961, contained new government requirements that addressed workplace issues and business practices other than engineering and production requirements typically covered in aircraft procurement. For example, Lockheed was required to be a "pilot plant in the South" for testing President Kennedy's policy of equal opportunity.[51] As a result, the plant integrated its cafeterias and employee facilities in 1961, three years before the Civil Rights Act of 1964 struck down segregation practices elsewhere. The desegregation of the plant generated tensions among workers, with some white employees threatening to disrupt the efforts, which ultimately proceeded successfully.[52] The C-141 contract called for Lockheed to subcontract 60 percent of the work and also to actively identify and subcontract with small businesses in an early manifestation of policies aimed at ensuring that small firms benefited from the billions of dollars channeled into federal contracts. The federal imposition of new business and workplace practices as contract requirements, and Lockheed's willingness to abide by these requirements demonstrates the leverage the government had over firms whose continued existence depended on new contracts.

One of the biggest experiments in defense procurement during the 1960s involved Lockheed's contract to design and build the C-5. The Department of Defense (DOD), under Robert McNamara, developed a concept called total package procurement system (TPPS) that was used for the C-5. TPPS embodied the concept that combining research and development of new aircraft with their production would save the government money by reducing contractor overruns and costly contract changes. Along with the TPPS contract came myriad new cost monitoring requirements and personnel, such as use of program evaluation and review technique (PERT) to plan and track production. Unfortunately, the TPPS approach failed to work as intended, because the C-5 program experienced huge cost overruns and the plane did not initially perform to expectations. As a result, Lockheed nearly went bankrupt in the late 1960s trying to meet contract obligations, and only extensive modifications to the contract and ultimately a $250 million federal loan saved the firm.[53] As the military transport planes that Lockheed made in Georgia grew in size, complexity, and cost, the work on federal contracts got increasingly riskier due to government demands that went beyond simply producing aircraft that performed well. However, Lockheed's business remained viable because the federal government, essentially its sole customer, would not allow it to fail.

Throughout its existence, the Marietta plant has depended on federal contracts to employ as many as 32,000 manufacturing workers and provide defense contractors with government-owned equipment worth $400–550 million.[54] The initial federal decision to build and own the plant has resulted in a continuity of operations since 1942 because its military owners remain reluctant to abandon a highly specialized and valuable asset that has had strong southern support in Congress. While other government-built plants from the World War II era have been sold to private firms (e.g., American Airlines bought the Tulsa plant for a maintenance depot, Boeing acquired the Wichita plant to manufacture commercial aircraft) or transferred to other agencies (e.g., a Kansas City engine plant became a nuclear weapons supply depot for the Atomic Energy Commission/Department of Energy), the Marietta plant continues under air force ownership. It is likely that the sheer size of the facility makes it harder to sell than smaller plants. (In 1965, after winning the C-5 competition, Lockheed considered buying the facility for $20 million, but the sale did not take place.)[55] With strong military and congressional support to keep it operating, the Marietta plant offers a clear example of what President Eisenhower termed the "military-industrial complex," and a continuous stream of federal contracts for building or modifying aircraft has indeed represented a de facto federal industrial policy, much as Markusen and Roessner have argued.

GOCO DEFENSE PLANTS AS INDUSTRIAL POLICY

As is typical of many large-scale economic development projects, the Marietta plant's siting occurred because of the confluence of several economic and political forces:

> Business boosters in Atlanta and Marietta were determined to attract an Army Air Corps installation to the region, touting a large regional pool of unemployed workers and offering a municipal airport as an incentive.

> The B-29 program called for the construction of an aircraft manufacturing plant of unprecedented size, and the government decided to build and own the plant because of the reluctance of private sector firms to make the necessary capital investment for what was deemed to be a temporary operation.

> The New Deal emphasis on economic assistance to the South was carried over to war planning agencies, with support from conservative Georgia legislators, who no longer supported Roosevelt's peacetime policies but were enthusiastic about efforts to win the war.

> Larry Bell's aircraft company benefited from the wartime mobilization effort that raised its annual revenues from $5.2 million in 1940 to $121.9 million in 1942. When the army asked, the firm willingly created the largest aircraft plant in the world in a southern industrial environment that must have seemed akin to a developing nation to the New Yorkers.

> Patriotic Georgia workers, including women and African Americans, stood ready to contribute to the war effort, even if it meant rigorous training and accepting workplace requirements (e.g., long commutes, unions, Yankee bosses, rigorous security) that ran counter to southern traditions.

Air Force Plant #6 offers policy analysts a unique case study since, together with Air Force Plant #4 in Fort Worth,[56] it is an aircraft manufacturing facility built by the military during World War II that has remained government-owned while being used for its original purpose. In addition to the economic benefits to

Georgia, manufacturing large, specialized military aircraft almost continuously since 1943 has

> Created a regional pool of skilled workers and thereby demonstrated the efficacy of training southerners for technologically sophisticated manufacturing;
>
> Been responsible for an in-migration of technical talent to the region;
>
> Provided important support for the development of regional engineering and technical training schools and a nearby market for their graduates;
>
> Pioneered the recognition of worker rights previously resisted by southern businesses;
>
> Symbiotically supported numerous smaller businesses through the development of a network of suppliers and subcontractors; and
>
> Spun off new technology-based businesses started by entrepreneurs working at the plant.

Continuing air force ownership of the Marietta plant has cast the government in the role of a major stakeholder in the success of the plant. This position was reinforced by political support of Georgia legislators, including Carl Vinson, Walter George, Richard Russell, Sam Nunn, and Newt Gingrich, who have wanted to contribute to the economic stability of Cobb County and the state. Other GOCO plants that have been sold by the government, such as the Boeing-Wichita facility that built B-29s during World War II, may have also been successful over the same period as the Marietta plant; aircraft manufacturing is the major industrial presence in the Wichita region and Boeing is the world leader in manufacturing commercial aircraft. However, in contrast to a successful private sector manufacturer, the Marietta plant looks more like a mission-oriented federal laboratory or space program facility that provides tens of thousands of high-paying manufacturing jobs. As such, Air Force Plant #6 has exerted a tremendous economic development influence on Marietta and Cobb County since 1942.

NOTES

1. See chapter 6, "Missiles and Magnolias," in Bruce Schulman, *From Cotton Belt to Sunbelt* (New York: Oxford University Press, 1999); chapter 7, "The Stimulus of War," and chapter 10, "The Sunbelt South," in Dewey Grantham, *The South in Modern America* (New York: Harper Perennial, 1994).

2. See Ann Markusen (with Peter Hall and Amy Glasmeier), *High Tech America* (New

York: Allen and Unwin, 1996); Markusen, *The Rise of the Gunbelt: the Military Remapping of Industrial America* (New York: Oxford University Press, 1991); and J. David Roessner, "Technology Policy in the United States: Structures and Limitations," *Technovation* 5 (1987): 229–45.

3. Grantham, *The South in Modern America,* quoting Franklin Roosevelt, 179.

4. Jacob Vander Meulen, *Building the B-29* (Washington, D.C.: Smithsonian Institution Press, 1995), 14–18.

5. Vander Meulen, 21.

6. Vander Meulen, 21–29.

7. Irving B. Holley Jr., *Buying Aircraft: Materiel Procurement for the Army Air Forces* (Washington, D.C.: Center for Military History, 1989), 164–65.

8. As recently as 1935, Congress had held hearings that vilified World War I military contractors as "merchants of death."

9. Holley, 305–8.

10. Numan Bartley, *The Creation of Modern Georgia,* 2d ed. (Athens: University of Georgia Press, 1990), 186–93.

11. Franklin M. Garrett, *Atlanta and Environs,* vol. 2 (Athens: University of Georgia Press, 1954), 851.

12. The depot at Wellston was later named Warner Robins and is currently one of four Air Logistics Centers for the U.S. Air Force. Wellston was a community of several hundred at the time the depot was built; today the Warner Robins ALC employs over 20,000 civilians and has anchored industrial growth in the middle Georgia region.

13. Copies of Shaw's letters to Rickenbacker and the Industrial Location Section are in James V. Carmichael's papers, Box 25, "Airport Correspondence," Special Collections, Emory University.

14. According to a 1965 proposal from Lockheed-Georgia to buy the Marietta plant from the air force, the plant site covers 709 acres (Carmichael papers, Box 37, Folder 8).

15. Vander Meulen, 36.

16. *Atlanta Constitution,* lead story in 24 January 1942 issue announcing the army decision to build the plant; 20 February 1942 story, "Plane Plant Site Official, Tarver Wires Mayor Blair"; 23 February 1942 editorial, "Welcome to New Atlantans," about ceremonies to welcome Bell Aircraft officials at a victory dinner.

17. LeCraw was a leading Atlanta booster who had served as president of the Atlanta Chamber of Commerce in the 1930s. He was elected mayor in September 1940, beating out William Hartsfield, and he left office for a military leave of absence in early 1942, just after the successful Bell plant siting (Garrett, 1002–4).

18. Rickenbacker Field was being constructed with three runways 4,000 feet long, with two expandable to 5,600 feet (Carmichael papers, Box 25, 27 August 1941 letter from Carmichael to Rickenbacker).

19. A. O. Willauer, "Outline History of B-29 Program at Bell Bomber Plant: Dec. 22, 1941 to Dec. 31, 1943," 5 (Air Force Historical Research Agency (AFHRA) collection, call number 208-1).

20. Willauer, 5, 22; "Bell Aircraft News," 15 April 1944 edition (Carmichael papers, bound volume of plant newsletters).

21. Speech by army general Kenneth B. Wolfe to Aviation Writers Association at the Bell plant on 12 January 1945 (AFHRA collection, 208-1, "Historical Report of AAF Plant Representative, 1/1–3/31/45").

22. Willauer, 15.

23. The B-29 program compressed design, research, production engineering and modification operations into a very short time frame; the first (experimental) plane didn't fly until 21 September 1942, while the Bell plant was still being constructed.

24. Willauer, 45.

25. Vander Meulen, 81.

26. "Bell Aircraft News," various issues (Carmichael papers, bound volume of newsletters).

27. The family day on 15 July 1945 is estimated to have brought 100,000 employees and visitors to the plant ("Bell Aircraft News," Carmichael papers, bound volume).

28. NYA report dated 18 June 1943 (Carmichael papers, Box 2).

29. Marietta newspaper clipping dated 6 November 1942 (Carmichael papers, Box 65, Folder 7).

30. "Bell Aircraft News," 24 September 1943 edition (Carmichael papers, bound volume of newsletters).

31. The Bell insistence on using lofting became a point of contention within the B-29 consortium (Vander Muelen, 78).

32. "Lofting for Super-Bombers," article in May 1944 edition of "Bell Ringer," newsletter for Bell's Buffalo, New York, plant (Carmichael papers, bound volume).

33. "Bell Aircraft News," 20 August 1943 article cautioning workers not to "discriminate against union supporters," and a 26 February 1944 article titled "NLRB to Hold Election Wednesday" (Carmichael papers, bound volume).

34. Interview with Ms. Frances Sewell Light on 12 May 1998.

35. "Historical Report of AAF Plant Representative: April 1–June 30, 1945," 208-1, AFHRA collection.

36. Vander Meulen, 54.

37. Biographical outline in Carmichael papers, Box 17.

38. Joseph E. Dabney, *Herk: Hero of the Skies* (Lakemont, Ga.: Copple House Books, 1979), 97.

39. Obituary for W. E. "Eli" Cook Sr., *Atlanta Journal*, 7 April 1998.

40. Willauer, 19, and Air Force Plant Representative Officer (AFPRO) report for 1 July–31 December 1967 (AFHRA archives).

41. C-5 wingspan is 222 feet, compared to the B-29 (141 feet), C-130 (132 feet), or the C-141 (160 feet).

42. Other aircraft built in Marietta included the JetStar, a small commercial jet; the C-140, a military version of the JetStar; and the GV-1, a marine tanker version of the C-130 built for the navy.

43. In 1993 the Lockheed Aircraft Division headquarters was moved to Marietta from Burbank, and in 1995 Lockheed Aircraft Corporation merged with Martin-Marietta Corporation to form Lockheed-Martin.

44. Dabney, 98.

45. Ibid.

46. The author's father, Richard C. Combes Jr., was working as a structural engineer at McDonnell Aircraft Corp. in St. Louis, Missouri, in 1952 when he answered a Lockheed recruiting ad and was hired by Lockheed-Georgia in 1953 to work in the C-130 program. He retired in 1979 and still lives in Atlanta.

47. Dabney, 119–20.

48. Lockheed Corporation did build another plant in Palmdale, California, during the late 1960s to build its new commercial airliner, the L-1011; it stopped producing this aircraft in the 1980s.

49. Gilbert C. Fite, *Richard Russell, Jr.: Senator from Georgia* (Chapel Hill: University of North Carolina Press, 1991), 444, 485.

50. This type of contract set a fixed price for R&D, design, and production of the C-5, with an incentive clause that increased the government payments if certain goals were met or exceeded.

51. AFPRO report covering 1 January–30 June 1961 (AFHRA archives).

52. Interview with former Lockheed engineer R. C. Combes.

53. Kathleen Heintz, "The C-5A," a case study conducted at the Kennedy School of Government, Harvard University, copyright 1976.

54. The AFPRO report for 1 January–30 June 1960 indicates Lockheed-Georgia was in possession of 280,000 items of government property worth $396 million; the report for 1 January–30 June 1966 indicates 431,412 items worth $556.8 million (AFHRA archives).

55. Lockheed proposal dated 26 March 1965 (Carmichael papers, Box 37, Folder 8).

56. This plant, also operated by Lockheed-Martin, manufactures the F-16 fighter and employs 12,000 workers.

The Politics of Exclusion

Wartime Industrialization, Civil Rights Mobilization, and Black Politics in Atlanta, 1942–1946

KAREN FERGUSON

In 1943, the *Atlanta Daily World* (ADW), Atlanta's black newspaper, published an editorial cartoon distributed by the Associated Negro Press. Entitled "This Is Your Responsibility," it presented a tableau of African American society. In the cartoon a dissolute couple, shown slouching and loitering at the corner of "Slum Boulevard" and "Any Street," with a factory in the distance, are encountered by a group representing the black elite, including a minister, a lawyer, and a "society woman," who look at the couple as if seeing them for the first time. In the lower right-hand corner, a white man addresses the elite group, admonishing them, "Better try to lift them! *You* can go no higher than *they!*" (See fig. 1.)

At first viewing, the fears represented by this cartoon seem to contradict entirely what historians have taught us about the democratic thrust of black activism during the Second World War. In a flowering of exciting recent research, scholars have uncovered the "lost years" of the civil rights movement in the war, showing how black activists, working as a broad, politically ecumenical coalition, struggled valiantly to turn the era's democratic promise into reality. Representatives of local, regional, and national organizations as diverse as the NAACP, the CIO, and the Southern Conference on Human Welfare shared a common goal to seize the unprecedented opportunities created by the era's urbanization, industrialization, and evolving Democratic Party liberalism, to lift the veil of Jim Crow, and to remove the barriers that excluded African Americans from the mainstream of the South's economic and political life. The linchpin of this effort was the South's black defense workforce and its fight for inclusion in the region's indus-

Fig. 1. *Atlanta Daily World*, 17 October 1943.

trializing wartime economy. This southern democracy movement embraced these workers' claims and employed their nascent autonomy and growing public visibility to further its goals of economic and political equality.[1]

In Atlanta, a center of black reform activism, the black elites represented by the *ADW*'s editorial board and in the cartoon were full partners in this apparently egalitarian movement, marking a turning point in their struggles for black citizenship. Their willingness to participate in this worker-centered movement marked their emancipation from a decades-long tradition of racial uplift ideology in which they had asserted their citizenship as educated elites by condemning and dissociating themselves from what white society considered the uncivilized and morally degenerate black masses. However, in the evolving movement toward southern democracy they understood, as the cartoon suggests, that their progress toward full citizenship was tied directly to that of the majority of the black community.[2]

Yet as the cartoon also suggests, elitism and mistrust of the black working class continued to mark these reformers' vision of the path to full black citizenship.

While they believed in the necessity and rightness of full citizenship for all African Americans, they did not think that the black masses were prepared for citizenship and felt that this lack of preparation imperiled the aspirations of the entire black community. Their project as self-defined race leaders not only was to agitate for civil rights or economic opportunity but also, urgently, to lift the black masses to the level of behavior they considered necessary for American citizenship. Therefore, while these leaders sought to democratize the South through mass action, theirs was not an egalitarian movement. They worked *for*, not *with*, the majority of the black community.

The efforts of the right wing of the South's wartime coalition for democracy are crucial to understanding the evolution of the postwar civil rights movement. Working in a broad coalition with labor leaders and leftist movements in the South and nationwide, these moderate reformers held very different notions about the meaning of citizenship and democracy than many of their more radical allies, despite their apparent united front and shared rhetoric. When this coalition disintegrated, and anti-Communism destroyed its left wing, the black freedom struggle was reshaped to fit the new political realities of the cold-war era and the ideological convictions of the black reform elite, who now dominated civil rights discourse and leadership.

Wartime industrialization was crucial to the democracy movement in the South. By modernizing the southern economy, it released hundreds of thousands of black southerners from the paternalism and dependency of traditional "Negro work." These African Americans escaped farm tenancy or domestic service at the first opportunity and became vital members of the civilian mobilization. Migrating to southern cities, they were more than ready to seize on or to push for work opportunities beyond the veil of segregation, in defense industries and the larger wartime economy. This economic emancipation was a crucial prelude to the postwar civil rights movement, creating a sizable autonomous and publicly visible African American industrial workforce, freed from the grossest forms of isolation, exploitation, and white scrutiny that marked their prewar employment, and ready to be mobilized as the postwar civil rights constituency.

Still, despite fighting for industrial opportunity in order to create these emancipatory possibilities, the black reform elite also sought to control this constituency according to its ideological preoccupations. This group's members worried about the increasing visibility of the black working class and its growing participation in public life. They feared that by becoming visible before being uplifted, the black masses would imperil the struggle for democracy and black citizenship by demonstrating African Americans' unsuitability or unpreparedness for such progress. Although they understood that the modernization of the South was crucial to achieving full citizenship, black reformers fretted that the veil was lifting too quickly for an unready majority of the black community. In particular, they felt that unprepared black workers were joining urban, industrial society, with grave consequences for the entire black community and black citizenship.

These anxieties shaped many wartime freedom struggles. While the black reform elite worked for full democracy, its mobilization efforts focused on those African Americans who could or would share its notions of citizenship and behavior, while excluding those who did not. In fact, black reformers refused to countenance, and even condemned, those working-class assertions of citizenship that did not conform to their notions of respectability, citizenship, or democracy. This exclusion had enormous consequences for black communities across the South during the war and after.

Atlanta in the 1940s was a national center for the black reform elite. Its numerous black postsecondary institutions provided a base that acted as a magnet for social workers and social scientists. Graduates of Atlanta University's sociology department and Forrester B. Washington's respected Atlanta University School of Social Work, former "Negro Division" administrators for New Deal social welfare programs, and black employees of a full complement of black- and white-run social-work agencies formed an unusually large and influential network of elite black reformers. This group was unified by its devotion to racial uplift, the hallmark of its professional efforts on behalf of the black community.

At the forefront of this group's wartime activism in Atlanta was the local Urban League chapter. Leaders of the Atlanta Urban League (AUL) recognized the enormous potential opportunities presented by industrial employment and sought to maximize black participation in war production. The AUL worked indefatigably to force open the doors of defense training and industry to black workers. Its efforts made it the most important broker between the black community and government and private industry, ultimately resulting in the AUL's becoming an essential partner in war manpower coordination in the city, and giving it the power to choose those black workers who would receive the limited number of jobs available for African Americans in defense plants.

Despite its growing power, the AUL could not obtain assembly-line defense jobs for more than a tiny minority of Atlanta's black workers. The AUL's triage in determining which workers would receive these jobs had enormous implications for the future of Atlanta's black community. The agency made its choices on the basis of its leaders' continuing conservative definitions of black citizenship. These handpicked workers became the critical core of postwar civil rights mobilization by the AUL, whose leaders from the beginning of the war had explicitly linked black incorporation into the South's modernizing society and economy to the attainment of civil rights. Those who were not chosen found themselves excluded from the upward mobility afforded by industrial employment and their concerns unrepresented by the emerging, narrowly defined movement for racial equality.

BLACK WORKERS' WARTIME FREEDOM STRUGGLE

In 1944, white liberal and Georgia Tech lecturer Glenn Rainey wrote to his friend, the ex-Atlantan and young historian C. Vann Woodward, about the trials of being a new father. Chief among them was the unwelcome novelty of having to deal with his infant son's dirty diapers. "Since the emancipation of the Negro is now consummated," he wrote, "we are largely doing our own work, with the blessed help of the Lullaby Diaper Service, though we find that ninety diapers a week are not more than a challenge to his excretory powers."[3]

Rainey's offhand remark suggests the fundamental changes experienced by Atlanta's black community in wartime, and the challenges these changes presented to the city's Jim Crow racial order. His assumption that under normal conditions, even his always insecure and insubstantial income as a sessional instructor at Georgia Tech could support a maid or a home laundry worker, and his equation of "the Negro" with domestic work is highly emblematic of prewar Atlanta's paternalistic racial order and black Atlantans' dependent position within it. Moreover, his observation that black workers had experienced a second "emancipation" highlights the changes for African Americans wrought in wartime Atlanta.

Black Atlantans' new emancipation was fundamental, but its importance has sometimes been obscured by whites' successful efforts to limit its scope. Both government officials and defense employers in the South collaborated in an effort to graft traditional southern labor practices onto the South's burgeoning industrial sector. Despite the massive war-induced labor demands and federal anti-discrimination policies, they continued to treat black workers as a separate caste, a "special and exogenous phenomenon,"[4] as historian Bruce Nelson put it, unwelcome on the assembly lines of the region's new economic sector. So important to whites was the exclusion of black workers from defense industries that the War Manpower Commission (WMC) created artificial labor shortages by ignoring black workers, resulting in both the importation of white workers to southern defense centers and the disruptive and dangerous overcrowding that plagued all Southern cities during the war.[5]

Atlanta was no exception to the pattern. Black workers were grossly underrepresented in industrial and government defense work during the war. Despite making up over 40 percent of Atlanta's population and workforce, African Americans never accounted for more than 30 percent of government workers and 15 percent of industrial workers. The employment they did find consisted of a replication of traditional Negro work translated to the industrial setting. At the Bell Aircraft plant in Marietta, the Atlanta region's largest defense employer and the largest industrial employer of black workers, between 1942 and 1945 only 2,500 black Atlantans found positions out of a total workforce that reached

The Politics of Exclusion

nearly 30,000. Unsurprisingly, the work black Atlantans obtained at Bell was overwhelmingly in menial positions. Only 800 black employees worked on the line, while the remainder were consigned to work as "industrial maids," janitors, or cafeteria workers.[6]

This exclusionary pattern is testament to whites' anxiety over the implications of industrialization for the future of white supremacy, and particularly whites' inability to prevent wartime industrialization from disrupting traditional racialized labor patterns. Even black workers' limited participation in the economic and social modernization implicit in wartime industrialization threatened the foundations of the Jim Crow regime. In the massive, impersonal munitions factories, bomber plants, and shipyards of the wartime South, ex-sharecroppers and ex-domestic workers could escape the exploitative paternalism and dependency on whites that defined traditional Negro work.

The first thing that the war offered black Atlantans was mobility. Ever since the Great Migration of the First World War, southern African Americans had seized upon industrial opportunities to free themselves from the paternalistic anachronisms and gross exploitation that had trapped them for generations. Until the 1940s, this movement took them out of the South's kitchens and cotton fields, but as the region industrialized and modernized with the Second World War, such freedom could also be created within the South. After an initial exodus of black workers in 1940 and 1941 in which over 14,000 African Americans left the city, Atlanta's black community mushroomed. By 1950 Atlanta's African American population had reached 121,416, representing a 16 percent increase over 1940 figures, or twice the rate of growth for the white population.[7]

These new Atlantans were drawn to a burgeoning and diversifying economy. Along with the defense plants, including Bell Aircraft's Marietta operation and a Firestone rubber factory, virtually every industrial concern in the city converted to war production. Over 8,000 black Atlantans found work in these "essential" defense establishments. In addition, government employment exploded with the opening of several military installations, including an army air base and ordnance depot, and Lawson General Hospital for military personnel. By 1945, fully 25,000 black and white Atlantans worked for the federal government, including civilians employed by the military, compared with only 7,000 in 1940. Opportunities also exploded for black Atlantans outside defense industries, especially in the service sector. Just as much of Atlanta's workforce left for military units or defense installations, demand multiplied for restaurant meals, hotel rooms, and commercial leisure with the influx of war workers, soldiers, and military officials into the city. Black women, for example, became waiters in the dining rooms of Atlanta's most exclusive hotels for the first time during the war, moving into this relatively lucrative work when the regular staff was drafted or sought defense work.[8]

Such a panoply of employment choices was unprecedented for black workers. For decades, black men's job options had steadily declined in the city, especially when white men turned such "black" work as brickmasonry or bellhopping into exclusively "white" occupations. The erosion of black male employment opportunities left black women to fill the breach through domestic work, the only job option open to most of them. In 1940, about as many black women as men worked in Atlanta, and almost 70 percent of black female workers toiled in domestic service, mostly as maids or home laundresses, at times earning less than a dollar a day for a workweek that often stretched to six-and-a-half twelve-hour days. The caste system that underlay African Americans' position in the labor market effectively perpetuated Jim Crow by marginalizing black workers through exclusion, and subjecting them to white control through poverty and economic dependency.

The war broke open this situation. For the first time, many black workers could pick and choose among employers and a variety of jobs. Although most did not find places on the assembly lines, their positions as waiters, janitors, or production helpers in Atlanta's new defense economy represented a crucial shift in their work lives. Even the move from being a maid or cook in a private home to a factory cleaner or cafeteria worker represented a real step up from traditional Negro work. Not only did these new jobs provide shorter and more regular hours and higher, even sometimes union-protected, wages, but they also largely freed workers from the paternalistic and dependent relationships that white domestic employers and planters tried to impose on their black help.

Black workers seized on the emancipatory possibilities of the tight wartime labor market. They shopped around for jobs, constantly seeking the kind of work and the employer offering the best conditions and pay, consequently yielding enormously high turnover rates for defense contractors. More fundamentally, they left the most demeaning of their prewar work sites in droves, often for good. By 1950, only about half of Atlanta's black female workforce toiled in domestic labor, a precipitous and permanent decline in this bulwark of black employment. "Negro women," wrote black sociologist Walter Chivers, "were so soured on the 'romance' of domestic service and so thoroughly disillusioned by the fickleness of the loyalty of 'their white folks,' whom they had served so 'loyally,' that they were ready for the . . . 'good money' dangling before their eyes as a reward."[9] Now Atlanta's Glenn Raineys would have to change diapers themselves.

As wartime wages eased their Herculean efforts merely to scrape by, black workers used their unprecedented economic security to distance themselves from workplace exploitation. Some black women, for example, retreated from the labor market during the war and remained at home with their children, a luxury made possible by spouses' defense-industry wages or servicemen's allotments high enough to cover all family expenses. One study found that most families who chose this option actually suffered some drop in income, suggesting their pent-up aspirations for family life, denied when both parents had to work long hours.[10]

By offering black workers jobs in the new war plants and breaking the bonds of persistent paternalism, industrialization brought black workers much greater public visibility. While the types of work they performed may not have changed, the workplace had. Again, the experience of ex-domestic workers provides the most dramatic example. These women and men no longer scattered through the city to toil in obscurity in white neighborhoods and homes. Rather, they joined a mass, biracial wartime workforce in Atlanta's most modern industrial settings, or they found work in government installations, office buildings, hotels, and restaurants, often in the city's central business district, bringing them to the geographic and economic center of the wartime city.

The new visibility of black workers and their centrality to the wartime workforce meant the forging of new relationships with white employers and workers. Wartime industrialization forced the city's white union establishment to acknowledge and include black workers, after decades of ignoring or deliberately excluding them. Black workers became an important constituency when the CIO initiated an organizing drive in Atlanta to correspond with the wartime industrialization of the local economy, culminating in an organizing victory at Bell Aircraft in 1943. Its success can be attributed, at least in part, to the union's willingness to organize and recognize black defense workers. The Atlanta Federation of Trades (AFT), representing Atlanta's AFL-affiliated union establishment, was caught off guard by the CIO's campaign. Although the CIO in Atlanta did little for black members once they were organized, it had a better record than the AFL's national and local pattern of racism and exclusion. Scrambling to maintain its preeminence among Atlanta's workers, the AFT began courting black workers openly in its contest with the CIO. But given that the Machinists' Union, one of Atlanta's most openly racist, led the AFT's organizing drive at Bell, black workers gave little credibility to this abrupt about-face, which reflected more a survival instinct than a desire to serve black workers.[11]

The CIO's victory at Bell showed the AFT the importance of black workers in Atlanta's new labor order. Consequently, the AFT's wartime effort at self-preservation, in conjunction with black workers' new economic position, achieved the greatest unionization victory to date for the city's black workers: the 1943 organization of commercial laundries. Prior to unionization, the city's 3,000 mostly female black laundry workers were among the city's poorest, sometimes earning less than $300 a year. The AFT supported the laundry workers in an eight-week strike in 1943 in which they defied the War Labor Board (WLB) and the AFL's wartime no-strike promise. Through the WLB's intervention, the laundry workers won a fifty-hour week, paid vacations, and overtime pay, with their base wages set at between thirty and fifty cents an hour. Although two segregated locals won the strike, in 1945 they merged into one organization, led and dominated by black members. Such recognition pointed to the fundamental changes experienced by black workers during the war. Not only did black women, like Glenn Rainey's imagined "Negro," leave home laundry work in droves but also, as they joined the commercial or industrial workforce, as at the Lullaby Diaper Service, their new visibility and autonomy allowed them to assert their rights as workers successfully. They continued to toil at tasks similar to those required by their prewar employment, but their changing workforce position produced fundamental improvements in their work lives.[12]

Other black Atlantans also used their newfound autonomy and visibility to push their rights as citizens and workers. With growing assertiveness, they fought the arbitrary limits placed on their economic and vocational opportunities. A rash of shop-floor incidents erupted during the war when black industrial workers defied their caste position and white supremacy by attempting to use machinery forbidden to them or by refusing to assume the subservient mien or behavior demanded by their position. Then they fought back courageously when incensed white workers attacked them violently for challenging Jim Crow.[13]

Similarly, if less dramatically, black defense workers used the visibility granted to them by federal government and labor movement recognition to assert their rights as workers and citizens. In droves, they used the complaint mechanisms opened to them by the Fair Employment Practices Commission (FEPC), allowing them for the first time to record officially their dissent to the discrimination they had always faced at work. In hundreds of FEPC complaints, Atlanta's black defense workers exposed hostile working environments where white supervisors, intent on limiting black workers' visibility and ensuring their subordination, established a myriad of roadblocks to hamper black success at defense plants. Among other complaints, these workers charged that their supervisors regularly barred them from the training that would allow them skilled work, demoted them from semiskilled positions to janitorial work without justification, forced them to work seven night shifts a week, required them to obtain passes to use the toilet while white employees went to the restroom at will, and issued them demerits that sometimes led to dismissal for coming back from breaks or the toilet a few minutes later than arbitrarily deemed necessary. While such complaints almost never resulted in sanctions against the offending employer, their number and scope reveal black workers' pent-up frustrations and their sense of entitlement to equal opportunity and treatment in the workplace. Their growing autonomy, along with the federal government's implicit recognition of their citizenship, allowed them finally to protest their treatment openly.[14]

Black Atlantans' increasing activism as workers also had important implications for their struggle for freedom outside of the workplace, allowing them to fight against white constraints on their citizenship more openly and assertively.

With increasing fearlessness, they claimed public space and defied segregation. As in Birmingham, the most dramatic of these struggles in Atlanta occurred on public transportation.[15] Given extreme wartime crowding on streetcars, black and white riders encountered each other more often than ever before as they made their way to the same defense workplaces. Many used this situation to play out the racial tension emerging out of African Americans' greater wartime mobility, visibility, and autonomy. In fact, the Federal Bureau of Investigation, in its "Survey of Racial Conditions in the United States," singled out public transportation as the most important stage for resentful blacks and whites to act on their mutual animosity. The survey's authors reported that African Americans chafed against Jim Crow segregation laws that "resulted in a scarcity of rapid and available transportation for Negroes. This scarcity, coupled with the reported change in attitude of Negroes in the South, is said to be the cause of numerous minor clashes and fights between Negroes and whites throughout the South."[16]

Certainly whites' day-to-day defense of the Jim Crow order became more violent during the war as they protected their traditional claims on increasingly limited public space. White passengers, who by custom had always entered streetcars before black riders, now asserted this right by shoving or assaulting blacks who dared enter before them, even when this occurred by accident. Streetcar drivers and passengers regularly cursed, beat, and sometimes killed black passengers who contravened racial etiquette by refusing to relinquish their seats when extra white passengers forced back the fluid line separating white and black. Streetcar motormen (who had police powers in Atlanta) frequently armed themselves with guns or used the "streetcarman's best weapon,"[17] the switch steering stick, to beat black passengers.[18]

Black Atlantans did not take this abuse sitting down, however. They often fought back or even provoked violence from white drivers and passengers by defiantly entering streetcars before whites, sitting in the white section of the streetcars, or answering white passengers' and drivers' abuse with curses and threats. As Robin Kelley has theorized, streetcars, being moving enclosed space, were places where African Americans could openly resist white authority. Even if whites brutally punished them for this behavior, as they often did, defiant black passengers had a captive white audience forced to witness their actions and acknowledge their presence in an important segment of the city's public space. Moreover, if black passengers constituted a majority of passengers on a streetcar, they could tip the balance of power for the time of their trip and, for a change, force whites to cower in their presence. In a terse digest of the "Racial Situation" in Atlanta, the War Department reported the following Atlanta streetcar incidents during a three-week period in 1945. On 12 January, "Three young Negroes slashed at whites on a street car after a white man reprimanded one for cursing. Some of the 60 other Negroes aboard pulled the trolley pole and others hung out windows stopping passing trolleys." On 23 January, "Negroes argued with a driver and one pulled the trolley pole." On 1 February, "A Negro girl threatened to cut a white girl after they fought on a streetcar when the Negro pushed the white," and on 2 February, "Twelve months on public works was the sentence for a Negro who cut a white man in a bus fight."[19]

Both black and white participants in these incidents realized that they were engaged in a hand-to-hand racial battle, a violent contest in which the very foundations of Jim Crow were at stake. As the war progressed, black passengers increasingly made explicit the connections between their defiant behavior and their entitlement to full citizenship. For example, in 1945 a police report detailed one incident in which a streetcar motorman was "victimized" by a black passenger supposedly "in a drunken condition" who called the motorman an "S.O.B." upon being ejected from the car. After beating the black man with the streetcar's control handle, the motorman found himself on the other end of the stick as the passenger returned the favor, ultimately leaving the "victim" with broken glasses, a badly cut ear, and a swollen left temple.[20]

This fight began when the black passenger told the insulting white motorman that he was "a man just like him," a common refrain during the war, when black Atlantans fought rhetorically as well as physically for recognition of their citizenship. On the streetcars, these protests often took the form of an angry "Greek chorus" commenting from the rear on specific incidents of discrimination as they occurred. In one incident, an elderly man who had to stand at the front of a very crowded streetcar asked the driver if he could exit by the front, rather than fighting the crowd to get to the rear door where African Americans usually had to exit. When the driver refused, black passengers protested vocally. As the streetcar left downtown and became less crowded, the driver roughly told black passengers standing in the front to get to the back where they belonged. An unidentified black man responded by retorting, "you don't have to talk to us like we were dogs." The incensed driver then demanded that the man behind the voice identify himself, which he did. The driver then drew his pistol and ordered the man to leave the car. Exemplifying the defiance and increased fearlessness of blacks during wartime, the man demanded his fare back from the driver, who was still aiming his gun. He got his token and coolly left the streetcar by the rear exit with the driver's gun pointed at his back.[21]

Thus, working-class black Atlantans protested Jim Crow at the workplace and on the streets. As the streetcar examples attest, these black Atlantans became more and more willing to assert their rights openly and militantly as workers and citizens. The war sparked their actions. They battled the deep contradictions implicit in the fight against Hitlerism in Europe while they continued to face Jim Crow at home. Yet what permitted their fight was the economic emancipation that wartime industrialization brought Atlanta's black community. Black Atlantans no longer would submit to the rules of deference and enforced inequality, and their newfound mobility, autonomy, and visibility meant they no longer had to.

REFORM ELITE IDEOLOGY AND THE WARTIME FREEDOM STRUGGLE

Like Atlanta's black working class, the city's black reform elite also seized upon the opportunities wartime industrialization presented. For years, this group of social workers, academics, and journalists had been working for the inclusion of African Americans into the mainstream of Atlanta's economic and political life, but to little avail. They understood such changes would require a fundamental transformation of the South's economic traditions of black exclusion and exploitation. They believed in the transformative potential of Atlanta's wartime industrialization to achieve their ends and intended that black Atlantans would play an integral role in modernizing the South's economy and society. Yet, instead of interpreting black workers' wartime mobility, visibility, and activism as essential to their goals, they often viewed these developments as detrimental to their dreams of full citizenship for African Americans. Understanding black elite ideology and particularly elite notions of black citizenship may explain this apparent paradox.

In probing black elite ideology in the first half of the twentieth century, the issue of respectability has emerged as its most enduring and important leitmotif. "The Politics of Respectability," as Evelyn Brooks Higginbotham puts it, was the preeminent Progressive-era expression of African Americans' response to their situation "within the larger structural framework of [white] America and its attendant social norms."[22] By teaching African Americans to live according to the behavioral norms of the white middle class, black reformers sought to escape the trap of their caste position by finding "common ground on which to live as Americans with Americans of other racial and ethnic backgrounds." Through advocating these shared moral and behavioral standards, black reformers fought to be seen as "both black and American," working against white rhetoric that would "deny this possibility by isolating the 'Negro's place' within physical and symbolic spaces of inferiority."[23] If African Americans proved respectable in every way, they could refute the racist stereotypes that whites used to justify their subordination. The rhetoric of respectability, then, was a tactic to demonstrate African Americans' citizenship, deny white justifications for their imposed marginality, and move toward full inclusion in public life.

However, by defining black citizenship in terms of behavior and morality, the politics of respectability was decidedly limited as an ideology of racial liberation. Most obviously, it excluded the legions of African Americans who would not or could not conform to the gender roles, sexual behavior, and economic activity deemed legitimate by white America. Instead of simply excluding this group from their purview, proponents of respectability asserted their own citizenship in opposition to and at the expense of the black masses.

This ideology was easy to sustain in the prewar South, when poverty, illiteracy, and dependency kept most African Americans invisible and immobile, thus allowing the black elite to claim legitimacy as the natural leaders and uplifters of the black community. Yet when wartime industrialization freed many black workers from their fixed status as farm tenants or servants, and when black workers' acts of resistance and group assertion became publicly visible, the black elite felt their self-proclaimed leadership challenged. Many of the most profound wartime changes for black Atlantans occurred without elite intervention. Black workers' migration to the city, employment in defense industry, higher living standards, and increasing public visibility all largely derived from the war and the labor demands of war industries, not elite reform campaigns. Furthermore, the most dramatic of these changes wrought by industrialization occurred among poor, working-class African Americans, whose agency and interests had heretofore been ignored by the reform elite, which had as much difficulty as whites in appreciating their strivings, if for very different reasons.

In their evolutionary notions of racial uplift, black reformers always envisioned the masses' progress toward full economic and political citizenship as a gradual, elite-led process. In fact, a key component of uplift ideology emphasized that the "pathologies" of black urban life stemmed from African Americans' supposed unpreparedness for the shift from peasant to modern city dweller. In a 1940 passage that echoed uplift rhetoric since the beginnings of the mass exodus of African Americans from the countryside, Forrester B. Washington of the black Atlanta University School of Social Work outlined what he considered black migrants' fundamental difficulties in adjusting to city life and urban employment. Migrants had "little conception . . . of the urban requirements of unskilled labor, such as prompt appointments, attitudes in applying for work, and ability to understand simple specifications of job analysis. Moreover, there is a minimum of personal appearance required on unskilled jobs in the city. . . . Neither the male nor the female ex-agricultural laborer can toil half-clad or semi-nude in the city as they could in the country."[24]

As such rhetoric suggests, the black reform elite did not accept that uneducated African Americans could engage in their own freedom struggle, believing the masses lacked even a basic understanding of modern life or elementary political consciousness. In fact, reformers based their claims to leadership of the black community on these beliefs. Before the war, they could sustain this myth, given black workers' marginality. But with events like the commercial laundry workers' unionization drive or the escalating tension on public transportation,

Atlanta's black reform elite had to reconfigure its ideology by adapting it to black workers' public activism on their own behalf.

The black reform elite reasserted their leadership's legitimacy by interpreting the wartime activism of African American workers as evidence of social pathologies and unreadiness for civic citizenship and membership in the industrial order. Thus the black passenger who asserted his manhood to the streetcar motorman was not making a legitimate claim for citizenship. His drinking, his swearing, and his violent retaliation disqualified him from respectability and, hence, citizenship. Proponents of uplift interpreted black Atlantans' street and workplace struggles as signs of their ignorance, laziness, and lack of self-respect and responsibility, instead of as a different quest for citizenship. This interpretation invalidated the importance of working-class black Atlantans' efforts to fight on their own behalf and blinded black reformers from seeing or acknowledging the war-era struggles of many black workers.

Elite reformers blamed black Atlantans' misbehavior on the war's dislocations and the "social disorganization" that they felt resulted when poor African Americans left their traditional social moorings without adequate supervision or support. For example, Helen Whiting, supervisor of teaching practice in Atlanta University's education department, lectured a group of Georgia's black teachers in 1943 about how the "high degree of mobility, vertical and horizontal," within the black community had created "severe stresses and strains" and an "intense crisis" that imperiled her goals for black citizenship "in a world of peace after the war."[25]

What exactly did Whiting and her fellow teachers mean by a "crisis"? For them, wartime mobility had broken down traditional kin and community ties, leaving children and youth adrift, just at the time when African Americans were moving into the mainstream through their expanded vocational opportunities. Luckily, in Whiting's view, black teachers could step into the breach by becoming parental surrogates to their students, guiding them to make "proper adjustments" to these enormous changes, and specifically according to Spelman College history instructor Margaret Curry, "educating [them] for democratic citizenship."[26] Black school teachers saw themselves on the frontlines of this effort, being the "Senior Technical Craftsmen" on "Freedom's Assembly Line,"[27] as the patriotic editors of the Atlanta black high school's yearbook put it.

While the citizenship training Whiting and the other teachers conceived included the kinds of universal rights rhetoric explicit in the South's wartime democracy movement, it also sought, in the spirit of uplift ideology, to teach black students a behavioral code of citizenship, hoping to prepare them for public visibility and participation in the mainstream. Spelman College English instructor Henrietta Herod's instructions to high school English teachers engaged in citizenship education concentrated almost completely on teaching students civility and the social niceties of bourgeois America. She wrote that the teacher "will endeavor to train his [*sic*] pupils so that they are able to converse graciously and intelligently with others, to agree or disagree with courtesy, and to carry on relationships with regard for social amenities." The teacher of English "will know that he [*sic*] must send out students who are able to use the English language with proper regard for those literacies of expression approved by cultivated men and women." For Herod, such skills were imperative to and inseparable from citizenship.[28]

While Herod sought to instill the civil behavior of good citizenship in black Atlantans through a campaign of positive change, many other reformers worked to change attitudes and behavior through criticism and condemnation of working-class black actions and attitudes. Such negative messages betrayed the black reform elite's impotence to control black workers' behavior. While teachers could intervene directly in the lives and behavior of young people through the schools, no comparable institution could guide adults. One of the most overt displays of this attitude of shame and mistrust of the black working class appeared in a series of editorial cartoons published between 1943 and 1945 in the *ADW*. Distributed by Continental Features, a black news service, and drawn by an artist with the pseudonym "Stann Pat," these cartoons, taken together, comprised a series of do's and don'ts—but mostly don'ts—for black behavior in wartime. The drawings portrayed graphically a series of situations in which black workers found themselves every day. They demonstrated the black elite's fear that the increased visibility of the black working class might jeopardize claims for full citizenship.

One of the most prominent themes of this series focused on proper street and public transportation behavior. Stann Pat depicted ordinary black people as uncouth boors, shoving others to get onto streetcars, eating and drinking on the street, and deliberately taking up more than their share of space. A caption condemning the ignorance, selfishness, and immorality of the action and warning of its danger for the entire black community accompanied each image. All the captions explicitly linked such behavior to the black freedom struggle, demonstrating the reform elite's awareness of the opportunities presented by wartime visibility for black citizenship and their terror that this same visibility might destroy this chance for black uplift. "Shoving others about in public conveyances for some slight satisfaction or convenience is selfish and small," complained one caption. "We fight jimcrow on trolley cars, trains and subways because we are human and deserve better treatment." Thus the cartoon implicitly invalidated working-class assertions against Jim Crow by condemning African Americans for undermining the elite's uplift program when they fought whites for their share of space on public transportation. "[A]ll forms of eating on the street are contrary to good conduct and taste," exhorted another cartoon. "You and I will have to learn these things, lest our protest for full citizenship be in vain." Thus Pat condemned black people for a practice that was nearly unavoidable during the war, demeaning black workers' struggles and the social realities of southern cities in wartime (see figs. 2 and 3).

Although the reform elite knew that its objectives could only be achieved through the increased visibility of African Americans, these cartoons demonstrated its members' fear of this visibility and their impulse to control it. Increasingly, reformers used their growing authority with whites to mobilize a constituency of the respectable poor and middle class to achieve their goals for the black community. Soon the visible organization of these groups, presented by black leaders as an example of virtuous and lawful black citizenship, would have an enormous impact on the future of the city and the black community.

THE ATLANTA URBAN LEAGUE'S BATTLE FOR DEFENSE TRAINING AND JOBS

Atlanta's black reform elite worried so obsessively about the behavior of the black working class because its members understood the importance of wartime industrialization to the future of the black community. They knew that the period's circumstances gave black Atlantans a window of opportunity to break into industrial work that carried enormous implications for their struggles to destroy Jim Crow. Because the stakes were so high and the industrial opportunities so limited, black reformers fought to control the black defense workforce so that it would represent and advance, not jeopardize, their goals for black citizenship. Thus, while their goal was economic and political democracy for the South, limited industrial opportunity along with uplift ideology produced a fundamentally elitist strategy to achieve this egalitarian end.

The Bell Aircraft plant stood as the most important symbol of the potential latent in Atlanta's wartime modernization. For Atlanta's leaders, both black and white, it represented a great new future for the city, the South, and its citizens. Atlanta, not a major manufacturing center, had never seen an industrial concern on the scale of this plant, built in Marietta, just north of the city in Cobb County. By luring Bell to the Atlanta area, local boosters hoped to make a great leap forward in modernizing the local economy. In the 1940s, no manufacturer could compete with the prestige of the aviation industry, which symbolized the pinnacle of American technological and industrial achievement. Local officials hoped the Bell plant's success would prove to the rest of the country that southern workers, traditionally perceived as too uneducated, inexperienced, and unskilled for complex industrial work, could manufacture bombers as efficiently as any group elsewhere. Bell officials often referred to their pioneering effort in Georgia. In 1944, company president Larry Bell called the Marietta plant "a great trade school," which would "prove of great value to Georgia in the difficult post-

WE ALL PAID OUR FARE
A fellow who exercises his sporting instincts in a game where he exchanges blow for blow, wouldn't do this. Shoving others about in public conveyances for some slight satisfaction or convenience is selfish and small. We fight Jimcrow on trolley cars, trains and subways because we are human and deserve better treatment.

Fig. 2. *Atlanta Daily World*, 22 September 1943.

"Of course you may not go this far, but all forms of eating on the street are contrary to good conduct and taste. There are just some things that people don't do. You and I will have to learn these things, lest our protest for full citizenship be in vain. Better stop kidding yourself."

Fig. 3. *Atlanta Daily World*, 21 April 1944.

war days ... when the industrial skills available here will be of great importance to this community and to the South as a whole."[29]

Not merely looming large in the city's imagination, the Marietta plant literally towered over any industrial concern the city had ever seen. With its main assembly bay "large enough to house the nation's total annual cotton crop," the plant's size tested the descriptive powers of one WMC official: "To look at the plant from a distance is to experience an emotional shock.... It is as though one had suddenly come across the architecture of a people from another and larger planet—people used to doing things on a scale that dwarfs the familiar buildings and dwellings of mere earth-men."[30] Appropriate to such an enormous and utterly modern industrial plant, Bell officials described the movement of the tens of thousands of workers inside the plant in language evoking machinery. "The flow of workers will be controlled with precision," one Bell news release explained. "They will enter the plant through tunnels into the basement containing locker rooms, showers and cafeterias. A network of stairways will enable each to go to his particular job area by the most direct route."[31]

This image contrasted sharply with stereotypes of a lazy, premodern South, with its personalized and paternalistic labor relations and its workers' supposed indifference to time discipline. Atlanta's black reform elite also interpreted the Bell plant's opening as the dawn of a bright future for the city's black community. Its members envisioned black workers' inclusion in the clean, technologically sophisticated aircraft industry as hammering the first nail into the coffin of Jim Crow and its traditions of black exclusion and exploitation. They believed that the Bell plant represented the potential modernization of the southern economy and society, and they intended that black Atlantans would play an integral role in this transformation.[32]

For this reason, the AUL spent the war years devoting its efforts to opening up black opportunities for skilled defense work, particularly at Bell Aircraft. Inclusion of black workers in war industry depended almost entirely on protracted grassroots struggles to force defense industries and federal manpower agencies to comply with federal antidiscrimination legislation. The weak authority of the FEPC, established to enforce Presidential Order 8802 (banning employment discrimination in defense industry), did not ensure compliance. Still, the presidential order had crucial importance in efforts to recognize the citizenship of racial minorities and their entitlement to full participation in the war effort. The AUL and other black reformers across the South used this moral authority to shift the status quo in the region. No longer did African Americans have to justify the benefits and utility of black employment in industry by proving the citizenship of African Americans. Instead, they could put local, state, and federal officials on the defensive by forcing them to justify the exclusion of African Americans from employment by federally funded defense contractors.[33]

In Atlanta, these efforts for inclusion began in 1942, after federal authorities granted $200,000 for aircraft manufacture training to local officials, who excluded African Americans from their instruction programs despite directives that these funds be distributed without discrimination. The black reform elite realized that if black Atlantans were to join the industrial mainstream, it would be crucial that they be included in the skilled labor pool for Bell's huge potential workforce. Bell made it clear that only qualified workers would be hired for aircraft assembly, yet none of the federally funded training equipment, intended to establish fifteen aircraft-assembly instruction centers in and around Atlanta, was made available to black Atlantans.[34]

Understanding the devastating implications of this exclusion, the AUL founded the Council of Defense Training (CDT) to focus on creating courses for black workers to match the white program for Bell. Composed of luminaries of the reform elite, including AUL secretary William Bell, public-housing manager and AUL industrial secretary Jacob Henderson, and ADW editor C. A. Scott, the CDT worked tirelessly throughout 1942 to achieve its goals, battling against the plots and subterfuges of white officials who sought to prevent the launching of a black training program. Borrowing their strategy from A. Philip Randolph's March on Washington Movement, the CDT mobilized black Atlanta to protest its exclusion from the program. It undertook a registration drive of all African Americans in Atlanta who wished to participate in the Bell training program. Prompted by the slogan, "Could you use $35 a week?" (through a skilled job at Bell), black Atlantans responded to the council's appeal in droves. While the council set 2,000 registrants as its original goal, between 5,000 and 10,000 black Atlantans, perhaps as much as 10 percent of Atlanta's black community, participated in the ten-day drive.[35]

The CDT's registration effort represented a strategic turning point for Atlanta's black reform elite, built on the groundwork of activism it had established in the 1930s. The campaign's success led this elite to abandon its decades-old strategy of backroom negotiation for an opposite strategy, making the black community as visible as possible and demonstrating its leadership of the black masses to government officials and Bell's management. Federal manpower agencies like FEPC or WMC also compelled this shift. The reactive policy of these agencies meant that the federal bureaucracy only acted on black workers' behalf when they themselves complained of their treatment or demonstrated their availability for defense work.

The CDT's effort forced federal officials to acknowledge black Atlantans as a significant segment of the local labor force, something that local manpower bureaucrats had refused to recognize. The council's registration drive deliberately paralleled that of the United States Employment Service (USES), the agency responsible for registering and referring all potential candidates for federal defense training programs. USES, like other branches of the WMC, ignored black workers as potential defense workers. The resounding quantifiable success of the council's registration drive compelled government officials to consider African Americans as part of the mainstream labor pool. Although that acknowledgment did not ensure defense training, it did force recalcitrant federal and state agencies to justify the exclusion of African Americans from training.[36]

The CDT used its registration campaign and federal policy to maneuver local officials into an increasingly defensive position. Using Washington contacts made in the 1930s, the CDT's members complained constantly to FEPC, WMC, and USES officials about the misuse of federal funds in Atlanta, bringing increasing pressure to include black Atlantans in the defense training program. Their campaign's effectiveness and their shrewd use of a national network of bureaucrats and activists meant that Atlanta became a crucial test site for federal antidiscrimination legislation and policy. Impressed by the CDT's campaign, the National Urban League chose to make the Atlanta situation the focus of its campaign to force Washington officials to redress the dismal state of defense training for blacks in the South and to end the unlawful practice of "earmarking" programs for African Americans by offering black workers training only in skills they had traditionally practiced.[37] Ultimately, this pressure and the strength of the case led to victory when the CDT filed a discrimination complaint against Atlanta and Georgia's defense-training officials after being chosen for representation at regional FEPC hearings in Birmingham in June 1942. The commission ordered Atlanta authorities to establish an aircraft assembly instruction program for African Americans. In November 1942, a center, the "first training program ever opened in the deep South for prospective [black] aircraft workers,"[38] opened with much fanfare at Booker T. Washington High School (BTWHS), Atlanta's only black secondary school.[39]

Through these extraordinary efforts the AUL became the most powerful black agency in Atlanta. While the CDT's registration efforts were initially designed to protest and publicize the actions of local officials and to publicize the availability of black workers, white officials now eyed the council and the AUL as potential allies in managing the local defense labor force. The AUL's actions demonstrated its access to black Atlantans, who were badly needed as unskilled workers in defense industries. Even USES officials grudgingly praised the efforts of the council in "stimulating the recruitment of . . . potential Negro trainees, and the proper registering of these trainees with the Atlanta office." Although the local USES office obstructed the aspirations of skilled black workers throughout the war, it did face pressure from above to register available black workers for unskilled positions. The registration drive demonstrated that the AUL could deliver these workers. One Washington administrator for the WMC, of which the USES was a part, suggested to the National Urban League that "comparable cooperative programs" to Atlanta's "be worked out between [the USES] and the National Urban League in other strategic defense centers." Moreover, the CDT's work also brought representatives of the labor-strapped southern shipbuilding industry to the AUL in search of black workers willing to migrate to Brunswick, Georgia, or Mobile, Alabama, for defense jobs.[40]

This recognition enormously increased the AUL's prestige and legitimacy with white officials. It became an important adjunct to federal manpower agencies in the city, emerging as a vital referral agency for black workers for the USES, Bell Aircraft, and the Civil Service Commission. In fact, these agencies often only dealt with black workers if they had been referred by the AUL, which registered and selected those black workers who attended the BTWHS defense school. The AUL also became an important buffer institution for black workers, steering them to the proper wartime agencies and preparing them for the hostility and bureaucratic hoops through which they would be required to jump.

After the success of the CDT's drive, the AUL continued to employ its new strategy of mass mobilization. It coordinated FEPC complaint campaigns among black workers against USES discrimination in job placement (and the lily-white policies at Atlanta's Firestone Rubber plant and in the UAW local at a nearby Chevrolet plant) to undergird its protest to government and union officials in Washington and Detroit. However, these campaigns originated with the AUL, not with workers, none of whom filed an independent FEPC complaint about Firestone's exclusionary practices. Rather, those workers who cooperated with the AUL sought to benefit from the agency's growing influence over black defense employment by supporting its programs.[41]

Not all workers could afford to support the AUL, nor did the AUL's wartime programs represent the majority of black Atlantans' wartime interests. The defense-training program that resulted from the CDT's registration campaign achieved virtually nothing for most black workers. The course, held during the day and for no pay, faced logistical and financial roadblocks that barred most working-class black Atlantans from participating. Other potential students were stymied by the prerequisite of a sixth-grade education. Further, given the history of black exclusion from industry, ordinary black workers recognized that there was no guarantee that they would be employed in skilled jobs at Bell or any other defense plant in Atlanta, even with qualifications. Only those able to afford three weeks without wages could seek better-paying jobs in defense industries through training.

Hence most black workers did not make the sacrifice the training program required, preferring instead to take the relatively well-paying unskilled jobs that became available in Atlanta in 1942–43 as military installations opened or expanded their operations and the draft tightened the local labor market. Further, many black Atlantans left the city before 1943 to work in southern shipbuilding centers where they could earn almost double the wages local employers offered. The AUL had to make constant appeals to rectify the severe underenrollment at the BTWHS day course, and even the night program that began in June 1943 suffered from small enrollments. Thus, while the AUL's campaigns sought to improve the situation of black workers and increasingly used mass-mobilization strategies, they did not necessarily benefit Atlanta's black workers or advance their most immediate wartime interests. Instead, the league's strategies represented both its own goals for the black community and its response to the bureaucratic demands of wartime agencies like the FEPC, which required official complaints to be filed by individuals in order to act on the AUL's behalf.[42]

Comprehending these differences of interest and goals between black workers and the AUL is crucial to understanding the achievements and limits of the reform elite's fight to obtain assembly-line work for black Atlantans at Bell. In order for the defense training drive to amount to anything concrete, the company had to make an unprecedented move by training and hiring skilled black workers. Through defense training, the AUL wanted to make it as difficult as possible for the company to exclude black workers from its Marietta production labor force. Although Bell repeatedly promised federal and local officials that it would exhaust the area's labor supply before looking elsewhere for workers, president Larry Bell also reassured local whites before coming to Atlanta that "there are certain traditions sacred to the South and we expect to abide by them."[43] Interpreting the contradiction in Bell's public rhetoric as an indication that Bell could be persuaded to hire black Atlantans in large numbers to operate machinery, the AUL exerted its new influence as power broker for the black community, attempting to wield as much influence as it could over company policy regarding black workers.

Repeating the effort of the registration drive, the AUL became the unofficial referral agency for black Atlantans desiring work at Bell, thus once again deliberately "supplementing the work of the United States Employment Service."[44] After all, the USES might work with company officials to underrepresent blacks when reporting the available workforce and to keep blacks out of the plant in all but the most menial, nonmechanical positions.

Delegations from the AUL also met regularly with Bell officials long before the Marietta plant opened to discuss ways in which they could work together "to increase understanding of the factors which influence the successful utilization and well-being of Negro workers."[45] Through these negotiations, AUL representatives like Jacob Henderson convinced company officials to hire African Americans for white-collar positions in the Marietta plant's personnel department. The AUL thus buttressed its efforts by positioning its agents within the company for the hiring of skilled African Americans. Bell conceded to this demand shortly after the plant opened, when it appointed two men handpicked by the AUL—

Milton White, principal of Atlanta's D. T. Howard Night School for black students, and Joel Smith, ADW reporter—as employment interviewer and personnel counselor respectively for Bell's black workers.[46]

Only through these efforts did Bell employ any black assembly-line workers. When the company opened its Marietta plant in late 1942, it hired African Americans only as janitors and maids, no matter their previous work or training experience. Even those who had completed aircraft training at BTWHS were offered only menial positions at the plant. Bell did not engage black workers for skilled positions until 1944. That shift derived from protracted backroom talks with AUL officials, after which the company took over the training program at BTWHS, upgraded its equipment and standards for training through intelligence tests, and began to pay sixty-five cents an hour to trainees, who having completed the three-week program were guaranteed skilled work.[47]

It soon became apparent that Bell's unprecedented offer of skilled work to black Atlantans would be extremely limited. Of the average of 2,500 Bell positions held by African Americans during the war, 800 were skilled. While this number represented nearly one-third of all black workers at Bell, it comprised only a tiny proportion of the total workforce at the Marietta plant, which employed 18,000 to 28,000 workers between 1943 and 1945. Furthermore, the skilled blacks hired by Bell represented only those who had managed to be selected by the AUL for the company training program before the unofficial quota of 800 was rapidly reached. After that point, Bell refused to assign any African Americans to skilled positions, regardless of their experience and of its often acute assembly-line labor shortages.[48] The skilled workers Bell did take on were segregated into all-black work units at the Marietta plant or an entirely separate facility on Roswell Road.[49]

The AUL remained silent regarding Bell's refusal to expand assembly-line work to other eligible black Atlantans once it reached its initial quota. Jacob Henderson remembered quietly encouraging qualified workers whom Bell refused to consider for skilled work to lodge complaints with the FEPC. Yet these clandestine efforts paled in comparison to the AUL's earlier, open campaign of mass mobilization against discrimination in defense training. The reform elite feared rocking the boat with Bell officials lest they might jeopardize the opportunity that limited employment of African Americans at Bell presented to challenge Jim Crow labor practices. This outlook, however, sometimes placed the AUL and its agents in compromising positions. For example, black FEPC complainants often named Milton White, one of the black personnel officers at Bell, as the company official who informed them that advertised assembly-line positions were for whites only, thus implicating him in the company's discriminatory policy.[50]

This collaborationist approach, stemming from black Atlantans' insecure foothold on industrial work, shaped the AUL's attitude toward and treatment of

Bell's black workers. As Atlanta's preeminent racial broker, and the quasi-official employment agency for the city's black defense workers, the AUL had enormous influence over the composition and assignment of Bell's black assembly-line workforce. Given the limited opportunities for skilled work, the AUL was forced to perform triage, selecting those who, in its opinion, would make the most of the available assembly-line positions, aiding in the goal to protect and expand black opportunity in industry. Its new prestige in the eyes of white officials intensified the AUL's tendency to exclude all but a very narrow segment of the black community from the focus of its reform efforts.

While they lobbied hard for black workers at Bell, black reformers also expressed their long-held concern that these same men and women, as much products of southern economic and social custom as whites, could not handle the demands of the modern industrial workplace. Therefore, in the AUL leadership's view, the future of black industrial employment rested not only on Bell's black pioneers' immediate adjustment to their new working conditions, but also on their quick transformation into paragons of the industrial workforce. With Bell's opening, the reform elite's perennial concern that working African Americans prove themselves efficient and indispensable took on new urgency. Although even unskilled work at Bell was unionized, well-paid, and regulated by modern industrial labor relations practices, the AUL worried that black war workers, many of whom were recent migrants to Atlanta, would not prove equal to the jobs. While it began its wartime campaign and gained legitimacy from white officials by mobilizing the masses, the AUL's ideological convictions and black Atlantans' tenuous hold on industrial jobs prompted the AUL to retreat to its familiar elitist strategy in its approach to Bell.

Given their ideological fears and the demand for skilled work attested to by the CDT's defense training registration campaign, AUL leaders unsurprisingly referred for training at Bell workers whose social and economic profile did not match that of average black Atlantans. In one study of Bell workers' wartime experience (in which 100 skilled black Bell workers were chosen at random), 44 had belonged to the elite ranks of the black community, having been either students or professional, white-collar, or skilled workers before being selected for training. The wages of Bell riveters, assemblers, or drill press operators, which far exceeded what they had been earning as teachers, insurance salesmen, or mechanics' helpers clearly attracted these black Atlantans. The impeccable qualifications (indeed overqualifications) of the skilled black workforce at Bell not only demonstrated worker demand for high-paying jobs. The AUL, having screened all applicants for skilled work at Bell, ensured that the company personnel office met only those whom the agency judged as the most educated, respectable, and responsible of Atlanta's black labor force.[51]

Whereas the AUL could provide Bell a skilled workforce that it had handpicked, it had little or no influence over the unskilled workers who comprised the majority of the company's black employees. The AUL dismissed these workers and their problems at Bell because their behavior did not set the example of black citizenship the agency advocated. Anxious about its inability to direct these African Americans, the AUL held a 1944 series of workshops for Bell employees titled "Hold Your Job." These meetings, intended to help "new employees to become adjusted to working conditions in a large industrial establishment," covered such topics as absenteeism and the "problems growing out of supervisor-employee relations" but were very poorly attended. Jacob Henderson, remarking on the virtual absence of unskilled laborers "in the Janitorial and Cafeteria Departments, and men employed as Common Laborers and Productive Helpers," complained that these workers were precisely the ones "who need expert advice on techniques of 'holding their jobs.'"[52]

Those who did attend found little empathy or understanding of their position as mudsills of the industrial workforce, plagued by "low pay and little or no chance to be upgraded."[53] At one typical "Hold Your Job" meeting, Ira DeA. Reid, a black sociologist and consultant to the Social Security Board, placed much of the burden of the future of black industrial employment on the shoulders of African American workers. Reid warned Bell workers "that if Negroes are to keep their present jobs after the war, they must throw out personal feeling and do their work efficiently. 'Don't carry a grudge out on the job,' he said." Reid also advised the workers to use the personnel services of the company and to work "through the regular channels" when dealing with any grievances, if they wanted to retain their jobs.[54] Such directives merely reinforced a message constantly reiterated implicitly and explicitly by the city's black reform elite, living up to its members' tacit bargain with Bell's management that in return for assembly-line jobs they would discipline the company's black workforce (see fig. 4).[55]

Black Bell workers knew from experience the absurdity of Reid's directives. Bell's personnel departments ignored their complaints of discrimination, even when they worked through the "regular channels" for making grievances and when they enlisted the help of the FEPC.[56] As dozens of FEPC complaints attest, shop-floor discrimination ran rampant at Bell, especially for unskilled workers who, unlike their skilled counterparts in their all-black unit, labored alongside or beneath white employees. Whether the AUL would even support these workers was unclear, given the agency's emphasis on respectable and efficient worker behavior and its unwillingness to push Bell once the company hired black assembly-line workers. However, the FEPC's Atlanta reports indicate that none of the complainants had anything but the most sophisticated understanding of the nature of industrial work, belying the AUL's and Bell management's characterization of their troubles. Still, their complaints indicate that white supervisors used racial

Fig. 4. *Atlanta Daily World*, 8 December 1943.

stereotypes of black laziness or inefficiency to keep black workers subordinate or to exclude them from the Bell workforce altogether.[57]

Thus, the AUL leaders' concern for community interest, as they defined it, superseded concern for the struggles of the majority of Bell's black workforce or for the social justice issues its members confronted in the workplace during the war. Constrained by the continuing realities of Jim Crow and their ideological priorities, they chose to concentrate their efforts on the "respectable" skilled workers they could help and lead, while ignoring and even condemning the majority they could not.

THE POLITICS OF EXCLUSION IN POSTWAR ATLANTA

On 12 February 1946, only six weeks before the Supreme Court struck down the white primary in Georgia, Atlanta voters went to the polls to elect a successor to their long-time U.S. congressman, Robert Ramspeck. This special election, in which black Atlantans could vote despite the persistence of the white primary in Georgia, represented a crucial test of African American electoral power for the black reform elite, which had been mobilizing black Atlantans to register to vote in this contest. When the ballots were finally counted, an underdog candidate, Helen Mankin, supported by black electoral organizations, won an upset victory over Ramspeck's handpicked successor, Thomas Camp. Mankin owed her success to the black electorate, which had swelled from 3,000 to nearly 7,000, thanks to the voter-registration campaign leading up to the election.

The success of the postwar voter registration effort was something of a surprise to the black reform elite, whose prewar registration efforts had rarely garnered more than 1,000 black voters, or less than 1 percent of the black population. Even after the repeal of Georgia's cumulative poll tax in 1945, this group had been able to convince only 3,000 black Atlantans to register that year, despite the destruction of this pillar of white supremacy. Buoyed by their success in the congressional election, black reformers decided to launch an unprecedented effort to reach all potential black voters in Atlanta and to urge them to register for the 1946 gubernatorial primary. This would be the first such opportunity for black Atlantans since 1899, due to the 1946 repeal of Georgia's white primary.

Drawing from their experience coordinating the struggle for defense training, AUL leaders organized an All-Citizens Registration Committee, including representatives from the city's black reform organizations, to run an intensive and extensive registration campaign. Dividing the city into the 1,162 blocks on which African American citizens lived, committee leaders recruited 870 volunteers to reach black Atlantans of voting age around the city. The AUL printed and distributed 50,000 handbills to prospective voters. The Committee enlisted ministers like Martin Luther King Sr. and William Holmes Borders to urge their congregations to vote and arranged carpools to deliver their members to the courthouse. This registration blitz garnered extraordinary results. In the fifty-one days of the campaign before the registration books were closed, nearly 18,000 new black names were added to the rolls, yielding a total of over 24,000 eligible voters and marking the spectacular debut of African Americans as a political force in the city.[58]

It is hardly surprising that the AUL led and controlled the mobilization campaign of the All-Citizens Registration Committee. While the local NAACP chapter and various other civic groups contributed greatly to the effort, the Urban League board members fashioned the registration campaign's strategy, and the organization's employees put the plan into practice. The league's leadership in this program was in some sense a matter of practicality; in 1946, it was the only black civic organization in Atlanta with the resources to accomplish such an ambitious campaign. That year, its $17,223 budget put it far ahead of the NAACP in terms of financial resources. What is more significant, however, was that in 1946, 85 percent of the AUL's budget came from the Community Chest, an organization dominated by the city's conservative white business and charitable elite. While the AUL's leaders contributed to the registration effort under the auspices of the All-Citizens Committee and sought to avoid public controversy by being "discreet" about the league's links to the campaign, they took no great pains to hide their central role in organizing the drive. In other words, the registration campaign that marked black Atlantans' debut as a significant force in the city's public life took place with the tacit approval of some of the most powerful white people in the city.[59]

White acceptance of the AUL's leadership role in the registration campaign simply marked the extension of the organization's wartime activities. It easily assumed its postwar role as a "central connector in the city's governing coalition,"[60] given its crucial efforts as a powerbroker between government and the black community during the war. The AUL's wartime campaigns for defense training and skilled work had established its power to represent the black community's interests successfully to white officialdom. Its backroom maneuvering between federal agencies and defense contractors had demonstrated a shrewd ability to manipulate competing bureaucracies to its own ends and a sophisticated understanding of the power of compromise. The AUL's tactics represented a synthesis of modern southern liberalism and black politics, emphasizing interracial cooperation and electoral trade-offs.[61]

The AUL's turn to politics represented its leaders' frustration over postwar roadblocks to continuing the expansion of African Americans' economic rights. After spending the war devoting its energy to expanding the vocational opportunities for black Atlantans, the AUL saw most of its progress nullified. Its leaders found themselves so stymied on this front that they dissolved their industrial department in 1946 and refocused on the more attainable goals of black voter registration and political representation.[62]

Peacetime reconversion was a difficult and tension-filled process in Atlanta, with blacks bearing the brunt of the resulting racial conflicts. Returning black veterans encountered hostility and ingratitude, coming home to a boomtown that had just gone bust for black workers. Although wartime migrants did not leave the city after the war, the jobs that had attracted them to Atlanta in the first place did. Bell Aircraft and Firestone shut down their plants as the city's military installations began to close up or scale back their operations in preparation for peace. These closings, accompanied by the return of black veterans with military experience in technical, clerical, or mechanical work, flooded the local labor market with skilled black workers. As elsewhere, they had no comparable place in the peacetime economy. Many African Americans, living off what they had saved from defense work or servicemen's allotments, stayed unemployed as long as they could before returning to the unskilled work to which they were again consigned and for which they were often vastly overqualified. Many veterans expressed vocational aspirations by taking advantage of the training and educational opportunities offered by the GI Bill. Sadly, they most often found that the high school, college, and apprenticeship training they received could not be put to practice in Atlanta or the South.[63]

Despite these serious setbacks, industrialization had achieved sustained upward mobility for a significant minority of Atlanta's black workforce. The precipitous and permanent decline of domestic work in the city was the most notable signifier of this achievement. In 1940, 36 percent of black workers toiled in domestic work; by 1950 only 22 percent did so. This decline was most dramatic for black women, almost half of whom found employment outside whites' homes in 1950 compared with just under one-third a decade before. Men experienced a similar, if less dramatic decline in service work positions as janitors, porters, and messengers that were the male equivalent of domestic work. By 1950, only 23 percent of employed black men fitted into this category compared with 30 percent in 1940. Even more important for black men was their increased opportunity to work in the wartime and postwar economy. By 1950, they comprised 58 percent of the city's African American workforce, a 7 percent increase over 1940, suggesting an easing of the chronic unemployment and underemployment that had plagued black men since the end of Reconstruction after the Civil War.[64]

African Americans continued to be relegated to the lowest-paid and most menial work in the city. Female ex-domestic workers moved in greatest numbers to service work, while men became unskilled laborers. However, for most of these black Atlantans, such occupational shifts represented significant upward mobility within the ranks of the city's unskilled workers. For many of these "deserters" there was no looking back. Maids became cleaners in commercial and industrial establishments, porters became production helpers, and previously unemployed men became laborers in Atlanta's postwar industries.[65]

While the duties of these workers may have been very similar to their prewar positions, their new employment was very different. By leaving white households, for example, domestic workers left the paternalism and dependency on whites that had defined work for them. Although these black workers continued to be beholden to their white employers, the terms of this subordination were much less oppressive and personalistic than in household work. Most postwar black employment continued to be hot, dirty, and poorly paid. But usually the hours were set, Sundays were free, and the wages were hourly and in cash, not in kind. The jobs might even be unionized, as in the case of commercial laundry work. These black Atlantans' improved work lives and economic situation had important implications for reformers' aspirations to mobilize them for full citizenship. Reformers believed that these workers' higher wages prompted them to want more for their families and communities. Their relative autonomy from whites also gave them more freedom to work openly for racial uplift. More practically, these workers had more time for reform efforts. Freed from the grossest exploitation of "Negro work," these black Atlantans were also less isolated from civic life and from other black workers, making them more accessible for reformers to contact and to organize. Thus changes in black employment made it easier to organize the African American community politically.

Black reformers could mobilize this group of striving black workers after the war because it was only then that they could effectively reach them. Only after the mobilization efforts of the war, such as the CDT's registration drive, could Atlanta's black reform elite touch a sufficient number of black Atlantans to create a mass constituency for its citizenship goals. Before the war, Atlanta's black reform elite had only the haziest and sometimes prejudiced notions of many of the city's black neighborhoods. Its members often wrote with frustration of the apparent impenetrability and parochialism of working-class and migrant neighborhoods like Summerhill or South Atlanta. Yet these neighborhoods did not lack respectable residents interested in racial betterment through vocational, economic, and political opportunity. Rather, black reformers, despite their best efforts, lacked the resources and authority to engage these communities and make the residents appreciate the economic and political benefits of joining their crusade. Generally, it was impossible for them to unite sympathetic black Atlantans from the city's disparate black neighborhoods for a common cause.

The reform elite's uplift efforts were always aimed at working for full citizenship for those black Atlantans most receptive and most able to conform to the politics of respectability. Black reformers limited their efforts and appeal in this way largely because of their circumscribed authority and resources. Ideologically linking respectability and citizenship, they had always aimed their reform efforts at the top, and from there extended downward both geographically and demographically, as far as they could. By the end of 1946, owing to their wartime efforts and the structural forces that improved the lot of many black Atlantans, they had reached farther than ever before, managing to register about 21,000 black voters, or just over one-quarter of the potential black electorate, as part of their constituency. But what of the other almost three-quarters of the black voting-age population?[66]

This group remained essentially untouched by the citizenship efforts of black reformers and outside the postwar constituency on which the reformers based their influence. Always perceived as marginal by whites, this majority of black Atlantans became even less perceptible to black leaders after the war, when they accomplished their goal of full citizenship for the respectable and "deserving" segment of the black population. It became easier and easier for black leaders to ignore the poorest black Atlantans as they gained political power and influence representing their respectable and growing postwar constituency. The reform elite thus split the black community into those who it determined were deserving of the fruits of inclusion into the polity and those who were shut out of the upward mobility afforded by wartime industrialization and political mobilization and consigned to remain at the margins of civic life.

Today, the legacy of the wartime efforts of Atlanta's black reform elite can still be felt. Governed by a black mayor since the Maynard Jackson administration, Atlanta continues to be a national center of black education, business, and culture. It boasts one of the most prosperous middle-class African American communities in the country. These black Atlantans owe their success and progress largely to the path paved by their peers fifty years ago. But Atlanta also contains some of the largest pockets of urban poverty in the United States.[67] Members of the city's "underclass" can also look back to choices made decades ago in difficult times for one of the keys to their continued exclusion from the public life of the city.

NOTES

1. The most complete work dealing with this wartime movement for southern democracy is Patricia Sullivan's *Days of Hope: Race and Democracy in the New Deal Era* (Chapel Hill: University of North Carolina Press, 1996). Her book builds on the work of labor historians who have examined the impact of wartime industrialization on black workers and southern society. See, for example, Robert Korstad and Nelson Lichtenstein, "Opportunities Found and Lost: Labor, Radicals, and the Early Civil Rights Movement," *Journal of American History* 75 (December 1988): 756–81; Bruce Nelson, "Organized Labor and

the Struggle for Black Equality in Mobile during World War II," *Journal of American History* 80 (December 1993): 952–88; Michael Honey, *Southern Labor and Black Civil Rights: Organizing Memphis Workers* (Urbana: University of Illinois Press, 1993), 177–278.

2. For a full examination of uplift ideology and its evolution, see Kevin K. Gaines, *Uplifting the Race: Black Leadership, Politics, and Culture in the Twentieth Century* (Chapel Hill: University of North Carolina Press, 1996).

3. [Glenn Rainey] to [C.] Vann [Woodward], 25 April 1944, Box 3, Glenn Weddington Rainey Papers, Special Collections Department, Robert W. Woodruff Library, Emory University (hereinafter EU). See also "Workers Unavailable for Jobs Open in Atlanta Area," *Atlanta Daily World* (hereinafter ADW), 11 October 1941.

4. Nelson, "Organized Labor and the Struggle for Black Equality," 957.

5. Ibid., 955–58; Pete Daniel, "Going among Strangers: Southern Reactions to World War II," *Journal of American History* 77 (December 1990): 898–901. For evidence of the WMC's policy in Atlanta, see [War Manpower Commission], "Preliminary Statement on the Atlanta and Marietta Labor Market," 10 December 1942, Box 1, Series 12, U.S. War Manpower Commission, Region VII Records, Record Group 211 (hereinafter WMC), National Archives Regional Office, East Point, Ga. (hereinafter NA); "Estimate of In-Migration into the Atlanta, Georgia, Labor Market Area during the Six Months Beginning November 1, 1943," 27 November 1943, Box 1, Series 12, WMC; War Manpower Commission, Division of Reports and Analysis, Region VII, "Estimate of In-Migration into the Atlanta, Georgia, Labor Market Area during the Six Months Beginning January 1, 1945," 28 December 1944, Box 1, Series 12, WMC.

6. Atlanta Urban League, "Timeless: The Task of Preventive Social Work among the Most Under Privileged," [1942], Box 5, Grace Towns Hamilton Papers (hereinafter GTH), Atlanta History Center Library/Archives (hereinafter AHC); War Manpower Commission, "Labor Market Developments Report," 15 April 1943, Box 7, Series 12, WMC; [War Manpower Commission,] "Labor Market Developments Report," 15 June 1943, Box 7, Series 12, WMC; War Manpower Commission, "Proposed Manpower Program for the Atlanta Area," 20 August 1943, Box 20, Series 11, WMC; [War Manpower Commission,] "Labor Developments Report for Atlanta, Georgia," 28 December 1943, Box 7, Series 12, WMC; War Manpower Commission, "Summary of ES-270 Reports," September 1944, III:565, Reel 124, *Southern Regional Council Papers* (Ann Arbor: University Microfilms International, 1984) (hereinafter SRC).

7. In the same period, Atlanta's white population increased by only 8.5 percent, from 193,393 in 1940 to 209,898 in 1950. Charles S. Johnson and Clifton R. Jones, "Memorandum on Negro Internal Migration, 1940–1943: An Estimate by the Department of Social Sciences, Fisk University," 16 August 1943, Box 4, OF 4245g, Franklin Delano Roosevelt Papers, Franklin Delano Roosevelt Library.

8. "Reports on War Production Centers, WPB Region 4, Atlanta-Marietta, Georgia Area," 14 February 1944, Box 17, Series 12, WMC; Clifford M. Kuhn, Harlon E. Joye, and E. Bernard West, *Living Atlanta: An Oral History of the City, 1914–1948* (Athens: University of Georgia Press, 1990), 364.

9. Walter R. Chivers, "Effects of the Present War upon the Status of Negro Women," *Southern Frontier* 4:12, December 1943, 5:30, Reel 30, *Commission on Interracial Cooper-*

ation Papers, 1919–1944 (Ann Arbor: University Microfilms International, 1984) (hereinafter CIC); Willie Mae Jackson interviewed by E. Bernard West, partial transcript, n.d., Box 37, Living Atlanta Collection, AHC; [War Manpower Commission,] "Labor Market Developments Report," 30 August 1943, Box 7, Series 12, WMC; Atlanta Urban League, "Timeless: The Task of Preventive Social Work."

10. Alan L. Ritter, "Annual Family and Occupational Earnings of the Residents of Two Negro Housing Projects in Atlanta, 1937–1944," n.d., Box 50, Charles Forrest Palmer Papers, EU; Daniel, "Going among Strangers," 895.

11. Minutes, 4 February 1943 and 11 February 1943, Box 139, Machinists Lodge #1 Records, Southern Labor Archive, Georgia State University; "Federation in All-out Drive to Organize Bell Bomber Plant," [Atlanta] *Journal of Labor*, 14 May 1943; "Organization Drive at Bell Bomber Plant Gaining Momentum," *Journal of Labor*, 5 November 1943; Daniel, "Going among Strangers," 898.

12. Willie A. Allen, "A Study of the Negro Members of the Laundry Workers' International Union, Local 218, Atlanta, Georgia" (master's thesis, Atlanta University, 1946), 3–10, 25.

13. Minutes, 19 February, 17 September, 9 July 1942, Box 138, Machinists Lodge #1 Records.

14. For Atlanta area FEPC complaints see Closed Cases boxes 2 through 7, Committee on Fair Employment Practices Records, RG 228, Region VII (hereinafter FEPC), NA.

15. Robin Kelley, "'We Are Not What We Seem': Rethinking Black Working Class Opposition in the Jim Crow South," *Journal of American History* 80 (June 1993): 103–10.

16. Robert A. Hill, ed., *The FBI's RACON: Racial Conditions in the United States during World War II* (Boston: Northeastern University Press, 1995), 254; Kelley, "'We Are Not What We Seem,'" 103–10.

17. Sanders Ivey interviewed by Cliff Kuhn, n.d., partial transcript, Box 37, Living Atlanta Collection.

18. "Atlanta NAACP Plans Appeal of $27 Fine Given in Trolley Case," ADW, 2 October 1941; [Minutes, Annual Meeting, Fulton-DeKalb Interracial Committee,] 20 October 1942, Reel 48, CIC; Spike Washington, "Brutality Victims Are Fined in Police Court," ADW, 14 January 1944; Douglas Carter and James O. Slade, "SRC, Inc., Transportation-Segregation Study, Municipal Transportation, Atlanta, Georgia," 7 August 1945, Reel 61, SRC.

19. War Department, Army Service Forces, Office of the Commanding General, "Racial Situation in the United States," 3 February-17 February 1945, Box 9, OF 4245g, Roosevelt Papers. See also Police Committee of Council, "Regular Meeting," 3 November 1943, Police Committee Minute Book, July 1938–January 1946, City of Atlanta Records, AHC; Spike Washington, "Brutality Victims Are Fined in Police Court"; Douglas Carter, "Schedule for Observation of Urban and Interurban Streetcars, Trackless Trolleys and Buses," 2 August 1945, I:1919, Reel 61, SRC.

20. Douglas Carter, "SRC, Inc., Trans-Seg. Study—Aggravated Assault on Trolley Car," 5 June 1945, I:1919, Reel 61, SRC.

21. [Incident report], [ca. 5 July 1945], I:1919, Reel 61, SRC.

22. Evelyn Brooks Higginbotham, *Righteous Discontent: The Women's Movement in the Black Baptist Church, 1880-1920* (Cambridge: Harvard University Press, 1993), 187.

23. Ibid., 188. See also Glenda Gilmore, *Gender and Jim Crow: Women and the Politics of White Supremacy in North Carolina, 1896-1920* (Chapel Hill: University of North Carolina Press, 1996), xix.

24. Forrester B. Washington, "Economic Problems of Rural Negro Migrants in Atlanta," *Georgia Observer*, supplement, August 1940, VII:106, Reel 49, CIC. Washington's portrayal of black migrants matched the "distaste and condescension" marking other observers' portrayal of white rural folk flocking to southern cities during the war. Daniel, "Going among Strangers," 902.

25. Office of Supervisor of Practice, Atlanta University, "Summary of High Points of Seminar on Secondary Education," 1943, Box 7, Georgia Department of Education Division of Negro Education, Director of Negro Education Subject Files, Georgia Department of Archives and History. See also Rubye Weaver, "As a Woman Sees It," ADW, 7 October 1945.

26. "Summary of High Points."

27. Senior Class, Booker T. Washington High School, "The Cornellian," Atlanta, Georgia, 1944, Samuel Howard Archer Collection, Auburn Avenue Research Library.

28. "Summary of High Points."

29. Larry Bell quoted in "Progress Report," n.d., *Bell Bomber Source*, Box 2, Series 17, WMC.

30. Bell Aircraft Corporation, Press Release, 14 March 1943, Box 2, Series 17, WMC.

31. Ibid.

32. Robert Weaver, *Negro Labor: A National Problem* (New York: Harcourt, Brace and Co., 1946), 109, 129-30.

33. For the most complete examination of these grassroots struggles to force compliance with federal nondiscrimination policies for defense workers, see Merl E. Reed, *Seedtime for the Modern Civil Rights Movement: The President's Committee on Fair Employment Practice* (Baton Rouge: Louisiana State University Press, 1991).

34. William Y. Bell Jr., "Defense Training for Atlanta Negroes," *Georgia Observer* 3 (September-October 1942), VII:106, Reel 49, CIC.

35. Sub-Committee of the Council on Defense Training for Negroes to E. A. Adams, 11 March 1942, Box 12, Series 2, WMC; Drive for Defense Courses Continues," ADW, 12 March 1942; "Registration for Defense Courses Gaining Impetus," ADW, 13 March 1942. Although the ADW claimed over 10,000 registrants resulting from the CDT's drive, the AUL only reported 5,000. "Over 10,000 File Cards in Defense Training Job," ADW, 23 March 1942; Atlanta Urban League, "Timeless: The Task of Preventive Social Work."

36. The USES situation in Atlanta was not unique to that city. In the first quarter of 1941, USES placed some 35,000 workers in industrial jobs nationwide, of whom only 245 were black. Daniel R. Fusfeld and Timothy Bates, *The Political Economy of the Urban Ghetto* (Carbondale: Southern Illinois University Press, 1984), 46. Even after the CDT won its battle for defense training for blacks, USES continued to undercount the city's black workforce, demonstrating this agency's national recalcitrance in integrating black workers into assembly-line jobs during the war. Weaver, *Negro Labor*, 145-51.

37. "WPB Chief Nelson Gets Protest on Failure to Train Negroes for Bomber Plant Work," *ADW*, 2 April 1942.

38. "Defense Training Classes Started," *ADW*, 24 November 1942.

39. Bell, "Defense Training for Atlanta Negroes"; Reed, *Seedtime for the Modern Civil Rights Movement*, 185–91.

40. John J. Corson to Franklin O. Nichols, 4 April 1942, Box 12, Series 2, WMC; Lawrence A. Oxley to James H. McGinnis, 25 March 1942, Box 12, Series 2, WMC; Mrs. G. T. Hamilton to Mr. Cy W. Record, n.d. [ca. June, 1943], Box 2, Series 18, WMC.

41. A. Bruce Hunt to Will Maslow, 3 April 1944, Closed Cases Box 4, FEPC; Amos Ryce Jr. to Bruce Hunt, 12 April 1944, RG 228, Closed Cases Box 4, FEPC; Sallie McCrary, "Complaint," 13 April 1944, Closed Cases Box 4, FEPC; Anon. to A. Bruce Hunt, n.d., [ca. July or August 1944], Closed Cases Box 4, FEPC; H. W. Sewell to A. Bruce Hunt, 5 September 1944, Closed Cases Box 4, FEPC; Atlanta Urban League, "United States of America before the President's Committee on Fair Employment Practice, Complaint" 20 October 1944, Closed Cases Box 1, FEPC; [Witherspoon] Dodge, n.t., [typed memo on scrap of paper,] [ca. 6 November 1944,] Closed Cases Box 1, FEPC.

42. "Aircraft Grads Hear Nicholson," *ADW*, 13 January 1943; "Urge Enrollment for Bell Bomber Courses," *ADW*, 29 March 1943; Robert Thompson, "Brief Report of Vocational Department of Atlanta Urban League, Sept. 1942–April 1943," Box 19, Rainey Papers; War Manpower Commission, "Labor Market Developments Report," 15 April 1943, Box 7, Series 12, WMC; "Day Classes at Aircraft School May Be Stopped," *ADW*, 23 July 1943; "Need More Students at Aircraft School," *ADW*, 1 August 1943; [War Manpower Commission,] "Labor Developments Report for Atlanta, Georgia," 28 December 1943, Box 7, Series 12, WMC; "Atlantans Urged to Use Aircraft School Facilities," *ADW*, 30 June 1944.

43. "Progress Report."

44. "Urban League to Register Group for Bell Work," *ADW*, 22 January 1943.

45. "Progress Report"; Atlanta Urban League, "Timeless: The Task of Preventive Social Work among the Most Underprivileged, Annual Report," 1943, Box 5, GTH; Sub-Committee of the Council on Defense Training for Negroes to E. A. Adams, 11 March 1942, Box 12, Series 2, WMC; Atlanta Urban League, "Timeless: The Task of Preventive Social Work," 1942; [War Manpower Commission,] "Preliminary Statement on the Atlanta and Marietta Labor Market," 10 December 1942, Box 1, Series 12, WMC.

46. Atlanta Urban League, "Timeless: The Task of Preventive Social Work among the Most Underprivileged," 1943; Joel Smith interviewed by Bernard West, partial transcript, Box 39, Living Atlanta Collection; Jacob Henderson interviewed by Duane Stewart, 8 June 1989, Georgia Government Documentation Project, Special Collections, Georgia State University.

47. A. Bruce Hunt to Frank Constangy, 8 January 1944, Closed Cases Box 2, FEPC; Madrid Boyd Turner, "A Study of One Hundred Skilled Negro Workers at Bell Aircraft Corporation and the Problems Encountered in Adapting to a Peacetime Economy" (master's thesis, Atlanta University, 1946), 2; William Shell to Dillard B. Lasseter, 30 June 1945, Box 1, Series 20, WMC.

48. Bell Aircraft advertised constantly for assembly-line workers in Atlanta's white

newspapers throughout 1944 and 1945, and even offered training to unskilled workers to fill these positions. African Americans were excluded entirely from these jobs and training opportunities. See Bell Aircraft FEPC complaints in Closed Cases Boxes 2, 6, and 7, FEPC.

49. "Occupational Classification of Negro Workers at Bell Aircraft during World War II," Box 1, Housing Center Files, 1933–1949, Atlanta Urban League Collection [unprocessed], Special Collections, Robert W. Woodruff Library, Clark-Atlanta University; Turner, "A Study of One Hundred Skilled Negro Workers," 2. Bell did such a good job of segregating skilled black workers from the rest of the Marietta workforce that many white workers were not even aware that the company hired blacks in skilled positions. Catherine Cohen interviewed by Adina Back, n.d., partial transcript, Box 36, Living Atlanta Collection.

50. See, for example, Minnie Harvey, "Complaint," 7 February 1944, Closed Cases Box 2, FEPC; Corria L. Durden, "Complaint," 26 June 1944, Closed Cases Box 2, FEPC; Lureline Thomas, "United States of America before the President's Committee on Fair Employment Practice, Complaint," 20 January 1945, Closed Cases Box 2, FEPC.

51. Turner, "A Study of One Hundred Skilled Negro Workers," 11; Nelson C. Jackson to Lester B. Granger, 27 April 1947, Box 1, Housing Center Files, 1933–1949, Atlanta Urban League Collection.

52. "Workers' Education to Be Topic for Bell Employees," ADW, 27 April 1944.

53. William H. Shell to Dillard B. Lasseter, 31 July 1945, Box 1, Series 20, WMC. See also Daniel, "Going among Strangers," 902.

54. "War Workers Warned to Work on and off Job for Security," ADW, 31 October 1944.

55. In this way, black reformers acted very much like wartime and postwar union leaders, who, in their new partnership with corporate leaders, took over "much of the company's personnel work" and became "the disciplining agent of the rank and file." C. Wright Mills, *The New Men of Power: America's Labor Leaders* (New York: Harcourt Brace and Co., 1948), 224.

56. All FEPC complainants protesting on-the-job discrimination at Bell told of white personnel officials dismissing their charges or, in the case of workers protesting discriminatory suspension, threatening them with permanent dismissal if they made an official grievance. See Bell files in Closed Cases Box 2, FEPC.

57. Annette Devine Giddings, "Complaint," 15 February 1944, Closed Cases Box 2, FEPC; Annie Mae Hightower, "Complaint," 16 February 1944, Closed Cases Box 2, FEPC; Lamar Ross, "Complaint," 3 March 1944, Closed Cases Box 2, FEPC; Spicey Simmons, "United States of America before the President's Committee on Fair Employment Practice, Complaint," 19 February 1944, Closed Cases Box 2, FEPC; Dora Smith, "United States of America before the President's Committee on Fair Employment Practice, Complaint," 19 February 1944, Closed Cases Box 2, FEPC Files; "Report by Flournoy on Cases No. 197–198," 30 May 1944, Closed Cases Box 2, FEPC; Sarah Madison, "United States of America before the President's Committee on Fair Employment Practice, Complaint," 1 May 1944, Closed Cases Box 2, FEPC.

58. Clarence Bacote, "The Negro in Atlanta Politics," *Phylon* 16, no. 4 (1955):344; Ronald Bayor, *Race and the Shaping of Twentieth-Century Atlanta* (Chapel Hill: University of North Carolina Press, 1996), 20.

59. This remarkable connection between the registration campaign and the city's white establishment, while beyond the scope of this study, warrants further investigation. "Table I: Source of Income, Atlanta Urban League, 1946–1949," 26 March 1958, Manuscript Collection Box 48, Ralph Emerson McGill Papers, EU; Lorraine Nelson Spritzer and Jean B. Bergmark, *Grace Towns Hamilton and the Politics of Southern Change* (Athens: University of Georgia Press, 1997), 111; Robert Thompson interviewed by Duane Stewart, 5 June 1989, interview transcript, Georgia Government Documentation Project, Georgia State University Archives.

60. Clarence Stone, *Regime Politics: Governing Atlanta, 1946–1988* (Lawrence: University Press of Kansas, 1989), 32.

61. Ibid., 32–34.

62. Robert Thompson interview; Spritzer and Bergmark, *Grace Towns Hamilton*, 89–90.

63. Lillian Virginia Evans, "A Study of Twenty-Five Negro Veterans Who Are 'On-the-Job' Training in Ten Establishments in Atlanta, Georgia" (master's thesis, Atlanta University School of Social Work, 1946), 20, 25; Turner, "A Study of One Hundred Skilled Negro Workers," 45; Sandy Gregg Reid, "A Study of the Social Problems of Fifty Veterans of World War II, Enrolled in Booker T. Washington High School, Atlanta, Georgia 1946–1947" (master's thesis, Atlanta University School of Social Work, 1947), 10–12, 14, 21.

64. Bureau of the Census, *Sixteenth Census of the United States: 1940, Population*, v. 3, part 2 (Washington, D.C.: GPO, 1943), 735–40; Bureau of the Census, *Census of Population, Seventeenth Census of the United States: 1950*, v. II, part 11 (Washington, D.C.: GPO, 1952), 297–99.

65. Twyler Wenona Griffin, "A Study of the Employment Changes since the Close of World War II and How These Changes Affect 100 Persons Seeking Services at the United States Employment Service Office in Atlanta, Georgia" (master's thesis, Atlanta University School of Social Work, 1946), 16–19; Turner, "A Study of One Hundred Skilled Negro Workers," 2.

66. Bureau of the Census, *Census of Population, Seventeenth Census of the United States: 1950*, 218. Black registration rates in Atlanta continued to be low into the 1960s. See Bayor, *Race and the Shaping of Twentieth-Century Atlanta*, 7, 18.

67. This apparent paradox is a favorite topic for journalists in Atlanta and elsewhere. Michael H. Trotter, "America's Public Housing Capital," *Atlanta Journal-Constitution*, 20 April 1997; Tracie Reddick, "Black Workers Find Tale of Two Cities," *Tampa Tribune*, 12 May 1996; Thomas D. Boston, "Black Middle Class Shifts over Time," *Atlanta Journal-Constitution*, 21 May 1995; Carrie Teegarden, "Is the City a Mecca for African Americans?" *Atlanta Journal-Constitution*, 14 January 1994.

Regional Advantage in the New South

The Creation of North Georgia's
Carpet Industry, 1945–1970

RANDALL PATTON

The small northwest Georgia community of Dalton has recently drawn scholarly interest. Douglas Flamming published a prize-winning study of workers and managers in the cotton mills of Dalton that detailed the building of Crown cotton mill and its mill village and eloquently described the birth, life, and death of organized labor in this small southern town. Flamming finished by describing the demise of Dalton's cotton mills and the simultaneous rise of a new local industry—tufted carpeting. By the early 1960s, carpet plants had eclipsed cotton mills as the largest employers in the Dalton area, and this enterprising "New South" city had become the "carpet capital" of the world.[1] As Flamming rightly noted, cotton mills such as the Crown company's represented the South's industrial past; the carpet mill boom was the wave of the future. The rapid growth in carpet manufacture in the Dalton area during the 1950s and 1960s, and post–World War II southern industrial development generally, deserve greater scholarly attention.

A study of Dalton's carpet industry can help expand a new line of inquiry for historians of southern industrialization. Most scholarship on post–World War II industrial development in the American South has focused on what James Cobb has called "the selling of the South": the feverish pursuit of outside investment by southern state and local governments and boosters. This focus has been quite understandable. From Henry Grady's "New South" addresses of the 1880s through Mississippi's Balance Agriculture With Industry (BAWI) program of the 1930s to Alabama's wooing of Mercedes in the 1990s, southern political and economic leaders have tended to look outside the region for solutions to the problems of poverty and underdevelopment.[2]

The complex of tufted carpet manufacturers that emerged around Dalton, Georgia, in the mid-twentieth century exemplified a different development strategy. The tufted textile industry built on a foundation laid by more conservative firms in textiles and by developers and industrialists in the nearby "industrial dynamo" of Chattanooga. This industry was characterized by small entrepreneurial firms utilizing new technologies. These firms developed a flexible method for mass-producing a wide array of slightly different goods. Local government added crucial support for the new industry by developing an infrastructure designed specifically to accommodate its needs. Rather than recruiting outside companies, Dalton-area leaders maximized their own particular "regional advantage" in tufted textile manufacture.[3] The development of the tufted carpet industry illustrates the attempts of manufacturers to combine flexibility with high throughput and mass-market production. In doing so, these new, mainly southern, entrepreneurs claimed control over an important segment of the textile industry during the 1950s.

In 1950, the word carpet implied a woven wool construction, but by the early 1960s, machine-tufted nylon rugs and carpets dominated the soft floor covering market. A handful of old, established companies in the Northeast controlled carpet manufacturing in the early 1950s; by 1965 the nation's largest producer of soft floor coverings was a new Georgia firm created with a $4,500 investment in 1949. In the early 1950s, U.S. households purchased about two square yards of carpet per year, a rate that had changed little since the early years of the twentieth century. By the end of the 1960s, annual household consumption of carpeting had risen to more than ten square yards. New firms—quite small initially and most of them located in and around the small town of Dalton, Georgia—played the leading role in transforming the carpet industry; such firms were primarily responsible for introducing and refining the new tufting technology, which supplanted weaving.

THE CRISIS OF THE OLD ORDER

Before the war, American textile manufacture, in virtually all its subdivisions, had been mired in a seemingly endless crisis. This "prolonged instability" was broken by a brief period of prosperity during and after World War II, but the sense of constant crisis reemerged in the early 1950s and has persisted ever since. Still, Annette C. Wright has described this prolonged slump as a period in which some individual entrepreneurs were able to survive and prosper. Spencer Love created his Burlington Mills during the textile depression and built it into the largest textile firm in the world. One of the secrets of Love's success was his willingness to commit fully to new man-made fibers—first rayon, then nylon. Philip Scranton has also described this prolonged textile crisis. In the late nineteenth century, the textile industry consisted of two relatively distinct groupings: a mass production sector that focused on cheap, bulk goods and a "batch production" sector in which small, flexible firms produced a variety of finished and semifinished specialty goods. Carpets fell into this batch sector. For a variety of reasons—including pressure from textile buyers, long-term design trends, adverse federal and state government policies—the batch sectors entered a long period of decline during the 1920s, and the mass production model took hold in virtually all textile fields by default.[4]

Much of the recent scholarship on manufacturing has revolved around the dichotomy of flexible versus mass production. As Scranton notes in his recent *Endless Novelty,* batch\flexible\specialty production was not the sole province of small and medium firms: "Specialty manufacturing took place at giant enterprises making the 'big stuff' of America's infrastructure." Scranton described three categories of specialty manufacturers. First, the large firms mentioned above, which he described as "integrated anchors." Then came two other formats that were closely related. "Networked specialists" were "clusters of smaller companies in urban industrial districts," which "offered diverse finished goods to households and enterprises, relying on thick webs of contact and affiliation." These networked specialists often "contracted with a third array, 'specialist auxiliaries,' for essential services," such as, in the case of textiles, dyeing and finishing. The carpet makers of Scranton's Philadelphia district fell into the networked specialist category.[5] The tufted carpet district of Dalton, Georgia, also can be categorized in this format.

U.S. carpet manufacturers had long faced a stagnating demand for their products. After World War II, the industry experienced a brief boom but quickly sank back into its prewar problems. Decolonization and the Korean War led to sharply rising wool prices and unstable supplies of the industry's chief raw material. Wool price and supply instability put cost pressure on the carpet manufacturer at precisely the time when other consumer goods were becoming more affordable to the American mass market. The dilemma of being a producer of an "upper-class" product in the midst of a "middle-class" consumption binge was not new for the industry in the 1950s. During the first half of the twentieth century, per-family consumption of carpets actually declined about 60 percent. *Business Week* noted in 1955 that the American carpet industry had endured several decades of near-stagnation by the 1950s, earning "the unhappy distinction" of being one of a few industries "where growth has nowhere near matched the potential market—or the growth of the economy generally."[6]

Established companies tried a variety of methods for boosting sales and cutting costs during the 1950s, including trade-in programs, financing of carpet purchases, and massive consumer advertising. These old firms also sought cost efficiencies in cheaper labor and new technology, both of which they found in the South. Most major carpet manufacturers moved their carpet-weaving operations to the South in the 1950s. By 1958, more than 60 percent of woven carpet was produced south of the Mason-Dixon line.[7] Yet a new technology had surfaced—tufting. The machine-tufting process evolved from a northwest Georgia handicraft tradition in the first half of the twentieth century. Even the early carpet tufting machines of the 1950s were 6–10 times more efficient than looms producing floor coverings. Small companies emerged in the Dalton area to produce tufted carpet, generally from cotton. Georgia Rug Mills, Cabin Crafts, and Barwick Mills, among others, began tufting area rugs and carpeting between 1946 and 1949.[8]

SOUTHERN INDUSTRIALIZATION AND THE TUFTED TEXTILE INDUSTRY

Jack Turner, a longtime carpet industry executive, insisted in a 1995 interview that during the Great Depression, "Dalton and northwest Georgia were still . . . suffering from the after-effects of the Civil War and Reconstruction; a lot of us today have difficulty realizing the degree of economic discrimination against the South," which was prevalent "as late as the Thirties." Turner referred to the colonial economy thesis in explaining the rise of the tufted textile industry in northwest Georgia, which came to dominate carpet manufacturing by the 1960s. Entrepreneurs in Dalton and other small neighboring communities in the state's long-neglected northwest corner created a homegrown industry, helping lift the area by its own bootstraps into the modern industrial world. Turner's remarks underscored the power of the colonial economy thesis as an explanation of the South's economic backwardness; his exposition of the rise of a new industry attested to the vitality of one solution to the vexing problem of southern poverty.[9]

At the close of World War II, southern leaders debated alternative development strategies. Some southern business and political leaders urged the encouragement of indigenous entrepreneurial capitalism. William H. Wilkerson, president of the Auto-Soler Company of Atlanta, Georgia, delivered the following admonition to a group of southern and Georgia business colleagues in 1946: "Dixie . . . Look to Your Bootstraps." Wilkerson detailed his assessment of the South's economic predicament to an audience at the annual meeting of the Southern Machinery and Metals Exposition in Atlanta. "It is a fact that we in the South are poor," Wilkerson noted, "and it seems to me, that to overcome our poverty, we need industry." However, Georgia and the South should foster "home-grown" industry. Three kinds of businesses operated in Georgia, according to the executive. First there were "branch plants" established by "Northern capital," where "the management is absentee," and the "profits are siphoned away to the North." This type of business did Georgia "only partial good." Another category of business was "the type . . . that is owned in Georgia, gets all its income from Georgia and keeps its profit here for the benefit of Georgia." This type of business was "perfectly all right," Wilkerson allowed, but still did not fill Georgia's most pressing need. "[T]he thing that we must have to take our place in the sun," Wilkerson argued, "is the third type of business—our *own* national industry—businesses that are Georgia-owned and Georgia-managed, bringing profits into Georgia from other states and countries." Georgia and the South, in other words, should strive toward *export-led* economic growth and development. Wilkerson urged Georgia's business leaders to invest in national market–seeking yet locally owned industry.[10]

Southern state governments and community leaders had followed a different path in attempting to promote economic development: the feverish pursuit of outside investment. In order to court external investors and entice northern corporations to open branch plants in or relocate to the South, southern political and business leaders publicized the region's social stability and favorable business climate: low taxes and no unions. As Numan V. Bartley has observed, it was not until the 1940s that "the southern states established the programs that were to mature during the postwar years into well-staffed, handsomely financed commissions." Throughout the South, the "campaign for locally originated industrial capitalism rapidly dissipated" in the aftermath of World War II. The old landlords were openly hostile to substantive changes, such as improved education, that would promote internally generated industrial development. Yet the region lacked a powerful, cohesive group of home-grown entrepreneurs in manufacturing. Consequently, southern state governments responded to the prevailing sentiments among their most powerful constituents and "channeled their efforts into cajoling northern corporations to expand into the region."[11]

In spite of state governments' increasing preoccupation with industrial recruitment, the pre–World War II South was hardly devoid of homegrown entrepreneurs. In North Carolina, James Buchanan Duke, among many others, helped create North Carolina's tobacco processing industry, and a host of enterprising individuals combined to create the High Point area's furniture district. Most significantly, industrial promoters throughout the region had sponsored the textile mill building boom of the late nineteenth and early twentieth centuries. While some of the South's textile mills were transplants, most were the result of local entrepreneurship. These local textile entrepreneurs continued to depend on northern machine builders and northern marketing structures, and especially on plant managers and engineers hired away from northern mills. As David Carlton has observed, "the ease with which these entrepreneurs could enter cotton manufacturing . . . came at a price." Entry into cotton manufacturing "required relatively little in the way of flexible and rapid adjustment to a dynamic environment," and "the diversion of entrepreneurial energies into textiles would in the long run exert a deleterious effect on North Carolina's [and the entire region's] industrial development, . . . encouraging an entrepreneurial conservatism" that inhibited innovation.[12] Those southerners who had advocated and practiced the encouragement of indigenous entrepreneurial capitalism have often almost disappeared in the mists of southern history.

U.S. textile manufacture shifted to the South during the first half of the twentieth century, largely due to the creation of a new southern textile industry that supplanted northern manufacturers and at least partly in response to state recruitment efforts. Carpet manufacture was one of the last segments of textile manufacture to be "southernized." When carpet makers relocated in the 1950s, they often received aid from southern state and local governments. Alexander Smith and Sons, for example, secured substantial aid in its shift from Yonkers, New York, to Greenville, Mississippi. Mississippi had long encouraged outside investment through its BAWI program, which dated from the 1930s. Under this program, Mississippi communities could offer five-year exemptions from county taxes and ten-year exemptions from municipal taxes to relocating companies. Communities could also build factories to company specifications, then lease those facilities to the firms at low rates. Local governments could also offer loans at interest rates below prevailing commercial terms. The Smith company announced in 1951 that management had accepted an offer from the city of Greenville, Mississippi, under the BAWI program. Greenville issued $5 million in municipal bonds to support construction of a modern carpet-weaving plant, which Smith would lease. Smith officials initially claimed that this new facility represented expansion and not a replacement for existing facilities. After the Mississippi plant was completed and functioning smoothly, however, Smith's managers changed their minds. In July 1954, Alexander Smith announced plans to close its century-old manufacturing facility in Yonkers, New York. Workers at Yonkers had been organized by the Textile Workers Union of America in 1937, following an industry trend. Although management and workers had cooperated effectively for more than a decade, the labor unrest of the late 1940s and early 1950s took its toll.[13] The lure of cheap and tractable southern labor proved powerful for Smith and other carpet makers in the 1950s.

THE ORIGINS OF THE TUFTED TEXTILE INDUSTRY

While the prevailing strategy throughout the South since 1945 has been the courtship of outside industry, small pockets of internally generated industrial development survived and occasionally thrived. The development of the tufted textile industry of northwest Georgia exemplified the approach advanced by advocates of entrepreneurial capitalism. Local entrepreneurs combined a native handicraft tradition with new technology to produce the tufted bedspread industry. Early in the twentieth century, led by Katherine Evans Whitener, women in northwest Georgia reintroduced an old method for producing designs and patterns on simple cotton sheets, making their sheets attractive as bed covers. Whitener taught local women to stamp designs onto sheets and then to sew long raised tufts to fill in the pattern. Once the tufts were hand-clipped, the sheet was washed in boiling water to promote shrinkage and lock in the yarn tufts. Whitener and hundreds of other farm families worked creatively to find markets for their products. One local handicrafter simply packed up a selection of her spreads and sent them to Wanamaker's department store in the 1910s, along with a note suggesting prices and asking that she be compensated if the spreads were sold. A few weeks later, she received payment along with an order for several dozen more spreads. As the industry grew, selling agents and merchants from a variety of ethnic backgrounds moved to northwest Georgia to take full advantage of this consumer phenomenon. By the 1920s, a "putting-out" system had emerged, with merchants providing raw materials and payment for labor, while handling the national marketing of the finished products. By the early 1930s, the stretch of U.S. Highway 41 that ran through Dalton, Georgia, had become known as "Peacock Alley," with local manufacturers lining the road with bedspreads for sale, usually hanging from clotheslines. Tourists driving south to Florida were their prime targets.[14]

As capital requirements were slight and demand remained high, spread houses proliferated. During the 1920s, department store buyers refined the tactic of playing one spread house off against the others, driving prices down. Manufacturers began to search for faster, more efficient ways to produce tufted spreads, trying to convert surplus Singer commercial-grade sewing machines to replace handwork. The origin of the first tufting machine is lost in a mélange of competing claims, though one may have been in use as early as 1922. The successful adaptation of sewing machines to the task of creating raised stitching on cotton sheets set the stage for an industrial revolution in northwest Georgia. The rapidly expanding market for tufted bedspreads and related products encouraged experimentation with machines with the aim of initiating mass production. By the early 1930s, several men laid claim to the invention—or adaptation—of a tufting machine. In Dalton, Georgia, local entrepreneurs established Cabin Crafts in 1930, and the tufted bedspread industry moved into factory production. This step was made possible by, and in turn encouraged, the further development of a regional machine-building industry. From quite humble beginnings, the original crude adaptations became more sophisticated. A host of machine shops, dealers, and parts makers rose to meet the demand for specialized sewing machine conversion parts and later tufting machines.[15]

The tufted textile industry continued to use small sewing machines for production through the early 1940s. The Cobble Brothers firm, headquartered in nearby Chattanooga, Tennessee (about 25 miles north of Dalton), played a central role in the development of larger tufting machines in the mid-1940s, which paved the way for carpet manufacture. Albert and Joe Cobble were hosiery mill mechanics who struck out on their own with a machine shop in the early 1930s. Joe Cobble, one of the company's founding brothers, patented in 1943 a tufting machine with a multineedle bar suitable for tufting wide-width bedspreads on a continuous basis. This first "yardage machine" became the model for later rug and carpet tufting machines, patented by Cobble in the late 1940s. At about the same time, Cabin Crafts mechanics and Mose Painter, a local Dalton welder, were independently tinkering with wide machines capable of tufting large rugs and carpets as well. Sometime in 1949 or early 1950, one of these firms sold the first "broadloom" (larger than four feet by six feet) tufted carpet; a host of others followed quickly. Thus the carpet segment of the tufted textile industry generally dates its origins to 1949.

Joe Cobble turned over direction of the machine shop to his nephew, Lewis Card, in 1950. By 1952, Card became general manager at Cobble. Lewis and his brother, Roy, developed several significant alterations and improvements for the basic tufting machine, such as pattern attachments that could produce geometric shapes. Lewis Card presided over the expansion of Cobble's product line, including the introduction of a larger machine capable of producing tufted floor-covering products in a seamless twelve-foot width. To stimulate sales, Card shipped machines on an installment purchase basis, often keeping the financing in-house, and devised a leasing plan based on a minimum rate with additional charges predicated on yardage actually produced. Leasing imposed strenuous financial demands on Cobble's resources, but it became Card's major marketing strategy to offer tufting equipment to customers who had more ambition than capital.[16] In the 1950s and 1960s, that category included most of the entrepreneurs entering the field.

The productivity of the tufting machine created an industry and annually threatened to ruin it. Former Cobble designer Max Beasley recalled that "every year was the last big year for tufting"; it seemed inevitable to many observers during the 1950s and 1960s that the rising demand for tufted carpeting would falter. Lewis Card observed that in the early 1950s, "We knew little about the tufting machine and our customers [the manufacturers of carpets and bedspreads] knew less."[17] All the interested parties understood was that year by year demand seemed to exceed supply. Card and Beasley kept innovating, and new entrepreneurs continued buying faster and faster tufting machines, banking on the future. Other machine makers followed Cobble's lead in offering liberal terms for financing tufting equipment purchases, thus almost eliminating machinery costs as an effective barrier to entry. New firms proliferated, and small firms characterized the expanding industry.

CARPET FINISHING

While barriers to entry into carpet tufting were low, the reverse was true in carpet finishing. Carpet finishing involved as many as four basic steps. All tufted carpets required a latex coating to lock in tufts. Rolls of carpeting then had to be dried. Cut-pile carpeting often required shearing, a process that brushed the carpet's surface and then trimmed the tufts to uniform height. Carpets that had been tufted using undyed yarn had to be dyed. All tufted goods, then, required some degree of finishing. Even very small firms that produced level loop goods from predyed yarn had to have their products coated and dried. Bigger manufacturers with a wider variety of cut and loop products might need shearing services. The manufacturers who participated in the largest segment of the carpet industry—the residential market—generally tufted sizable quantities of gray goods in a variety of cut and loop constructions, preferring to dye carpets to suit distributors and retailers on short notice. This practice allowed tufters to minimize the risk inherent in storing inventories.

Carpet finishing equipment was large and required a great deal of space. Moreover, it was quite expensive. Tufting machines could be purchased for $10,000, and manufacturers like Cobble Brothers would often finance the purchase in-house. A carpet coater, for the application of latex, cost over $200,000 by the late 1960s. An oven, for drying, might run as much as $500,000. The introduction of printing machines and continuous dye units in the late 1960s and early 1970s raised the stakes even higher. These imported machines—generally from Germany—began at around $750,000, and an investment in both printing and continuous dyeing units represented a gigantic capital expenditure (in terms of this industry). Some of the largest tufting firms, like Barwick Mills, installed such machinery for their own use, but less well capitalized manufacturers looked to finishing companies to provide these services.[18]

A smaller number of finishing companies arose in the 1950s and 1960s to serve the needs of dozens of small and mid-size carpet tufting operations, dyeing and coating carpets on a commission basis. Most of these carpet finishing companies emerged from the old bedspread finishing industry. Star Finishing will serve as an example. Robert and J. C. Shaw had taken over their father's bedspread and small rug-dyeing business, Star Dye Company, in 1958, after the elder Shaw's death. The Shaw brothers moved quickly into the emerging business of broadloom carpet finishing. By 1967, Star had grown into the largest commission finishing firm in the industry.[19]

Carpet finishing firms grew and proliferated in number (though not as rapidly as tufting companies) as tufted carpet sales boomed. Finishing companies shared risks with tufting firms in a variety of ways. Star Finishing, for example, held inventory for its customers, thus cutting the overhead costs of tufting mills. Finishing companies allowed manufacturers to avoid heavy investments in dyeing equipment, while still enabling tufters to delay the crucial color decision in carpeting to the last possible instant. Finishing companies benefited from serving a variety of customers, thus minimizing the risks associated with choosing the wrong color for the marketplace. Finishers and tufters formed a network of associated producers, spreading risks and sharing rewards in a rapidly expanding market.

LOCAL GOVERNMENT AND REGIONAL DEVELOPMENT

Alongside the evolution of a local technology, local government also played a large part in the development of the Dalton district, chiefly in the form of the Water, Light, and Sinking Fund (WL&SF), Dalton's municipally owned utility company. The district's bedspreads and later carpets had to be finished and dyed. These processes required large amounts of water. The spread and carpet finishing plants also needed "soft" water. Individual companies at first tried to install water-softening facilities, but these generally yielded less than satisfactory results, and were quite expensive as well. During the late 1930s and early 1940s, the WL&SF used public funds to conduct experiments and then implemented a series of renovations at its water purification plant. The WL&SF used community funds to tailor the region's water supply to the needs of industry. The city's utility company added the right mix of water softening agents, and also increased acidity levels in the local water supply to augment the bleaching effect in bedspread laundries.[20]

The relationship between the tufted textile industry and the city's utilities became even closer when V. D. Parrott assumed the leadership of the WL&SF in 1945. Parrott was committed to promoting the interests of indigenous manufacturers and used the public utilities to foster the concentration of tufted textiles in the Dalton area. He immediately initiated plans to expand the city's water supply, anticipating future industrial growth. Parrott "created a series of rural reservoirs," and increased filtration capacity. By 1949, the utility had doubled its plant capacity to more than 4 million gallons per day, and doubled this again by 1960. As early as 1963, Dalton ranked second—behind only Atlanta and ahead of many more populous cities such as Augusta and Macon—in daily water consumption among Georgia communities. Parrott also changed the WL&SF's rate structure "so that increased industrial demand was rewarded by decreased costs for [business] consumers." Parrott proved so effective that the mayor and city council gradually ceded total control of the utility to him, making it a government within a government. Parrott's plans called for large capital expenditures, which entailed changes in utility policy. Before 1949, "Dalton's schools, churches, and the hospital" received free water and power, and the utility regularly turned over surpluses to the city treasury. Parrott's ambitious plans forced him to abandon these policies, as he increasingly invested in expanding services to industry. Unsurprisingly, Parrott and his policies received near-unanimous support from mill owners.[21]

The WL&SF struggled to keep pace with the growth of the carpet industry throughout the 1950s and beyond. New mills opened regularly, and the demand of the new production facilities for electricity and water at times threatened to overwhelm the municipal utility. Parrott made it his chief goal, however, to accommodate the needs of this burgeoning local industry. The local utility pioneered in using natural gas in the 1950s to offset electricity costs. Parrott convinced the WL&SF commission and the city government to fund construction of a pipeline to connect with the Southern Natural Gas Company's main line, and a project was completed in 1955. By the early 1980s, Dalton led all of Georgia's municipally owned utilities (there were 89) in natural gas sales; industry accounted for 85 percent of natural gas usage in Dalton. Dalton Utilities and the WL&SF also entered several joint ventures with Georgia Power Company to help reduce electricity costs. The utility invested in Georgia Power's controversial nuclear facility, Plant Vogtle.[22]

It was water—quantity and quality—that caused the greatest concern for both the utility and the carpet industry in the 1960s and 1970s. Parrott devoted his full energy to facilitating the growth of carpet manufacture in the Dalton area. He constantly sought new sources of water—needed in ever-increasing amounts by the finishing segment of the carpet industry. However, this constant demand for more water brought Dalton Utilities into conflict with the emerging public concern for water quality in the late 1960s. State authorities regularly chastised Dalton Utilities for encouraging too-rapid growth and pushing local water treatment facilities past their limits. As new federal and state regulations in the early 1970s assigned to corporations the responsibility for cleaning the wastes they dumped into the nation's waterways, Parrott subsidized local carpet manufacturers by having Dalton Utilities accept the task of removing dangerous chemicals from the local water supply.[23]

NEW FIRMS AND THE DECENTRALIZATION OF THE U.S. CARPET INDUSTRY

Regional machine manufacturers like Cobble Brothers and new carpet manufacturers like Cabin Crafts generated most of the major innovations that made the new tufted carpet industry possible. Other ambitious individuals used such innovations to build successful carpet companies and challenge the dominance of long-established woven carpet manufacturers. Many of these new manufacturers had backgrounds in sales. E. T. Barwick had worked for years buying tufted textile goods such as small rugs for Sears. He became perhaps the most influential individual in the new tufted carpet industry in its 1950–1960s boom period. No other individual, according to the unanimous testimony of his competitors and contemporaries, made a greater contribution to the growth and development of tufted carpeting. Certainly he was the most flamboyant "outsider" to enter the tufted textile business in the Dalton district. Born in Lake City, Florida, in 1914, Barwick came from a self-described modest background and attended the University of North Carolina at Chapel Hill on a football scholarship. In 1961, *Sports Illustrated* named Barwick as a member of its silver anniversary college football team.[24]

Barwick Industries quickly became the early leader among local Dalton-area carpet manufacturers. Gene Barwick began buying and selling tufted goods for Sears in the late 1940s. He bought out one of his chief suppliers, McCarty Chenille of Chatsworth, Georgia, in 1949, and formed his own company, promptly hiring former owner Frank McCarty to continue running production while Gene concentrated on sales. Risking his entire life savings—$4,500—on the venture, he logged over 100,000 miles traveling to hawk his rugs and carpets in 1949, returning with orders totaling $998,000. Barwick's sales doubled in 1950, and he began expanding his facilities. The small company that had started with "one superannuated tufting machine in an old grocery store in the backcountry town of Chatsworth, Ga." grew into a firm that claimed to produce 25 percent of America's tufted floor coverings in 1954. (Barwick Mills' sales topped $26 million that year.) In addition to price advantages, tufted floor coverings offered color and styling variety. The cotton and synthetic carpets produced in Barwick's mills brought new choices to consumers, according to its owner. Woven wool carpets were limited to dark, murky colors. Postwar consumers wanted something brighter, "more modern," Barwick argued, and cotton and synthetic tufted carpets offered a much broader, and brighter, range of colors. By 1955, a network of twenty-two distributors scattered throughout the country sold Barwick's carpets, and the company sponsored showrooms in New York, Dallas, San Francisco, and Chicago. Despite this rapid growth, Barwick continued to travel extensively, showing up unexpectedly at all these facilities.[25]

Barwick's strategy combined marketing with product innovation. Barwick Mills introduced several all-nylon lines of carpeting in 1956, along with new rayon styles. The company worked with DuPont and American Viscose to promote the new products, and with department stores such as G. Fox & Company of Hartford, Connecticut. Indeed, the success of Barwick and other new manufacturers in expanding the market for carpeting prodded DuPont and other fiber-producing firms to accelerate their research and development efforts. Barwick used a variety of methods to promote tufted floor coverings. His primary targets were home furnishings retailers and distributors, though the firm advertised directly to consumers in the late 1950s. Symbolic of Barwick's personal energy and salesmanship was the DC-3 airplane that the company purchased in 1955. *Retailing Daily* reported in April 1955 that Barwick had flown a group of Detroit floor covering retailers down to Lafayette, Georgia, for a tour of a Barwick manufacturing plant. Barwick escorted another group of midwestern floor covering dealers to Lafayette and Dalton in June 1955.[26] These junkets became a company trademark. While other manufacturers did not share Barwick's flair for the dramatic, they did share his strategy, marketing most of their tufted carpeting to wholesale distributors of floor coverings and home furnishings, with a lesser portion going directly to retailers, during the 1950s and 1960s.

Barwick Mills and a few other pioneering enterprises of the early 1950s also played a key role as a training ground for future entrepreneurs in carpet manufacturing. Former Barwick salesmen and shop floor manufacturing supervisors started a half-dozen or more companies, including two major mills of the 1960s and 1970s. Frank McCarty, the man who organized Barwick's manufacturing operations early on, teamed with salesmen Eddie Evans and Art Black to form E&B Carpets in 1958. This company soon grew to become one of the industry's top ten firms before it was purchased by Armstrong in the late 1960s. Former Barwick and E&B employees started Galaxy Mills, a top ten company of the 1970s. E&B and Galaxy were only two of dozens of new firms spawned by the success of Barwick and other mills in the 1950s.

In 1949, tufted carpeting quite literally did not exist. By 1955, sales of tufted carpets had surpassed those of traditional wovens. Even though most tufting operations then used inferior fibers—cotton, rayon, and staple nylon, all less than perfect for floor coverings—and though most consumers had never heard of these manufacturers, their products were flowing off the shelves at wholesale distributorships and retail stores all over the country. By the mid-1950s, the established woven carpet companies recognized the magnitude of this challenge and responded.

THE WOVEN INDUSTRY RESPONDS

The American Carpet Institute launched a new advertising campaign in the mid-1950s to try to shore up dwindling markets, shape consumer tastes, and counteract the growth of the new tufted mills. The institute revived an old campaign from the late 1940s, proclaiming in a 1955 print and television advertising campaign that "Home Means More With Carpet on the Floor," boosting its annual marketing budget from about $750,000 to $1.25 million per year for three years. This marketing blitz targeted consumers with full-page ads in national magazines and newspapers, television spots, and booklets for consumers. The goal of the campaign was "to enlarge the total market for soft floor coverings," according to Alexander Smith president James Elliott. The institute began to promote the "functional benefits" of carpeting—"quiet, beauty and warmth."[27]

Advertising Age took note of the carpet campaign in March 1959, reporting that in 1958 broadloom carpeting "became the most strongly retail-advertised item in the home furnishings field—usurping the No. 1 spot headed by TV sets . . . since 1948." The advertising journal summarized the results of a study of the number of lines of advertising copy conducted in nine major cities, including New York, Philadelphia, Cleveland, and Chicago. The survey revealed that most carpet ads targeted the growing "middle-priced market," or carpets that cost between $5 and $10 per square yard. The established carpet industry was selling for all it was worth by the end of the 1950s.

Herbert Jay, Mohasco's director of public relations and advertising, explained his company's marketing strategy and the company's return to television after an eight-year absence in 1960. "As the largest company in the industry, we feel that it's our duty to first sell the concept of carpet—the generic of carpet," Jay asserted. If consumers weren't "sold on carpet per se, it doesn't matter how much we advertise the Mohawk line." This statement reflected the general strategy of the Carpet Institute and individual large companies within the industry.[28] The established carpet oligarchy evidently assumed that if the public were sufficiently "sold on carpet per se," consumers would obviously turn to firms with the skill and experience of more than a century of carpet craftsmanship. In making this assumption, the established firms were wrong.

In general, the results of intensively advertising soft floor coverings were mixed for the members of the elite Carpet Institute. With the industry facing both a brand name identification crisis and rising tufted production by new firms entering the carpet market, all manufacturers, not just weavers, benefited from their approach. Even though almost all of the old-line woven firms had entered tufted production by the end of the 1950s, these companies still had heavy investments in woven carpet facilities and equipment. Cheaper tufted carpets took a larger and larger market share in the 1950s, and that declining market share squeezed woven manufacturers. Mohasco, Bigelow, and other woven giants slashed "excess capacity" and consolidated in the face of a variety of challenges. The American carpet industry, after decades of virtual stagnation, took on a new look by 1960 as southern firms benefited most from the developments of the 1950s.

THE CARPET MARKET

In 1955, John S. Ewing and Nancy P. Norton published a history of Bigelow, one of the carpet industry's largest, oldest, and best-known companies, which was synonymous with woven wool carpets and rugs. Ewing and Norton, writing in the midst of the revolutionary changes sweeping through the carpet trade, noted that the chief "imponderable" with which Bigelow's management had struggled in the postwar period was "the long-range trend of the industry." While noting that the Bigelow company had "diversified" by purchasing a tufted rug mill in Georgia in 1950, neither the authors nor Bigelow's managers could have foreseen the virtual replacement of woven wool carpets by tufted constructions made from synthetic fibers, or the rise of a host of small firms in the American South that would dominate the new production process.[29]

In 1968, William Reynolds, longtime treasurer of the American Carpet Institute, published a study of his industry's post–World War II innovations. Reynolds examined the demand for carpeting and found a strong correlation between rising per capita income and increases in carpet sales. U.S. carpet sales gained about 1.3 percent for every 1 percent increase in real income in the period 1947–1963. Carpeting had long been associated with comfort and luxury in the home. Before World War II, relatively high carpet prices had limited consumption to the upper and upper-middle income strata. The postwar global economic boom, a "golden age" according to Eric Hobsbawm, generated rapid income growth and an unprecedented surge in new housing construction. The general economic boom coincided with the emergence of tufted floor coverings, and consumers freely substituted tufted carpets for woven.[30]

The old woven establishments had long struggled to achieve brand name recognition and a consumer franchise, but these efforts had proven less than successful. In 1961, the American Carpet Institute sponsored a market survey of consumer attitudes toward carpets. The survey's findings confirmed the worst fears of woven carpet executives. More than 40 percent of consumers who had purchased carpet within the past six months could not hazard a guess as to its brand name. Of those consumers who mentioned a brand name, almost 10 percent mentioned Sears or some other retail chain. Less than 40 percent of those surveyed mentioned a manufacturer. Most consumers were unable to differentiate between woven and tufted constructions by sight. The most important factors in consumer purchase decisions were color, style, pattern, price, and durability. Consumers almost never mentioned fabric construction or method of manufacture as factors.[31]

The inability of woven manufacturers to build brand name recognition combined with another trend to work against increased consumption of woven carpets and in favor of the tufted variety: the decline of ornamental designs, which had been popular until the 1920s. From the Great Depression through the 1960s, "demand homogenized steadily in apparel and furnishings textiles." For carpets, this trend favored monocolor constructions rather than the intricate multicolor patterns long associated with high-end woven goods. According to Philip Scranton, this trend was accompanied by a seemingly contradictory demand on the part of home furnishings and apparel buyers for "a wide stylistic variety" within these newly established boundaries.[32]

Tufted carpeting made an attractive bargain for floor covering distributors, retail buyers, and consumers. The new tufting machines could make solid color carpeting that closely resembled pile-inserted Axminster woven goods. Lewis Card and others worked to create new attachments and designs for tufting machines that could create new styles. Lewis and Roy Card, working for Cobble Brothers, developed a variety of cut-pile, loop-pile, and cut-and-loop style machines. By mixing cut and loop piles in the same carpet, the new machines could create simple geometric patterns (though none as elaborate as the old carpet looms). The Cards also developed an attachment that could vary the length of cut or loop tufts by "back-robbing," or pulling back on a few of the yarn strands along the tufting machine's needle bar. Along with an almost endless variety of colors, these variations on the tufting machine helped carpet manufacturers produce an almost "endless novelty," to borrow Scranton's phrase. Yet this novelty arose within the new homogenized boundaries of the American consumer market. A solid color, tufted carpet with a simple pattern "sculpted" by cut-and-loop effects, or through the "back-robbing" attachment, was indistinguishable to the average consumer from a solid color Axminster. Indeed, the woven industry's advertising campaigns of the 1950s may have backfired. The marketing blitz extolled the virtues of carpets in general, though few consumers had any understanding of different constructions or manufacturing methods. As per capita incomes rose in the 1950s and 1960s, consumers based their purchases on style (including color) and price. Tufted carpeting was substantially cheaper than woven; and Reynolds found that price was, in the final analysis, the key factor in consumer decisions.

Many observers at the time and since have questioned the quality of tufted carpets relative to woven goods. Clearly, however, relative prices accounted for the dramatic increase in tufted carpet sales. By the end of the 1950s, tufted carpeting had replaced woven carpeting as the consumer's choice. The American Carpet Institute's statistical handbook for 1962 starkly summarized the differences in manufacturers' costs between the tufting and weaving processes. Using statistics for 1958 (the most recent year for which complete figures were available), the institute reported that sixty companies were engaged in the manufacture of woven carpets, operating sixty-nine plants and employing about 15,000.

The woven plants shipped 82.6 million square yards of carpet in 1958, achieving a productivity level of about 1.7 square yards per man-hour of labor. For this work, they paid more than $55 million in total wages that year.[33]

In contrast, eighty-eight companies operated ninety-two tufting mills, where fewer than 10,000 production workers managed to turn out more than 113 million square yards of tufted carpets and rugs. Even factoring in scatter rugs, which had lower productivity than broadloom tufting, the entire tufted floor covering industry managed to produce 5.8 square yards per man-hour. For this output, tufting mills paid about $27 million in wages, less than half the woven mills' total. The bottom line was painfully obvious to veterans of the old woven industry: tufting produced more carpet with fewer workers at lower cost. Tufting plants also outspent woven mills on capital improvements, $8 million to $5.8 million.[34]

Wholesale carpet prices, the consumer's top priority, also demonstrated the efficiency of the tufting process. Using the 1947–49 average price for broadloom carpeting as a base, the wholesale price index for wool Axminster carpets (the most popular wovens) stood at 144.4 in 1956. By 1960, Axminster prices had risen slightly, to 148.6. This price increase was quite small in contrast to the sharp hikes in the years immediately following World War II, and reflected woven industry efforts to modernize and regain a competitive posture with tufted carpets and imported wovens. Tufted carpet prices actually fell in the same period. The price index for cotton tufted carpets and rugs was 117.1 in 1956; by 1960 it had dropped to 96.0. Tufted products made from synthetic fibers showed the same pattern of steady price index decreases, from 118.4 to 104.1.[35]

Carpet consumption followed the price trend. The increasing availability of tufted goods brought the average per-square-yard mill value of broadloom carpeting (combined tufted and woven) down from $6.26 in 1950 to $3.56 in 1970 (in current, not constant, dollars; the cost-depressing effect of the tufting process was remarkable). Broadloom carpet shipments per household rose from just under two square yards (1.97) in 1950 to about three yards (2.81) in 1960, reflecting the efficiencies of tufting. As the technology matured and the public began to accept manmade fibers, per-household consumption jumped to 8.5 square yards by 1970, creating even more opportunity for producers of tufted floor coverings.[36]

BARWICK, DUPONT, BCF NYLON, AND THE COMPLETION OF THE TUFTING REVOLUTION

The emergence of tufting as an alternative to carpet weaving and the rapid rise of tufted carpet sales during the 1950s prompted DuPont to speed up its development of new textile fibers. Carpet manufacturers experimented with existing nylon fibers during the early 1950s. Nylon was a continuous filament fiber; nylon yarns for hosiery and other purposes did not require a laborious process of carding and blending to produce long strands. Such continuous filament yarns were more durable than "staple" yarns which consisted of short strands of cotton, wool, or other fibers blended and twisted into longer yarn strands. Especially in "cut pile" carpet constructions, continuous filament nylon yarns were valuable in reducing fuzzing and preventing the yarn's being pulled away from the carpet backing. Unfortunately for carpet makers, continuous filament nylon had insufficient bulk for use in carpet manufacture. Yarn producers made carpet yarn from nylon by chopping the continuous filaments and baling them like cotton or wool. This "staple" nylon was then processed just like any natural fiber by a process of spinning and crimping to produce the bulk necessary for carpet manufacture.

DuPont researchers recognized the shortcomings of continuous filament nylon for carpet manufacture and other purposes requiring thicker yarns. Company scientists realized in the 1940s that it would "be far less costly to crimp the original filament yarns as a means of obtaining the bulk of spun staple yarns." The company sponsored some experimentation with methods of creating bulked continuous filament fibers, but the demand for such fibers was then too small to encourage massive investment in such research. In 1951, DuPont researchers Alvin Breen and Herbert Lauterbach developed a method of using "hot fluid jets to relax yarn continuously." Lauterbach even had a small sample carpet produced with this yarn to illustrate the potential of the new technique. A DuPont internal history noted, however, that "the business climate of 1951–1952 was not propitious" for such a "carpet development." Demand for carpeting had remained relatively stable for decades, and traditional manufacturers of woven wool carpets were reluctant to make a wholesale move toward synthetic fibers. In addition, the process developed by Breen and Lauterbach needed refining to produce consistently good yarn for carpet manufacture. While working on the bulking process, Breen serendipitously discovered a process for bulking rayon and other nonthermoplastic yarns that became the "Taslan" process. Taslan proved more commercially promising and the company diverted manpower and funding to it and away from the bulking of nylon.[37]

By early 1957, however, "the atmosphere had changed," for the carpet tufting process had now "become commercially viable." Per capita carpet sales had increased substantially in the period after 1950, reversing a decades-old trend; indeed, tufted products accounted for *all* of the industry's growth in the 1950s (and beyond as well). The new tufted manufacturers never hesitated to explore alternative fibers, and were especially attracted to cheaper synthetic fibers. Working with cotton, rayon, staple nylon, blends of all or some of these, and a few other less-used fibers, tufted carpet enterprises had already revolutionized the manufacture of carpeting in the United States. In early 1957, DuPont researchers "reexamined" Breen and Lauterbach's earlier discoveries and began an intensive effort to perfect the bulking of continuous filament nylon. That April, DuPont created a task force to refit some manufacturing facilities to produce bulked continuous filament nylon (BCF). In June 1958, the company announced the new product as Type 501 BCF nylon. DuPont reached agreements with two large carpet manufacturing firms to introduce all-nylon tufted carpeting in the fall of 1958, James Lees and Sons and E. T. Barwick Mills.[38]

By the end of the 1950s, Barwick Mills had settled on nylon as its principal fiber, announcing in March 1958 that 95 percent of its carpets were currently being made of nylon. Barwick and retailer G. Fox collaborated on a succession of impressive marketing drives for the new nylon carpeting. In April 1958, the manufacturer and the retailer decided to "torture test" Barwick nylon carpeting at Fox's Hartford store to kick off a new promotion. Store management placed two carpets at the main entrance to G. Fox & Sons. A third strip of nylon carpeting was placed in the store's garage at the package pickup counter. This latter carpet would be subjected to both foot and automobile traffic. After a few weeks, half of each carpet strip was to be cleaned to demonstrate both durability and cleanability. DuPont and Barwick sent representatives to Hartford to be available for customer questions during the promotion.[39]

Barwick also set about educating retailers and distributors on the advantages of nylon. The tufted innovator conducted a series of fifty-one seminars on nylon carpeting in various important market cities between August 1957 and April 1958. Barwick advertising chief John Hoff told *Home Furnishings Daily* that carpet dealers and distributors were much more willing to accept nylon carpeting at the end of the seminar series than before. The nylon seminars were so successful that Barwick decided to repeat the series beginning in summer 1958.[40]

Barwick cooperated with DuPont to take the nylon story to television in the fall of 1959. *Home Furnishings Daily* characterized an upcoming Barwick television campaign as "the biggest promotional assist yet" for "retailers of the E. T. Barwick Mills' line of nylon carpeting." That September Gene Barwick announced plans for a joint advertising campaign to be shared with DuPont. The campaign called for Barwick and DuPont to tell "the manufacturer's story" in a series of ads on NBC's "Today Show" on three successive days, September 29 through October 1. The ads would "name personally more than 200 Barwick dealers." In addition, similar ads would air during the DuPont-sponsored "June Allyson Show" on CBS. Barwick claimed that "never before has a carpet promotion been scheduled to so big an audience." Tufted carpeting's top manufacturer and marketer predicted that "more customers than ever before will learn what the DuPont label means to them in the purchase of carpet for their home. Our dealers can expect their biggest selling push this fall."[41]

Barwick developed a close relationship with DuPont, which was crucial to this marketing blitz. Barwick Mills, with about $30 million in sales in 1958, could not

Regional Advantage in the New South

finance a national television advertising campaign of this magnitude on its own. Huge fiber companies like DuPont could, and the tufted carpet industry needed help in national marketing and advertising. DuPont needed to expand the potential market for its nylon fibers. It was a marketing marriage made in heaven, much to the chagrin of the old established woven companies. As more and more tufting operations turned to synthetic fibers such as DuPont's "501" nylon, the fiber producers saw the obvious advantage in promoting increased carpet sales.[42]

MANAGING AN EMERGING INDUSTRY: CREATING A TRADE ASSOCIATION

Dalton district bedspread manufacturers created a workable trade association in 1945. Membership in the Tufted Textile Manufacturers Association (TTMA) was open to all makers of tufted textile products. The association was headquartered in Dalton and dominated by firms located within a twenty-five mile radius of the future carpet capital. Initially, the TTMA's main purpose was to negotiate with government for scarce raw materials on behalf of a group of small companies. The organization soon grew into an effective body of medium-sized tufted textile manufacturers. By the mid-1950s, TTMA promoted cooperative research efforts; sponsored workmen's compensation and other insurance plans for tufting companies; compiled statistics on tufted textile sales and shipments for use by members; adopted minimum quality standards for tufted bedspreads; organized market shows for tufted carpets and rugs (beginning in the early 1960s); and perhaps most significantly, advised and trained members in labor-management relations.[43]

As carpet manufacturing came to dominate the tufted textile industry, tufted carpet mills began to dominate the trade association. TTMA took a leading role in helping its members try to cope with the tight labor market in the Dalton area. Convinced that the Dalton district faced a labor shortage, TTMA leaders urged employers to use every available means to mobilize local workers. The association took a leading role in compiling an extensive set of job descriptions for the state department of labor. TTMA executive vice president Henry Ball made clear to his membership that these descriptions would be useful in making certain that experienced workers in the Dalton district could be mobilized by the state employment service. Indeed, a long-time TTMA officer recalled that the greatest challenge facing the carpet industry in the 1950s and 1960s was labor relations.[44] TTMA spent most of its time and efforts in this period helping firms cope with what members called the "labor problem."

TTMA played a crucial role in crushing a union organizing campaign aimed at the tufted textile industry during the mid-1950s. In this initial organizing drive, it focused its anti-union propaganda on a maverick community organizer named

Don West. West had ties to left-wing organizations dating back to the 1930s, and TTMA engaged in a red-baiting smear campaign, which tarred the Textile Workers Union of America along with West. The strategy worked. TWUA lost a critical election at Belcraft Chenilles in December 1955 (840 workers voted for "no union," only 625 for TWUA), and the first attempt to organize the tufted textile industry rapidly fell apart in the aftermath of the Belcraft defeat. TTMA played a role in defeating the union, but members understood that red-baiting tactics might not work a second time. In 1956, TTMA established an Industrial Relations Club to encourage member companies to adopt new personnel policies, and to educate managers in the field of personnel management. TTMA and Dalton-area tufted textile manufacturers faced another challenge from TWUA in the early 1960s, and the union made certain that there would be no hint of Communist influence in that drive.[45]

TWUA leaders renewed efforts to organize Dalton's carpet mill workers in 1961. By the early 1960s, carpet had almost completely eclipsed all other forms of tufted textile manufacturing; bedspread and robe manufacture was in serious decline as demand for these novelty goods waned. Carpet manufacture, in contrast, was more profitable, and the carpet market seemed limitless. It appeared that carpet makers could afford wage and benefit increases. TWUA's John Chupka visited the Dalton district in late 1960 to assess the prospects for a new organizing drive. In early 1961, the union decided to press ahead.

TTMA responded to this with a new strategy, given that TWUA had made certain that there were no hints of "communist influence" in its new campaign. This time, TTMA officials and members focused on defending the growth of the past decade, and emphasized the danger that unionization might pose for future growth in the tufted carpet industry. The trade association argued that the communities of northwest Georgia must maintain "a favorable business climate" and made it clear that unions had no place in such an environment. TTMA helped create and cooperated closely with an organization called the Dalton Boosters, a group of local merchants and suppliers to the industry. The Boosters were particularly active in distributing anti-union literature and placing newspaper ads. TTMA and the Dalton Boosters developed a powerful argument against union organization. Dalton and surrounding communities had experienced rapid industrial growth, outpacing the manufacturing growth of Georgia and much of the Southeast. "The good, reliable labor supply" was "certainly one of the reasons" for Dalton's economic good fortune. "[T]he most important reason the tufted industry is continuing to expand in this region is simply because of the FAVORABLE BUSINESS CLIMATE that exists here" [emphasis in original]. TTMA also distributed anti-union leaflets of this sort to members for use on bulletin boards, and brought in seasoned professionals in textile labor like Atlanta attorney Frank Constangy. Constangy urged TTMA members to moderate their treatment of workers, boost wages and benefits, and institute rational personnel procedures to discourage employees from joining the union.[46]

In spite of the anti-union campaign waged by the Boosters and TTMA, the textile organizers won an important victory in November 1962 when more than 600 workers at a carpet mill in Calhoun, Georgia (20 miles south of Dalton), voted in favor of TWUA representation. Success at Dixie Belle Mills appeared to give TWUA a "foot in the door," according to a documentary produced by an Atlanta television station in early 1963.[47] However, the union's election victory at Dixie Belle represented only the beginning of a difficult process. The matter of negotiating a contract remained, and negotiations were delayed while the company appealed the National Labor Relations Board's certification of election results. The agency ruled against the company on April 1, 1963.[48] Union leaders expected Dixie Bell Industries to remain defiant and try to surrender as little as possible in the contract. Dixie Belle management announced early in 1963 that some 200 jobs at the Calhoun plant would be eliminated as the company consolidated many of its operations. The timing appeared to indicate that management was sending a message about job security to workers in "Tuftland." This move was obviously intended to have a chilling effect on the union drive in the area.

National TWUA officials debated alternative strategies for dealing with the Dixie Belle situation. This internal debate reflected the difficulties generally faced by organized labor in southern textiles. One faction advocated a strike. Edward Wynne and others at the national level argued that only by winning a contract that produced a substantial increase in the workers' standard of living could TWUA hope to build on its Dixie Belle victory. Some TWUA officials saw the Dixie Belle negotiations as a turning point, not just in the carpet campaign, but in southern textiles. Others were more cautious and advocated a more conservative strategy. Ultimately, the national union leadership chose to accept a contract offer from Dixie Belle management that produced much less than the union had promised workers during the campaign. TWUA's leadership concluded that a strike was too risky and might jeopardize the entire carpet drive. Leaders like Paul Swaity argued that by getting a contract—no matter how bad—without a strike, TWUA might build a reputation as a reliable negotiating partner and defuse some of the rabid opposition to organization among the small and medium-sized mills of the Dalton district.[49]

TWUA leaders decided to compromise. On 10 June 1963, Local 1592 approved a contract with Dixie Belle management. Dixie Belle workers got an average 5.5 percent pay increase, or about eight cents on the average hourly wage of $1.48. Local 1592 also secured several paid holidays (a first for Dixie Belle workers), time-and-a-half pay for working holidays, and increased health benefits. The union backpedaled on the issue of seniority and control over promotion. The contract recognized management's ultimate right to make key personnel decisions, requiring only that seniority be taken into account. While all permanent vacancies had to be filled from a list of "qualified" applicants on the basis of seniority, the company retained "the right to make the determination of qualifications for any job." If the local union objected to a management decision, a grievance could be filed, but "the burden of proving that the Company's determination was discriminatory or inherently wrong" rested "at all times" with the union. The low level of the wage increase and the union's lack of control over hiring and promotions generated public relations problems for TWUA in the area.[50]

THE MANAGEMENT RESPONSE TO THE DIXIE BELLE ELECTION

The Tufted Textile Manufacturers Association held a mass meeting of owners and managers on 16 July 1963 to discuss the Dixie Belle contract and the industry's response. TTMA officials had the meeting transcribed, and this remarkable document gives a rare glimpse into the private deliberations of a trade association's members. TTMA vice president R. E. Hamilton opened the meeting by criticizing many in his audience of more than 100 mill executives for keeping wages too low and engaging in arbitrary personnel practices: "We have too many people who assume that only a few large, major concerns are paying good wages, paid holidays, paid vacations, etc." Hamilton cited the TWUA's charge that the average wage in the tufted industry was around $1.40, noting that while it was in the union's interest to minimize the figure, it was not far from the mark. He appealed to those in the room who paid less than the industry average to boost wages. Hamilton also urged managers to cultivate better relations with employees.[51]

Hamilton then turned the meeting over to Frank Constangy and Lovic Brooks, Atlanta lawyers who served as counsel to TTMA and several companies on labor matters. Constangy had substantial experience in southern textile labor relations, and both had also represented Dixie Belle in its contract negotiations with TWUA. They came to Dalton to explain the Dixie Belle contract to the rest of the industry and recommend policies designed to keep the union from expanding beyond the Calhoun mill. Constangy told the assembled owners and managers that the tufted textile environment had changed dramatically in the preceding few months. The companies had "lost one of their major arguments—namely, that TWUA could never get a contract in the tufted industry without a strike." The union had done that. The TWUA's strategy of playing along with management had worked to that extent. The resulting contract, however, had been much weaker than TWUA had promised during the organizing campaign. This gave the companies a new argument: "that the TWUA's promises are not what they say they are because when it comes time to deliver, they not only get considerably less than what they promised, but in the end the people don't get [any of the things] that they committed themselves to the union to get changed."[52]

"The Dixie Belle contract was painfully and painstakingly negotiated," Constangy noted, given "that when a union is certified you've got to sit down and at least go through the motions of bargaining in good faith. When the union makes demands, you've got to make counter-proposals. Unfortunately, when they accept your counter-proposals, you can't back out of them." Constangy referred to TWUA's ratifying of contract terms that the company believed were unacceptable to the union. He did not quite say that the company had hoped to provoke a strike, but he certainly allowed that impression to be drawn from his comments. The contract "was designed by management ... to give the fullest possible freedom of action to the company." Constangy did bemoan the loss of managerial freedom inherent in any union contract, but he clearly believed that TWUA had surrendered control over the workplace to Dixie Belle management. As previously mentioned, just after the election, Dixie Belle had announced the elimination of certain operations at the plant, with a consequent loss of 200 jobs. TWUA protested and promised to get those jobs back, but the company held firm. Constangy recalled that he had participated in numerous contract negotiations over the years, and "if anybody has devised a stronger management rights clause and a greater freedom of action in terms of the elimination of jobs than we got at Dixie Belle, I haven't seen it." The company won the right to eliminate jobs at management's discretion, with the union merely winning the right to be notified.[53]

Constangy lectured the tufted textile executives on rudimentary personnel policies. The content of Constangy's remarks and his familiarity with the industry give valuable hints to the nature of labor relations in the carpet industry. Constangy wanted to point out a few elements of the contract "because these are not things Dixie Belle gave away because it was soft-headed or soft-hearted or under the gun." These were policies "that are inherent in any decent relationship between management and its people." Managers of unorganized plants simply had no choice but to adopt these policies "in order to avoid the union [being voted in] simply [to bring] some semblance of order out of the chaos of your industrial relations." He urged a preemptive strike against the union movement in Dalton. Once an election was set, employers faced numerous restrictions, but in the current period no elections had been slated. While organizers were trying to get workers to sign cards, management was free to campaign against card signing with few restrictions. Owners should take the offensive in the wake of the Dixie Belle contract, Constangy urged. "We should open an anti-union campaign in virtually every plant."[54]

TTMA members had already been practicing what Constangy preached at this meeting. In early March 1963, several large mills had announced a general

5.5 percent wage increase. By late spring 1963, TTMA's membership had swelled to over two hundred, an increase of thirty-three new members in an eight-month period beginning in the summer of 1962, when the TWUA organizing drive began to heat up. The trade organization touted this increase as the "greatest growth in membership in any similar period since the Association was founded." The new members included a substantial number of smaller mills.[55]

The union's organizing campaign in the Dalton area fell apart after the Dixie Belle contract was signed. The trade association used the tactics urged by Constangy in helping the Collins and Aikman company defeat TWUA in a 1963 election. During that campaign, TTMA made a particular point of criticizing the Dixie Belle contract as inadequate. Announcing the election results in its 9 September newsletter, the association wasted no time in drawing a connection with the "failed" contract at Dixie Belle. "The union's 'great victory' and the three-year contract at Dixie Belle in Calhoun is turning out to be considerably less than an asset" in the Dalton organizing campaign, TTMA told its members. "The surest way for TWUA to lose an election," TTMA concluded, "is to base its campaign on 'what the union got in the Dixie Belle contract.'"[56] The TWUA organizing drive lost all momentum and never recovered.

The Tufted Textile Manufacturers' Association effectively countered all union efforts to build on the victory at Dixie Belle by organizing carpet manufacturers more effectively than ever before. The union struggle did have lasting consequences for the industry, however. The existence of a union in the area prodded owners to modernize their personnel procedures and increase wages and benefits. The trade association successfully marketed a "growth" ideology. In the final analysis, Dalton-area carpet workers remained unorganized, but wages and benefits rose. TTMA and its legal counsel also urged companies to treat workers with greater respect and avoid arbitrary hiring and firing practices. The industry also made well-publicized investments in the local hospital and new recreational facilities, claiming credit for improving the standard of living for the entire community. Carpet manufacturers continued to refine their personnel practices and announced occasional general wage increases, which mitigated workers' worst complaints. TTMA continued to sponsor management seminars and train industry supervisors in anti-union tactics throughout the 1960s.[57]

Timothy Minchin has recently noted that even though southern textile workers chose not to join TWUA, the union deserved much of the credit for improving the standard of living throughout the region. The threat of union organization prodded southern textile firms to raise wages and improve management practices in the late 1940s and early 1950s. This appeared to be the case in the Dalton carpet district a decade later. The material benefits gained by workers in the carpet industry should not be minimized. Raymond Roach, a former president of the TWUA local at Dixie Belle, remembered with great pride the paid holidays, rational personnel procedures, and higher wages his union won at Dixie Belle. These benefits were small compared to those achieved by steel and auto workers, yet for workers in the carpet industry, those gains were real and substantial. Roach was convinced that the progress made by Local 1592, halting though it may have been, helped pressure other carpet firms into improving wages, benefits, and working conditions.[58]

Dalton's carpet mill workers also benefited from the multiplication of manufacturing companies in the district. By 1963, tufted carpets and rugs dominated the marketplace, accounting for $2.56 in shipments for every $1.00 in woven carpet shipments. More than half (101 of 181) of the nation's tufting mills were located in Georgia. Specifically, Dalton clearly was the new center of the soft floor covering industry: Whitfield County was home to 67 of those mills, and most of the rest were scattered in surrounding counties like Murray, Gordon, and Walker. Whitfield County carpet mills produced 56 percent of the value added for the entire industry in 1963, and the trend toward concentration showed no signs of abating. With new mills springing up regularly, it was a simple matter for an experienced mill hand to choose his or her place of employment. High turnover rates in Dalton-area mills reflected the array of choices available to workers. Even mill workers could occasionally get into the manufacturing game (generally by buying secondhand machines and doing commission tufting work for larger companies), and upward mobility through tufting was a real possibility, at least for a time during the 1960s and 1970s.[59]

THE IMPACT OF THE NEW INDUSTRY

By the mid-1960s, entrepreneurs and workers in northwest Georgia had created a new industry. Carpet sales soared throughout the 1950s and 1960s, and despite a brief slowdown in the early 1970s, growth continued and opportunities for new firms multiplied until the 1981–82 recession. The saturation of the existing housing market, the severe recession, and shifting consumer demand combined to push the new industry toward consolidation. Carpet's share of consumer spending in the floor covering market had risen from barely a third in the early 1950s to more than 80 percent by the early 1980s. The tufting process created products that meshed perfectly with the housing boom of the post–World War II generation: cheap floor coverings for the mass housing market. That trend had reversed itself by the late 1990s. As the *Wall Street Journal* succinctly noted in 1998, "The American Dream no longer requires wall-to-wall carpeting." Consumer tastes shifted toward hardwoods, tiles, and other alternative floor coverings. Carpet still dominated the market, but its influence was slipping: in 1997, carpet's share of floor covering spending dipped to 58 percent.[60] Tufting machinery had proven quite flexible within the boundaries established by the American marketplace of the 1950s through the early 1970s. The emergence of an ever more segmented market, in which price was important but not the sole determinant of floor covering purchasing decisions, presented an intriguing challenge to carpet manufacturers.

The establishment and concentration of this industry in northwest Georgia had produced tangible economic benefits for Dalton and other surrounding communities. Per capita income in Whitfield County, for example, rose from 81.7 percent of the national average in 1959 to 91.2 percent in 1984. Of Georgia's 159 counties, only the five that made up the core of metropolitan Atlanta had a per capita income higher than the national average. Whitfield was one of only nine other counties with per capita incomes above the state average. These income statistics reveal the impact of the concentration of the carpet industry in the Dalton area. The United States as a whole garnered 23.8 percent of its income from manufacturing employment in 1984; the state of Georgia was a little behind the national rate at 22.1 percent. Whitfield Countians received more than 55 percent of their earnings from manufacturing.[61] The concentration of the tufted carpet industry in the Dalton area created opportunities for self-employment and wealth accumulation among the region's workers, as well as a labor shortage that kept unemployment rates low and allowed workers substantial freedom of movement. At the end of the 1980s, citizens of Whitfield County, the heart of the district, enjoyed a per capita income of about $16,000 compared with a Georgia state average of $15,267; Whitfield County's per capita income was about 97 percent of the national average, compared to the state's 92 percent.[62]

Conversely, the Dalton district's very reliance on carpet manufacture and lack of economic diversification made the region particularly vulnerable to recession. The downturn of 1974–75 produced an unemployment rate of more than 15 percent in Whitfield County; in 1981–82, that county's unemployment rate reached almost 18 percent. By contrast, Georgia's more diversified urban economies fared better—Columbus had the state's highest urban unemployment rate in March 1982 at just over 10 percent. The state average was about eight percent.[63] With the number of mills declining rather than increasing after 1980, the bargaining power of individual workers eroded as well. It was no longer a simple matter to go down the street and find a new job with a new employer. Community leaders complained about the overreliance of Dalton and surrounding towns on a single industry, but alternatives were difficult to find.

Regional water supplies also suffered for the concentration of the carpet industry in Dalton. By the end of the 1990s, the Environmental Protection Agency had ordered massive improvements in the city's water treatment facilities and began demanding that companies take some responsibility for pretreatment of waste water. Neighboring Alabama threatened a lawsuit over the industry's contamination of shared waterways, and a citizens group had formed to protest pollution of the Conasauga River. In spite of the emerging problems, local industry leaders attested to the public utility's centrality to the success of carpet manufacture in the region. As the EPA cracked down on Dalton Utilities in 1995, Whitfield County Chamber of Commerce economic director John Rhodes observed that the municipal water and power company had been "a great protectionist of the carpet industry" and acknowledged that the city of "Dalton has borne that burden [of water treatment] to shelter the carpet industry from the federal and state regulations." Queen Carpets CEO Julian Saul insisted that Dalton Utilities "grew us all. You shut down Dalton Utilities and you shut us down."[64]

The development of the tufted carpet industry illustrated the positive and negative aspects of the regional approach to economic development suggested by Annalee Saxenian. Pursuing "regional advantage," carpet manufacturers and government officials in the Dalton area created a homegrown industry that changed the way American consumers furnished their homes. Local government fostered the growth of the industry by tailoring the policies of the local municipal utilities to the needs of local manufacturers. The industry grew rapidly and offered opportunities for employment and self-employment, but that very economic growth put a tremendous burden on local water resources and threatened water quality for the entire region. Boundaries among firms were porous, and new firms proliferated, encouraging creativity and experimentation; local manufacturers cooperated as often as they competed. That cooperation had a darker side, however. Manufacturers formed a relatively strong trade association but used it in the 1950s and 1960s chiefly to coordinate anti-union campaigns. The cooperative community atmosphere did not extend to workers, at least not unionized workers. Manufacturers cooperated with local government through Dalton Utilities. The industry grew, but as was often the case with industrial development, the environment suffered.

As economist Paul Krugman has noted, Dalton's carpet industry, like many other highly localized manufacturing complexes, resulted from a historical accident—Mrs. Whitener's bedspread. The new industry produced great opportunity for many entrepreneurs, and local workers benefited from the carpet boom as well. The carpet industry was, in Krugman's estimation, the ninth most geographically concentrated in the United States (on his list of more than a hundred industries).[65] What factors contributed to this concentration? The South's carpet industry grew slowly from modest handicraft roots in bedspread production, and local mechanics adapted old machines to new purposes with remarkable ingenuity. A dense web of economic relationships evolved in the Dalton region, and information flowed freely (sometimes purposefully, sometimes accidentally). It was not the result of investors looking for a suitable way to invest capital and create local industry but was homegrown in a very deep sense.⁶⁶ The Dalton district shares more in common with California's Silicon Valley (in spite of important limitations) than with many of the other, earlier examples of particularly "southern" industrialization. The Dalton district illustrates the complex and contingent nature of successful industrial development for any community or region.

NOTES

1. Douglas Flamming, *Creating the Modern South: Millhands and Managers in Dalton, Georgia, 1884–1984* (Chapel Hill: University of North Carolina Press, 1992); Randall L. Patton with David B. Parker, *Carpet Capital: The Rise of a New South Industry* (Athens: University of Georgia Press, 1999).

2. The best overview of post–Civil War southern industrial development is James Cobb, *Industrialization and Southern Society, 1877–1984* (Lexington: University of Kentucky Press, 1984). James Cobb, *The Selling of the South: The Southern Crusade for Industrial Development, 1936–1980* (Baton Rouge: Louisiana State University Press, 1982), is the definitive work on the southern strategy of courting of outside investment and its costs in the twentieth century. The options facing the South's political and economic leaders at the end of World War II are nicely summarized in Numan V. Bartley, *The New South, 1945–1980: The Story of the South's Modernization* (Baton Rouge: Louisiana State University Press, 1995), 7–21.

3. For discussion of "regional advantage" and specialization in one industry, see Annalee Saxenian, *Regional Advantage: Culture and Competition in Silicon Valley and Route 128* (Cambridge: MIT Press, 1994); and Saxenian, "Lessons from Silicon Valley," *Technology Review* (July 1994), 42–51. The Dalton story resembles the evolution of Saxenian's Silicon Valley in many respects, though the connections and similarities should not be overstressed. The tufted carpet industry—in spite of important technical innovations, a high degree of cooperation among producers, the ease and frequency of new firm creation, porous boundaries among firms, and so forth—was still closer to the old textile industry than the new wave of high tech, high skill industry represented by computer and electronics manufacture.

4. Annette C. Wright, "Strategy and Structure in the Textile Industry: Spencer Love and Burlington Mills, 1923–1962," *Business History Review* 69 (Spring 1995): 42–79; Philip Scranton, "'Have a Heart for the Manufacturers!': Production, Distribution, and the Decline of American Textile Manufacturing," in Charles Sabel and Jonathan Zeitlin, *World of Possibilities: Flexibility and Mass Production in Western Industrialization* (Cambridge, U.K.: Cambridge University Press, 1997), 310–43.

5. Philip Scranton, *Endless Novelty: Specialty Production and American Industrialization, 1865–1925* (Princeton, N.J.: Princeton University Press, 1997), 20–21.

6. *Business Week*, 24 December 1955, 46.

7. *Business Week,* 1 November 1958, 110.

8. William A. Reynolds, *Innovation in the United States Carpet Industry* (Princeton, N.J.: Van Nostrand, 1968), 87.

9. Author interview with Jack Turner, 10 February 1995, Kennesaw State University Carpet History Series, Kennesaw State University Library, Kennesaw, Ga. All interview citations, unless otherwise noted, are from this collection. Turner's analysis was familiar to southern business and political leaders of the immediate post–World War II era. For example, see Georgia governor Ellis Arnall's *The Shore Dimly Seen* (1946; reprint, New York: Acclaim Publishing Co., 1966). Southern reformers like Arnall argued that the South functioned as a colony of the industrial North. The region specialized in producing raw materials and unfinished goods while relying on northern firms for higher value-added manufactured goods. This colonial status was enforced informally through discriminatory freight rates, minuscule expenditures on public education, and absentee "Yankee" ownership of much of the South's low-wage industry. The classic statement of the colonial economy thesis is in C. Vann Woodward, *Origins of the New South, 1877–1913* (Baton Rouge: Louisiana State University Press, 1951), 291–320. A thoughtful reappraisal of the thesis may be found in Gavin Wright, *Old South, New South: Revolutions in the Southern Economy since the Civil War* (New York: Basic Books, 1986), 156–97.

10. Address by William H. Wilkerson to the Southern Machinery and Metals Exposition, 25 April 1946, reprinted by Higgins-McArthur Company, copy found in Morgan Papers, "Boost Birmingham Club" file, Birmingham Public Library, Birmingham, Ala.

11. Bartley, *The New South,* 19, 21; Cobb, *The Selling of the South,* 3–63; and Cobb, *Industrialization and Southern Society,* 43.

12. David L. Carlton, "Entrepreneurship and Southern Industrialization: The Case of North Carolina," paper presented at the Business History Conference, 6 March 1999, paper in the possession of the author.

13. Jack A. Tupper, "The Impact of the Relocation of the Alexander Smith Carpet Company upon the Municipal Government of Yonkers, New York" (master's thesis, New York University, 1963), 43–44.

14. "The Tufted Story," *Tufted Textile Manufacturers Association Directory,* January 1950, 26. The Tufted Textile Manufacturers Association (TTMA) Directories, clipping files, correspondence, and other papers are housed at the Carpet and Rug Institute (CRI), Dalton, Ga., along with the institute's papers. For a more detailed account of the rise of the bedspread industry, based largely on oral histories, see Thomas Deaton, *Bedspreads to Broadloom: The Story of the Tufted Carpet Industry* (Acton, Mass.: Tapestry Press, 1993).

15. "The Tufted Story," *Tufted Textile Manufacturers Association Directory,* 27–28; Spencer Wright Industries, "A Chronology of Significant Tufting Developments," Historical Files of Cobble Division, Dalton, Georgia. The key innovation in turning a sewing machine into a tufting machine lay in the addition of a hook (or "looper") which would catch yarn loops inserted by needles and hold the yarn as the needle retracted, creating a raised yarn loop. Knife attachments were quickly added, and the hooks also acted as cutting devices which created the characteristic cut loops associated with hand-tufted bedspreads. Machine operators could use single-needle tufting machines to sew raised de-

signs on cotton sheeting to create bedspreads that were identical to the handmade variety. By the mid-1930s, many manufacturers had moved toward using tufting machines to produce other textile goods. The tufting process was applied to create area rugs (called "scatter rugs" locally) by covering the entire surface of a piece of backing material (still usually cotton) with raised tufts of yarn. The process was also used to create "chenille" bathrobes, toilet tank and seat covers, and a variety of other goods. All these products were produced by inserting pile yarns into a piece of backing material using a tufting machine. The development of area rugs by firms such as Cabin Crafts particularly pointed toward the future possibility of larger tufted carpets.

16. Lewis Card interview, 18 May 1994, Panama City, Fla.

17. Max Beasley, "Cobble: The Name That Is Synonymous with Tufting Machinery," Historical Files of Cobble Division; Card interview.

18. This discussion of carpet finishing relies primarily on James B. Flemming, "The Northwest Georgia Carpet Finishing Industry: Its Operation and Financing" (master's thesis, Stonier Graduate School of Banking, Rutgers University, 1974), esp. 21–29. The Census of Manufactures has never differentiated between tufting mills and finishing companies, instead combining statistics for both segments of the industry into an aggregate. This makes analysis of finishing as a distinct segment of carpet manufacture difficult.

19. J. C. Shaw interview, April 11, 1998.

20. Clark M. Jones and W. L. Avrett, "Solving a Flashy Water Problem," *Water Works Engineering* (10 September 1941): 1140–42.

21. Robert McMath and Bruce Sinclair, "Infrastructure for the New South: Dalton Utilities and the Development of an Industrial City," paper delivered at the Southern Historical Association annual meeting, 7 November 1995, paper in the possession of the author.

22. Dalton *Citizen-News*, 3 December 1955; Dalton *Daily Citizen-News*, 29 January 1982.

23. Peggy Whaley, "Taking the Novel Approach," *Carpet and Rug Industry* (December 1982): 18–21.

24. Deaton, *Bedspreads to Broadloom*, 55; *Business Week*, 15 January 1955, 72–74.

25. *Business Week*, 15 January 1955, 72–74.

26. *Retailing Daily*, 25 April 1955; and 14 June 1955, TTMA Clipping File.

27. Alexander Smith *Annual Report*, 1954.

28. *Printer's Ink*, 18 November 1960, 36–37.

29. John S. Ewing and Nancy P. Norton, *Broadlooms and Businessmen: A History of the Bigelow-Sanford Carpet Company* (Cambridge: Harvard University Press, 1955), 359–65. For an examination of the technological changes in the carpet industry after World War II, see Reynolds, *Innovation*. A colorful account of the rise of the carpet industry in Dalton, based on extensive oral interviews, is Deaton, *Bedspreads to Broadloom*.

30. Reynolds, *Innovation*, 47–48; Eric Hobsbawm, *The Age of Extremes* (New York: Random House, 1995), 257–86; Robert Heilbroner *The Economic Transformation of America, 1600–Present*, 3d ed. (New York: Harcourt Brace, 1994), 329–30.

31. Reynolds, *Innovation*, 43–46.

32. Scranton, *Figured Tapestry: Production, Markets, and Power in Philadelphia Textiles, 1885–1941* (Cambridge, UK: Cambridge University Press, 1989), 386–87; Scranton, "American Textile Manufacturing," 340–41.

33. American Carpet Institute, *Confidential Statistical Handbook*, 1963 edition, 31, CRI Library.

34. Ibid. Since no figures for man-hours of labor and output for broadloom carpeting were kept separately, it is difficult to estimate the productivity of broadloom manufacturing. Certainly, if it were possible to factor out scatter rug production, the productivity numbers of the tufted industry would be even higher.

35. American Carpet Institute, *Statistical Handbook*, 1962 edition, 26–27.

36. Carpet and Rug Institute, *Directory and Report, 1974–75*, 65, 70.

37. This summary is based on D. F. Holmes, "A History of DuPont's Textile Fibers Department," 64–66, Box 10, DuPont Textile Fiber Records, Hagley Museum and Library, Wilmington, Delaware (hereinafter cited as Holmes, "Textile Fibers").

38. Ibid., and *Financial World*, 28 January 1959.

39. *Retailing Daily*, 28 March 1956; *Home Furnishings Daily*, 10 April 1958, TTMA Clipping File.

40. Hoff quoted in *Home Furnishings Daily*, 15 April 1958, TTMA Clipping File.

41. *Home Furnishings Daily*, 17 September 1959.

42. *Business Week*, 29 December 1956, 92; and *Barron's*, 6 July 1964, 19.

43. All these functions are detailed in the *Annual Directory and Yearbook of the Tufted Textile Manufacturers Association*, 1950–1968, CRI Library.

44. Interview with Truitt Lomax, 7 May 1995.

45. For an extended and insightful discussion of this campaign, see Douglas Flamming, "Christian Radicalism, McCarthyism, and the Dilemma of Organized Labor in Dixie," in Gary M. Fink and Merl E. Reed, eds., *Race, Class, and Community in Southern Labor History* (Tuscaloosa: University of Alabama Press, 1994), 190–211.

46. Material and quotations drawn from clippings of Booster newspaper advertisements found in TTMA Papers. All the advertisements appeared in the local *Daily Citizen-News*. Many were reprinted and mailed to employees of plants involved in pending elections. The material on Frank Constangy and his advice to manufacturers is from the TTMA meeting transcript, 16 July 1963, TTMA Papers, Carpet and Rug Institute, Dalton, Ga.

47. This organizing campaign is explored in detail in Patton, "Textile Organizing in a Sunbelt South Community: Northwest Georgia's Carpet Industry, in the Early 1960s," *Labor History* 39 (August 1998): 291–309.

48. *Atlanta Journal*, 5 April 1963, 22.

49. Memorandum for Mr. Pollock's use, "Dixie Belle," 11 April 1963, TWUA Papers, Mss 396, Box 627. The authorship of the memo is unclear.

50. *Calhoun Times*, 13 June 1963; and "Contract between Dixie Belle Mills, Inc., and the Textile Workers Union of America," 10 June 1963, copy found in TTMA Papers.

51. Transcript of TTMA Meeting, 16 July 1963, TTMA Papers.

52. Ibid. The role of union busting specialists like the Constangy law firm has been largely overlooked in attempts to explain the decline of unionism in the United States

since the mid-1950s. For an examination of this theme, see Robert Smith, "Using Knowledge Rather Than Goons," *Michigan Academician* 27 (August 1996): 401–19.

53. Transcript of TTMA meeting, TTMA Papers.
54. Ibid.
55. TTMA "Newsletter," 15 March 1963, TTMA Papers.
56. "Labor Bulletin," 9 September 1963, TTMA Papers.
57. TTMA "Newsletter," 10 April 1962; TTMA "Labor Bulletin," 9 September 1963, TTMA Papers. There are programs of annual industrial relations training institutes, sponsored by TTMA, in the organization's Industrial Relations Club file that extend to 1969. The union organizing drive is examined in detail in Patton, "Textile Organizing." The experiences of the small TWUA local at Dixie Belle and the broader experiences of workers in the region in the aftermath of the union campaign are explored in Patton, "'A World of Opportunity': Labor Relations in North Georgia's Carpet Industry, 1963–1980," *Georgia Historical Quarterly* (Summer 1997).
58. Timothy Minchin, *What Do We Need a Union For? The TWUA in the South, 1945–1955* (Chapel Hill: University of North Carolina Press, 1997), 206–9. On the benefits of limited unionization in the Dalton district, see author interview with Raymond Roach, April 6, 1994, Kennesaw State University Carpet History Series, Kennesaw State University Library.
59. U.S. Bureau of the Census, 1963 *Census of Manufactures*, vol. 2, *Industry Statistics*, 1964, 22D-5, and vol. 3, *Area Statistics;* Steven S. Plice, "Manpower and Merger: The Impact of Merger upon Personnel Policies in the Carpet and Furniture Industries," Manpower and Resources Study No. 5, Industrial Research Unit, University of Pennsylvania, Philadelphia, 1976, 118–19; Patton and Parker, *Carpet Capital*, chapter 6. For a spectacular example of a rags to riches story, see the Ed Weaver story, 224–26.
60. Wall Street Journal, 31 March 1998, 15.
61. Charles F. Floyd and Thomas M. Springer, "The Georgia Economy," report compiled for the Georgia Department of Transportation, 1988, Kennesaw State College Library. Statistics for the report were drawn from census data.
62. Georgia Department of Labor, "Area Labor Profile: Whitfield County," 1990.
63. *Atlanta Journal and Constitution*, 21 March 1982, 8-A.
64. *Atlanta Business Chronicle*, 20 October, 1995; *Atlanta Constitution*, 2 February 1997.
65. Paul Krugman, *Geography and Trade* (Cambridge: MIT Press, 1992), 60–61.
66. Unlike cotton mills and furniture, two other highly concentrated industries crucial to the South, the carpet industry did not import much machinery (at least in the crucial area of tufting) or mechanical and managerial skill. For an excellent and finely detailed summary of the furniture industry, see David Nolan Thomas, "Early History of the North Carolina Furniture Industry, 1880–1921" (Ph.D. diss., University of North Carolina at Chapel Hill, 1964). On early post–Civil War textiles, see Carlton, "Entrepreneurship and Southern Industrialization." Carpet manufacture bore a greater resemblance, perhaps, to the tobacco industry as portrayed by Carlton.

Dismantling the South's Cotton Mill Village System

TOBY MOORE

At the close of World War II, most textile mills in the South still housed workers and their families in private and paternal company towns. Mounting political and economic pressure had spurred some textile companies to start selling their mill village housing in the late 1930s, but only a handful had been converted to individual home ownership when the outbreak of hostilities postponed any further activity. In South Carolina alone, some 185,000 people lived in mill villages in 1945, comprising 17 percent of the state's white population.[1] In major textile counties such as Gaston, North Carolina, and Greenville and Spartanburg, South Carolina, upwards of a third of the white population lived in places owned and operated by textile companies.

With the end of the war, the South's cotton mill village system resumed its rapid decline, although it would be another forty years before Cannon Mills finally sold its houses in the last bastion of the village system, the sprawling mill complex of Kannapolis, North Carolina. By 1955, the southern textile industry had unloaded most of its tens of thousands of aging houses, usually to the working families who lived in them. Shifting its capital into new factories and new machines to keep pace in an intensely competitive industry, the textile industry radically altered the formerly close relationship between work and home in hundreds of mill communities from Virginia to Alabama.

Despite the recent wave of scholarship on the southern textile industry, the dismantling of the mill village system has received only passing attention, part of the broader scholarly neglect of the industry and its workers after 1945. Harriet Herring's 1949 book, *The Passing of the Mill Village*, written at the midpoint of the process, remains the only full-length study. The magisterial *Like a Family*, which has become for many the standard work on southern mill villages, ends as the sales were just commencing. The effects of terminating the mill village system receive some attention in studies of postwar textile communities, such as those by Flamming and Janiewski, and the consequences of home ownership for textile workers during union organizing campaigns and strikes following the war are a focal point in Minchin's recent book. But the sales themselves, and the broader impact of the end of the regional village system, have not been studied to the degree that the village system's creation and maintenance have been examined.[2]

This dismantling merits further study because it was the tool with which the textile industry switched from one mode of regulating labor to another. With the sale of the villages and the creation of a large group of working-class property owners, factory owners swapped the social control mechanism of paternalism for the social control of the mortgage note, accompanied as it was by increasing social and occupational fragmentation across the South. Many mill officials entered into the change with great reluctance, and significant continuities remained between the paternal mill village system and its successor: in neither case, for example, did textile companies consider labor unions to be part of the bargain. But in many ways the end of the mill village system of labor control represented a decisive break with southern cotton mill traditions. It ushered the industry and its workers from an avowedly southern form of welfare capitalism to a lukewarm variant of the Fordism of the rest of the country.

Divided into three sections, this essay is a first step in reexamining the end of the cotton mill village system and the effects its demise had on the region's political and social landscapes. The first section explores why the mills sold their villages and weighs the evidence that the divestiture was in part a reaction to a perceived weakening of the effectiveness of the village system as a means of labor control. The second part of the essay details how the villages were sold, drawing from oral histories and newly available real estate records, with special attention paid to the role of race. The final section examines the transformation of the mill villages as *places* by looking at concurrent changes in several important social institutions in the villages.

INTRODUCTION

The first sales of southern mill villages came soon after the last ones had been built. Textile companies continued to construct villages around new mills through most of the 1920s, as Pacific Mills did in Spartanburg County in 1924, naming the new town Lyman after its company president. Pepperell built a new mill and village in Opelika, Alabama, in 1925, constructing 100 houses that year, 50 more in 1926, and another 56 in 1934.[3] Other companies expanded their villages over the same period of time, adding houses as they enlarged their plants or introduced shift work.

These last village constructions combined the industry's traditional paternalism and southern regionalism with new ideas of scientific management. As factory managers across the country hired experts to study the efficiency of their production lines, southern textile companies hired landscape architects and urban planners to construct "model" villages. This last round of construction reached its apogee in the village that Chicopee Manufacturing constructed on farmland three miles outside Gainesville, Georgia, in 1927. "This work has been done by Southern engineers and contractors, using Southern labor and materials and concentrating the benefits of the entire investment as far as possible in Southern territory," trumpeted a company booklet, echoing the industry's traditional parochialism. However, the booklet argued, "Chicopee Village is as different from most mill communities as the mill itself is different from most mills. It is a village of beauty, healthfulness and home-like comfort—a community planned in advance and laid out in detail by our landscape architects and engineers." The engineer who supervised construction later remembered Chicopee for the glazed tile factory walls and its brick houses, and the care that Chicopee demanded for its design and construction: "They wanted it to be absolutely spotless." The mill was built to supply surgical gauze to the Johnson & Johnson pharmaceutical company, and the company sought to use old-style village paternalism to extend the aseptic cleanliness of its shop floor both to the village and to the bodies of the mill workers and their families. "We, therefore, expect the workers and the residents of Chicopee to keep the mill, the streets and houses clean as well as to keep clean in person," the company announced.[4]

The textile industry began to slip into recession in 1927; then it experienced the tumult of the Great Depression and the sweeping changes of the New Deal. Mildred Gwin Andrews, a longtime textile writer and trade official, placed the beginning of the sales in the mid-1930s and credited Spencer Love with starting the trend as he put together Burlington Mills. Burlington initiated its sales not long after the General Strike of 1934. According to Andrews, "As he bought a mill, he sold the village." Although an exact starting point for the village sales is difficult to pinpoint, Andrews's estimate seems plausible. Such early sales sparked a growing interest among textile officials, with further encouragement coming from positive articles in trade journals, including the publication in 1940 of a widely distributed series of stories on the future of the village system in *Textile World*. In the spring of that year, Herring found only seventeen mills selling their villages; by fall, her estimate had risen to thirty-five mills and 3,700 houses. North Carolina mills led the way. By 1941, fifty-four of the sixty-seven villages sold in the South had been sold in North Carolina, including those belonging to Marshall Field and Company, which had unloaded almost all of its 1,500 houses in and around Spray, North Carolina, by the spring of 1941. However, as Herring wrote a colleague, while mill village sales in the prewar period represented a significant trend, "it is as yet a small thing, and may not work any quick transformations."[5]

This movement to sell off the southern villages began as the last of the New England company housing was being auctioned off, partly as a result of northern textile companies shifting production to the South. A 1934 Bureau of Labor Statistics survey found that 25 of 60 northern mills still provided housing, compared to 126 of 131 southern mills. Urban growth and competition from southern mills had accelerated northern sales of company housing, but Herring judged the New England experience to have little value for southern mill owners looking for guidance on how to conduct their sales. New England mill housing more often consisted of multifamily tenement buildings than the single-family, detached homes that dominated the southern villages, and such tenements tended to be sold to investors rather than employees. By 1940, northern real estate companies who had handled village sales were looking south for future business, reporting that mill villages had been "largely eliminated" in New England.[6]

The war suspended nearly all sales activity, as mills clung to any housing they had as a means of attracting scarce labor. At the end of the war, however, managers moved quickly to resume the divestiture. By 1949, Herring estimated, nearly half of the southern villages had been sold; a 1952 survey of twenty-three Georgia mills found that about one-third had sold all or part of their housing, and only 40 percent of the mills' employees lived in company-owned villages. The trend peaked in 1949 and 1950 but continued at a heavy pace through most of the 1950s, with a prominent real estate agency estimating in late 1958 that 73 percent of village houses had been divested. Only isolated village sales took place in the 1960s, until the impending passage of new federal housing and civil rights legislation in the last years of the decade prompted a flurry of sales. Few villages remained by the early 1970s, although Cannon Mills continued to own 1,600 houses and a square mile of commercial property in downtown Kannapolis into the 1980s.[7]

The transfer to private ownership of mill houses in the South took place during, and contributed to, an era of sharply increasing home ownership rates across the country. Increasingly, home ownership was seen as a key to the new, postwar economic order; the end of the village system was inextricably woven into this national trend (and ideology) of private home ownership. "The desire to own his home should be constant in the mind of every man," posted announcements of upcoming village sales often began.[8] From 1940 to 1970, the home ownership rate in the United States increased from 43.6 percent to 62.9 percent. In southern states, and in textile counties in the Piedmont, the increase was even more marked; by 1980, each of the six states with counties in the southern textile region had exceeded the national average.

In many prominent textile communities, home ownership increased even more sharply, a direct result of the mills' decision to convert their villages. Greenville County, South Carolina, for example, increased its home ownership rate from 1940 to 1970 from 28 percent to 67.4 percent; Greenwood County, just to the southeast, more than doubled its rate, from 32.5 percent to 67.7 percent, in just twenty years from 1950 to 1970. It was not uncommon for textile counties to see a fifth or more of their housing units become owner-occupied in a decade.[9]

WHY THE VILLAGES WERE SOLD

The hundreds of textile mills in the Piedmont sold their villages at different times for different reasons, or more exactly, for different combinations of reasons. The forces prompting the end of the village system included social and economic changes, both in the nation as a whole and in the southern textile industry; the sweeping changes prompted by the Great Depression and the New Deal; and the rising perception among mill officials that there was a more attractive means of labor control than village paternalism.

Perhaps the most critical of the social changes that prompted the dismantling was the rise of the affordable automobile. More cars and better roads allowed textile workers to commute much longer distances to work. The automobile freed workers to live on cheap land in the countryside, which many preferred in any case, or in neighboring towns, allowing them to avoid the often crowded conditions in the villages. "Henry Ford is certainly emancipating the average Southern small town worker," Stuart Cramer, a Gaston County mill owner, told the Southern Industrial Conference in 1922. "Even the most casual observer has noticed the amazing number of automobiles of all vintages now in mill communities."[10] Cramer may have been somewhat premature in his assessment of the prevalence of cars among low-paid textile workers, but over the next several decades, spurred by higher, post-Depression wages and increased leisure time, automobiles became a common part of the average mill worker's world.

The rise of the automobile was only one of many variables changing the complex economic equation by which mill owners calculated the costs and benefits of operating a village. The widespread adoption of shift work, for example, tended to reduce the percentage of a mill's total workforce that lived in its village.[11] Mill owners complained that a shortage of company housing in some communities fomented discontent among those operatives forced to pay market rents, while elsewhere companies reported having a difficult time keeping their houses filled as new opportunities opened up around the village. At the same time, the number of employees the mills could draw from each village house fell as the family labor system declined. New job choices for spouses and tougher child labor laws made it more difficult for mills to employ families. An aging workforce, with longtime village residents becoming too old to work but still needing housing, may also have prompted the decline in the average number of employees coming from village housing.

The houses themselves had aged and increasingly needed renovation in an era of tightening local housing codes and a heightening national awareness of substandard housing. In 1950, FHA inspectors at the Mayfair Mills village in Arcadia, South Carolina, found that "practically all" the 150 houses built in 1905 had leaking roofs, and 90 percent of window frames and sashes had rotted. Inspectors noted substandard foundations, and determined that most chimneys needed repointing.[12] Utility systems, particularly sewer systems, remained a problem in many villages; dumping raw sewage into the local river was a common practice. Textile companies, already under competitive pressure to implement expensive modernization projects in their factories, had little desire to invest scarce capital in dilapidated residential property.

Mill villages also operated under rapidly changing corporate structures, as the locally owned, single-mill operation that had characterized the industry's earlier years in the South gave way to integrated corporations headquartered in far-off cities. The postwar years brought a rapid series of mergers and acquisitions. In 1949, a study by the Textile Workers Union of America (TWUA) found that "northern interests" controlled 60 percent of South Carolina spindles, up from only 13 percent in 1931. The three largest employers in the state, J. P. Stevens, Deering Milliken & Co., and Springs Cotton Mills, comprised 30 percent of the state's textile industry, and more than half of the 120 plants in the state had changed hands during the 1940s. Union president Emil Rieve noted, "Textile employers in South Carolina can no longer claim a neighborhood relationship with their workers; the average mill is in the hands of owners whose homes are elsewhere and whose interests spread far beyond the confines of the state."[13] The union study had a political aim, of course, in countering mill owners' traditional portrayal of union organizers as "outsiders," but the trend was real. Textile executives in New York or Boston judged mill communities in a less personal way, and more often saw the villages and the cost of running them more narrowly as entries on a balance sheet. The increasing distance between the villages and the men who controlled their future made the villages easier to sell.

Ending company housing was an explicit goal of the New Deal, and measures aimed at undercutting the cotton mill villages of the South made their way into much of the new textile legislation. The first code written by the National Recovery Administration was the textile code, which reduced the standard workweek from fifty or fifty-five hours to forty, set the minimum weekly wage in the South at $12, limited plant operations to eighty hours a week, and eliminated child labor. Each of these requirements made villages less cost-effective, but the code directly opposed the village system as well. It required textile companies to "consider the question of plans for eventual home ownership of homes in mill villages" and make a report to the NRA by 1 January 1934. According to the code, "there is something feudal and repugnant to American principle in the practice of employer-ownership of employee homes.... It is hoped that, with the creation of real industrial self-government and improvement in the minimum wage, an impetus will be given by employers to independent home ownership." In 1938, the Fair Labor Standards Act restricted employers' ability to charge rent for housing. New Deal legislation worked against the maintenance of the villages in a more oblique way by forcing on the region a more modern definition of the relationship between labor and capital. The encouragement of union organizing, the inducements to collective bargaining, and the implementation of formal mechanisms for mediating labor disputes pushed mill owners toward a relationship altogether different from the paternalism they had practiced through the institution of the village.[14]

Simmering beneath these legal and societal changes was the growing consensus among textile officials, middle-class reformers, and academics that paternalism and company housing had created something like a political and social monster in the Piedmont, one that was, by the 1930s, threatening to escape from the textile companies' control. The village system, these people feared, was generating a "social type" of villager-worker, particularly as children were born and raised within its confines; second- and even third-generation textile workers and village residents had begun to appear in southern mill villages. Company officials feared that this "social type" was more inclined to such dangerous sympathies as class consciousness, unionism, and Communism, or at the least, was more susceptible to mob violence and bloc voting. This prospect particularly scared southern elites because it undermined the carefully constructed notion that white mill owners and white mill workers were members of the same social group, what Cash termed the "proto-Dorian convention."[15] If white textile workers began to perceive a division of identity and interest between themselves and their white bosses, they might eventually see the gap between themselves and poor blacks as being less severe.

People living in or near mill villages before World War II remembered vividly the villages' social and geographic isolation. Robert Moore, who later helped dismantle vestiges of paternalism as a personnel manager for Fieldcrest Mills, grew up in the countryside between Statesville and Mocksville, North Carolina, where few of his family's acquaintances worked in the mill. The East Monbo Mill village, where he attended Fourth of July baseball games with his father in the 1930s, was "sort of a strange, isolated little place," and "hardscrabble," set apart in his child's mind from both the countryside and the town. Among country people, he remembered, it was considered "something of a tragedy or a failure to go into industrial work at low wages." Hoyle McCorkle, born in the Highland Park #3 village in Charlotte, played accordion, guitar, and a little violin with a boy his age whose father was an editor for the Charlotte News. "So I got to socializing with him, playing with one another, sitting in with one another. One night we went to his parents'—he'd been coming here—and he says, 'Don't tell them your parents works in a mill village.' Now, I never did play with him anymore." Or as Ada Mae Mosely Wilson put it, "Oh, we was nothing but trash . . . they thought [mill] people ought to wear overalls and brogan shoes to church, you know. They didn't think we should have anything."[16]

The academics, clergymen, and journalists studying and critiquing the village system picked up on this sense of alienation. In 1927, a group of forty-one southern churchmen signed what came to be known as the "Bishops' Appeal," which criticized the village system for being "unfavorable to education, to religion, and to understanding and sympathy between the citizens of the mill village and those of the larger community." Pope observed that in Gastonia, "housing arrangements have helped to create and symbolize the gaps between the three social classes. Residence in a mill village soon became a distinctive badge of class affiliation, and a stigma in the eyes of independent farmers and uptown people alike." Even Broadus Mitchell, whose *The Rise of the Cotton Mills in the South* remains the classic boosterist account of southern textiles, noted in 1921 the potential trouble brewing in the villages: "The mill village, especially the company-owned town, has crystallized this sentiment, and politics and the lack of any other considerable industry in the South have made their unfortunate contributions. Dislike of the operatives' station is undoubtedly greater at present than in the years when the mills were building." Rhyne warned that the cotton mill village was "an institution which sets apart rather definitely a portion of the population. . . . These factors tend toward the development of a social type."[17]

While bound to the textile industry by "social type" or occupational skills, many mill families had looser ties to any particular mill or village. Poor and with no leases or mortgages, textile workers in the first half of the century were notoriously mobile, particularly when times were good and the industry flush with jobs. J. M. Robinette, who started working in a Charlotte cotton mill in 1907, described his family's travels through the Piedmont textile industry. Their first move came in 1910, when they followed an overseer in the Charlotte mill to his new job in nearby Belmont, where they worked for twelve months before moving back to Charlotte. Robinette, late in returning after a visit to relatives, wasn't rehired immediately, so he went to the East Monbo mill in Iredell County. He married and moved to a mill in Hickory, quit and returned to East Monbo, then moved on to Landis and Altamahaw before finally settling down at the Plaid Mill in Burlington, where he worked in the dye house for twenty-two years. Mobility rates varied widely from village to village and across time and occupations, and between men and women, and the young and old; as Wright points out, mobility could also be a sign of a shortage of steady work during hard times. Certainly there were moving costs to overcome, even for families with few possessions, but mill-owned housing could make it easier for workers to leave their jobs and served to tie together distant mill villages as newcomers brought news from afar. Mobility allowed an outlet for worker discontent, while forcing mills to match their competitors in terms of school offerings and the provision of housing. A substantial portion of a mill's workforce, particularly in the early years of the village system, could simply "vote with its feet" when it encountered a despotic foreman or poorly kept homes. Mill superintendents wearied of high turnover rates in their factories, while high mobility encouraged the formation of the villager-worker "social type" that the mill owners and the middle class feared.[18]

This social type had begun to express itself at the polls, too, even before the Depression. The politics of place that developed along with the mill village system is a story perhaps best told in Carlton's *Mill and Town*, which focuses on the role of the mill villages in the rise to power of South Carolina's Cole Blease and his followers before World War I. Blease's gubernatorial and U.S. Senate campaigns "brought to a focus the sharpest class confrontations between white men ever to appear in the Palmetto State." Utilizing a base of committed village operatives drawn from fraternal groups such as the Improved Order of the Red Men, he played textile workers against middle-class townspeople. Blease offered little to the workers by way of a solid program of reform, and much of what he did offer appeared contradictory—for example, Bleasites opposed national unions but were "fervent advocates of the right to strike." The Bleasite challenge triggered renewed support for Progressive-style social reform among middle-class townspeople, and, together with periodic outbreaks of mob violence, exacerbated the fear among mill owners that the villages might loosen themselves from company control.[19]

The village system certainly made the mechanics of political organizing along class lines easier. Villages often comprised their own precincts, and their density made reaching millhand votes simpler for politicians and their machines. Blease "often barnstormed the little textile towns of the upstate.... During the weeks preceding each primary election for the various jobs he sought in the 1920s, Blease frequently hired itinerant organ-grinders to tour the little textile mills... endlessly braying out a campaign slogan on street corners." On the day before the 1926 election, Blease reportedly spoke at thirty villages in Spartanburg County alone. His strategy made sense, for more than a third of all votes cast in the county came from the villages. At lower levels of government, mill workers sometimes elected their own to office outright. Mack Duncan remembered a loom fixer who won a seat in the state legislature. One night, he and other mill workers were sitting in the loom fixer's car when the mill owner leaned in the window to talk politics, saying, "What are *we* going to have to do...." Such incidents gave the loom fixer a reputation as a "cat's paw" for the mill, and operatives took notice when he voted against legislation to limit working hours. When the man ran for county auditor, he lost badly.[20]

Mill owners weighing the future of the village system were well aware of this social and political gulf, and of the rising criticism it was generating among townspeople and the owners' fellow elites. Selling the villages could give them a way to overcome it. Caesar Cone, contemplating in 1950 the sale of Cone Mill houses in Greensboro, speculated that breaking up the company's mill villages would pacify his current workers and make mill employment more attractive in the wider labor market. Cone's 1,504 houses, most built before the turn of the century, needed renovation, a project the company had decided was too expensive to undertake. But the sociology of the mill village system was more important to the company than the financial costs. Scattering Cone's workers among the general population, Cone wrote, and making them home owners could break down what he called "the mill village psychology." "It is felt that at some future time the company's labor relations will be on a sounder basis if all of its employees live among the general citizenry of the community.... It is conceivable that next door neighbors who are employed by a multiplicity of employers would be less inclined to criticize the individual employer who might be paying the highest wage... granting the greatest fringe benefits and... providing the best working conditions."[21]

It quickly became apparent to mill owners that selling a village did not have a calamitous effect on a mill's ability to produce textiles profitably. "We have talked with many superintendents, some of whom were hesitant or actually resisted the sale of their villages," a real estate company wrote F. E. Grier of Abney Mills in 1958. "However, after the sale, it is their unanimous opinion that instead of being more difficult to operate a plant, the employees are more stable, better citizens and less likely to be absent." A North Carolina textile promoter put it this way: "When you get a lot of people living in one community, living in one mill village, they're naturally objects of concern—and, of course, exploitation—by labor unions. But scattering these people out all over the county turned out to be a very healthy concept." After the first sales, mill owners considering the unloading of their houses could see these effects of both home ownership and rising consumerism among mill workers. Purchases of homes, as well as televisions, furniture, automobiles, and other items, were typically handled "on time," which mill families had long used to make ends meet. Minchin found the new, larger debt burdens to be a critical factor in the failure of the Dan River Mills strike in Danville, Virginia, in 1951. Wages at Dan River had increased by more than 200 percent between 1941 and 1951, and in 1949 and 1950 the company sold its village homes. During the strike, a mortgage company responsible for the financing of five hundred mill homes reported only 10 percent of their purchasers had fallen behind in their payments, which Minchin interprets as evidence that homeowners returned to work during the strike more quickly than other workers. Even those who were not buying their houses from the mill were at risk, as commuting generally required a car, which was also likely to be financed.[22] Mill companies worrying that selling their own villages would undermine control of their labor force had to be encouraged by the Dan River experience.

The relative importance of these myriad forces on textile mills is difficult to assess. Village circumstances varied widely from mill to mill; some enjoyed good relations with their employees, while others had long histories of labor unrest. Some villages in remote areas had little outside housing available, while other villages were being swallowed by postwar urban growth. Corporate structures and attitudes varied widely, as well. What is clear is that textile companies did not seek to end their control of the textile workers living in their villages, but rather to secure that control by different means.

HOW THE VILLAGES WERE SOLD

Textile companies operating mills in the South divested themselves of their villages in several different ways. Some firms sold properties as a unit to real estate companies or local entrepreneurs, who retailed the individual homes themselves or continued to rent the houses. The Bynum, North Carolina, housing authority purchased one of the last of the Piedmont mill villages in 1977 and refurbished the houses for resale to low-income residents. Other mills offered their houses to employees directly, using real estate agents and attorneys to handle the paperwork. Some mills sold entire sets of villages at one time; others stretched the process over several years. Some villages never reached the market at all but were torn down in part or as a whole to open room for plant expansion or highway improvements. Much of the Camperdown Mill village, located in downtown Greenville, South Carolina, was demolished to make room for a highway interchange.[23]

The records of the Alester G. Furman Company, a Greenville-based brokerage company with long ties to the textile industry, reveal much about the demise of the southern mill village system. Beginning in the late 1930s, Alester Furman III and his father, Alester Furman Jr., sold mill houses for textile companies from Delaware to Alabama, at one point handling more than 9,000 houses in a four-year span. In all, the company sold an estimated 27,000 village homes, maintaining for many years an eight-man sales team.[24] The records are particularly revealing because of the Furmans' personal familiarity with many of the mill owners and managers with whom they corresponded.

Mill houses sold through the Furman agency were nearly always offered first to the families living in them, then to other employees, and finally, if necessary, to the general public, though employees bought the vast majority of the houses. In the late 1940s and early 1950s, prices ranged from $1,000 or less (for the smallest dwellings, or those in particularly poor condition) to $7,000 or more, with most falling in the $2,000 to $3,000 range. They varied in size from simple, three- or four-room single-story homes to eight- or nine-room buildings; most were of such standard design that the Furman company developed a typology that allowed the agency to make quick appraisals of entire villages in a day or two.

While mill houses followed standard designs, the villages the Furman company helped sell varied widely in size and condition. The smallest contained only a few dozen houses, while other jobs could involve several different villages under common ownership, at times totaling thousands of houses and millions of dollars. In addition, most mill village sales involved the disposal of miscellaneous pieces of property that could not so easily be dispatched. Churches and minister's houses, for example, and large boarding houses, retail stores, and hotels, not to mention farmland and recreational facilities, presented special challenges to the real estate company. At Piedmont, South Carolina, the property to be sold along with the village in 1950 included the downtown commercial area, comprising eleven retail and office buildings containing everything from a magistrate's office to a theater to the meeting hall for the town's fraternal orders.[25] Such properties had to be disposed of with great care, in the name of community relations; the disposal of houses occupied by ministers presented a particularly sensitive issue.

A 1954 letter to the Boston headquarters of Pacific Mills from Alester Furman Jr. indicates the range of issues involved in selling a mill village. First, there was the choice of methods. Auctions and sales to single investors had proven unpopular in the South, it was reported, since "personnel relations are excluded in both plans." (Such methods might also have provided less in commissions to Furman's agency.) Then there was the question of utilities; mills traditionally had their own water and sewer systems, but outside financing agencies such as the FHA generally required that utilities be operated by a local governmental entity, and many mills wanted to be out of the utility business as well. Setting up utility districts or merging village systems with existing networks took time and often money. As to price, most mills gave employees a slightly lower figure than the market might otherwise bear, "to obtain his good will by giving him an additional equity." The FHA guaranteed loans at 5 percent, savings and loans offered 6 percent, while company financed plans ranged from 4 to 6 percent. Standard down payments ranged from 5 to 10 percent, with 10 percent the most common. The condition of the housing was an important consideration if FHA guarantees were being sought as federal inspectors would require that the houses be in good shape, but condition was not so important if the company was doing the financing. Generally, Furman advised, firms in the South chose one of two methods in selling their villages. The first strategy was to set the prices at a low level and finance the sales "in-house," requiring no down payment from purchasers and deducting monthly payments from the payroll. The second established prices closer to market value, transferred utilities to public entities, and secured outside financing.[26]

Groundwork for a sale often commenced in company-owned publications or in the local press. Joanna Mills, reorganizing following the death of its largest stockholder, decided to sell its houses in the vicinity of Joanna, South Carolina, in early 1960. The company devoted the October 1959 issue of *The Joanna Way* company magazine to "Families at Home in Homes Which They Own." The magazine's cover featured a photograph of the W. E. Davis family relaxing on a couch in their living room, a book open on the mother's lap and the three children crowded around. Inside, mill families posed on their porches or in their gardens. Joanna employees weighing the chance to buy their own homes could read interviews in which nine Joanna families "who have already purchased homes reveal their feelings: pride in ownership, joy in developing homes that suit them, financial security—a home—for payments as reasonable as rent." Another article traced the career of Joanna's own LeGrande Shealy, who had left the spinning room of the Joanna plant to become a professional interior designer for a department store in Shreveport, Louisiana. Where no company publication was available, mill officials were encouraged to "bring some pressure to bear" on local papers to do advance stories on home ownership and the community improvements that were said to follow.[27]

The entire process required a certain amount of discretion and even subterfuge, as rumors could sour the atmosphere quickly. Mill companies and real estate officials considered the villages to be fertile breeding grounds for gossip; Furman employees making initial surveys occasionally traveled under the guise of insurance adjusters to prevent tipping off residents that a liquidation was imminent. Once a mill had decided to sell, Furman preferred to post a general notice in the mill and village to explain the presence of such people as surveyors and inspectors, and then to hold back details such as price and terms until plans were finalized. Two or three months later, the company presented its "package" to the employees at meetings in a community center or vacant house over a period of up to four weeks before closing the individual sales.[28]

Not all purchasers passed muster with mill officials, who saw no reason to cede their last opportunity to manipulate the neighborhoods where their workers lived. Real estate agents often consulted mill superintendents before offering workers a house, and a poor report from a supervisor could doom a prospective home buyer. Outsiders faced similar scrutiny. Annie Stephens, seeking a house in the Bibb Manufacturing village in Macon, Georgia, passed an initial review of her credit record. "I thought we had a good prospect here," the mill's vice president for finance confided to Furman in the midst of its 1964 sale. "But in checking further I find that she is not the type person we would want in the village.... What I want you to do is get me off the hook by turning her down." Stephens did not get a house.[29]

Financing was the most vexing issue for both the mills and the real estate company. Ideally, Furman preferred to complete the sales through a local savings and loan under FHA guarantees, an arrangement that offered better terms to the buyer and an immediate cash payment to the mill. FHA guarantees also helped mills to place the mortgage in cases in which no local savings and loan arrangements could be made. The cooperation of a savings and loan effected a swifter and surer divorce for the mill, since payments were made to an outside lender by the employee with no company involvement in any foreclosure or delinquency proceedings. But local savings and loans at times proved to be reluctant to finance village sales, or unable to handle the volume of business. Even when they agreed to take on the task, their idea of the value of mill village housing could diverge sharply from that of the real estate agents and mills. At Fitzgerald, Georgia, in 1956, where the houses were in such poor shape that Fitzgerald Mills considered simply giving the houses away, the local savings and loan appraised their value at $500 each, well below the Furman estimate of $850. "We recognize that these houses are in poor shape, and do not have modern bathroom conveniences. However, we sold poorer houses just outside Selma, N.C. (a smaller town than Fitzgerald) without any running water on the lot at all for $1,000." Furman blamed the appraiser for being biased against mill villages; in the end, the company financed the sale itself, grossing $74,500 from eighty-eight houses.[30]

So eager were mills to distance themselves from their previous role as landlords that they often worked with Furman to disguise the continuing debt relationship between the mill and the new homeowners. In instances in which no outside financing could be attained and mills had to finance the mortgages themselves, Furman encouraged companies to use its subsidiary, General Mortgage Company, as a front to cover continued mill ownership of the houses. Mortgage notes and security deeds were taken in the name of General Mortgage and immediately assigned back to the mills, although this last assignment was not recorded, leaving employees to make their payments to General Mortgage. Furman suggested that "using General Mortgage Company as nominee conceals from the employee and the general public that [the mill] is actually going to own the paper." Even collection agreements with banks to handle the monthly payments could serve to obscure the continuing real estate relationship between mill and worker, as happened in Cherryville, North Carolina, in 1964. Furman stated: "You will note that I have tried to incorporate Cherryville National Bank into the picture as much as possible, due to the advisability of any employee purchaser feeling that he is obligated to Cherryville for the payments and not to Carlton [Yarn Mills]."[31]

Local FHA officials actively encouraged the mills to sell, often soliciting the business of guaranteeing the loans. State FHA director H. E. Bailey urged Furman officials to handle the proposed sale of the Graniteville, South Carolina, village in 1950: "It is a very fine community and the houses are in excellent condition.... we would like very much to work this deal through and any other village you have in mind." However, FHA financing brought its own set of problems for mills. The agency insisted that village houses it guaranteed be in good repair, and many older mill employees could not meet FHA requirements for solvency, forcing the mills to make special arrangements or risk angering their workers.[32]

The sums realized from selling village property could be considerable. Crown Mills in Dalton, Georgia, raised more than $100,000 in 1954, a year in which textile production netted only a $25,490 profit. Crown eventually earned $522,701 from its 350 houses. Mills with more extensive property holdings made even more money. Abney Mills announced in January 1959 that it planned to sell more than 2,000 houses at various villages in South Carolina, an announcement that prompted banner headlines on the front pages of local papers. Six months later, Abney had reaped more than $7 million. Burlington Industries bought Henrietta Mills' Henrietta and Caroleen plants in Rutherford County, North Carolina, in September 1957, and within a year sold 359 houses for $774,360. Greenwood Mills unloaded 562 houses at its Mathews plant in Greenwood, South Carolina, for almost $4 million in 1962 and two years later announced plans for a new $6 million plant.[33]

Attitudes toward making the greatest possible profit varied from company to company. Adopting a supportive stance, United Merchant and Manufacturers made it a policy to pick up the first five months' payments for employees, "in order to enable the employees to get a good start as home owners." Canton Mills, recovering from a strike in 1963, discounted the 275 houses in its Canton, Georgia, village by 20 to 25 percent and accepted 2 percent down payments. Canton worked through a local savings and loan but guaranteed the loans itself to ensure better terms for workers. Meanwhile, other firms sought to squeeze the last few thousand dollars from their properties. While selling a village for Atlanta's Fulton Bag Company in 1956, Furman officials asked the company to pick up the bill for the first year's fire insurance on the houses, in order to spare purchasers additional costs at closing, when cash was especially scarce. An attorney for the mill replied, "While it is true that the amount of money involved is not very great, nevertheless, it will amount to approximately $2,000 to $2,500 and to some extent involves a matter of principle."[34] Other companies raised Furman's proposed prices after deciding that the sales had to yield more money to be worthwhile.

On the other side of the transaction, mill families by and large welcomed the chance to buy their homes. With monthly payments not much more than rent, the financial burden was generally not onerous, and buying a house offered a future free of payments altogether. Building equity through home ownership operated as a savings account for many working couples, who could look forward to a more secure retirement once the mortgage was paid off. Paul and Pauline Griffith bought their home in Greenville's Judson Mill village about 1940. "Our payment was ten dollars a month, and I had so many years to pay for it. My wife was working then. It was eleven and a quarter and that left us with a thousand dollars (to finance) . . . and we paid it off in about three years, no more."[35] Mill workers knew they were generally getting below-market prices, and some looked to turn a quick profit by reselling soon after the purchase from the mill.

At the same time, some workers greeted the change with wariness, or found prices too high or pressure to buy too intense. Employees often felt they had little choice but to buy on company terms, as companies were reluctant to negotiate with individual workers. Declining to buy also could mean paying higher rents or leaving the village. Older workers in particular were less likely to be enthusiastic home buyers. Charles Hatley and his wife had lived in their Wiscassett Mills house in Albemarle, North Carolina, for thirty-nine years and were in failing health when the mill made its offer to sell in 1972. "My husband felt the price they set was too high. I believe this house is about 80 years old. My uncle helped build them. But we couldn't find any place to live, and the down payment was low and the monthly payments are low, so we're in the process of buying it." Mrs. Henry Chance, forty-two years in her family's house in the same village, was more blunt: "I think we've paid for a mill house three or four times living here."[36]

Workers had some leverage in resisting sales plans they considered unfair, because circumstances dictated that mills sell the houses quickly and without controversy. The best, and often only, market for houses in many locations were the tenants already living in them; this was true particularly in the more isolated villages. If employees did not purchase a high percentage of the homes, the mill risked having to carry leftover properties for years or sell them at a deep discount, which in turn would anger employees who had paid the original asking price. Moreover, a major motivation in selling a mill village in the first place was to eliminate maintenance and utility responsibilities and to streamline profitable textile production in the plants. The village sales were often seen by the people conducting them as an exercise in personnel relations first, with maximizing immediate returns a secondary consideration.[37]

In addition to these implicit pressures on textile companies, workers, particularly where they were unionized, could resist high prices or unfavorable plans in more formal ways. When Marshall Field sold its houses in and around Spray in 1941, the TWUA local formed the Tri-Cities Tenants' League, which called for federal inspectors to investigate the sale. The Tenants' League asked for reappraisal of the houses; a reduction in the down payment from 15 percent to 5 percent; an extension of the financing period; and a 4¼ percent interest rate. Marshall Field resisted the workers' efforts at least initially, but by mid-June the company had extended the period for buyers to gather down payments, and was averaging twenty-one sales a day.[38] Similarly, union leaders at Aragon Mills in Georgia insisted on using seniority to assign houses for sale in 1953, and the mill agreed to let the union collect the monthly payments. Union efforts, predictably, irritated mill owners and their agents. "Although I am not enthusiastic about the sale, I think it will eventually pan out after lots of hard work," a frustrated Alester Furman III wrote Aragon's parent company, A. D. Juilliard & Co., in New York. "You asked me once while we were in Aragon if I thought the South could keep Unions out forever. We, in the South, must keep them out unless we want to be ruined."[39]

In at least one village, discontent led directly to a strike. In July 1949, nine hundred workers at M. Lowenstein and Sons' Aleo Manufacturing plant in Rockingham, North Carolina, walked out over plans to sell company-owned houses. TWUA officials said employees were unhappy with the conditions of the sale, which the company refused to discuss with the local. Discontent apparently centered on the length of time employees were given to come up with their down payments. The strike lasted for nineteen days while union officials threatened to strike other Lowenstein mills in the South and the mill's manager hinted that the company might close the mill altogether. In the end, union officials blamed the strike on a "regrettable misunderstanding," and work at the plant resumed.[40]

Unrelated labor unrest could also have an impact on a sale. An organizing drive or a strike not only poisoned the goodwill that many mill owners felt was necessary, but any work stoppage or slowdown also dried up savings that might be used for down payments.[41] During the 1951 sale of a large number of houses at Erwin Mills in Durham, for example, a strike date was scheduled for 31 March and the closing date on one set of houses for 2 April. Workers walked out on schedule but settled in May, and the company eventually netted more than $2 million.[42] Strikes tended to postpone, not cancel, company plans to sell their villages, and some went on without any problems despite strikes or a bitter relationship between management and labor.

As the general postwar boom in U.S. consumer spending continued in the 1950s but textile wage hikes slowed, mills found themselves competing for their workers' consumer dollars. "The sale of houses today and 7 or 8 years ago is quite a different thing," Alester Furman Jr. lamented in 1955 to L. O. Hammett, president of the Chiquola Manufacturing Co., "because there are no savings accounts to make down payments as formerly there were, and, therefore, we have to be patient with people." The increasing ease of obtaining credit put many village residents into debt with local merchants or car dealers before they had the opportunity to buy their village house. In 1968, the real estate company warned its new customers in Graniteville, South Carolina, to be wary of solicitations from "home-modernization people," "at least until you have built a substantial equity."[43] The boom in consumer spending also could lead to poor credit reports, which jeopardized financing for home purchases.

At least one set of textile workers experienced the village sales in a very different way: African Americans. While relatively few blacks were employed in southern textile mills until the 1960s, most mills had at least some black employees, who worked outside or in loading areas; one typical "black" job was on maintenance crews in the villages themselves. Many mills provided houses to their black employees. Housing for blacks was usually along a street or alley separated from the rest of the mill village, sometimes on the opposite side of the plant from the rest of the village. As might be expected, mill houses for black employees were smaller and of poorer quality than houses in the rest of the village, sometimes merely two- or three-room shacks.[44]

Moreover, white mill owners and workers socially constructed the mill villages as white places, a convention that survived the sales. As the race-based labor system elevated white labor in the textile mills by designating less desirable jobs as "black" work, so too did the mill owners elevate the status of the sometimes-squalid mill villages in the eyes of their white workers by making them "white" places, with even more squalid "black" places located nearby for comparison. Even with their own low wages, many mill operatives could afford to hire black domestic help from nearby neighborhoods, a relationship that helped bolster white textile workers' fragile social position.[45] When Pope remarked that "it would be as unthinkable in most uptown houses of Gastonia to invite a 'common millhand' to dinner as it would be to invite a Negro," he was alluding to the danger that class distinction held in such an intensely race-conscious society.[46] The equation of "common millhand" with nearby African Americans was resisted violently by white textile operatives, and the preservation of white and black areas of the mill village supported that resistance.

Cotton mills sold their villages along racial lines; houses occupied by white workers were sold to whites and houses occupied by blacks to blacks, although some black houses may eventually have been sold to whites as well.[47] There is no evidence in the Furman correspondence of any sales to blacks of white houses until federal intervention in the 1960s. However, once the decision had been made to sell houses to black employees, the mills apparently followed much the same procedures, although at times special effort was made to reduce the down payment and monthly payments required.

While much of the preservation of the racial segregation of mill housing occurred informally, or resulted from white domination of the workforce at the time the villages were sold, formal restrictions on the purchase of mill houses by blacks persisted for a surprisingly long time. In 1948, the U.S. Supreme Court ruled racial restrictions in property deeds, a common practice in the South for decades, to be unenforceable. Despite the Supreme Court ban, such covenants were still under discussion in mill sales as late as 1960.[48] In 1959, as Joanna Cotton Mills prepared to sell its houses in Joanna, South Carolina, the Furman company wrote to the mill: "We have wrestled with the caucasian race item and realize that some of the houses will be offered to Negroes for Negro occupancy. Consequently, it would be impossible to have a uniform set of restrictions for all houses." Joanna dropped the clause.[49] Representative of earlier covenants was the one placed in deeds on mill houses at a Victor Monaghan Company village near Greenville in 1942. The deeds stated that "no portion thereof shall be used for any purpose, other than single family residences for white persons only, except as servants of occupants, and shall never be sold, rented or otherwise disposed of to any person other than an American of the white or Caucasian race." That restriction was deleted in 1955.[50]

The formal and informal discrimination practiced by the mills and their agents did not, however, preclude them from publicizing sales involving blacks when it could suit their purposes. When Alex Williams, an elderly black man living in the black section of Riegel Textile's Ware Shoals, South Carolina, village, bought his house in 1953, he penned a short letter of thanks: "I wish to thank Mr. W. J. Erwin vice president and general manager of Riegel Textile Corp. extending the opportunite to all in Briar Hollow to own a home.... I have lived in Ware Shoals for more than 18 years and have found Christanty with white and colored there is great favors in the white peoples of Ware Shoals." Furman officials sent copies of the letter to trade publications in the North, as "indicative of the spirit that is found in the textile communities of the south." *America's Textile Reporter* reprinted the letter in its 23 April issue, along with a story on textile workers buying village homes. Its editor replied to Furman officials: "Isn't it wonderful to have such a nice inter-racial feeling, and isn't it a shame that there aren't more Easterners who understand the situation[?]"[51]

The passage of civil rights and fair housing legislation in the 1960s confronted textile companies and their agents with a new set of legal requirements and practices. Of particular concern to those few mills still owning villages was the 1968 signing of the federal Open Housing Bill, which immediately banned discrimination in the sale or rental of multi-unit dwellings insured or underwritten by the FHA or the Veterans Administration; the bill extended the ban to single family houses sold or rented through brokers effective in 1970. Coverage of mill villages began on 1 January 1969.[52] By the time of that bill, textile companies with large government contracts, such as the St. Louis-based multinational Bemis Corporation, were already under scrutiny by federal officials. Bemis sold a village of more than three hundred houses near Jackson, Tennessee, in 1968 under the supervision of a government attorney, with government officials traveling to the village to oversee the process. They required Bemis to assure credit to black applicants and to follow government directions in drawing up the deeds. Federal government involvement complicated the sale for both Bemis and the real estate agency; they greeted it with much the same irritation as union involvement. "I think we all recognize that your current relationship with the government makes it possible for the village sale to fail, in whole or in part, through no fault of our performance but because of the forced introduction of a social concept by the government bureaucracy using its economic power. The Bemis Company and my company may be maneuvered into the position of making a real effort to successfully 'integrate' housing in Jackson, Tennessee," Alester Furman III wrote Bemis's director of textile operations. In the end, the circumstances did not prevent the company from netting $1.3 million.[53]

The legislation sparked a rush of sales as companies moved to beat the deadlines for the new laws, while other mills found that the changed legal landscape precluded sales altogether.[54] Cannon Mills operated its village in the early 1970s under a consent order from the U.S. Department of Justice, an order that required it to rent its next 150 vacant houses in Kannapolis to black employees. Cannon at the time still owned 633 acres in the heart of Kannapolis and more than 1,600 mill houses, and its interest in selling its villages remained tepid. In 1971, company president Donald S. Holt issued a statement with the grudging admission that private home ownership was "generally desirable."[55]

The impact of gender on the sales is more difficult to ascertain, although North Carolina real estate law during the era provided for an interesting set of circumstances during the sale of the Erwin Mills villages in Durham in 1951. Of the 525 houses sold by mid-February, thirty-five had been bought by women: sixteen of the women were widows, three divorcees, and four single, while twelve married women bought under their own names. However, sales of houses to five of the married women were more complicated. North Carolina law at the time did not allow married women to convey an interest in real estate without the written consent of their husbands, and it was not unusual for women in mill villages to have been separated from their husbands for years without obtaining a legal divorce. One of the women at Erwin Mills had been separated from her husband for twenty years; another thought her husband had obtained a divorce and remarried but wasn't certain and anyway had no proof of it. Real estate agents advised these women either to pay cash or to obtain proof of their divorce. In the end, one of the women had the deed recorded in her mother's name; the other four were given additional time to obtain divorces or track down proof.[56]

Whether they were dealing with black or white workers, men or women, the mills' intent in selling the villages is clear: to divorce the villages financially, socially, and geographically from the mills that had built them. This divorce extended to the symbolic realm as well. A letter from a Canton Cotton Mills official to the Furman company in 1964 indicates how far the mills were willing to go to detach themselves symbolically from their former villages. Canton officials were busy drawing up the plats from which the houses would be sold:

> We agree that the wording in the title section should be changed and this is being done, which will eliminate any reference to Mill Villages. We have decided to call the plat marked "Mill No. 2 Village" Riverview Subdivision; Mill No. 1, Section 1, will be Hillcrest Subdivision; Mill No. 1, Section 2, will be Riverdale Subdivision. The plat which shows our colored Mill Houses will be called Eastside Subdivision.[57]

DECLINE OF THE MILL VILLAGE SENSE OF PLACE

Place as a central focus for academic research has undergone something of a renaissance in recent years in geography and other disciplines. Geographers have looked at place as an important but often neglected organizing framework through which individuals negotiate the larger economic and social structures of their lives. Scholars in geography, anthropology, cultural studies, and other disciplines insist that "people don't just dwell in comfort or misery, in centers or margins, in place or out of place, empowered or disempowered. People everywhere act on the integrity of their dwelling." The term remains difficult to define succinctly, but an important distinction is drawn between place and community. Communities can exist without being in a single place, and places can contain more than one community.[58]

The mills' divestiture of employee housing did not end the villages' sense of place overnight. The neighborhoods continued to be filled with blue-collar workers, overwhelmingly white, a large number of whom continued to make the short trip every day to the nearby textile mill. However, coincident to the changes in the legal ownership of the mill houses, a variety of local institutions entered into a period of rapid transformation or decline. Neighborhood grocery stores, factory baseball teams, and local schools in the villages had been closely tied to the textile mills, and each institution would undergo dramatic changes in the postwar era. In each case, the result would be a dilution of the textile influence on the residents' sense of place, as workers in the mills and others living in the villages found their work lives increasingly severed from their lives outside the factory.

An example of these changes can be seen in the career of Herman Newton Truitt, who returned after college to the family grocery business in North Carolina's Glen Raven mill village. Truitt could remember as a boy selling food grown on his grandparents' farm, riding in a horse-drawn buggy with his grandfather from mill village to mill village on Tuesdays and Saturdays. Truitt's father operated several stores before settling in at Alamance County's Glen Raven mill, where his store became a gathering place for mill workers on Saturday nights. "At that time they had a bunch of pretty regular customers who would maybe celebrate a little bit by . . . smelling the bottle, or tasting a little when they'd come by. Sometimes there was a jew's harp, and a violin, what you'd call a fiddle . . . they had pig feet in the barrel, crackers in the barrel." Across the street from the store was a field where the family grew corn; when a customer wanted an ear, Truitt ran across the road and picked one. The grocery store took barter from farmers and mill workers, who lived on a diet of dried beans, cooked up with a piece of fatback, Irish and sweet potatoes and onions, with chicken the most popular meat. Most customers kept an account at the store, and credit terms were flexible. "Of course, we tried to pick out the customers that were good pay. Those we were acquainted with and those we knew. If there was a sickness in the family, hardship, somebody lose a job and had to be out of work for a while, we would extend him credit a little longer." The personal relationships and local nature of the store did not survive long after the war. Truitt's store had grown into the second largest in the county by the early 1940s, but then the large, chain grocery stores began to appear in town. With their advertising campaigns and "loss leaders" enticing customers, the chains triggered a battle for shoppers that local neighborhood groceries could not win. "Then the local owned grocery stores began to lose out, fading away." By the late 1970s, Truitt was closing out his business.[59]

Other retail businesses in the villages faced the same kinds of competition, either through the introduction of franchise operations or through urban growth. The rise of Wal-Mart and other discount stores at the expense of the neighborhood clothing or hardware store is perhaps the most familiar example of these changes, but other small businesses also faced increasing competition. When Albert Faulkner opened his Coffee Pot diner a half block north of the Dunean Mill in Greenville in the early 1940s, the competition consisted of only three restaurants within four miles. By 1996, when Faulkner finally retired at the age of eighty-one, he estimated there were three hundred.[60]

A similar fate awaited another prominent feature of the cotton mill world: textile baseball, which grew to great popularity before the war and enjoyed a brief renaissance after it. Textile companies underwrote the mill baseball teams, often giving players do-nothing jobs in exchange for their efforts on the diamond. A

1926 survey of 322 North Carolina mill villages found that while most companies had begun to abandon their welfare programs, they still supported 127 baseball teams. In the glory days of textile league baseball, during the 1930s, 15 or more leagues could be found operating simultaneously in upstate South Carolina. Textile baseball served as an unofficial farm league for the major leagues, with games drawing thousands of fans and sometimes being broadcast on local radio stations. Black millhands had their own teams and leagues, often drawing large crowds of white fans; for a brief time there was even a Textile Girls Baseball League in Anderson.[61]

Mill baseball brought together outside the factory people who worked together inside it, and promoted a place identity among workers living in the villages. With meager disposable income and limited transportation, recreation opportunities were limited, and mill baseball allowed working people the opportunity to participate in the national pastime. Hoyle McCorkle remembered that at night, "that's all we would go to, ball games," at Highland Park Mill #3 in Charlotte. The mill recruited ballplayers from Gastonia and South Carolina, "so we got to where we had a good team. It was really a source of great pride to us. We'd always looked up to the hosiery mill, but now we began to beat them at the baseball, and it did us a whole lot of good."[62]

Renewed interest following the war peaked in 1949 and 1950, when the season started with twenty leagues composed of 120 teams and 2,000 players in South Carolina alone. Yet as mills began to give their teams widely divergent amounts of support, a growing gap emerged in talent levels. Crowds of several thousand were still not uncommon, but weaker teams began to have trouble drawing. Sagging attendance prompted the mills to cut back their support, as the long-term trend toward cutting welfare program expenditures finally hit the baseball teams. The author of a book on the rise and fall of textile baseball in South Carolina tied its demise directly to the end of the village system. "One by one, the owners began to sell the houses in the mill villages and that fierce community pride was lost. For the first time, there were folks living in the village whose personal welfare was not tied to the fortunes of the company." By 1954, the textile leagues had begun winding down.[63]

Like neighborhood groceries and mill baseball teams, schools in the villages had been closely linked to the cotton mills. Through the first half of the century, in fact, mill village schools operated almost as a parallel educational system in many textile communities, one with striking similarities to the separate schools provided for blacks. Most mills ran elementary schools for the children of their employees, providing a building and often the teachers as well. Many children quit school at an early age to work with their parents in the mill; village children usually had to pay tuition at the local town or county high school if they wanted to continue past the grades offered by the mill. Even if they could afford the cost, village children regularly found town high schools inhospitable. Mack Duncan, who worked for thirty years at Poe Mill in Greenville, told the story of a mill friend who went to school in town. One day a classmate asked the friend where he lived. "So he said, 'I live at 15-something Buncombe Road.' They said, 'That's Poe Mill, ain't it?' So he said, 'No, I live on Buncombe Road.' He tried to better his standing, you know, in the sight of his peers."[64]

South Carolina even appointed a state mill school supervisor in 1915; he oversaw some two hundred school districts. Supervisor William Banks suggested in 1923 that a summer training course be held for teachers bound for mill schools. "It would be unpardonable for the state to foster anything like class consciousness, and mill children are just children," Banks reported. "But there are certain lines of living in mill communities for which the teacher should be adapted." Textbooks should reflect the needs of the mill children, Banks wrote. "Our textbooks are totally unsuited to mill schools. Problems in arithmetic—measuring acres of ground, computing size and value of piles of wood—these are all right, but what the mill child should be taught especially is to measure cloth, to compute the number of strands in a yard of cloth, etc." In Greenville, mills formed the Parker District to operate schools in the villages; six thousand students enrolled in the district's twenty schools, and the district had the largest tax base of any district in the state.[65]

Mill schools did not long survive the end of the war. Greenville County had 82 school districts in 1950, with 128 schools for white children; one school board member recalled that "we didn't even know where they were." The next year, however, South Carolina launched a massive school district consolidation effort, hoping to stave off legal challenges to segregation. By consolidating small school districts into countywide districts, and by investing millions of dollars in new school construction and rehabilitation, the state hoped to prove that it was meeting its own Jim Crow assertion of separate but equal education. In Greenville County, the state reduced the 82 school districts to one; from 1951 to 1964, the county abandoned 108 small schoolhouses, many in the already fragmenting mill villages.[66] School consolidation was another blow to the vulnerable sense of place of the villages.

CONCLUSION

The divestiture of mill villages by southern textile companies irrevocably changed the relationship between work and home, and between capital and labor, in the Piedmont South. The village system had set the parameters of labor relations in the textile South between Appomattox and Pearl Harbor, when large numbers of poor, rural whites were introduced to the rhythms of the town and the factory. While company control of the villages could and did stifle organizing efforts and hamstring the formation of class consciousness, the very existence of the factory-centered villages and their separation from both the surrounding countryside and the emerging towns made possible a place-based labor politics that eroded in the decades following the Great Depression, although as Carlton points out, its remnants can still be found.[67]

Textile companies sold their villages for a variety of reasons, ranging from the increasing freedom of mill workers to live outside the village to internal finance and investment considerations, and the perceived need for a more effective system of labor discipline. Mill owners were acutely aware of the potential the break-up of the villages had for improving the stability of their workforce. By encouraging mill workers to enter into debt relationships with outside finance organizations, the mills transferred a key coercive responsibility for reproducing their labor force. Mills found that they were no longer responsible for evicting recalcitrant workers from mill-owned housing, yet striking workers still faced eviction if they failed to keep up with their house payments. In fact, eviction under the new system represented an even greater loss to the workers and their families because they risked losing years of accumulated equity and damaging their credit rating.

While some mills attempted to maximize short-term revenues from their villages, most companies saw the sales as a way to garner new working capital while improving labor relations. Limited by their potential customers' low incomes and often by the narrow outside market for mill housing, most gave favorable terms. But textile companies were not above manipulating the process for their own ends. Mills used a variety of means, including obscuring the true identity of the financing institution to which the workers were indebted, to hasten the real and perceived divorce of the mills from the villages.

By and large southern textile workers welcomed the chance to buy the mill houses, and benefited from the opportunity. The transfer of local governance away from the mills expanded local democracy, giving mill workers a real say in how their communities would be run; the end of the village system meant the beginning of a fuller citizenship. The postwar Fordism adopted by southern textile companies after World War II was not the sort identified by most scholars: the purchasing power of workers remained tenuous, labor had little leverage to counter the power of the employers, and government remained in the grasp of the business community. Yet despite its problems, the system of labor relations that replaced village paternalism was a distinct improvement for most mill workers and a significant accomplishment by them.

The full effect of the racial discrimination practiced during the mill village sales is difficult to ascertain, but a few tentative conclusions can be ventured. The timing of the sales, coming as they did prior to the passage of federal fair housing laws, deprived many black southerners of a historically unique opportunity to move into the ranks of home ownership, an opportunity made available to white members of the working class. In the Piedmont textile counties, mill village houses represented a large supply of affordable homes at reasonable and often favorable terms. Prevented from working in the mills and thus from participating in the sales, Piedmont blacks largely missed out on the most significant leap in home ownership rates in the history of the region and of the nation. Because of this discrimination, the mill village sales served to reinforce residential patterns put in place by the prior racial segregation of the village system. Had divestment taken place after the passage of fair housing legislation—had textile companies been forced to sell to blacks, as occurred at Cannon Mills—a higher degree of integration might have been attained. The continued segregation of the villages and their surrounding neighborhoods also had an important impact on the political unity of textile workers. While southern textile factories have integrated, the former mill villages have largely remained white places. In the mill village era, village institutions paralleled the racial segregation of the shop floor. In the post–civil rights era, mill workers in the home spheres have remained spatially divided between black and white.

Once cast into the private housing market, mill villages and the institutions that operated within them gradually lost much of their sense of place as work-centered neighborhoods. Where families once attended industry-sponsored baseball games with their co-workers, they could now stay home and watch commodified forms of entertainment on television. Local groceries gave way to chain supermarkets, which drew customers from many miles around. Mill and town schools merged and began to bring together different segments of society. All of these changes diluted the work-centered sense of place that had developed in communities in which people shopped, slept, learned, and worked in a factory or its shadow.

On a broader level, the sales of the mill villages represented both a break from the past and a continuity with it. As for continuity, workers in the end still depended on their employers for the provision of their housing. The credit system replaced the company, but there was no change in who controlled the paychecks that covered the monthly mortgage. The former mill villages remained places populated by working-class, mostly blue-collar and service-industry people and their families, dependent on an economic system designed to minimize their wages, despite new guarantees of minimum wages and maximum hours intended to support purchasing power.

However, the sales represented a break with the region's past by shifting the relative mobility between labor and capital, and by divorcing home and work socially and geographically. With savings invested in property, mill workers faced higher moving costs if fired, or if they quit their jobs to pursue other opportunities. Unlike textile work under the village system, when families could show up at a mill in the morning and be housed by nightfall, moving now meant selling the family home, absorbing the costs associated with the sale and the ensuing relocation, and finding new housing and employment at another site. At the same time, mills shed a substantial, immovable, and decaying capital investment at favorable terms. Such companies had a difficult time playing spatial games of blackmail with localities over taxes and wage rates when a high proportion of their investment had been sunk in the village property; that is, when they were part of locally dependent capital. Shorn of this commitment, textile enterprises could better chase lower tax burdens or cheaper labor, although the textile industry was less prone to this sort of movement than the more labor-intensive apparel industry.

Mill houses, through the mechanism of the sales, shifted from belonging to the fixed assets of productive capital into what Marx termed the "consumption fund." Unlike fixed capital items (such as factories and railroads and so on), the consumption fund includes those parts of the built environment that soak up surplus production, storing it in the form of houses, roads, and parks.[68] Mill houses, owned now by individual workers instead of the textile companies, transferred their key function in the postwar economy from production to consumption, not coincidentally at the same time that faster looms and spinning machines produced increasing amounts of cloth and yarn with fewer and fewer workers. Furthermore, this shift to the consumption fund changed the mill villages as *places*. As textile workers planted lawns around their newly bought houses, added porches, and installed washing machines, their neighborhoods increasingly reflected their new role as reservoirs for the commodities of an increasingly Fordist Piedmont economy. As the new consumerism flourished, many former villages lost their mills, as the multistory brick factories were replaced by single-story plants on cheap land in the suburbs or in the country. Children whose parents and grandparents had grown up within sight of a mill now lived in neighborhoods without the physical presence of any form of industrial capitalism.

These changes did not put an end to a politics of work in the textile Piedmont, but it did mean that the places in which the workers lived tended to support a politics of consumption rather than a politics of work. Issues such as property and income tax rates, roads, and schools assumed a more prominent position in the new homeowners' lives (and neighborhoods) as the twentieth century wore on. In many ways, this new politics reflected the improved conditions in the mill villages: despite the continued imbalance of power between labor and capital in the South, the living standards of most Piedmont textile workers improved significantly in the years following the Great Depression. The dismantling of the cotton mill village world was the price of that prosperity.

NOTES

1. South Carolina Department of Labor, *Annual Report* (Columbia: South Carolina Department of Labor, 1945), 17, 38.

2. Harriet Herring, *Passing of the Mill Village: Revolution in a Southern Institution* (Chapel Hill: University of North Carolina Press, 1949); Jacquelyn Dowd Hall, James Leloudis, Robert Korstad, Mary Murphy, LuAnn Jones, and Christopher B. Daly, *Like a Family* (New York: W. W. Norton, 1987); Douglas Flamming, *Creating the Modern South* (Chapel Hill: University of North Carolina Press, 1992); Dolores Janiewski, *Sisterhood Denied: Race, Gender, and Class in a New South Community* (Philadelphia: Temple University Press, 1985); and Timothy Minchin, *What Do We Need a Union For? The TWUA in the South 1945–1955* (Chapel Hill: University of North Carolina Press, 1997).

3. Evelyn Knowlton, *Pepperell's Progress: History of a Cotton Textile Company 1844–1945* (Cambridge: Harvard University Press, 1948), 336.

4. *Chicopee, Georgia* (n.d.), company publication in South Carolina Room, Greenville Public Library; Abner D. Asbury Jr., interview by Brent Glass, transcript, 6 April 1976, Piedmont Series, Southern Oral History Collection, University of North Carolina, Chapel Hill (Piedmont Series).

5. Mildred Gwin Andrews, interview by Mary Murphy and James Leloudis, transcript, 15 June 1979, Piedmont Series; see also Hall et al., *Like a Family*, 356; Jonathan Daniels, "A Native at Large," *The Nation*, 21 September 1940, 246; Anthony J. Badger, *North Carolina and the New Deal* (Raleigh: North Carolina Department of Cultural Resources, 1981), 39; Harriet Herring to Douglas C. Woolf, 9 March 1940, folder 50, Harriet Herring Papers, Southern Historical Collection, University of North Carolina, Chapel Hill (SHC).

6. Bureau of Labor Statistics, "Personnel Policies in the Cotton-Textile Industry," *Monthly Labor Review*, June 1936, 1477–95; Herring to Woolf, 4 November 1940, and W. F. Hooey to Herring, 18 November 1940; both in folder 54, Herring Papers, SHC.

7. Stuart D. Brandes, *Welfare Capitalism: 1880–1940* (Chicago: University of Chicago Press, 1976), 145; Alester Furman III to F. E. Grier, November 14, 1958; folder 6, box 1, Alester Furman Company Records, Special Collections, Clemson University Libraries, Clemson, S.C. (Furman Records); "Cannon's Hometown Feels Winds of Change," *New York Times*, 17 March 1981, D1.

8. See, for example, notice dated 3 June 1958, posted in the Bellevue Manufacturing Company village in Hillsboro, N.C.; folder 20, box 2, Furman Records.

9. Rates of owner-occupancy taken from Census of Housing, 1940, 1950, 1960, and 1970 (Bureau of the Census: Washington, D.C.).

10. Stuart W. Cramer, "Some phases of the Human Element in Southern Industrialization," pamphlet reprint of 15 July 1922 speech to the Southern Industrial Conference, folder 242, Herring Papers, SHC.

11. Gavin Wright, *Old South, New South: Revolutions in the Southern Economy since the Civil War* (New York: Basic Books, 1986), 209–10.

12. H. E. Bailey to Alester Furman III, 3 January 1951 and 8 February 1951, folder 97, box 10, Furman Records.

13. *South Carolina Textiles: Southern Workers, Northern Bosses* (New York: Textile Workers Union of America, 1949); quotation from foreword.

14. Roger Biles, *The South and the New Deal* (Lexington: University Press of Kentucky, 1994), 59; Brandes, *Welfare Capitalism*, 142–43; Herbert Lahne, *The Cotton Mill Worker* (New York: Farrar and Rinehart, 1944), 42.

15. W. J. Cash, *The Mind of the South* (1941; reprint, New York: Vintage Books, 1969), 40.

16. Robert Moore, interview by author, tape recording, Eden, N.C., 9 March 1998. Hoyle McCorkle, interview by Jim Leloudis, transcript, 11 July 1979, Piedmont Series. Ada Mae Mosely Wilson, interview by Allen Tullos, transcript, 1 February 1980, Piedmont Series.

17. Liston Pope, *Millhands and Preachers: A Study of Gastonia* (New Haven: Yale University Press, 1942), 63, 189; Broadus Mitchell, *The Rise of the Cotton Mills in the South* (Baltimore: Johns Hopkins University Press, 1921), 196–97; Jennings J. Rhyne, *Some Southern Cotton Mill Workers and Their Villages* (Chapel Hill: University of North Carolina Press, 1930), 209–10.

18. J. M. Robinette, interview by Cliff Kuhn, transcript, July 1977, Piedmont Series; Wright, *Old South*, 150.

19. David Carlton, *Mill and Town in South Carolina, 1880–1920* (Baton Rouge: Louisiana State University Press, 1982), 221, 252.

20. David Robertson, *Sly and Able: A Political Biography of James F. Byrnes* (New York: W. W. Norton, 1994), 88; Marjorie Potwin, *Cotton Mill People of the Piedmont* (New York: AMS Press, 1968), 98; Mack Duncan, interview by Allen Tullos, transcript, 7 June and 30 August, Piedmont Series.

21. Caesar Cone to Herring, "Long range program for modernization of Cone Mill's Greensboro villages," 1 March 1950, folder 254, box 12, Herring Papers, SHC.

22. Alester Furman III to Grier, 14 November 1958, folder 6, box 1, Furman Records; Hall, et al., 356–357; Minchin, *What Do We Need*, 141–43, 199–209.

23. Douglas DeNatale, "Traditional Culture and Community in a Piedmont Textile Mill Village" (master's thesis, University of North Carolina, Chapel Hill, 1980). For the demise of Camperdown, see various documents, folder 45, box 5, Furman Records.

24. Alester Furman Jr. to J. W. Medford, 9 June 1952, folder 123, box 13, Furman Records; Alester Furman III, interview by author, tape recording, Greenville, S.C., 29 May 1998.

25. "Business Property to Be Offered for Sale at Piedmont," folder 106, box 11, Furman Records.

26. Alester Furman Jr. to F. S. Whitesides, 16 January 1954, folder 102, box 11, Furman Records.

27. *The Joanna Way*, October 1959, folder 91, box 10, Furman Records; Alester G. Furman Company to George Riegger, 15 July 1952, folder 51, box 6, Furman Records.

28. For the general methodology employed by the Furman company, see "Typical Timetable for Village Sale," folder 19, box 3, Furman Records; for traveling incognito, see J. J. Hinds to George DeBrule, 8 January 1960, folder 33, box 4, Furman Records.

29. Hugh M. Comer to Alester Furman III, 16 November 1964, folder 26, box 3, Furman Records.

30. Various documents, folder 71, box 8, Furman Records; quotation in Alester Furman III to Mark M. Hoblitt, 18 July 1956, same folder. Other real estate companies had different ideas of how the sales should be conducted. A Greensboro, N.C., agency, the Hugh Pinnix Realty Company, reported in 1950 that most mills it was familiar with had done the financing themselves, even though outside money was available, in order "to go through this weaning period along with their employees and help to guide them through the first few years of home ownership." Mills could suspend payments during slow periods, according to Pinnix, and employees tended to be "suspicious and resentful" of outside financing programs. Furman officials in 1964 estimated that 40 percent of village houses had been sold under mill-provided financing. It is likely that securing outside financing became more common as the sales went on and the credit system matured. See Mrs. Hugh Pinnix to Herring, 24 August 1950, Herring Papers, SHC; Alester Furman III to J. Mack Holland Jr., 3 November 1964, folder 50, box 6, Furman Records.

31. Alester Furman III to Gardiner Hawkins, 26 April 1952, folder 149, box 15, Furman Records; Alester Furman III to J. Mack Holland Jr., 6 November 1964, folder 50, box 6, Furman Records.

32. H. E. Bailey to Alester Furman Jr., 14 November 1950, folder 74, box 8, Furman Records; various documents, folder 97, box 11, Furman Records.

33. Flamming, *Creating*, 270; "Abney Mills to Sell Houses," *Greenville Piedmont*, 8 January 1959, 1; "Analysis of Village Sales," 26 August 1959, folder 6, box 1, Furman Records; sales report, 2 July 1957, and memo, 18 April 1958, both in folder 38, box 5, Furman Records; price list, 9 August 1962, folder 79, box 9, Furman Records; G. O. Robinson, *The Character of Quality: The Story of Greenwood Mills* (Columbia, S.C.: Greenwood Mills, 1964), 57, 94–95.

34. David Levy to Alester Furman III, 15 March 1954, folder 145, box 15, Furman Records; "memorandum to file," 9 September 1964, folder 49, box 5, Furman Records; Ben Kohler to Alester Furman III, 2 November 1956, folder 72, box 8, Furman Records.

35. Paul and Pauline Griffith, interview by Allen Tullos, transcript, 30 March 1980, Piedmont Series.

36. "Wiscasset [sic] Mill Workers Buying Their Company Homes," Phil Moeller and Helen Arthur, *Charlotte Observer*, 21 Febuary 1972, 1.

37. Alester Furman III to Greenwood Mills, 8 May 1963, folder 77, box 8, Furman Records; Furman interview.

38. "Report Sale of Houses Progressing While TWUA Seeks Government Action," 29 May 1941, *Leaksville News*, 1; and "Record Sales Reported by Realty Agency; More Time Given Prospective Buyers," 12 June 1941, *Leaksville News*, 1. Herring helped mediate this dispute, drawing on her previous experience as a village social worker in Spray.

39. Alester Furman III to Charles R. Dear, 22 August 1953, folder 15, box 2, Furman Records.

40. *Columbia* (S.C.) *State*, 17 July 1949, 2–D, and 23 July 1949, 16; *Greenville News*, 2 August 1949, 1; and Thomas H. Leath to Alester Furman Jr., 15 July 1949, folder 81,

box 9, Furman Records. For more information on the Aleo strike and the home sales there, see Minchin, *What Do We Need,* 189–92.

41. See, for example, various letters, folder 49, box 6, Furman Records.

42. Alester Furman III to Carl Harris, 17 March 1951, and Alester Furman III to John McArthur, 15 August 1951, both in folder 67, box 7, Furman Records.

43. Alester Furman Jr. to L. O. Hammett, 29 April 1955, folder 52, box 6, Furman Records; Alester Furman III to William C. Lott, 21 April 1956, folder 74, box 8, Furman Records; undated notice, "To our new Graniteville customers," folder 75, box 8, Furman Records.

44. Rupert Gaddy to B. B. Snow, 13 May 1964, folder 26, box 3; handwritten description and price list of houses, folder 17, box 2; both in Furman Records; also, Potwin, 46.

45. Hall et al., *Like a Family,* 157.

46. Pope, *Millhands,* 68.

47. Alester Furman III to J. W. Wood, 20 October 1950, and memo, Alester Furman III, 28 August, 1950, both in folder 89, box 10, Furman Records; Furman interview.

48. Robert Trudgian to Rupert Gaddy, 1 August 1960, folder 31, box 4; and Alester Furman III to James E. McDonald, 27 November 1959 and 1 December 1959, folder 91, box 10; both in Furman Records.

49. Alester Furman III to James E. McDonald, 1 December 1959, folder 91, box 10, Furman Records.

50. Memo, n.d., folder 153, box 15, Furman Records. It is unclear in the correspondence exactly what the circumstances surrounding the covenants were; that is, whether these discussions were a result of efforts to sustain the covenants or part of the process of removing them from existing contracts. However, as late as August 1960, printers' proofs of purchase contracts still contained such provisions (see folder 31, box 3, Furman Records).

51. Various letters, folder 116, box 12, Furman Records.

52. Leo Hill to James L. Sanderson, 1 May 1968, and Alester Furman III to W. C. Lott, 17 May 1968; both in folder 75, box 8, Furman Records.

53. Quotation from Alester Furman III to K. H. Hoffman, 19 April 1968, folder 25, box 3, Furman Records; sales figure in "Village Sales Report," 9 July 1968, same folder. See also Alester Furman III to Don Holt, 5 May 1971, folder 25, box 3, Furman Records.

54. Alester Furman III to George Hightower, 18 April 1968, folder 138, box 14, Furman Records.

55. Alester Furman III to Julien L. McCall, 19 July 1971, folder 48, box 5, Furman Records; and "Cannon Doesn't Own Wiscasset," *Charlotte Observer,* 21 February 1971, 13A. Phil Moeller, "'The Mill' Loosening Its Grip on Kannapolis," *Charlotte Observer,* 2 April 1972, 1A.

56. Alester Furman Jr. to William B. Umstead, 16 February 1951; Umstead to Alester Furman III, 20 February 1951; and Umstead to Carl R. Harris, 6 March 1951; all in folder 67, box 7, Furman Papers. A question for future research would be the changes in household power relations resulting from the change from tenancy to home ownership.

57. C. K. Cobb to Alester Furman III, 3 March 1964, folder 49, box 5, Furman Records.

58. Steven Field and Keith Basso, eds., *Senses of Place* (Santa Fe, N.Mex.: School of American Research Press, 1996), 11. For general discussions of place see Doreen Massey, *Space, Place and Gender* (Oxford: Oxford University Press, 1994); R. J. Johnston, *A Question of Place: Exploring the Practice of Human Geography* (Cambridge, Mass.: Blackwell Publishers, 1991); John Agnew, "The Devaluation of Place in Social Science," in John Agnew and James Duncan, eds., *The Power of Place: Bringing Together Geographical and Sociological Imaginations* (Boston: Unwin Hyman, 1989); and Nicholas Entriken, *The Betweenness of Place: Towards a Geography of Modernity* (Baltimore: Johns Hopkins University Press, 1991).

59. Herman Newton Truitt, interview by Allen Tullos, transcript, 5 December 1978, 19 and 20 January 1979, Piedmont Series.

60. "Seventy Years a Businessman," *Greenville News*, 8 September 1996, Upstate Business section, 6–9.

61. Jack Temple Kirby, *Rural Worlds Lost: The American South 1920–1960* (Baton Rouge: Louisiana State University Press, 1987), 302; Thomas Perry, *Textile League Baseball: South Carolina's Mill Teams, 1880–1955* (Jefferson, N.C.: McFarland and Company, 1993), 49–51, 55–58, 63–64.

62. McCorkle interview, Piedmont Series.

63. Perry, *Textile League*, 67, 80–81.

64. Duncan interview, Piedmont Series; Mary Thompson, interview by James Leloudis, transcript, 19 July 1979, Piedmont Series.

65. *50th Annual Report of the State Superintendent of Education, 1918* (Columbia, S.C.: Gonzales and Bryan, 1919), 31; *Annual Report of the State Superintendent of Education: South Carolina, 1923* (Columbia: Gonzales and Bryan, 1924), 114–30; Allen Tullos, *Habits of Industry* (Chapel Hill: University of North Carolina Press, 1989), 180–81.

66. Asbury interview, Piedmont Series; William Bagwell, *School Desegregation in the Carolinas: Two Case Studies* (Columbia: University of South Carolina Press, 1972), 33, 126; *1951 Annual Report of the State Superintendent of Education* (Columbia, S.C.: State Budget and Control Board, 1951), 12, 274–75.

67. Carlton, *Mill and Town*, 271.

68. Karl Marx, *Capital*, vol. 2 (New York: New World Paperbacks, 1967), 210; also see David Harvey, "Labor, Capital and the Class Struggle around the Built Environment in Advanced Capitalist Societies," in Kevin Cox, ed., *Urbanization and Conflict in Market Societies* (Chicago: Maaroufa Press, 1975), 9–37.

Texas v. the Petrochemical Industry

Contesting Pollution in an Era of Industrial Growth

CRAIG E. COLTEN

Oil and gas development anchored the Texas economy during the first half of the twentieth century. Particularly after 1930 Texas sought to build on its natural resource base and establish a strong petrochemical refining and processing industry. This endeavor was well underway before the onset of World War II, although it received a considerable stimulus from wartime expansion. Accompanying the oil-fueled boom came a less desirable by-product: industrial effluent. During the 1940s, the use of watercourses for waste disposal prevailed in Texas and caused increasing damage to valuable fresh- and saltwater species, thereby attracting the displeasure of Lone Star sportsmen. Poised between the polluters and the fishermen were the game wardens of the Texas Game, Fish and Oyster Commission, charged with enforcing the principal pollution law of the state but armed with limited powers.

During two brief intervals in the late 1940s and mid-1950s, the Texas conservation agency took vigorous steps to abate industrial pollution. They assessed fines and filed suits to restrict pollution by small producers, while they sought cooperative solutions with major manufacturers. This chapter examines the emerging conflict between an industry and the state that was actively courting it as an example of rising environmental concerns and as a measure of the efforts taken by states against most-favored industries.

HISTORICAL CONTEXT

Two overlapping and concurrent processes served as the crucible in which Texas industries found themselves in the postwar years. The first involved regulation of polluting activity. Samuel Hays contends that Americans' pursuit of outdoor recreation expanded after the Second World War and led to public policies that managed natural resources for human enjoyment, including protection of high quality water. While Hays found national environmental "impulses" between 1958 and 1965, efforts to preserve water quality in postwar Texas preceded full-blown national action.[1] In Texas, a state with a strong hunting and fishing tradition, pursuit of game and fish flourished.[2] Responsibility for protecting outdoor resources fell to the state conservation organization, which followed a progressive-era mission to promote wise use. The Texas Game, Fish and Oyster Commission served both commercial and sport fishermen and recreational hunters and had a responsibility to protect terrestrial and aquatic life in the state's forests, streams, and marine environments. By statute, the game wardens had the responsibility to enforce the state's water pollution law.[3] The obvious objective was to prevent polluting substances from killing fish, but it placed the game wardens in a situation where they had increasing environmental, as opposed to conservation, responsibilities. Their mission was not just to sustain the yield of sport and commercial species but also to prevent needless damage to species that were not the object of recreational or commercial exploitation and to protect public water supplies.

During the 1940s, manufacturers relied heavily on water bodies for waste disposal. Wartime industrial expansion sacrificed waste treatment to military priorities and left the streams in an undeniably deteriorated condition. Both the federal government and the states responded by taking action to revise their water pollution laws. In 1948, Congress finally enacted a federal water pollution statute, which largely encouraged states to take the lead in pollution control. In response to federal incentives and also independently, most states created pollution-control organizations and sought to restrict discharges to waterways.[4] These measures brought pollution under closer scrutiny, and with federal assistance, the petrochemical industry became one of the manufacturing groups under the government's gaze.[5] Texas had taken a first step to revise its pollution laws in 1943, when it prohibited the pollution of surface waters and authorized the Game, Fish and Oyster Commission to enforce the statute.[6] In 1953, in accord with the national trend, Texas created a Water Pollution Advisory Council to undertake "a more comprehensive program in the public interest for the prevention, abatement, and control of pollution." The council included a member from the state conservation agency, and also brought in representatives from the Board of Water Engineers, the Railroad Commission (which regulated the oil and gas industry), the Department of Health, and the Attorney General. This obviously broadened the scope of pollution concerns well beyond the conservation agenda and gave a voice to the regulated community. Also, it explicitly declared that state policy was to "conserve its waters for public water supplies, for domestic, municipal, agricultural, industrial, *recreational* [uses], for the propagation of fish and aquatic life, and for other beneficial uses," thereby including concerns of sportsmen and other recreational water users.[7]

Despite the existence of antipollution laws, state governments, especially those in the South, earned a reputation for accommodating the industry that drove the state's economic engine.[8] State regulators in North Carolina permitted a paper mill to use the Pigeon River as an outlet for its effluent in the interest of preserving jobs.[9] In the 1870s Massachusetts passed pollution control laws that were largely ineffective due to the absence of enforcement.[10] Pennsylvania effectively exempted major industries from enforcement with provisions in its 1937 Pure Streams Law that outlawed only discharges to "clean waters" of the state. Implicitly, it sanctioned continued use of already polluted waters, as did New York's 1950 stream classification system.[11] Louisiana's Stream Control Commission consistently granted permits to manufacturers seeking to discharge effluent to the Mississippi River during the 1950s and 1960s.[12]

Ineffective enforcement did not mean states ignored environmental concerns until the 1960s. The emergence of conservation-based pollution control ideas stemmed from late nineteenth-century actions that sought to preserve water quality for aquatic life.[13] Community leaders and state legislatures challenged the coke industry, a major economic force in the Ohio River valley, during the 1920s, exemplifying an episode of public concern with water pollution well before the national impulses.[14] Even though states had a reputation for accommodating favored manufacturing interests, when pollution caused undeniably extreme conditions, they took steps to reduce it. Nonetheless, state efforts typically focused on a single class of industries and not pollution control in general. Additionally, state efforts were largely ineffective in terms of interstate water quality. Federal pollution control action associated with the "national impulses" did not represent the birth of public concern, merely a congressional attempt to coordinate and provide interstate oversight for multiple state programs.

A second point of intersection between polluters and the environment can be found in the geography of industrial activity. Defense-oriented industrial expansion in the early 1940s initially concentrated in the nation's manufacturing belt—the Northeast and Midwest. After America entered the war, the South became an increasingly important locale for new plants seeking to take advantage of available space and labor. Shipyards from Norfolk to Houston grew, and aircraft manufacturing emerged in Texas and Georgia. Metals processing in Louisiana and Texas produced goods for use in ship and aircraft fabrication. Wartime expansion also took place in the petroleum and chemical industries. Ordnance plants opened in every southern state. Petroleum refining expanded in the producing states of Texas and Louisiana, and related chemical facilities spread along the Gulf Coast. Construction of major pipelines to northern states enabled safe transport of refined products. Although much of the ordnance and ship building disappeared after the war, petroleum, chemical, and metal processing remained extremely important to the Gulf Coast economies after 1945.[15] These industries, at least in Texas, selected coastal or riverfront locations near important aquatic resources and generated sizable amounts of effluent.

At the close of the war, Texas sportsmen were keen to resume hunting and fishing and trusted the state to preserve their prey. Oil production and related industries, which had increased along the prime fishing grounds, discharged sizable quantities of waste to the state's waterways. As a consequence, conditions were ripe for conflict between the conservation agency, with its newfound environmental responsibilities, and economic development/industrial interests. In Texas, there was substantial overlap in these communities, which led to a surprisingly vigorous response to the pollution threat—at least under certain conditions.

PETROCHEMICAL BUILDUP

Efforts to lure industry to Texas began before World War II and represented an active program by officials to capitalize on the state's natural resources.[16] Petroleum served as the most obvious lure for manufacturing. Just before the war (1937), Texas boasted 77,360 producing wells. By 1947 this number rose to 106,738 and climbed to 176,705 in 1957. Crude production nearly doubled in the same time period (1937: 510 million barrels; 1957: over 1 billion barrels). The east Texas field developed early in the century, while exploration and production spread to the panhandle, the high plains, the Houston area, and central Texas by the 1920s. Ample raw materials streamed from these prodigious oil fields and supplied a growing number of refineries.[17]

Joseph Pratt's excellent analysis of the Gulf Coast's refineries points to several important conditions for the dramatic expansion of oil processing. During the prewar years, the availability of crude oil enticed major refiners to construct Texas plants. Other fundamental economic factors such as low labor costs and inexpensive natural gas prompted the selection of Gulf Coast plant locations. Indeed, by 1941, the Gulf Coast had the largest regional refining capacity in the country (27.9 percent). Developments during the war enhanced Texas's favored position among refiners. Demand for aviation fuel and artificial rubber feedstock prompted massive government investment in refining capacity along the Texas coast. Military planners saw the Gulf of Mexico as a somewhat protected coast and diverted additional federal dollars to Texas and Louisiana. Furthermore, with the decision to construct pipelines from the southern coastal region to the Northeast, expansion of production capacity made economic sense. In the years following the war, the Gulf Coast remained the dominant refining region, claiming 32.2 percent of all refining capacity by 1956. Household demands for automobile fuel and also the development of chemical plants that consumed petroleum feed stocks drove the postwar expansion.[18]

Within Texas, crude oil extraction and petroleum processing represented vitally important elements of the economy. This was not lost on Texas politicians. Even before the war, Governor Lee O'Daniel made industrial expansion a cornerstone of his campaign in the late 1930s. He claimed that "the main thing is to build factories for our products and for our men and women to work in."[19] Organizations such as the Texas Industrial Commission worked to attract new industry to the state and to expand the sectors already present, particularly those that processed the state's natural resources. Their efforts paid off.[20] Texas crude processing increased from slightly more than 700,000 barrels per day in 1937 to over 1,300,000 in 1948.[21] Before the war (1937) seventy-nine petroleum refineries existed in the state. Shortly after the war, eighty-four establishments processed petroleum; by 1958 this number had climbed to eighty-eight. While the number of plants increased slightly between 1937 and 1957, the employee totals spiraled from 24,000 to over 41,000, reflecting internal expansion of plants along with the addition of new facilities. More important, dramatic growth occurred in the related production of petroleum feed stocks in chemical plants. Having only nine chemical plants in 1937, Texas attracted more than 400 new facilities by the end of the war. Between 1947 and 1957 the number of chemical plants increased from 433 to 543.[22]

Texas's petrochemical industry clustered in several key districts strung out along the Gulf Coast. The Houston–Galveston Bay area saw expansion of its well-defined node during the postwar period. Corpus Christi and Beaumont/Port Arthur also witnessed growth of established refinery clusters. Smaller coastal centers, such as Port Neches and Port Lavaca, and inland centers like Victoria and Alvin also experienced the construction of major facilities in the early 1950s.[23] By 1948 over 80 percent of the refining capacity of Texas existed in the coastal region.[24]

Access to petrochemical raw materials, Gulf of Mexico shipping, and fresh water at the mouth of seaward-flowing streams led to the clustering of petroleum and chemical processing along the Gulf Coast. This area of industrial concentration overlapped with important fisheries and an expansive habitat for migratory waterfowl.

EMERGING CONFLICTS

Conflicts between the state and oil and gas interests first erupted at numerous locations downstream from producing oil fields. In 1930 brine and oil releases

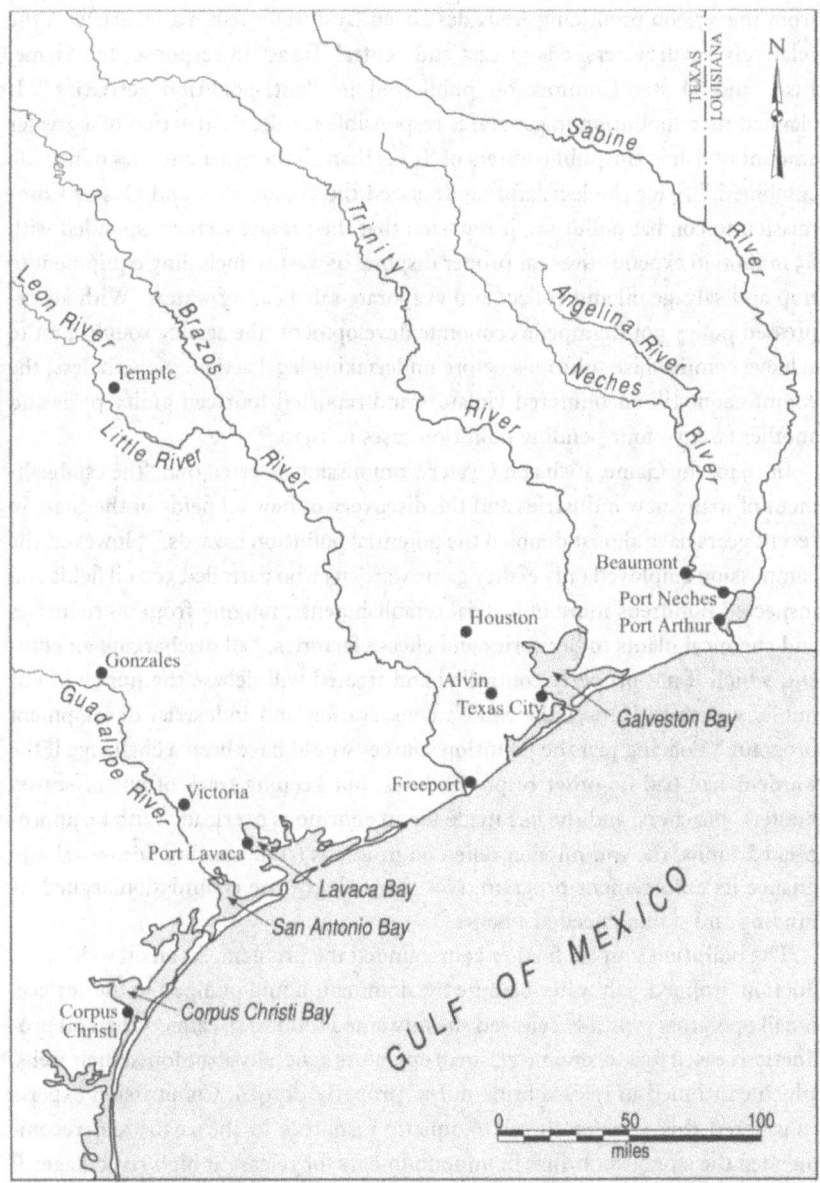

Map 1. Texas Gulf Coast Petrochemical Clusters and Rivers Involved in Pollution Incidents. Cartography by Mary Lee Eggart.

from the 37,000 producing wells destroyed freshwater fish, particularly in the relatively small watersheds of east and central Texas. In response, the Game, Fish, and Oyster Commission publicized its "anti-pollution activities." It claimed that "pollution in general is responsible for the destruction of a greater amount of fish in the public waters of Texas than all the other enemies of fish life combined." After the legislature authorized the Game, Fish and Oyster Commission to combat pollution, it reported that the private sector responded with $5 million in expenditures for proper disposal of wastes, including equipment to trap and salvage oil and collect and evaporate salt-bearing waters. With an expressed policy not to impede economic development, the agency sought first to achieve compromise solutions before undertaking legal action. Nonetheless, the commission still encountered violators and reported fourteen guilty pleas and another twenty-four pending pollution cases in 1930.[25]

In 1940, the Game, Fish and Oyster Commission asserted that "the establishment of many new industries and the discovery of new oil fields in the State in recent years have almost doubled the potential pollution hazards." However, the commission employed only eighty game wardens who patrolled 500 oil fields and inspected hundreds more industrial establishments, ranging from oil refineries and chemical plants to breweries and cheese factories, "all discharging an effluent, which if not properly controlled and treated will debase the purity of our public waters and upset the State's conservation and industrial development program." Policing just the pollution sources would have been a challenge if the wardens had had no other responsibilities, but keeping track of out-of-season hunters, poachers, and the like made for an enormous overload. With no appropriated funds, the commission relied on proceeds from hunting license sales to finance its enforcement program. Not surprisingly, the commission argued its funding and staffing needed a boost.[26]

The pollution sources further compounded the problem. As an oil well's production dropped, salt water became the dominant liquid pumped to the surface. Small operators typically released the unwanted fluid to streams. When oil production ceased to be economical, small operators generally abandoned their wells, which continued to release brine unless properly capped. Commission experts considered this a major threat to aquatic resources in the 1930s and recommended the storage of brines in impoundments for release at high river stages.[27]

Brine remained a primary concern of the Game, Fish and Oyster Commission in the early 1940s. It reported that "some of the most outstanding chemical and sanitary engineers in the Nation are employed by oil operators and industries to solve their waste problems" and claimed that "progress is being made." One solution involved injecting oil-field brine back into the earth. Done properly, this eliminated surface water pollution problems by returning the salty water to deep geologic formations.[28] Under pressure from the commission, oil producers in east Texas began deep-well injection of brine in 1938. Producers organized the East Texas Salt Water Disposal Company, and by 1943 it returned half the brine to subsurface formations. This relieved three rivers—the Sabine, the Angelina, and the Neches—of much brine pollution and provided protection against unwanted groundwater pollution.[29] Reinjection proved viable in the dense well fields of east Texas, but elsewhere, widely scattered producers commonly relied on earthen pits to hold the brines until released during flood stages. The commission recommended that the pits should be lined with "impervious material to prevent seepage into the ground waters."[30] When operators introduced excessive quantities of brine to a stream and caused salinity to exceed 2,000 parts per million (ppm), the state could and did assess fines and file suits requesting injunctions against polluting actions. The adoption of preventive measures led the commission to report in 1941 that complaints declined because operators sympathized with the law and responded to the commission.[31] Indeed by the end of the 1940s, operators of the East Texas Salt Water Disposal Company touted their system to industrial waste managers at the prestigious Purdue Industrial Waste Conference. They bragged that stream pollution there had been "eliminated" and that reinjected brine exerted pressure on oil deposits, enabling the recovery of huge quantities of oil. Thus, they were seeing direct economic benefits from efforts originally designed to stem stream pollution.[32]

Minimal enforcement during the war years resulted from limited supplies of gasoline for the game wardens and low revenues from sportsmen, many of whom were occupied elsewhere. Also, the commission was lenient with industries producing war materiel, particularly since they could not obtain the requisite equipment for adequate waste treatment systems. Nonetheless, complaints filed by commercial fishermen in Galveston Bay prompted the commission to investigate pollution caused by the Tex-Tin smelter at Texas City. A greenish discharge from the tin smelter caught the attention of fishermen, who suspected it was killing fish and oysters. Biologists sampled the water and sediments near the point of discharge and found accumulations of precipitated iron, but state investigators concluded that industrial pollutants had not damaged the oyster beds. Indeed, the prime oyster beds had been in decline since well before the smelter commenced operation. Despite some uncertainty about the cause of the oyster reef die-off, the state induced the smelter to investigate processes to reduce its iron discharges.[33] In sum, the state investigated the incident and sought a cooperative solution. This encounter between the commission and private industry shaped future practices.

Immediately following the war, the commission noted that wartime diversion of resources to production, at the expense of waste treatment, had contributed to stream pollution; and it charted a renewed antipollution effort for the coming years.[34] This program placed great demands on the Game, Fish and Oyster Commission's law enforcement division. Rapid industrial expansion, combined with a dry summer and low stream flow in 1947, created a troublesome situation—namely, too much effluent for streams to dilute. In a stepped-up effort, the commission appealed to oil-field operators and industries to control pollution at its source and install pollution abatement equipment in order to save the state's depleted waters from contamination. The response, apparently, was far from satisfactory. The following year (1948), the commission boasted that it had filed 113 criminal complaints and two injunction suits. In addition, fines collected jumped from $7,700 in 1947 to over $12,700 in 1948.[35]

Pollution problems began in the Guadalupe River basin before 1940, but climaxed during the late-1940s drought, when the state filed injunction suits against several oil-field producers. During the early stages of the field's development, producers near Luling discharged brines and oil wastes to the San Marcos River, which carried them into the Guadalupe River. As early as the 1920s, local entrepreneurs saw the economic potential in collecting the waste oil and constructed a trap that collected over 300,000 barrels of "fugitive" oil. The brines, however, remained a problem with no viable economic solution. After fouling the stream to the point where it could no longer serve as a domestic water source, the producers drilled water wells for two communities that had lost use of river water. In addition, they built a large brine retention pond to hold the effluent until the river was at flood stage and could accommodate the heavy salt loads. By the mid-1940s many wells in the Luling area were producing over 90 percent brine, causing severe stream pollution. Oil-field spokespeople assured state authorities that brine production would decrease as they shut down the declining wells. Nonetheless, brine continued to pour forth and destroyed the mussel population in the Guadalupe River.[36]

By the late 1940s, the Guadalupe and San Marcos (a principal tributary) rivers regularly carried brine in a concentration that exceeded the U.S. Public Health Service's standard of 250 parts per million (well below Texas's 2,000 ppm threshold for action in the 1930s). This endangered the downstream public water supply of Gonzales, and threatened planned water systems for Victoria and Cuero. Furthermore, the salt concentration destroyed aquatic life in certain stretches of the river. In response to these conditions, the state, in collaboration with three cities located along the Guadalupe River, filed a suit against operators in two oil fields and in 1948 won an injunction against several oil producers.[37] The state demonstrated to the court's satisfaction that the river had a low salt content above the point where the oil producers released their effluent and that the concentration below the oil field consistently exceeded safe levels. It also produced testimony that plant life and aquatic animals had disappeared from much of the stream. Based on the state's case, the district court held that several small producers created the high salt content, that their discharges posed a threat to community water supplies and to ranchers, that the brine was harmful to fish, and ultimately that these factors produced a public nuisance in violation of state law.[38] Cities Service, a larger and better financed operator, diverted its brine from the river via an injection well and earned an exemption from the injunction. On appeal, the oil producers argued that they had a right to discharge some of their effluent to the river and that an injunction was tantamount to a closure order. The appeals court affirmed the lower court's ruling and pointed out that the law simply prohibited the pollution of public water and that techniques were available to control discharges while continuing operations.[39]

This case merged public health and conservation concerns, without which the Attorney General might not have prosecuted. The State Department of Health assisted the conservation agency by dispatching engineers to evaluate the salt content of the water.[40] The fact that three downstream communities relied, or were planning to rely, on the river water, along with actual damage to fish and mussel life, provided sufficient impetus for legal action. Some of the most convincing testimony came, not from state game wardens, but from the State Department of Health, emphasizing the dual, if not more important, public health concern. Furthermore, the ruling turned on the state's public nuisance and trespass laws, and not the antipollution law that authorized the Game, Fish and Oyster Commission.

In subsequent cases, the state took legal action when pollution jeopardized public health as well as aquatic life. After oil producers fouled Tehuacana Creek (a tributary of the Trinity River, south of Dallas) in 1950, the state again filed suit asserting in its complaint that oil producers were killing fish while also damaging other water uses, such as irrigation and household consumption. On the eve of the trial, several producers sought a settlement, promising to install brine containment pits that were subject to inspection by the Game, Fish and Oyster Commission wardens. The named defendant constructed retention pits and also began injecting some brine back into the ground. This action prompted the state to seek a continuance while the remaining defendants complied. The other operators, however, continued to permit brine to escape into the river, according to the state inspector.[41]

Elsewhere, when oil field producers released brine to the Leon River (upstream from Temple), the state responded to the threat to a municipal water supply. After experiencing increasingly saline water, the City of Temple passed a resolution urging the state to take action. The Game, Fish and Oyster Commission, the Attorney General, and the Department of Health jointly held a public hearing in 1950 to evaluate the evidence. Following presentations from both sides, the state convinced the producers to install injection wells and holding pits to abate pollution of the Leon River. When high salt content in the river persisted during the summer of 1950, public health officials made regular inspections and reported on the slow progress made by the oil-field operators to construct pits and injection wells.[42] Thus, although the state conservation agency had policing and enforcement responsibilities, it cooperated with the public health agency, and in fact public health concerns triggered enforcement actions. Even joint action did not impel prompt remedies.

While these lawsuits all targeted relatively small oil-field producers, the industrial community was aware of the pollution suits.[43] The Game, Fish and Oyster Commission reported prosecuting 94 pollution cases in the fiscal year 1950–51 and issuing "notices of pollution" to "a large number of persons, firms, and corporations." These notices gave polluters time to remedy their situations before additional damages occurred.[44] In 1954 when the state first itemized the type of businesses it took action against, it reported taking enforcement steps against 55 oil field polluters and four against industries.[45] In subsequent years, a comparable ratio persisted.[46] Evidence that industry took note of the actions of the Game, Fish and Oyster Commission appeared in the trade literature. Chemical industry publications carried numerous stories about the pollution control efforts of large corporations moving to Texas. At the very least, the articles indicate that chemical producers sought a public relations benefit from their efforts while also evading conflict with the state.

When DuPont constructed a new plant on the banks of the Guadalupe River (the locale of the 1948 lawsuit Texas v. Magnolia Oil Company), it took steps "to avoid contamination of the Guadalupe River, of the fresh ground water, and of the atmosphere." In fact, a DuPont employee pointed out that "downstream are rice growing, shrimping, and fishing industries that are vital to the welfare of many residents and du Pont is obligated to avoid river contamination."[47] Toward that objective, DuPont brought in a team of biologists from Philadelphia's Academy of Natural Sciences to determine baseline stream conditions. By monitoring aquatic life, any change would reveal the deleterious effects of waste discharges. Such studies also provided DuPont with knowledge of conditions before its operation began so that it could defend itself against charges of stream damage. The biologists worked cooperatively with state agencies in compiling their data. They carried out two surveys before the plant opened, and a third a year and a half after it began operations. All three surveys found the stream in a "healthy" condition. In addition, they analyzed the shrimp and oyster populations where the Guadalupe River discharged into San Antonio Bay. A total of seven surveys found no evidence of bay pollution from the river.[48] Indeed, DuPont continued to support shrimp and oyster investigations in the bay into the early 1970s. When observers detected a massive oyster die-off in 1957, they attributed it to sediment brought into the bay by the floods that ended the 1950s drought.[49] Such an extensive pollution detection survey in a watershed where the state had sued polluters in the past suggests an awareness on the part of the manufacturing community and indicates an effort to avoid legal action oil-field producers had faced. A review of circuit court records in the coastal counties found no pollution cases filed against the new petrochemical manufacturers in the postwar years.[50] Nonetheless, when DuPont took on water-quality monitoring responsibilities, it assumed the state's duties and became its own watchdog. The lack of legal action, therefore, should not be a surprise.

In the wake of the Tex-Tin smelter waste controversy, Monsanto undertook a significant investigation of its wastes when adding a new production facility to its Texas City plant. It did not have data on the toxic effects of its wastes, and sought guidance from the Texas Game, Fish and Oyster Commission and its Marine Laboratory.[51] Working cooperatively with the state, investigators analyzed hydrocyanic acid and industrial wastes to determine what concentrations would harm aquatic life in Galveston Bay.[52] To establish the safe levels, they used existing laboratory methods on nongame species. The truly significant aspect of this investigation was that Monsanto and Texas employees coauthored the findings. Such cooperation was rare but indicated a capacity to produce results to which both the company and the state could attach their names. Even without established state standards, Monsanto was able to determine harmful levels of its wastes and develop a waste treatment system that it felt would safeguard the local environment.[53]

In the Houston–Galveston Bay area, industrial expansion and the associated risk of pollution was most pronounced. Drainage of some east Texas oil fields into the bay via the Trinity River accentuated the situation. Authorities recognized that industrial wastes presented different problems than sanitary sewage. Refinery effluent did not commonly carry the waterborne diseases found in municipal effluent, but it could contain toxic ingredients, deadly to humans or to the organisms that assisted in stream self-purification. One chemical plant in Houston had released arsenic, in high concentrations, just upstream from a popular swimming hole. Although no fatalities resulted, local authorities instituted a regular pollution survey. Yet their effectiveness was hampered by limitations in their analytical methods and by their inability to trace pollutants to specific sources in a highly industrialized district. Local officials recognized that industry was the life-blood of the southeast Texas economy, but sought to impress on manufacturers that surface water was a common resource and not a sink to be used exclusively as a sewer for industrial waste.[54]

One way to reach industry and encourage waste treatment was education. In 1950, as part of its regular short school on sewage treatment, Texas A&M University hosted a special symposium on industrial waste, which agency and industry personnel attended. R. F. Poston of the U.S. Public Health Service pointed out that industrial waste treatment lagged behind municipal treatment. In a state such as Texas, pollution of scarce waters actually could impede industrial expansion. Poston suggested that if industry accepted its responsibility to consider waste treatment as part of the manufacturing process and included treatment in its plants, then recourse to the courts might be unnecessary.[55] Industry presenters from DuPont and Humble Oil also expressed the view that treatment of troublesome wastes was important and that proper waste management was good business.[56] Sessions on industrial wastes remained on the program for the next several years and presented advice on treatment methods.[57]

Texas, through its conservation and public health agencies, actively promoted industrial waste treatment. Such a stance provided little hindrance to industries willing to accommodate the state, and suits against manufacturers remained a small portion of the total enforcement picture. Texas also implicitly turned over monitoring responsibilities to industry, and as one might expect, few enforcement actions followed such a delegation of authority. Consequently, enforcement actions focused on the smaller companies without resources to placate state officials. Changing environmental conditions, however, ushered in a second era of confrontation.

CHANGING CIRCUMSTANCES

Prosecution of small oil-field producers did not stem the flow of large industries relocating or expanding in Texas during the 1950s, but it made them aware of state pollution concerns and prompted them to tout their waste management systems in the trade literature. Taking this posture reflected both the public relations nature of the issue and the expressed position of major trade organizations to control pollution, especially at new or expanding plants. As early as 1948, the Manufacturing Chemists' Association (MCA) encouraged member companies to incorporate pollution control "from research through design to operation" in plant construction. This involved an assessment of local laws and environmental conditions. The MCA advised

> Whether so dictated or not, it is essential that investigations be made of location conditions, requirements, and trends concerning waste disposal, so that the design of the plant will include the facilities required for abating the discharge of excessive amounts of waste.[58]

By 1952 Union Carbide had constructed a petrochemical plant in Port Lavaca, on the upper end of Matagorda Bay, and included treatment facilities as part of the plant design. The waste treatment system's objective was to remove all traces of production materials before releasing the effluent to the environment. Union Carbide used a series of lagoons as its primary control method. The first lagoon collected oils on the surface, where they were burned. A vacuum truck removed heavier oils and solids to a second basin where biodegradation consumed them. From the lagoons, effluent drained into the bay where regular biological surveys, carried out in cooperation with DuPont, monitored for any adverse changes.[59]

The Jefferson Chemical Company opened a refinery at Port Neches in the late 1940s. Facing state concerns about effluents in the Neches River, the plant carried out internal investigations to develop a suitable treatment system for its waste—consisting largely of stripper bottoms (a process residue) and insoluble oils mixed with soluble organic compounds and some inorganic solids. At the time companies typically utilized biological treatment to break down organic wastes, but Jefferson Chemical's waste had an excessive oil content, plus the inorganic component. Over the course of several years Jefferson Chemical Company developed a means to separate a portion of the oils, adjust the pH of the process waste, and then treat the remaining effluent by biological means. To deal with the stripper bottoms, the company conducted toxicity studies to assess their effect on aquatic life. Its tests revealed that if diluted, filtered, and carbonated, the stripper bottoms were not toxic to fish in the Neches River. Although Jefferson carried out this work independent of the state, its efforts reflected the prevailing attitude of industry in the coastal area to cooperate with the state in preventing damage and its ability to find relatively simple solutions to effluent problems.[60]

Larger petrochemical plants being placed on line during the 1950s demanded more intensive waste management systems than previous operations. After a series of suits filed by the Harris County Health Department in 1955 and a request from the Game, Fish and Oyster Commission that industries along the Houston Ship Channel take steps to reduce pollution, Humble Oil publicized its pollution control efforts at its Baytown facility.[61] As a first step, Humble sought to diminish the overall volume of discharges. By installing cooling towers and reusing cooling water, the plant reduced one discharge component from 44 to 17 million gallons per day. Oil recovery systems eliminated the release of highly objectionable oily emulsions. Chemical wastes, particularly caustics, were neutralized and sent to a settling basin to reduce direct discharge to the channel. Humble also installed systems to recover chemicals for reuse, or if they could not be recovered economically, simply to remove them from the liquid waste stream. From 1950 to 1958, the refinery reported lowering oil content of its effluent from over 100 parts per million (ppm) down to an average around 32 ppm. Humble established a consistently neutral pH and reduced the suspended solids from over 150 ppm to below 60 ppm. These steps cut the biochemical oxygen demand of the waste stream from over 200 ppm to 53 ppm.[62] While Humble's presentation seemed impressive, it reflected a diversion of much effluent from water to land. This of course satisfied the Game, Fish and Oyster Commission with its responsibility for marine life.

Despite the efforts of some companies, sportsmen still voiced concern about producers overtaxing Texas streams' ability to handle large volumes of industrial effluent. In a public hearing before the renamed Game and Fish Commission, a resident on Adams Bayou (near Beaumont) pointed to refineries and chemical plants as the chief sources of damage to aquatic life. He cited eleven years' experience fishing along the bayou and noted that fishing had declined and that riparian forests were dying out. In his opinion, these were the consequences of pollution released from several major chemical producers in the vicinity. A spokesman explained the Game and Fish Commission's uneasy position. He pointed out that state government, with public support, was working diligently to attract industry and its payrolls to the state. He claimed that the commission was "fighting an uphill battle to try to bring these people [manufacturers] under regulation" and argued that the commission was making progress. He lamented that "we have to go and prove beyond any reasonable doubt in a Court-at-Law that they are harming, killing our fish population in our streams. Now, when you go to a Court with something like that, you really have to have the proof that they are harming the fish in the stream." He claimed that "a number of our worst cases, we have brought into Court and they have cleaned up. Under existing law, we can bring them into Court and fine them, but that doesn't mean much." He expressed the overall sentiment of the commission by saying that "if industry shows us that they are earnestly looking for methods to control it [pollution] by putting out an honest effort to clean it up, there is not much we can do but go along with them."[63] A retired game warden also vented his frustration with the system of the 1950s. He remarked that is was very difficult to convince a district attorney to file a suit against a local manufacturer for killing a few fish if the company also supported the local economy.[64] Although the state invested pollution control authority in the commission, the realities of local and state politics and economics limited its power. Still, there were exceptions to state officials' usually compliant stance.

The aggressive head of Harris County's Air and Water Pollution Control Unit, Dr. Walter Quebedeaux, challenged industries during the late 1950s, but he too found the system ineffective. When Quebedeaux sought to file complaints against major industries, the county attorney was reluctant to prosecute or called for unreasonable amounts of evidence. Nonetheless, Quebedeaux filed numerous suits with a few symbolic victories that imposed modest fines of $100 on the manufacturers. He also filed criminal charges against company executives, again with mixed success. His efforts got the managers' attention, but industrial growth outpaced pollution control efforts and water quality continued to deteriorate in Galveston Bay.[65]

Factors other than technology, politics, and the economy also entered into the equation, as severe drought embraced most of Texas in the mid to late 1950s and low precipitation resulted in low stream flows. Industrial and oil drilling expansion since the late 1940s meant more petrochemical processors and wells had lined the numerous small streams. This brought about an increased pollution load combined with diminished stream flow during the dry spell, which resulted in severe damage to aquatic life. Pollution enforcement actions had dropped to 86 cases in the fiscal year ending in August 1954. Two years later, during the serious drought, the number leaped to 143. The commission reported that it had received many fish-kill complaints and investigated them all. Of prime concern were releases from oil fields, but wardens found several other industries with "inadequate waste treatment facilities." The commission, recognizing that the drought was temporary, requested that the manufacturers "enlarge or improve their installations."[66] The following year (1957), when increased precipitation broke the drought, enforcement actions dropped to a still high 119, then fell back to 85 in 1958.[67] Diminished stream flows resulted in more pronounced pollution and prompted a vigorous response by the state, although once again the small producers situated on smaller streams were the primary target. During the mid and late 1950s, the pollution control laws remained virtually unchanged, yet enforcement actions varied considerably. Drought upset the delicate balance between cooperation and enforcement and revealed a state ready to challenge a segment of its most favored industry in extreme circumstances.

Legal actions taken by private citizens also targeted industry on occasion. In the mid-1950s a farm family that used Trinity River water for irrigation sued American Cyanamid for damages. They claimed that salts released by the company to the river from which they drew irrigation water stunted their crops. The local court found that the company had a right to use the stream for waste removal, but that right was limited and that its discharges posed a risk of injury to downstream water users.[68] State suits against major chemical producers were nonexistent in counties (other than Harris) where chemical companies reported installing major waste treatment systems during the 1950s.[69] Official state action, through the Game and Fish Commission, consisted of cooperative efforts with major petrochemical companies. Industry's response to state concern calmed the state's enforcement body and prevented frequent litigation.

CONCLUSION

The pollution control effort in Texas during the 1940s and 1950s contains two distinct currents: the consolidation of conservation and public health concerns and the inconsistent enforcement of state laws.

As Texas revised its pollution control laws during the 1940s and 1950s, it broadened the responsibilities of the enforcement community from sport and commercial aquatic life to include species that were not the object of fisherfolk, along with public water supplies. This merger of traditional conservation and public health concerns demonstrated a drift toward modern environmental issues by the late 1940s. Indeed, in order to make an effective case against stream polluters, state agencies had to collaborate and show damage to wildlife and water supplies. Even in a southern state with a reputation for guarding a favored industry from environmental regulation, there was an emerging "impulse" to abate industrial pollution.

Enforcement was inconsistent, however. Forceful action in the 1930s led to novel and cost-effective pollution control programs that benefited the oil drillers and the state. During the 1940s, the Game, Fish and Oyster Commission took aggressive action against small oil-field producers. Large manufacturers, although the object of some actions, assumed water-quality monitoring and standard-setting responsibilities and thereby usurped a role normally held by the state. They touted their pollution control programs in the trade literature and parlayed this campaign into a comfortable relationship with state agencies. Although county officials near Houston were not satisfied with the pollution control progress of manufacturers, the state did little to discourage industrial growth. Only during drought years did the state step up enforcement action.

Geographically, pollution control enforcement efforts focused on the upper reaches of small rivers, far from the Gulf Coast manufacturing districts. On these segments, brine or oil could obviously pollute streams and cause observable damage. It also presented a greater threat to municipalities drawing their drinking water from the streams. Near the river mouths and in the marine bays, dilution minimized the impact of effluent and made the detection of specific sources of pollution problematic. State policy and action concentrated on the most susceptible environments while sacrificing waterbodies in the coastal zone.

Industrial public relations did not ensure clean water; however, neither did the limited state efforts. By the early 1960s, there were obvious pollution problems that became more extreme as industry continued to grow. The ineffectiveness of Texas's water pollution control program rested in its inconsistent application of state law, and this contributed to the ultimate passage of environmental laws at the federal level in the 1970s.

Sweeping claims that the southern states ignored environmental concerns obscure the details of internal struggles at the local scale. Local citizens objected to pollution, and conservation agencies began the effort to protect wildlife and water from industrial discharges. Conflicting state policies that sought to lure industry while protecting water quality led to inconsistent pollution control efforts in Texas during the 1940s and 1950s. How common was this in other southern states? Was there a consistent balance of power between industry advocates and clean water proponents? Answers to these question will add texture to our understanding of pollution control in the postwar South.

NOTES

I would like to thank Phil Scranton, Joe Moore, Nancy Leigh, and an anonymous reviewer for useful comments on a preliminary draft, and Lisa DeChano for assistance with the fieldwork. Research support came from a Faculty Enhancement Grant from Southwest Texas State University. Also, I need to thank Mary Lee Eggart, who created the map.

1. Samuel P. Hays, "Three Decades of Environmental Politics: The Historical Context," in Michael J. Lacey, ed., *Government and Environmental Politics* (Baltimore: Johns Hopkins University Press, 1989), 19–80.

2. An excellent review of early wildlife exploitation and conservation policy development is found in Robin W. Doughty, *Wildlife and Man in Texas: Environmental Change and Conservation* (College Station: Texas A&M University Press, 1983).

3. In 1931 the Texas legislature prohibited the release of oil and oil-field wastes into the waters of the state, with some limited exceptions, and empowered the Game, Fish and Oyster Commission to enforce the act. "Prohibiting the Pollution of Streams: Chapter 42," *General and Special Laws of the State of Texas* (Austin: State Printing Office, 1931), 88–89.

4. See Water Resources Policy Commission, *Water Resources Law*, vol. 3 (Washington: Water Resources Policy Commission, 1950); Marvin Weiss, *Industrial Water Pollution: Survey of Legislation and Regulations* (New York: Chemonics, 1951); Manufacturing Chemists' Association, *Water Pollution Abatement Manual: Compendium of Water Pollution Laws* (Washington: Manufacturing Chemists' Association, 1959).

5. Federal dollars supported investigations of major sources of pollution. See Rolf Eliassen Associates, *Report of Study of Major Industrial Wastes from the Petrochemical Industries* (Cincinnati: U.S. Public Health Service, Robert A. Taft Sanitary Engineering Center, 1957).

6. See, "Anti-Pollution Bill: Chapter 285," *General and Special Laws of the State of Texas* (Austin: SPO, 1943), 418–19.

7. Emphasis added in quote, "Water Pollution Advisory Council—Creation—Powers: Chapter 353," *General and Special Laws of the State of Texas* (Austin: SPO, 1953), 868–69.

8. James C. Cobb, *Industrialization and Southern Society 1877–1984* (Lexington: University of Kentucky Press, 1984), 121–35.

9. Richard A. Bartlett, *Troubled Waters: Champion International and the Pigeon River Controversy* (Knoxville: University of Tennessee Press, 1995).

10. Theodore Steinberg, *Nature Incorporated: Industrialization and Water in New England* (Amherst: University of Massachusetts Press, 1991), 227–32.

11. Francis Gafford, "Antipollution Measures in Pennsylvania," *Journal, American Water Works Association* 41 (1949): 309–14; California State Water Pollution Control Board, *Water Quality Criteria* (Sacramento: California State Water Pollution Control Board, 1952), 423–32.

12. Louisiana Stream Control Commission, Proceedings of Meeting held at Baton Rouge, 15 May 1958–22 September 1966. Housed at the Louisiana Department of Environmental Quality, Baton Rouge, La.

13. John T. Cumbler, "The Making of an Environmental Consciousness: Fish, Fisheries Commissions, and the Connecticut River," *Environmental History Review* 15 (1991): 73–92; Donald J. Pisani, "Fish Culture and the Dawn over Water Pollution in the United States," *Environmental Review* 8 (1984): 117–31.

14. Joel A. Tarr, "Searching for a 'Sink' for an Industrial Waste: Iron-Making Fuels and the Environment," *Environmental History Review* 18 (1994): 9–34.

15. George B. Tindall, *Emergence of the New South 1913–1945* (Baton Rouge: Louisiana State University Press, 1967), 687–730; James C. Cobb, *The Selling of the South* (Baton Rouge: Louisiana State University Press, 1982).

16. James E. Anderson, Richard Murray, and Edward Farley, *Texas Politics: An Introduction* (New York: Harper & Row, 1971). When the state legislature assigned the Railroad Commission regulatory authority over the oil and gas industry, it reduced the economic chaos and fostered a friendly relationship between the industry and its regulator. The regulator also worked to keep taxes low and restrain pollution control efforts.

17. Railroad Commission of Texas, *Annual Report of the Oil and Gas Division* (Austin: Railroad Commission of Texas, 1940), 5–6; Railroad Commission of Texas, *Annual Report of the Oil and Gas Division* (Austin: Railroad Commission of Texas, 1948), 8; Railroad Commission of Texas, *Annual Report of the Oil and Gas Division* (Austin: Railroad Commission of Texas, 1959), 1.

18. Joseph A. Pratt, *The Growth of a Refining Region* (Greenwich, Conn.: JAI Press, 1980), esp. 65–95. See also Peter H. Spitz, *Petrochemicals: The Rise of an Industry* (New York: John Wiley & Sons, 1988).

19. "Industrial Texas!" *Epic Century Magazine* 5 (January 1939): 5–8.

20. "Raw Materials Situation in Texas, Parts 1 and 2," *Texas Business Review* 19 (November and December 1945): 7–17 and 4–17.

21. Dahl M. Duff, "Gulf Coast Refining," *Oil and Gas Journal* 47 (24 June 1948): 174–78, 226–30.

22. U.S. Bureau of Census, *Biennial Census of Manufactures*, Part 1 (Washington, D.C.: U.S. Department of Commerce, 1939), 644, 772; U.S. Bureau of Census, *Census of Manufactures*, 1947, vol. 3, Statistics by States (Washington, D.C.: U.S. Department of Commerce, 1950), 587; U.S. Bureau of Census, *Census of Manufactures*, 1954, vol. 3, Area Statistics (Washington, D.C.: U.S. Department of Commerce, 1955), 142-10-11; U.S. Bureau of Census, *Census of Manufactures*, vol. 3, Area Statistics (Washington, D.C.: U.S. Department of Commerce, 1961), 42-12.

23. See Arch L. Foster, "Celanese Corp.'s New Bishop Texas Petrochemical Operation," *Oil and Gas Journal* 47 (22 July 1948): 64–66, 75–77; J. V. Hightower, "Chlorine—Caustic Soda," *Chemical Engineering* 55 (December 1948): 112–16; "Petrochems at Corpus Christi," *Chemical Industries* 62 (May 1948): 738–40; "Gulf Coast Chemical Industry Continues to Expand," *Chemical and Engineering News* 26 (26 April 1948): 1214–15; F. Lawrence Resen, "E. I. du Pont de Nemours & Company, Orange, Texas," *Oil and Gas Journal* 51 (14 July 1952): 122–23; F. Lawrence Resen, "Shell Chemical Company, Houston," *Oil and Gas Journal* 51 (23 June 1952): 62–64; "Allied Dedicates Texas Plant," *Chemical and Engineering News* 32 (31 May 1954): 2184; F. H. Dotterweich, "Texas Top Spot in Petrochemicals—Here's Why," *Oil and Gas Journal* 53 (24 May 1954): 170–72;

and F. Lawrence Resen, "Dow Adopts Petroleum Techniques in Texas," *Oil and Gas Journal* 53 (24 May 1954): 165–69.

24. Duff, "Gulf Coast Refining," 176. For a discussion of plant location criteria, see Florence Escott, *Texas Plant Location Survey, 1955–1963* (Austin: University of Texas, Bureau of Business Research, Texas Industry Series No. 9, 1964).

25. Texas Game, Fish and Oyster Commission (TGFOC), *Year Book on Texas Conservation of Wild Life* (Austin: TGFOC, 1930), 97–101.

26. Texas Game, Fish and Oyster Commission, *Annual Report, 1939–1940* (Austin: TGFOC, 1940), 18–19.

27. A. H. Wiebe, J. G. Burr, and H. E. Faubion, "The Problem of Stream Pollution in Texas with Special Reference to Salt Water from the Oil Fields," *Transactions of the American Fisheries Society* 64 (1934): 81–86.

28. TGFOC, *Annual Report, 1939–1940*, 18–19.

29. J. G. Burr, "Preservation of Texas Streams," *Texas Game and Fish* 4 (September 1946): 18–19.

30. TGFOC, *Annual Report, 1939–1940*, 19.

31. TGFOC, *Annual Report, 1940–1941* (Austin: TGFOC, 1941), 24–26.

32. W. S. Morris, "Disposal of Oil-Field Salt Waters," *Proceedings of the Fifth Industrial Waste Conference* (Lafayette, Ind.: Purdue University, 1949), 243–51.

33. J. G. Burr, "Ferric Salt Deposits vs. Fish and Oysters," *Texas Game and Fish* 3 (1945): 16–17.

34. TGFOC, *Annual Report, 1942–1943* (Austin: TGFOC, 1943), 1; *Annual Report, 1943–1944* (Austin: TGFOC, 1944), n.p.; *Annual Report, 1945–1946* (Austin: TGFOC, 1946), 7.

35. TGFOC, *Annual Report, 1946–1947* (Austin: TGFOC, 1947), 8; *Annual Report, 1947–1948* (Austin: TGFOC, 1948), 10. Although the totals may seem trivial by today's standards, such fines could have significant impact on small producers. Furthemore, the difference between 1947 and 1948 represented an increase of nearly 65 percent.

36. J. G. Burr, "Luling Oil Fields and the San Marcos River," *Texas Game and Fish* 3 (May 1945): 10–11, 19.

37. State of Texas v. Magnolia Petroleum Company et al. (No. 81145), 126th District Court, Travis County, 1948. See also State of Texas v. Cities Service Oil Company et al. (No. 81247), 126th District Court, Travis County, 1948.

38. Magnolia Petroleum et al. v. State of Texas et al., Brief of Appellees, Court of Civil Appeals for the Third Supreme Judicial District of Texas at Austin, No. 9761 (1948), 8–9, Texas Attorney General Files (RG 302), Box 199/57-17, Archives Division–Texas State Library, Austin, Tex.

39. Magnolia Petroleum et al. v. State of Texas, 218 S.W. 2nd 855 (1949).

40. Texas State Department of Health, *Biennial Report, 1946–1948* (Austin: Texas State Department of Health, 1948), 46–48.

41. Case File, State of Texas v. C. L. Brown Jr. et al., District Court of Freestone County, Tex., 87th Judicial District (1950–52), Texas Attorney General Files (RG 302), Box 1991/51-17, Texas State Library–Archives Division, Austin, Tex.

42. Case File, State of Texas v. Lone Star Producing Company et al. (1949–51), Texas

Attorney General Files (RG 302), Box 1991/17-25, Texas State Library–Archives Division, Austin, Tex.

43. In the case State of Texas v. Allied Oil Company et al., the Texas Attorney General sought an injunction against oil fields along the San Marcos River in 1950. As in previous cases, the oil fields were releasing brine to the river. This situation prompted officials at DuPont in Victoria to express concern about the high chloride content of the river water they used at their plant. See Case File, Texas v. Allied Oil Company et al., Texas Attorney General Files (RG 302), Box 1991/17-25, file 50-131, Texas State Library–Archives Division, Austin, Tex.

44. TGFOC, *Annual Report, 1950–51* (Austin: TGFOC, 1951), 32.

45. TGFOC, *Annual Report, 1953–54* (Austin: TGFOC, 1954), 26.

46. In 1955 the state reported 65 actions against oil-field producers and 11 industries; in 1956 the numbers were 109 and 7 respectively, and for 1957 they were 80 and 10. TGFOC, *Annual Report, 1954–55* (Austin: TGFOC, 1955), 38; *Annual Report, 1955–56* (Austin: TGFOC, 1956), 45; *Annual Report, 1956–57* (Austin: TGFOC, 1957), n.p.

47. H. O. Henkel, "Surface and Underground Disposal of Chemical Wastes at Victoria, Texas," *Sewage and Industrial Waste* 25 (September 1953): 1044–49.

48. H. W. De Ropp, "Chemical Waste Disposal at Victoria, Texas, Plant of the DuPont Company," *Sewage and Industrial Wastes* 23 (February 1951): 194–97, and Henkel, "Surface and Underground Disposal."

49. Dabney Hart, Geraldine M. Gurka, and C. W. Hart, *Shrimp and Oyster Studies, San Antonio Bay, Texas, 1950–1972* (Philadelphia: Academy of Natural Sciences, 1975).

50. During the summer of 1997, with support from a Faculty Enhancement Grant from Southwest Texas State University, Lisa DeChano reviewed district court records in the primary refinery counties (excluding Harris County). She searched for cases with the refining companies as named defendants. No pollution cases existed for the years 1945 to 1960. The lack of cases does not prove either lack of enforcement or compliance with the laws, merely the absence of litigation.

51. Jack T. Garrett, "Toxicity Considerations in Pollution Control," *Industrial Wastes* (January–February 1957): 17–19.

52. F. M. Daugherty Jr. and Jack T. Garrett, "Toxicity Levels of Hydrocyanic Acid and Some Industrial By-Products," *Texas Journal of Science* 3 (September 1951): 391–96. See also F. M. Daugherty Jr., "A Proposed Toxicity Test for Industrial Waste to Be Discharged to Marine Waters," *Sewage and Industrial Wastes* 23 (August 1951): 1029–31.

53. Jack T. Garrett, "Toxicity Investigations on Aquatic and Marine Life," *Public Works* 88 (December 1957): 95–96. The lack of precise state standards was not uncommon at the time. Most enforcement actions relied on case-by-case determinations of what constituted pollution.

54. Frank Metyko, "Industrial Effluents and Marine Pollution," *Texas Journal of Science* 1 (March 1951): 45–52. This paper was presented to a seminar hosted by the Texas Game, Fish and Oyster Commission at its Rockport Marine Laboratory in 1949.

55. R. F. Poston, "The Stream Pollution Control Program and Some of its Aspects Related to Industry," *Proceedings of the 32nd Texas Water and Sewage Works Short School* (College Station: Texas A&M College, 1950), 138–40.

56. E. Q. Camp, "Simplifying Treatment by Separation of Wastes at the Source," *Proceedings of the 32nd Texas Water and Sewage Works*, 141–44, and H. W. de Ropp, "Possibility of Waste Disposal to Sub-surface Strata," ibid., 144–45.

57. See *Proceedings of the Texas Water and Sewage Works Short School* (College Station: Texas A&M College, 1951, 1952, and 1953).

58. Manufacturing Chemists' Association, *Organization and Method for Investigating Wastes in Relation to Water Pollution* (Washington, D.C.: Manufacturing Chemists' Association, 1948), 4.

59. R. L. Wright, "Treatment of Petrochemical Wastes at Port Lavaca, Texas," *Sewage and Industrial Wastes* 29 (September 1957): 1033–37.

60. Stripper bottoms were a process residue containing suspended solids in an alkaline solution. W. B. Davis, "A Laboratory Study for Biological Treatment of an Industrial Waste," *Pre-Printed Papers of the Third Annual Industrial Water and Waste Conference* (Houston: Rice University, 1963), 67–77.

61. See Bob Eckhardt, "How We Got the Dirtiest Stream in America," *Texas International Law Journal* 7:1 (1971): 9; TGFOC, *Annual Report, 1953–54*, Austin: TGFOC, 1954, 27.

62. Larry Resen, "Humble Attacks Pollution at Baytown," parts 1 and 2, *Oil and Gas Journal* 57 (5 October 1959 and 12 October 1959): 176–81 and 172–75.

63. R. S. McCauley (private citizen) and Charley Gray (Game and Fish Commission) Testimony, *Second Series of Game and Fish Commission Public Hearings* (1958), 48–49, Texas Parks and Wildlife Administrative Files (RG 802), Box 996–102, Archives Division–Texas State Library, Austin, Tex.

64. Carl Covert (retired game warden), telephone interview with author, 2 May 1997.

65. Eckhardt, "How We Got the Dirtiest Stream," 10–12.

66. TGFOC, *Annual Report, 1954–55*, Austin: TGFOC, 1955, 38; *Annual Report, 1955–56*, Austin: TGFOC, 1956, 45.

67. TGFOC, *Annual Report, 1956–57*, Austin: TGFOC, 1957, n.p.; *Annual Report, 1957–58*, Austin: TGFOC, 1958), n.p.; Robert Lowry, *Study of Droughts in Texas* (Austin: Texas Board of Water Engineers Bulletin 5914, 1959).

68. American Cyanamid v. M. G. Sparto, 267 F. 2nd 425 (1959).

69. Using a pair of contemporary state business directories, we compiled a list of new industries in the coastal counties. A review of circuit court defendant indices identified no pollution suits against the industries identified in the directories, excluding Harris County. The lack of suits suggests that industry made "good faith" efforts to prevent serious pollution. See Bureau of Business Research, *Directory of Texas Manufacturers*, (Austin: University of Texas, 1947 and 1952).

The Forest Is the Future?

Industrial Forestry and the Southern Pulp and Paper Complex

WILLIAM BOYD

> About five years ago I came to the conclusion that the Union Bag and Paper Corporation—without a Southern plant—would make about as much progress on the road to fame and success as Colonel Lindbergh would have made without an aeroplane.
>
> —ALEXANDER CALDER, President, Union Bag and Paper Corporation, 1936[1]

The 1930s proved to be a rather auspicious time for pulp and paper firms to establish operations in the South. Though there were already a dozen or so mills operating in the region, lingering concerns over the destruction of the southern timber resource and the appropriateness of immature southern pine as a furnish (raw material) for papermaking continued to raise questions in the board rooms of major northern paper manufacturers into the 1920s. By the 1930s, however, the so-called sap problem had been dispensed with,[2] and the preliminary results of the first forest surveys indicated that the southern forest, which had been under virtually continuous assault since the collapse of Reconstruction, was capable of rapid regeneration. Indeed, despite a series of government reports and hearings as well as rising public concern over the possibility of a national timber famine during the 1920s,[3] the so-called second forest that was growing up in the wake of the destruction of the South's old-growth forest testified both to the resilience of the timber resource and, more importantly, to the rapid growth rate of southern pine. At the same time, of course, southern states and towns, still reeling from the Depression, were eager for any sort of industrial development and provided generous incentives to pulp and paper mills seeking to locate in their areas.[4] Key raw materials—wood, water, and energy—abounded. Land and labor were plentiful and cheap. Unions were virtually nonexistent, and the big eastern markets lay close at hand. By the end of the decade, the South had radically reshaped the industry's competitive landscape.[5] Without a southern mill, as Alexander Calder suggested, it was unlikely that one would be able to remain in the business for long.

Thus began the "grand march South."[6] Between 1935 and 1940, fifteen new kraft mills were established in the region and pulping capacity more than doubled.[7] After a brief interruption due to war, the procession resumed at an even faster pace. By 1950, the South accounted for 55 percent of the total woodpulp production capacity in the United States, up from only 15 percent in 1929. Two decades later, the South had emerged as the undisputed leader in the production of pulp and paper, accounting for almost two-thirds of domestic woodpulp production and one-half of paper and paperboard production (see figure 1).[8]

If there were a signal event in this rather dramatic process of industrial relocation, it would have to be the 1936 decision by the Union Bag and Paper Company to build what would become the world's largest pulp and paper complex in Savannah, Georgia. With this move, the race was on to find and develop the most suitable sites for pulp and paper mills in the region. Because the new mills were massive by the standards of the day, reflecting the huge economies of scale available in kraft pulp and paper manufacture, their investments in fixed capital dwarfed anything previously seen in the forest products sector.[9] Unlike the small "peckerwood" sawmills that could be moved in search of new timber supplies, these new pulp and paper mills weren't going anywhere. Operating under an imperative to keep their fixed capital in motion, many of these mills ran twenty-four hours a day, seven days a week. Their appetites for water, energy, and timber were almost inconceivable.[10] As a result, the mills depended for their timber on what could be grown in their immediate procurement areas (a 100–150 mile radius). The earlier extractive logic employed by the lumber industry no longer sufficed. A new regime in forest management would be necessary.[11]

As the pulp and paper industry expanded in the South, industrial advocates throughout the region heralded the dawn of a new age. Echoing the boosterism of Henry Grady, the *Savannah Morning News* proclaimed that the Union Bag plant signaled a "New Industrial Epoch" for southeast Georgia, noting that the "lowly pine tree . . . has taken on a new aura of grandeur and significance as a symbol of vast potential wealth."[12] Speaking at a banquet celebrating the formal opening of the Union Bag plant, Savannah mayor Thomas Gamble pointed to the vast new opportunities awaiting his city and the South: "No one can safely limit the possibilities which center in the pine tree and its various possible products. . . . We apparently are on the threshold of discoveries which will incalculably broaden the use of products common to our section. The South, especially

Figure 1: Woodpulp Production in the Southern United States

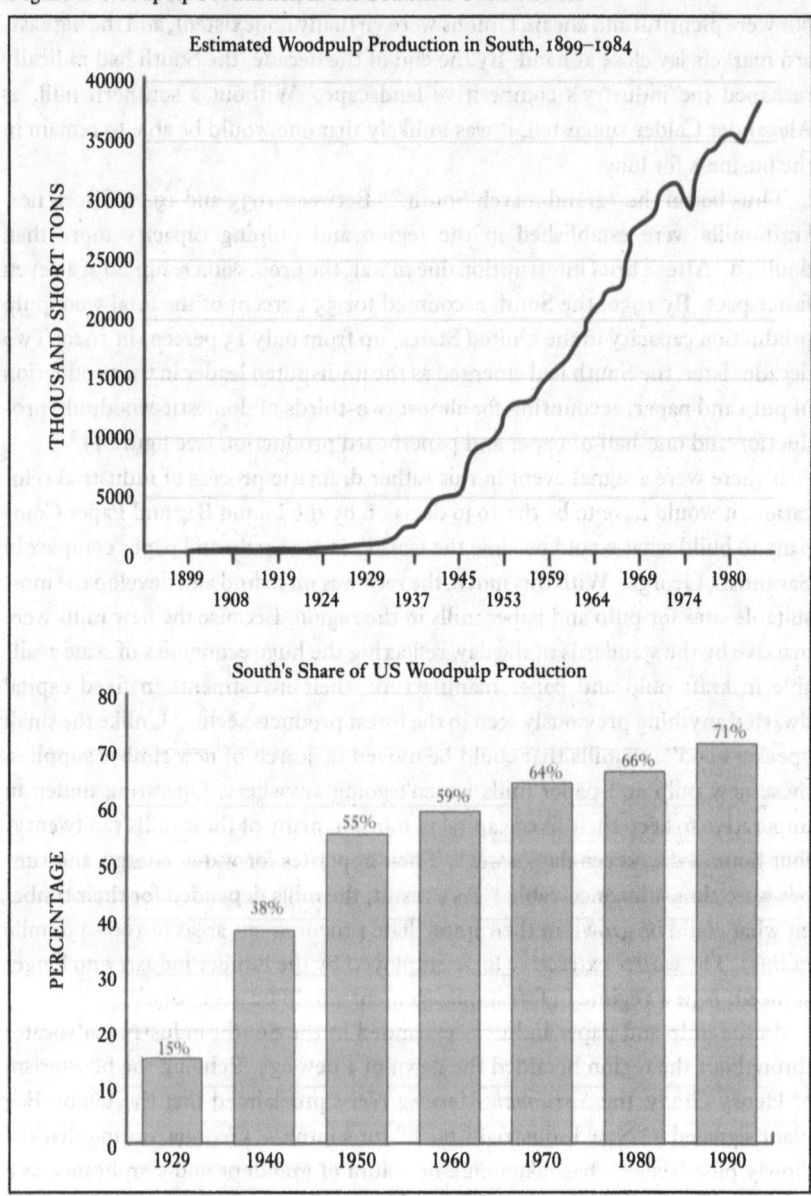

Sources: U.S. Forest Service, *The South's Fourth Forest: Alternatives for the Future*, Forest Resources Report no. 24 (Washington, D.C.: GPO, 1988), 329, table 2.27; U.S. Forest Service, *An Analysis of the Timber Situation in the United States: 1952-2030*, Forest Resource Report no. 23 (Washington, D.C.: GPO, 1982), 298-99; American Forest & Paper Association, *Paper, Paperboard, and Woodpulp Statistics* (Washington, D.C.: AF&PA, 1995), 49. South includes: Del., Md., Va., W.Va., N.C., S.C., Ga., Fla., Tenn., Ky., Ala., Miss., Tex., Okla., Ark., La.

our own immediate territory, is recognized as a coming industrial empire. A new world seems to be opening before us. Savannah must be prepared to enter and possess it."[13] By the end of 1947, slightly more than a decade after Union Bag opened its mill, Savannah's last cotton compress had been dismantled. King cotton, which had shaped the fortunes of the city for so long, had been replaced by the pine tree as the new staple of regional economic development.[14] As a *New York Times* reporter put it: "The industrializing of the New South is being dramatically illustrated in Savannah, as cotton is no longer brought here and the old river and wharves support a new business that still draws upon the countryside and the farmer. The cotton farmer has been succeeded by the tree farmer in a large section of the South. The pine tree has become the new cash crop."[15]

Such proclamations, of course, had to be tempered with the massive logistical and institutional challenges involved in providing these new pulp and paper mills with a continuous source of fiber. This supply problem had two essential components. First, a new forest management regime would have to be constructed to ensure that timber was treated as a crop rather than as a mine. Moreover, because small farmers and other small private landowners owned two-thirds or more of the timberland in the South (a fact which meant that pulp and paper mills depended on such owners for more than half of their overall fiber supply), it was not enough to establish such a regime solely on industry-owned lands. The small southern landowner also had to be persuaded, through education and incentives, of the "virtues" of viewing timber as a crop. Given the long time lags associated with growing timber, the tremendous risks and uncertainties involved, and the perverse incentives embedded within prevailing tax and credit systems, this was no easy task. The second component of the supply problem, which was perhaps even more challenging, involved securing access to the small landowners' timber and getting the wood to the mills. Accomplishing this, of course, meant that the new mills would have to engage the institutional realities of the rural South, particularly those involving land and labor. Again, no easy task.

This chapter will focus explicitly on the first of these two aspects of the timber supply problem. After a brief discussion of the state of the southern forest in the 1920s and 1930s, it will examine the transition to industrial forestry that transpired in the South during the interwar and postwar years and transformed timber into the region's number one cash crop.[16] This transition, which went into high gear during the 1950s, had its origins in the progressive conservation era and the New Deal and represented a rather remarkable example of public-private cooperation aimed at rationalizing the use of a renewable resource in the interest of efficiency and industrial development. Three major phases marked the transition: (1) *Rationalization:* the creation of a more stable environment for investment in timber growing, particularly through improved fire protection and management; (2) *Regeneration:* the reforestation and afforestation of cut-over and marginal agricultural lands; and (3) *Intensification:* the acceleration of biological productivity through advances in forest genetics and tree improvement. Within these three phases, which were overlapping and complementary, a complex and changing division of labor between federal, state, and private actors emerged. New institutions would have to be constructed. Extensive cooperation would be required. The whole process, moreover, was part of the larger agrarian transition taking place in the post–New Deal South—a transition marked by the decline of cotton tenancy, the industrialization of agriculture, the opening up of rural labor markets, and the transformation of southern land use. By the 1960s, the combined effect of such processes was manifest in the establishment of the South's "third forest," much of which was the result of artificial regeneration.[17] The South was on its way to becoming the wood basket of the world.

The emphasis of this chapter is thus decidedly more upstream than most studies of the pulp and paper industry, not to mention those of southern industrialization. There are two main reasons for such a focus. First, most general studies of twentieth-century southern industrialization and southern economic history have paid very little attention to the forest products sector and almost none whatsoever to the attendant rise of industrial forestry in the region during the interwar and postwar decades. Second, to divorce a study of the pulp and paper industry from the timber supply issue would miss some of the more important and distinctive elements associated with resource-based industrialization. Indeed, one could argue that, in the South at least, the complex set of challenges involved in subordinating biological systems to the dictates of industrial production, in the context of a particular regional institutional matrix, represented one of the more difficult tests facing firms attempting to construct a viable and competitive industrial form in the region. The outcome, as suggested, depended heavily on the construction of new institutions for public-private cooperation and new patterns of state intervention.

Given the importance of such state actions and the overall instrumentalization of nature that resulted, one could view the entire process as an example of what James Scott calls "state simplification," that is, a state-directed project aimed at achieving legibility and control over nature in pursuit of commercial gain.[18] Such an emphasis, however, would miss important elements of a story that is also very much about industrialization as a process of regional collective learning, whereby the institutional arrangements that facilitated the "making" of industrial timberlands function as vital elements of a larger industrial system.[19] Viewed in this way, the evolving organizational capabilities of particular firms, to use Alfred Chandler's language, are embedded in a larger process of building what Gavin Wright refers to as networks for collective learning and knowledge accumulation.[20]

That these networks were primarily regional in scope raises some interesting questions regarding southern industrialization. In contrast to arguments about the lack of an "indigenous technological community" that served to reinforce the South's status as late developer, it is quite clear that in the case of industrial forestry just such a community was starting to emerge in the region during the interwar years.[21] Moreover, because this community played such an important role in the rise of the South as a national and international leader in the forest products sector, one has to question the utility of applying traditional comparative advantage approaches to southern industrialization. The emergence of a distinctively southern pulp and paper industry, in other words, cannot be explained simply as the result of regional comparative advantage in key factors of production and the successful attraction of branch plants controlled largely by northern corporations. One must also attend to the ways in which these firms, in concert with other actors, mobilized and organized the productive capacities of southern land and labor and integrated them into a highly competitive industrial form. Regional advantage, from this perspective, is not simply derivative of factor endowments, but is instead a historically situated process of social construction.[22]

THE SLAIN WOOD

> The plain truth of the matter is that in county after county, in state after state of the South, the piney woods are not passing but *have passed*. Their villages are Nameless Towns, their monuments huge piles of sawdust, their unwritten epitaph: "The mill cut out!" Locally the catastrophe has already arrived of a vanished industry, unreplaced by any new industries remotely adequate to redeem the situation.
> —R. D. FORBES, "The Passing of the Piney Woods," 1923[23]

From the end of Reconstruction to the close of World War I, the southern forest suffered unmitigated destruction. Spurred by a growing domestic market for lumber and the prospect of timber depletion in the heavily cut-over Great Lakes states, speculators and lumbermen moved into the South during the last decades of the nineteenth century to capture the spectacular resource rents available in extensive stands of old-growth timber being sold at nominal prices. As they had done in the Lakes states, the lumbermen cut the southern forest with unprecedented haste. They operated according to a logic of extraction, their imperative: "cut and get out." By 1920, their work was virtually complete, with the cut-over area in thirteen southern states estimated at more than 156 million acres. Most of this cut-over land, perhaps as much as 100 million acres, was in the yellow pine belt stretching from South Carolina to Texas. In that region, estimates indicated that less than 24 million acres of old-growth pine timber remained in 1920.[24] One government forester, who surveyed the region at the height of the cutting, assessed the situation as "probably the most rapid and reckless destruction of forests known to history."[25] William Faulkner called it simply: "the slain wood."[26]

The forces driving such rapid exploitation are fairly easy to discern. By the early 1880s, concern over timber depletion in the Lakes states was mounting. In 1884, Harvard Professor Charles S. Sargent issued his famous *Report on the Forests of North America*, arguing that current rates of timber extraction in the Lakes states were unsustainable while also highlighting the vast expanse of old-growth timber available in the states of the South and the Pacific Northwest.[27] Meanwhile, the South was emerging from war and Reconstruction, with the newly ensconced "Redeemer" governments intent on opening up the region to outside capital. Land policies, such as the numerous state sales to railroads and other interests and the 1876 repeal of the Southern Homestead Act of 1866, which permitted unrestricted cash entry into the public land states of the region, provided substantial opportunities for acquisition of vast tracts of timberland. The availability of a mobile, "flexible" workforce made up largely of itinerant freedmen ensured that labor costs would be well below those prevailing in other lumber-producing regions.[28] Finally, the growing national consensus that yellow pine made good merchantable lumber, combined with the proximity to eastern markets and the massive expansion of railroads in the region during the post-Reconstruction decade, gave the South considerable comparative advantage vis-à-vis other lumber-producing regions.

Although early conservationists had voiced concern over timber depletion and the lack of conservation in the South since the turn of the century,[29] it was not until the 1910s and 1920s that the issue began to receive serious attention at the national level. During this time, the voice heard most often on the subject was that of Gifford Pinchot, the man credited with introducing the term "timber famine." In 1919, Pinchot authored a report for the Society of American Foresters that predicted an imminent timber shortage. This prompted Kansas Senator Arthur Capper to request a Forest Service study of the timber supply situation. The resulting document, known as the Capper report, fueled the ongoing debate over timber supply and the role of federal policy in regulating forest practices.[30] Based on an assemblage of previously collected information, the report provided data on trends in depletion, prices, trade, and concentration of timberland ownership in all of the major producing regions. The authors identified timber depletion as the "fundamental problem" underlying the decline of interregional competition, increased scarcity of timber products, rising prices, and the growing concentration of timberland ownership in the United States.[31] In the southern pine region, the Capper report estimated that four-fifths of the original yellow pine forests had been cut since 1870, and classified more than 30 million acres of cut-over lands (almost a third of the original pine forest) as "not restocking."

With an annual cut that exceeded annual growth by a factor of three, the report predicted that the southern yellow pine industry would soon cease to be a national factor and that by the early 1930s the South would be importing lumber from the Pacific Northwest to meet its own consumption needs.[32] In light of the systematic neglect of conservation, state and federal foresters feared that the second-growth timber in the region would be unable to support a substantial forest products industry in the future. Major George P. Ahern of the U.S. Forest Service captured such fears when he concluded in 1928 that "The end of virgin timber in the South is definitely in sight, while already the younger timber is being cut as fast as it grows."[33]

Had the South traded the possibility of a stable, long-term industry for short-term profit, much of which was captured by interests from outside the region? Would there be enough timber to support a lumber industry in the future, not to mention the nascent pulp and paper industry? No one really knew for there had been no systematic survey of the forest resources of the South. Many simply assumed the worst. Added to such uncertainty were the tremendous obstacles to be faced: investments in conservation, funds for forest regeneration, and the imposition of a new forest management regime. Forest fires, for example, ravaged the southern woods well into the 1940s, undermining efforts to promote the long-term investments required for timber growing. Tax policies, particularly at the county level, also provided a source of risk and uncertainty as to the long-term tax obligations associated with timberland ownership. Insects and disease threatened the viability of young trees, especially those already weakened by turpentining and wildfire. Finally, the unpredictability of timber markets, exacerbated both by endemic overproduction and the growing concern over the future of the industry in the region, added to a highly unstable and shifting investment environment that offered few incentives to invest systematically in forest protection and regeneration. In short, before the forest could be regenerated, before prudent investments in tree improvement could be made, the landscape of timberland investment would have to be made amenable to rational economic calculation.

RATIONALIZATION

> The chief obstacle to forestry in the South is the destruction caused by forest fires. Fires run riot in the pineries, lay waste the cut-over lands, and constantly endanger, often seriously damage the virgin timber. They set a premium upon premature, hasty, and destructive logging, and effectually discourage the holding of forest land for a continuous succession of crops, even for a single additional crop. As long as they go unchecked they will furnish lumbermen and forest owners with an unanswerable argument in support of their present de-

> structive methods. Unless fires are checked, forestry in the Southern pineries will never appeal to men of good business sense.
> —GIFFORD PINCHOT, "Southern Forest Products, and Forest Destruction and Conservation since 1865," 1910[34]

Fire was, by virtually all accounts, the chief obstacle standing in the way of rational, scientific forestry in the South during the early twentieth century. Yet the fire problem was compounded by the almost complete lack of reliable information on the state of the southern timber resource. Any successful effort in fire control, as part of a larger program of scientific forestry, thus required an accurate assessment of the volume and distribution of the timber resource, its condition and quality, the various threats facing it, and the ratio of annual growth to annual drain.[35] In the absence of such information, systematic forest land-use planning would be impossible, and the large investments in fixed capital and forest management necessary for a successful pulp and paper operation would be very difficult to justify. Indeed, despite all the reports and hearings about timber depletion and forest destruction during the 1920s, no one could speak with certainty about the actual state of the southern forest resource. The task of accomplishing a regional forest survey (there were almost 200 million acres of timberland in the twelve states of the South) was mind-boggling. Even in a single state, the financial and logistical requirements of developing an accurate assessment of the timber resource greatly exceeded the capacities of state governments and private firms. Such an undertaking clearly required federal assistance.

In 1928, the McSweeny-McNary Forest Research Act authorized the first nationwide forest survey. Major objectives included a field inventory of timber supplies, an accurate estimate of annual growth and annual drain, and an assessment of management options and public policies necessary for "the most effective and rational use of land suitable for forest production."[36] For the southern states, the survey began in 1931 under the direction of the Southern Forest Experiment Station in New Orleans.[37] Professional foresters carried out field-level inventories and assessments for individual states, which were divided into clusters of counties known as Forest Survey Units. It was, at one level, a gigantic timber cruise. Nothing on such a scale had ever been attempted before.

Given the magnitude of the task, it took the better part of a decade before the final results were available. As the preliminary results of early subregional surveys were released in the mid to late 1930s, however, they revealed a somewhat surprising recovery of the southern pine forest.[38] Despite decades of extensive logging, an almost complete neglect of conservation, and widespread incidence of forest fires, young second-growth pine had naturally regenerated over a wide area, including large acreages of abandoned or idled cropland.[39] Timber, which was already reclaiming many abandoned fields, was arguably the highest and best use for such lands.

Yet, although the surveys revealed a larger volume of timber than previously thought to exist, they also showed considerable pressure on the timber resource. In roughly half of the area surveyed, timber drain exceeded timber growth. The vast majority of southern timberlands, moreover, exhibited widespread damage due to fire, adding to the general lack of positive incentives for investment in scientific forestry. In the state of Georgia, for example, the forest survey found that fires had occurred in the previous few years on more than three-fourths of the state's total forest area. Half of the damaged area lay in south Georgia, where cattlemen and turpentine operators used fire extensively to improve grazing conditions and to protect turpentine orchards from uncontrolled fires. Overall, fire represented the direct or indirect cause of three-fourths of the state's pine timber mortality. For 1937 alone, some 3.75 million acres (18 percent of the total forest area) had been burned over. Echoing Pinchot and others, the report concluded that "frequent and indiscriminate forest burning has long been the most important factor militating against the development of well-stocked timber stands" and that the "first and most important step in the rebuilding of Georgia's forests is the control of the fire situation."[40] In short, without systematic investment in forest fire protection and forest management, southern timberlands would never reach their economic potential.

The forest survey was thus far more than a gigantic timber cruise. In addition to providing southern states with the first accurate assessment of their respective timber resources and the ratio of growth to drain, the survey came at a time when many pulp and paper firms were considering whether or not to establish operations in the South. By providing a realistic portrait of the southern timber resource as well as an indication of its potential, it undoubtedly stimulated an already growing interest in the South and facilitated the further expansion of the industry in the region. Yet the survey also raised concerns about the future of the southern timber resource, particularly if large pulp and paper mills continued to establish themselves in the region, consuming an ever larger share of the young second-growth timber in the area. In this respect, the survey represented a very important intervention in the emerging discourse on forestry practices in the South, particularly in the context of fire control.

Forest fires, of course, had long been a vital part of the landscape of the rural South. Annual woods-burning, a common practice throughout the region since the arrival of the first human inhabitants, was practiced extensively during the late nineteenth and early twentieth centuries, both to control the so-called rough or understory that grew so vigorously in the southern forest and to improve livestock grazing and eliminate pests. In times of drought, southern fires often assumed massive proportions. Most fires, however, burned low, marching slowly through the woods damaging grown trees and destroying younger trees and seedlings. As statistics on wildland fire began to be collected in the early twentieth century, it became clear that the South accounted for the vast majority of wildland fire in the United States, in terms of both frequency and acreage burned.[41] According to the Regional Committee on Southern Forest Resources, during the 1920s and 1930s, the South accounted for 85 percent of all forest fires in the country and more than 90 percent of the burned-over acres, despite the fact that it contained less than one-third of the nation's total forest area. Roughly 40 percent of these fires were suspected to be of incendiary origin, a consequence of the deep-seated cultural practice of annual woods-burning. Fire, in short, was part of the very fabric of rural life in the South.[42]

With the advent of industrialized logging—railroads, steam skidders, and trucks—fire simply had alternative vectors along which to travel. As rail and road opened up new tracts of timber, the scope of fire increased. Such widespread and growing incidence of fire, however, was hardly compatible with industrial forestry. Not only did fire prevent natural regeneration of certain pine species on cut-over lands, but it also provided a major disincentive to invest in artificial regeneration. With wildfires ravaging the southern woods, investments could all too easily go up in smoke. For early conservationists such as Gifford Pinchot, this represented the single greatest challenge facing southern forestry. Echoing these sentiments, W. W. Ashe, the secretary for the national forest reservation committee, wrote in 1925 that "Without adequate protection [from fire], especially for cut-over lands, all methods of management on private lands are futile."[43] By the early twentieth century, conservation and forest regeneration had become intimately bound up with the political economy of fire in the rural South.

Put simply, for industrial forestry to succeed, a new "cycle of fire" would have to be constructed for the region—one subordinated to the needs of industrialism and scientific management rather than to the rhythms of rural life.[44] Given that the majority of the region's timberland was owned by small farmers and private landowners, many of whom practiced annual woods-burning, the institutional challenges of systematic fire protection were very large indeed. People had to be persuaded of the value of the forest and the detrimental effects of woods-burning. The physical and institutional infrastructure for fire protection had to be established. Huge sums of money would be needed.

Institutionally, such a program would have to be built upon cooperation between state and federal agencies, the forest products industry, and private landowners. Because fire did not respect political or administrative boundaries, moreover, a successful strategy required a regional focus. Fire control, to put it crudely, represented a collective action problem that demanded new forms of coordination. Thus, although organized fire protection had been practiced piecemeal in the South since the turn of the century—primarily on the lands of several large lumber companies and through the experimental activities of several state agencies and cooperative associations—it was not until the 1910s and 1920s that the first systematic efforts at developing a coordinated effort were made. The U.S. Congress took its first statutory steps in this direction in 1911, when it enacted the Weeks Law, which provided matching funds for state agencies engaged in fire protection. Although progress under the law proved to be quite slow in the South, due to limited funding and a general reluctance among state governments to embrace the new regime of fire protection, the Weeks Law did establish fire protection as a legitimate area of cooperation between federal and state agencies. Picking up where Weeks left off, the Clarke-McNary Act of 1924 gave fire protection efforts a significant boost. By 1930, federal cooperative funding for fire control in the South had grown in nominal terms from nothing to about $400,000, while state funding had increased to $750,000.[45] Almost 70 million acres of southern timberland (out of roughly 230 million) received some form of fire protection (see table 1). Of course, this was a modest share of what would ultimately be required to realize the goal of regionwide fire protection in the South. But it was a start.

Beyond the challenge of establishing an institutional infrastructure and providing adequate funding for fire protection, perhaps the most difficult task associated with fire control was that of educating and persuading rural southerners to abandon their deeply ingrained practice of woods-burning. Federal and state agencies, conservation groups, and forestry associations all worked throughout the 1920s and 1930s to spread the gospel of fire protection through publications, films, rallies, conferences, informal meetings, and technical reports. Calling for "strict accountability" for "the man who burns the woods," one U.S. government pamphlet compared the southern woods burner to the "boll weevil, the malaria germ, and the cattle tick." "Because of him," the report charged,

> land values have suffered, industries and population have moved out, and idle acres have multiplied. Because of him every year millions of young forest seedlings, which in short time would have constituted a valuable asset to landowners, have been licked up by flames. . . . The South cannot afford to let the woods burner block economic progress. . . . The irresponsible burner must be banished from the woods, and the well-intentioned burner must squarely face the responsibility incurred when he starts fire on his own land."[46]

The report then concluded with a plea for collective action: "No one agency alone can cope with this situation. All private landowners, all Southern States, and the Federal Government must agree on a common course of action and work together to put an end to forest destruction."[47]

As state forestry associations developed throughout the South, new rules and regulations stiffened the penalties for arson.[48] Woods-burning was criminalized, while fire control was transformed into a moral crusade. Starting in 1928, the American Forestry Association launched a three-year, multistate tour of the South to educate rural folks about the dangers of woods-burning. The Dixie Crusaders, as the members of the fire prevention caravan were known, traveled 300,000 miles through the deep South, holding rallies, distributing pamphlets, and showing self-produced movies to some three million people. One state forester described the fire prevention caravan as one of the most important events in the history of southern forest protection—"the first mass effort toward the solution of the South's woodland fire problem."[49]

Drawing explicitly on the military analogy, fire control and fire protection assumed an unprecedented sense of moral urgency during the early 1930s.[50] The establishment of the Civilian Conservation Corps in 1933 created a virtual army of firefighters. Though most often remembered for their efforts in planting trees throughout the United States, the young men of the CCC also fought fires and constructed the roads, bridges, trails, fire towers, and telephone lines that provided much of the physical infrastructure needed for fire control in timber-producing regions such as the South. By 1942, when the CCC disbanded, the amount of southern acreage under fire protection had increased to almost 90 million acres.[51]

Through its fire protection work, the CCC also bestowed a certain legitimacy upon the use of prescribed burning as a tool for fire control in the South, an issue that provoked considerable debate among foresters in the United States well into the 1940s.[52] Early proponents of prescribed burning, such as Austin Carey and H. H. Chapman, argued eloquently for "proper" burning as a means for controlling wildfires and, more importantly, as a tool for stimulating forest regeneration in the South. In an early article (1912), Chapman argued that "to keep fire entirely out of southern pine lands might finally result in complete destruction of the forests."[53] Later, in 1926, Chapman issued his famous Yale School of Forestry Bulletin number 16, which caused a great stir throughout the southern forestry profession, arguing directly for the use of fire in longleaf pine regeneration.[54] Six years later, the U.S. Forest Service adopted a policy statement which admitted that fire could play a constructive role in longleaf pine culture. The following year, the Southern Forest Experiment Station issued its own twenty-three point "Fire Statement," allowing for the judicious use of fire for both silvicultural and forest management practices.[55] Not until 1935, however, did the prohibition on controlled burning under the Clarke-McNary Act formally end. Moreover, only after another series of disastrous fires between 1941 and 1943, fueled by a combination of drought and the accumulation of debris on the forest floor, did professional opinion actually begin to shift in favor of prescribed burning. In the wake of these fires, Lyle Watts, chief of the U.S. Forest

Service, reversed policy and initiated a program of prescribed burning in southern national forests.[56]

It was not until the 1950s, however, that southern states developed formal institutions for multistate cooperation in fire control and for forest fire research. In 1956, state governments signed two regional fire protection compacts (southeastern and south central) to coordinate efforts and resources among the various southern and federal agencies involved in fire control.[57] Three years later, the U.S. Forest Service established the nation's first forest fire laboratory in Macon, Georgia. The Southern Fire Lab, as it was known, conducted research on fire ecology and hosted a series of important seminars on prescribed burning for the fire control community. Beginning in 1962, the Tall Timbers Research Station at Tallahassee, Florida, also began hosting a series of annual fire ecology conferences. In the view of one southern fire expert, the Tall Timbers organization "became almost overnight the outstanding force for exposition and promotion of fire ecology and controlled burning in the entire world."[58] By the 1960s, the southern forestry community had firmly established itself at the vanguard of industrial fire control.[59]

For the twelve southern states,[60] as table 1 indicates, fire protection expenditures increased consistently throughout the post–New Deal period, peaking in 1970, while the amount of protected acreage grew until the early 1980s, at which time roughly all of the timberland in the region was under some form of fire protection. In Georgia, a leading state, fire control expenditures increased by 150 percent between 1950 and 1957, while protection expanded to roughly 21 million acres of timberland (close to 90 percent of the state's timberland).[61]

As a result of the increased investment in fire protection, between 1925 (a peak year for fire damage) and 1965, timberland burned annually in the southern states fell from over 21 million acres to slightly less than 600,000 acres. With increased fire protection, investments in timberland ownership and forest regeneration could proceed with much less risk and uncertainty.[62] Fire control, in short, brought a much needed calculability to the landscape of timberland investments. By 1980, "the great fire problem of the South," as one 1940 government report had put it, was little more than a memory.[63]

The high incidence of forest fires in the South during the 1920s and 1930s, however, was simply the most spectacular obstacle to systematic investment in forest regeneration and sound forest management. A number of other major problems stood in the way of industrial forestry. Like the fire problem, insects and diseases threatened long-term investments in forest management and represented a similar sort of collective action problem. The Forest Pest Control Act of 1947 provided for federal-state cooperation in insect and disease control in much the same way that Clarke-McNary provided for cooperative fire protection. Yet pest control has historically involved much more public controversy

Table 1: Timberland Burned and Fire Protection in the Southern United States, 1916–1983

	TIMBERLAND BURNED (1,000 acres)	PROTECTED ACREAGE (1,000 acres)	FIRE PROTECTION EXPENDITURES (1,000 dollars, 1982 value)		
			Total	Federal	State
1916	6,624				
1920	2,271				
1925	21,325				
1930	2,747	69,923	14,818	5,078	9,740
1935	1,514	73,658	11,200	4,933	6,267
1940	2,095	88,351	21,629	6,938	14,680
1945	1,204	89,031	33,780	12,008	21,771
1950	2,547	135,113	57,595	17,571	40,025
1955	1,850	157,296	71,170	16,597	54,573
1960	1,093	168,225	78,077	15,518	62,559
1965	557	183,709	90,174	17,754	72,420
1970	724	185,307	109,049	16,448	92,601
1975	469	218,582	99,003	14,295	84,708
1980	747	232,251	88,932	7,450	81,481
1981	1,405	232,651	96,310	5,791	90,519
1982	464	233,255	94,959	3,630	91,329
1983	279	233,255	87,855	3,591	84,264

Source: U.S. Forest Service, *The South's Fourth Forest: Alternatives for the Future,* Forest Resources Report no. 24 (Washington, D.C.: GPO, 1988), 287, Table 2.10.

than fire protection efforts, primarily because of the heavy use of chemicals. At the regional level, the forest products industry assumed primary responsibility for dealing with insect and disease issues and formed the Southern Forest Disease and Insect Research Council as a mechanism for coordinating research and allocating funds to southern universities for investigation of pest problems.[64]

Other obstacles were more of an institutional nature. The forest survey, for example, noted the need "to remove those causes that threaten the stabilized land ownership necessary for long-time forest management, such as unfair tax treatment, discriminating freight rates, hard credit terms, and unfavorable legislation."[65] In particular, the credit system that prevailed in the rural South meant that both small woodland owners and small sawmill owner-operators had limited access to the long-term financing necessary to invest in sustained-yield operations. In part, this derived from the fact that timberland was vulnerable to forest fires and other destructive agents and was thus seen as a bad investment by financial institutions. More important, it reflected the relative lack of capital market institutions in the rural South. Major credit providers, primarily local merchants and local banks, focused almost exclusively on agriculture, with its yearly cycles of planting and harvesting. This created a preference for short-term financing, which, when combined with the high debt burdens and various risks associated with forest investments, reinforced incentives for small timberland owners to liquidate their holdings as quickly as possible. Indeed, not until the 1950s did long-term credit become available for the majority of southern nonindustrial timberland owners.[66] Based on a recognition of the improvements in fire protection and forest management, the U.S. Federal Reserve Board amended its regulations in 1953 to allow financial institutions to lend money on timberlands.[67] As a result, life insurance companies, southern banks, the federal land bank, and, a bit later, the Farmer's Home Administration, began making long-term credit (from five to forty years) available for forest loans.[68] Timberlands had finally become creditworthy investments in the eyes of the financial community.

Closely related to the credit issue and commanding far more attention was the question of forest taxation—a major public-policy concern throughout the first three decades of the twentieth century. For some observers, much of the destruction of the southern forest during the half century after Reconstruction resulted from a perverted tax structure in which timber "was forced to pay revenues as though it were an annual crop."[69] The famous southern regionalist Rupert Vance referred to this treatment of timber under the *ad valorem* property tax as "merciless taxation," arguing along with many others for adoption of a severance tax to be levied only when the timber was cut.[70] In Vance's view, the disadvantage of the prevailing property tax system lay in the long time lags associated with timber growth. While timberland owners paid property taxes on a yearly basis, they often had to wait years or even decades before they received any timber-related income. According to the proponents of tax reform, the loss of interest on the investment in long-term timberland ownership, combined with the possibility of tax increases and the various risks associated with holding timberlands for extended periods of time (i.e., damage from fire, insects, and disease), encouraged the premature cutting of timber while discouraging investment in forest regeneration. Seen in this context, clear-cutting followed by abandonment made far more fiscal sense than holding timber as a permanent investment.[71] This compounded the related problem of tax delinquency. As local timber supplies were liquidated and sawmills cut out, many timber-dependent counties suddenly found themselves facing massive reductions in their tax base. Short of revenue, these local governments responded by increasing their tax rates on the lands not in default, which simply added to the incentive for timber owners to liquidate their holdings.[72] It was a fiscal catch-22.

Even as early as the 1910s, however, a number of states, including several in the South, amended their property tax systems in an effort to promote better forestry practices. During the 1920s and 1930s, in the face of mounting concern over forest destruction and depressed economic conditions throughout rural America, the tax problem began to garner national attention.[73] The 1920 Capper report, for example, called for both federal and state-level investigations into forest taxation.[74] Four years later, the Clarke-McNary Act vested the secretary of agriculture with the authority to investigate "the effects of tax laws, methods, and practices, upon forest perpetuation."[75] Pursuant to these provisions, in April 1926 the Forest Service established the Forest Taxation Inquiry under the leadership of Professor Fred Rogers Fairchild of Yale University.[76] Based on a nine-year investigation, the 1935 Fairchild report, which ran to almost seven hundred pages, provided exhaustive detail on state and local taxation practices and their effects on forest management. It focused, not surprisingly, on "the principal instrument of local taxation—the property tax,"[77] arguing that state and local methods of property taxation "subject[ed] the forest business to an influence directly opposed to conservation."[78] In short, the committee found the property tax systems of many state and county governments inherently unfavorable to deferred-yield property such as timberlands. Moreover, it was not so much the actual tax burden, but the *uncertainty* of future tax obligations that discouraged sound forest management. This presented a problem because it promoted rapid cutting of old-growth timber and provided a disincentive to invest in reforestation of cut-over lands and proper management of immature timber.

Nonetheless, the committee did not find the property tax system to be the unitary force responsible for forest depletion and the general lack of conservation, as so many believed. According to the report, taxation figured as only one of several important factors shaping the landscape of forest investment and management. The threat of fire, vulnerability to insect damage, the vicissitudes of the lumber market, and the long time lag needed for timber to reach maturity also discouraged investment in conservation.[79] "Taxation," the committee concluded, "is only one of the carrying charges that tend to bring about the rapid cutting of virgin timber and only one of the reasons why private capital is not embarking in timber-growing enterprises. There is no magic in forest-tax reform."[80]

More than anything else, then, the Fairchild report debunked the notion that there was a single, easy solution to the timber tax problem. Writing in the *Journal of Forestry* in 1938, R. Clifford Hall, a U.S. Forest Service economist, noted that with the Fairchild report, "The idea of a simple tax panacea, or even a model law that will fill the need in any and every state, ought to be dead. Anyone who examines the findings of this study [Fairchild report] can hardly fail to be convinced that no single and simple solution is possible."[81] Simply put, because the taxation of timberlands under the property tax was essentially a local and state issue, it required action at these levels. By the time Fairchild released his report, moreover, the Depression was in full swing, and forest taxation no longer had the urgency it held during the pre-Depression decade. Tax delinquency and declining tax revenues still concerned local governments, but legislators and government officials effectively shelved the issue of systematic property tax reform in the face of larger and more immediate concerns.

Eventually, all southern states adopted some sort of special tax code provisions recognizing the distinctive nature of timberland investments and providing incentives for industrial forestry.[82] As state and county governments throughout the South realized that the forest products industry constituted a vital part of their economic development prospects, they recognized that a low and stable tax rate provided an important incentive for future investments. Finally, as cheap, long-term credit for timberland investments became available in the 1950s, much of the "tax problem" of previous years disappeared, as annual timber taxes could be paid more easily.[83]

By mid-century, forest taxation no longer elicited the concerns that it had during the 1920s and 1930s.[84] Substantial progress had been made in rendering forest taxation more hospitable for timberland investments. Such progress, combined with advances in fire control, the increased availability of long-term credit, and the development of a systematic and ongoing forest survey, meant that forest management could now proceed as a rational business enterprise rather than as a speculative venture.

REGENERATION

> Here are two big birds of ill omen to be killed by one stone. We can put our unplowed acres to work growing a profitable crop for which there is no glutted market; repopulate our deserted forest regions and abandoned farm districts; give both the earth and the people something to do; and meet the impending shortage of forest products—by growing wood, east, west, north and south as part of a rational scheme of land use, with somewhat the same intelligence and skill that we put into the growing of cereals and fruit. National reforestation should command the interest and support of every thinking American citizen.
> —HENRY C. WALLACE, U.S. Secretary of Agriculture, "Forestry and Our Land Problem," 1923[85]

Regenerating cut-over lands in the South occupied a prominent place in national and regional policy debates during the first two decades of the twentieth century. Numerous government officials decried the destruction and waste evident in vast areas of cut-over lands and called for government intervention to deal with

The Forest Is the Future?

the problem.⁸⁶ The 1908 Conference of Governors on the Conservation of Natural Resources and the Weeks Act of 1911 both stemmed in part from concerns over how to utilize cut-over forest lands, though neither had much impact. The first Southern Forestry Congress, held in 1916, also devoted considerable attention to the challenge of regenerating southern forests.⁸⁷ Indeed, by this time, the problem had become so acute that in August 1917 a Southern Cut-Over Land Conference was convened in New Orleans, under the auspices of the Southern Pine Association and the Southern Settlement and Development Organization, to address the problem directly and to develop a program for restoring barren lands. Rather than focusing on reforestation, however, most of the discussion at the meeting evaluated the possibilities for conversion to pasture and cropland. Of the 340 people who attended the conference, only 4 had trained as foresters. Few considered forest regeneration a viable option, despite the fact that the vast majority of cut-over lands simply could not support commercial agriculture. Southern agriculture, moreover, would soon be having its own problems.⁸⁸ By the early 1920s, as the southern farm sector sank into depression, the prospects of converting barren lands to cropland had dimmed considerably. With fears of a national timber famine on the rise, the attitude toward forest regeneration on cut-over and marginal agricultural lands began to change. Timber was finally beginning to be seen as an alternative land use—as crop rather than as mine.

The first major commercial reforestation effort in the South was initiated by Henry Hardtner, president of the Urania Lumber Company in Louisiana, who developed an extensive program for "natural" regeneration on his company lands during the early twentieth century. Though well publicized, his efforts were not widely emulated by his contemporaries, and, more importantly, they offered little solace to those seeking a solution to the cut-over land problem.⁸⁹ In 1920, however, shortly after Hardtner began his venture, the Great Southern Lumber Company of Bogalusa, Louisiana, initiated the South's first large-scale artificial reforestation program. Under the direction of F. O. Bateman, Great Southern converted thousands of acres of cut-over longleaf pine lands to loblolly pine plantations to provide fiber for the company's lumber and pulp mills. To support these efforts, Bateman also established the first industry nursery at Bogalusa and pioneered the use of nursery seedlings as planting stock—a practice that became the standard for future southern pine regeneration efforts. By the early 1930s, the company had regenerated approximately 30 thousand acres.⁹⁰

Several years after the Bogalusa program commenced, the Clarke-McNary Act of 1924 authorized limited funding for state efforts to cultivate seedlings for planting on private lands. This led to the creation of a network of state nurseries throughout the South during the 1920s and 1930s, which in turn functioned as the biological foundation for southern regeneration efforts after 1930. Equally important, Clarke-McNary also established the institutional precedent for federal-state cooperation in assisting private timberland owners in forest regeneration and management.[91]

In both of these areas, as in fire control, Clarke-McNary ushered in an era of cooperation between the federal government, state governments, and private actors on matters of forest policy and management. As such, the statute represented the first tangible legislative result of a debate over public regulation of private forest practices that began at the close of World War I and lasted into the 1950s. This debate, which centered on whether the federal government should regulate private forestry directly or assist state governments and industry through cooperative institutions and programs, stemmed from the growing concern among professional foresters and political leaders over the extent of forest destruction in the U.S. during the 1910s and 1920s. Although the proponents of regulation included prominent foresters such as Gifford Pinchot and congressional leaders such as Senator Arthur Capper, those favoring the cooperative approach, including industry leaders and the head of the U.S. Forest Service William B. Greeley, carried the day.[92]

The onset of the Depression and the beginning of the New Deal, however, rekindled the debate over forest regulation. By lending an increased legitimacy to those voicing concern over the exploitative practices of natural resource industries, the Roosevelt administration created an administrative space for realizing some of the principles of earlier progressive conservationists.[93] Rational and efficient use of natural resources based on government planning became a mantra for many New Dealers. An early example of such convictions, the 1933 Copeland report, known formally as *A National Plan for American Forestry*, contained the most extensive account of forest conditions and practices in the United States ever completed and demonstrated convincingly that private timberland owners, even with the assistance of federal and state programs, had so far failed to initiate a significant program of rational, scientific forestry. Of the many recommendations made by the report, the most controversial was a massive program of public acquisition of timberland—totaling some 224 million acres, with 177 million acres in the East—as a way of ensuring that the nation's timberlands would be properly managed.[94] Although this particular proposal was never acted upon, the Copeland report boosted efforts aimed at establishing forest conservation and scientific management as both civic duty and sound business practice.

Such efforts found their most prominent expression in the National Industrial Recovery Act (NIRA) of 1933. Article X of the Lumber Code (the so-called "conservation article") legally committed the lumber industry to principles of conservation and sustained yield. Even though the Supreme Court declared the Act unconstitutional two years later, Article X provided a basis for the forestry policies and practices adopted by forest products companies during the late 1930s and 1940s.[95]

The most immediate and tangible impact of the New Deal on southern forest regeneration, however, involved the work of the Civilian Conservation Corps (CCC) in forest protection and forest regeneration. As with fire protection, the CCC helped transform reforestation into a moral crusade. By 1942, when the CCC closed shop, more than 1 million acres of timberland had been planted in the South (see figure 2).[96]

Nonetheless, by the end of the 1930s, despite the best efforts of the CCC and the Roosevelt administration, it was far from certain that the South's timber resource would be able to support a growing forest products industry for the indefinite future. During this period, as firms in the pulp and paper industry accelerated their efforts to move south (15 new mills were built between 1934 and 1940 and regional pulping capacity more than doubled), forestry professionals along with representatives of other wood-using industries began to voice concern that the huge new mills would quickly strip the region of its young second-growth timber without making any attempt to regenerate it. Although the pulp and paper industry accounted for a small portion of the timber consumption in the region (approximately 7 percent by 1939), the industry's growth potential combined with its preference for small trees raised concerns. Lumbermen and naval stores operators in particular opposed the new mills—fearful that younger trees would not be allowed to mature enough to provide raw materials for their own operations. Federal policy makers also voiced apprehension. In his annual report of 1937, the chief forester of the United States, F. A. Silcox, noted that pulp and paper firms' recent purchases of timber rights on large acreages of land from numerous small farmers and landowners in the South had not involved any commitment to regeneration. In Silcox's view, this set the stage for "re-exploitation." "If such a practice continues," he noted, "the land, the farmer, and the whole social and economic set-up must inevitably suffer. The South stands now at the crossroads."[97]

The following year, in March 1938, President Roosevelt entered the fray with a letter to Congress requesting an investigation of the "national forest problem." "The forest problem," he wrote, "is a matter of vital national concern, and some way must be found to make forest lands and forest resources contribute their full share to the social and economic structures of this country, and to the security and stability of all our people." Evoking images of "denuded" watersheds and "crippled" forest communities "still being left desolate and forlorn," Roosevelt urged the Congress to study the problem and propose legislation that would include "such public regulatory controls as will adequately protect private as well as the broad public interests in all forest lands." "[T]he fact remains," he concluded, "that... most of the States, communities, and private companies have, on the whole, accomplished little to retard or check the continuing process of using up our forest resources without replacement. This being so, it seems obviously necessary to fall back on the last defensive line—Federal leadership and Federal Action."[98] Two months later, the Joint Congressional Committee on Forestry, under the direction of Alabama Senator John H. Bankhead, launched a multi-year investigation of the nation's "forest problem." Based on extensive hearings in every major forest-producing region, the committee concluded that the management of commercial forest land under private ownership represented the crux of the so-called forest problem.[99] For pulp and paper firms moving into the South during the late 1930s, the threat of federal regulation proved quite serious indeed.

Many of these firms, however, had already begun to adopt practices of systematic forest conservation and regeneration. Because the new southern mills required a continuous supply of pulpwood at a reasonable cost, which effectively constrained mill procurement to the surrounding area, commitment to forest protection and forest regeneration on company-owned lands, as well as on the lands of the small owners who provided more than two-thirds of their total timber, was an economic imperative. From the mills' perspective, the overall objective was to generate a steady supply of timber to meet their needs without depleting the growing stock of timber in the immediate procurement area—a 100–150 mile radius from the mill site. Though most firms moving into the region during this period quickly acquired enough land to supply one-half to two-thirds of the wood necessary to support their mill operations on a continuous basis, they continued to depend significantly on nonindustrial timberland owners for the bulk of their timber, using their own timberlands to stabilize local pulpwood markets. By the late 1930s, for example, Union Bag already owned or controlled "considerably more" than the 400,000 acres it had estimated would be needed to supply its operations. With such a land base, the Savannah mill could effectively set the price for pulpwood in the region. Much of this land, however, was cut or burned over and thus required systematic investment in regeneration in order to reach its potential. To accomplish this, and in response to the mounting threat of regulation, Union Bag initiated a Forest Conservation Program in 1937 (one of the first in the industry) committing the company to establishing and maintaining high-productivity forests on company-owned land through fire protection, regeneration, and timber stand improvement.[100]

As important as such efforts were, however, they were not enough in themselves to stem the threat of federal regulation. Only a credible, industrywide commitment would successfully preempt government intervention. Seeking to avoid such an outcome, representatives of the pulp and paper industry met in New Orleans in May 1937 to formulate an industrywide program for forest utilization and conservation in the South. The resulting "Statement of Conservation Policy of the Southern Pine Pulpwood Industry" committed firms in the industry to promote selective cutting practices, forest regeneration, and fire protection on company and noncompany lands. Two years later, in 1939, the major firms with southern operations formed the Southern Pulpwood Conservation Association (SPCA). Financed by the industry and headquartered in Atlanta, Georgia, the SPCA provided technical forestry assistance and education to nonindustrial private timberland owners throughout the South. Its motto—"Cut wisely, prevent fires, and grow more trees to build a better South"—symbolized the extent to which forest protection and forest regeneration were being framed in the language of moral duty. Over the course of its existence, SPCA provided assistance to thousands of southern timberland owners. Although such a program was undeniably in the long-term interest of the pulp and paper industry, perhaps its most important impact was in silencing critics who claimed that pulp and paper firms were doing nothing to promote sound forest management among small private landowners in the South.[101] Thus, even though the push for regulatory controls over private forest practices during the New Deal did not produce any long-lasting legislative results, the very threat of such regulation added to industry leaders' incentives to adopt minimum standards of forest protection and management on their own lands and promote such standards among nonindustrial private landowners.

Notwithstanding such efforts to regulate private forestry directly, the most dramatic impact of the New Deal on southern forestry came not in the area of industrial policy but through agricultural policy and the profound restructuring of postwar land use that resulted. By initiating an agrarian transition in the South that radically reshaped the institutions that had governed land and labor since the end of Reconstruction, New Deal agricultural policies (and their successors) opened up unparalleled opportunities for forest regeneration. As administered, these acreage-reduction programs generated strong incentives for landlords to shift to wage labor, displacing tenants and sharecroppers.[102] At the same time, however, the shift to wage labor also compelled many rural southerners to seek work elsewhere. As off-farm opportunities increased, particularly during World War II, labor costs began to rise and many farmers accelerated their efforts to mechanize. Such incentives were given a further boost by the infusion of capital from government agricultural programs, which effectively allowed the larger southern farmers to invest in mechanization and more input-intensive agriculture. By the early 1950s, as the tractorization and mechanization of planting and harvesting reached full force, the introduction of new, high-yielding crop varieties and the extensive application of fertilizers and pesticides transformed southern agriculture into an industrial enterprise. At the same time, facing a weak international market, the rise of industrial substitutes, and government production-control programs, many large farmers switched from cotton to soybeans and other crops. Meanwhile, more than a million other farmers, many of them tenants, left the land as southern agriculture concentrated on larger farms in the more productive regions. Between 1950 and 1975, total farms declined from 2.1 million to 722,000 while average farm size increased from 93 to 216 acres (excluding Texas and Florida).[103] In the process, over 40 million acres of cropland became available for other uses.

With this rationalization of southern agriculture, new opportunities for forest regeneration emerged. By creating structural opportunities and incentives for land-use change, the system of agricultural production and regulation established during the New Deal opened the door for the rise of timber as the South's number one cash crop. The era of farm forestry had arrived.

In response, small timberland owners developed representative organizations to pursue their collective interests. The Forest Farmers Association, for example, organized in Valdosta, Georgia, in 1941, provided a greater voice for small timberland owners in regional and national matters, such as credit and tax policy for timberlands, and offered technical assistance to timberland owners. That same year, the American Tree Farm System began offering education and certification to private tree farmers (most of whom were large private landowners under industry sponsorship) throughout the United States and particularly in the South.[104]

By the early 1940s, then, the institutional foundations for southern forest regeneration were in place. After a short hiatus during World War II, forest planting and seeding accelerated significantly (see figure 2). Drawing on the network of state-supported nurseries established in the 1920s and 1930s under the Clarke-McNary program, seedling production moved into high gear.[105] This yielded something like a golden age of southern forest regeneration, stimulated largely by the Soil Bank Act of 1956.

In many respects, the Soil Bank program simply extended the system of agricultural regulation established during the New Deal. As in the 1930s, the basic problem was overproduction, and the overall policy objective was to provide incentives for farmers to take acreage out of production—to bank soil. What was different about the Soil Bank program, however, was that it provided explicit provisions and financial incentives for forest regeneration as an alternative use for idled cropland. Thus, the 1956 Soil Bank Act had two primary components— an acreage reserve program designed to take cropland out of production temporarily in order to reduce overproduction problems for key commodities and a conservation reserve program designed to provide incentives (cost-share arrangements) for landowners to convert their idled cropland to other uses such as timber production. Under the cost-share arrangement, the government reimbursed landowners who planted trees for 80 percent of their costs and provided annual payments determined by the estimated value of their land for the follow-

Figure 2: Annual Forest Planting/Seeding in the Southern United States, 1925–95 (by Acreage)

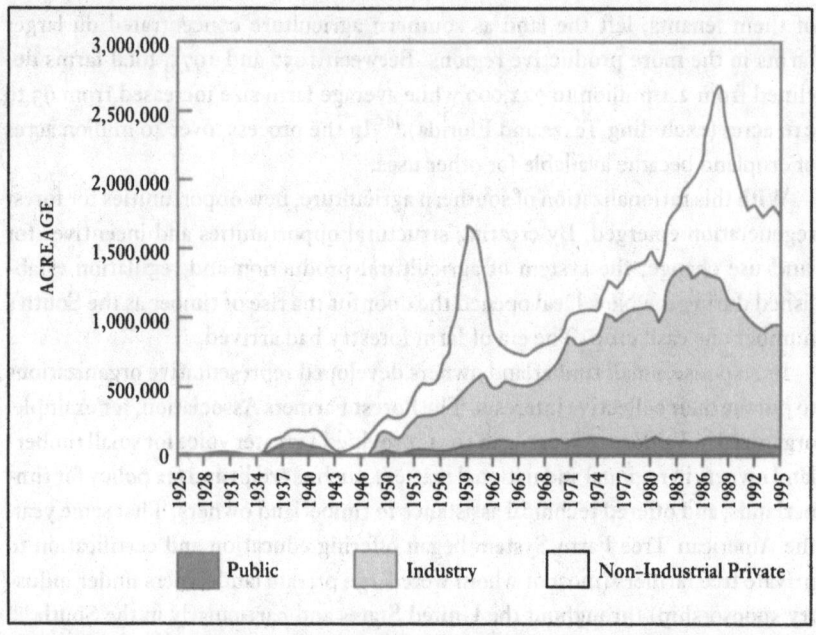

Sources: U.S. Forest Service, *A Statistical History of Tree Planting in the South, 1925–1985*, Misc. Report SA–MR 8 (Washington, D.C.: GPO, 1986); U.S. Forest Service, *U.S. Forest Planting Report 1986–1989* (Washington, D.C.: GPO, 1986–89); U.S. Forest Service, *Tree Planting in the United States 1990–1995* (Washington, D.C.: GPO, 1990–95).

ing ten years.[106] Many southern farmers obviously found the offer attractive. Over the course of the program (1956–1960), they converted more than two million acres of cropland to timber plantations. During the peak year of 1959, southern nurseries (public and private) produced more than one billion pine seedlings for planting on some 1.7 million acres of industry and nonindustry land. As the charts in figure 2 indicate, moreover, more than 70 percent of the total area planted and seeded in the region during this period was on nonindustrial private lands.[107]

As an extension of New Deal agricultural regulation, the Soil Bank program illustrated the power of government incentives and subsidies to alter land use patterns and transform economic institutions. Without government assistance, southern landowners would find it difficult to embark on a substantial program of artificial forest regeneration. Indeed, as figure 2 documents, significant acreages of nonindustrial private timberland were not artificially regenerated in the South again until the advent of another government program of assistance to landowners—the Conservation Reserve Program (CRP) of the mid to late 1980s.[108] From the perspective of the forest products industry, the Soil Bank program was thus a phenomenal success. Indeed, most of the cropland converted to timber plantations under the Soil Bank program remained in timber well after the annual cost-share payments ceased. A 1980 survey of Soil Bank lands in the South, for example, found that over 90 percent of the original plantations were still growing pine.[109] The program, though, was only a success for those whose interests it served. By creating incentives for established (white) farmers to bank soil and by channeling the program through county political machines, the federal government gave a significant boost to the ongoing capitalization of southern agriculture—forcing marginal farmers and tenants, many of whom were African American, to leave the land.[110] The conversion of cropland to timberland from this perspective turned out to be a highly effective form of enclosure.

In the absence of government programs such as the Soil Bank and the CRP, many southern landowners simply allowed their lands to restock "naturally," often with management assistance from forestry consultants and forestry professionals working in industry-sponsored landowner assistance programs. The overall result was a substantial transformation of land use in the postwar period. Between 1948 and 1968, some 10 million acres of agricultural land in the South converted to timberland through natural and artificial regeneration.[111] In contrast to earlier years, by the 1970s most private timberland owners no longer actively engaged in farming. Many simply saw timberland as part of a larger portfolio of investments.[112]

As for industry lands, as figure 2 indicates, forest regeneration efforts grew steadily throughout the post–World War II period. By the early 1980s, the forest industry was regenerating more than 1 million acres per year in the South.[113] As land values increased, the premium on intensive forest management grew. For firms that owned large acreages, maximizing biological productivity became an economic imperative. Tree improvement represented the next frontier for industrial forestry.

INTENSIFICATION

> Why . . . should the forester be satisfied to gather his seeds from the wild, unimproved forms that are only partially adapted to his needs? Should he not take steps to develop better strains of trees, and especially those capable of more rapid growth?
> —LLOYD AUSTIN, "A New Enterprise in Tree Breeding," 1927[114]

> Eventually, through the application of breeding methods, we may expect to produce high yielding and otherwise desirable genotypes at will.
> —SCOTT S. PAULEY, "The Scope of Forest Genetics," 1954[115]

Though few foresters would likely have challenged the basic maxim of early inheritance studies that "like begets like," the science and practice of forestry was relatively slow in appreciating and incorporating the role of genetic variation and "parentage" in influencing the viability and success of trees. Despite the widespread use of improved seeds in agriculture, most American foresters in the 1930s and 1940s did not think twice about using unimproved seeds in their reforestation efforts. Unlike farmers, foresters typically had little appreciation for genetics and made almost no effort to match seeds to particular sites. In effect, the rediscovery of Mendel's work on inheritance at the turn of the century took almost fifty years to find its way into forestry practice. For some reason, foresters saw trees as different—beyond the scale of practical human manipulation.[116] Most operated on the working assumption that trees of a given species were genetically uniform and that intraspecific variation was entirely the result of environmental influences.

Of course, there were those who did not accept such assumptions. Writing in 1929, Aldo Leopold chastised the forestry community for what he called "the highly improbable assumption that 'all trees are born free and equal.'"[117] Leopold, along with Lloyd Austin and a few other pioneers, felt that forestry was missing an important opportunity, and that both genetics and environment had to be taken seriously in forestry practice. By controlling both genetic and environmental variability, timber growing could achieve much-needed calculability. In Leopold's view: "what we are trying to create is not timber, but confidence that valuable timber can be made to grow; not dividends, but confidence that dividends can be made to accrue."[118] Part of the difficulty, of course, lay in the long biological time lags involved in tree growth. As Austin himself noted, "It is, at the present time, hard to interest people in the planting of trees that they know will not reach merchantable size in their generation."[119]

For those interested in applying classical breeding techniques to tree improvement, a number of obstacles stood in the way.[120] Compared to crop breeders, tree breeders had to deal with very large, immobile organisms with long nonreproductive periods and generation cycles that often exceeded human life expectancy. In contrast to most commercial crops, basic knowledge on forest and tree biology was quite thin, particularly regarding the relationship between the genetic structures of trees and tree characteristics.[121] Given the large heterozygosity of forest trees, finding superior trees and seeds, matching them to particular sites, and controlling the selection process in the context of open pollination posed numerous logistical challenges not found in crop breeding. Furthermore, the relative difficulty of controlling the biotic and abiotic environment of a particular stand of trees over the long time frame needed to judge breeding successes strongly limited the application of conventional breeding techniques.[122] Finally, from an operational standpoint, any successful tree improvement program would also have to produce improved seeds in commercial quantities sufficient to meet the needs of forest regeneration—a daunting task in a region such as the South where almost two million acres per year were being regenerated in the late 1950s.

Of all the obstacles facing tree improvement, though, it was the time constraint—time to achieve phenotypic stability, time to reach reproductive maturity, and time to harvest—that presented the greatest challenge. Maximizing the rate of return on investments in tree improvement would thus depend fundamentally on optimizing the amount of genetic gain per unit of time.[123] As gains accrued, the incentives to invest in tree improvement would increase. The problem, however, was that even under the best conditions, such gains would not be apparent until a decade or more after the initiation of a formal tree improvement program. Given the risk and uncertainty associated with such long time lags, combined with the tremendous logistical and institutional challenges involved in such an effort, systematic investment in tree improvement greatly exceeded the scope of any individual firm's investment horizon. Developing a tree improvement program in the South would thus have to be based on cooperation among firms, as well as between private industry and the state—all of which would take time. As Harvard professor Scott Pauley indicated in the mid-1950s, directed manipulation of forest genetics on a commercial scale was still a rather distant prospect.

Yet, even as Pauley wrote, the institutional foundations of industrial tree improvement were being established in the South. Although early breeding efforts, particularly in the development of hybrid pines, had taken place on an *experimental* scale at the Eddy Tree Breeding Station in Placerville, California,[124] there had been no systematic effort to develop a tree improvement program on an *industrial* scale in the United States until the early 1950s. During this time, a particular constellation of factors in the South—the growth of the pulp and paper industry and its appetite for wood, the rising value of timberlands, the increased demand for seedlings to furnish regeneration efforts, and the growing appreciation and acceptance of population genetics as a tool for tree breeding—created the opportunity for those interested in tree improvement to move toward operationalizing an applied tree breeding program for the region.[125] One of the first formal steps in this direction came in early 1951, when a group of southern foresters convened in Atlanta to develop a tree improvement strategy for the South. This meeting, which led to the formation of the Southern Forest Tree Improvement Committee (SFTIC) later that year, underscored the growing concern among some in the forestry profession that southern regeneration efforts then underway were missing important opportunities by giving only passing attention to forest genetics. Since 1951, the SFTIC, which operates under the auspices of the U.S. Forest Service, has sponsored biennial conferences on southern forest tree improvement and has served as a coordinating body for regional research efforts in the areas of seed source (also known as provenance), forest genetics and breeding, and production of superior seed.[126]

In one of its first and most important undertakings, the SFTIC established the Southwide Pine Seed Source Study under the direction of Philip Wakeley—the man known as "Mr. Southern Pine."[127] Up until this time, disregard for seed source in seedling production was the rule rather than the exception among seed collectors in the South as well as the rest of the country. Most southern state nurseries obtained loblolly pine seed (the most widely used planting stock) from the cheapest source available, without making any real effort to match seed source to the particular region where seedlings would be planted. This was a major problem in that it led to unnecessary planting failures.[128]

Wakeley's seed source study, which involved provenance research for the four major pine species of the South (loblolly, slash, longleaf, and shortleaf) marked a radical departure from the traditional views of many foresters in that it explicitly identified genetic factors within tree species as a source of variation.[129] It was a massive undertaking, requiring the cooperation of federal, state, industry, and university actors in spreading the costs and dividing the labor. Such a study, moreover, proved vital not only to efforts to plant "unimproved" seedlings in areas to which they were adapted, but also to designing future tree improvement programs in the region. Without attention to provenance, planting stock could all too easily end up on sites to which it was ill suited. Likewise, without knowing the geographic origin of particular seeds, forest geneticists would be unable to make accurate assessments of breeding successes and develop reliable pedigree analyses.[130] In Wakeley's words:

> Genetic differences between individuals or local strains within a geographic race ... seem likely to be overshadowed by the genetic unsuitability of the race as a whole when stock is transferred to a less favorable place. The inescapable conclusion is that selections and hybrids must be made separately region by region, within the framework of existing geographic races. To the extent that this is true, provenance studies designed to identify such races and define their territorial boundaries are fundamental to other phases of tree improvement.[131]

Put crudely, geography mattered. Provenance studies would henceforth be the foundation of any successful tree improvement program. As a result of Wakeley's work, the importance of seed source was widely accepted and southern states adopted formal seed certification programs. By the end of the 1950s, virtually all state and industry efforts in artificial regeneration drew seed from local sources.[132]

As artificial regeneration efforts increased in the South during the 1950s, early tree improvement supporters also began to argue for selecting seed stock from superior trees. Impressed by the productivity gains being recorded in agriculture, particularly with hybrid corn, some suggested that an intensive breeding program might also bring large benefits to industrial forestry. If you were going to plant, they argued, why not plant the best. Intensive breeding with forest trees, however, represented a substantially greater challenge than that involving agricultural crops, and it was far more complicated than provenance studies. Procuring seed from phenotypically superior trees throughout the South and using this seed as the basis for the commercial production of seedlings represented a major hurdle facing those who wanted to operationalize tree improvement on an industrial scale. Such a program would have to be carefully planned and, due to the biological time lags involved, it would necessarily take more than a decade to achieve any tangible results. Writing in 1954, Clemens Kaufman, the director of the School of Forestry at the University of Florida, reminded his fellow foresters that they were still operating in "what might be termed the fire protection-planting stage of forestry practice." "We must remember," he continued, "that at this time we have neither super trees nor seed from trees of proven quality, or even stands of average quality or better, phenotypically, which have been selected to supply the quantity of seed required annually." Kaufman thus suggested that the principles of genetics could be employed immediately in an *extensive* manner by selecting and leaving phenotypically superior trees as seed trees for natural regeneration.[133] The *intensive* application of genetics to tree improvement, however, would have to wait until reliable volumes of improved seed could be produced for artificial regeneration—a challenge that, more than any other single factor, led to the creation of the industrial tree improvement cooperatives in the South during the 1950s.

The first university-industry tree improvement cooperative in the United States was established at Texas A&M University in 1951. Initially, the cooperative included eight companies, which together provided most of the financing, while the university provided facilities and staff. Bruce Zobel, who had just received his Ph.D. in forest genetics from the University of California, was hired as the first director. Influenced by Scandinavian and Australian research in forest genetics, most of the early work focused on developing an applied breeding program oriented to the members' areas of operation in Texas, Louisiana, and Oklahoma. Because of the relative lack of basic knowledge of tree biology and forest genetics, however, participating firms saw the whole effort as something of a gamble.[134] These companies were investing in a long-term effort that no one could say for sure would actually result in tangible gains.

Shortly after the establishment of the Texas cooperative, industry leaders, in concert with members of the forestry community, initiated two more tree improvement cooperatives—one at the University of Florida (1955) and one at North Carolina State University (1956).[135] In 1956, Zobel moved to Raleigh to became the director of the new North Carolina State cooperative and a professor of forestry at the university. The cooperative at North Carolina State, which focused primarily on loblolly pine, quickly emerged as the largest and most well known of the three. Its principal objective was to develop strains of trees with desired characteristics—yield, quality, and adaptability—and to produce seeds of these strains on a commercial scale. Reducing turnover time was the critical challenge. As Zobel put it: "The objective of our tree improvement program is to get as much improvement as possible as quickly as possible.... We are interested in gain per unit of time."[136]

From an organizational standpoint, the program was unique. There were no formal contracts or written agreements. Members (about thirty-five in the early 1970s: thirty-two from industry and three state agencies) paid yearly dues and participated on an equal basis. Any member could withdraw at any time, and any member could be asked to withdraw if its contribution was considered inadequate. Members who withdrew, however, would not be allowed to return. The cooperative's university-based managers designed, analyzed, and interpreted field tests, while professional foresters employed by the member firms performed fieldwork under the guidance of cooperative staff. More fundamental research, which was not a primary focus of the cooperative, enlisted associated graduate students, some of whom would later become employees of member firms. The entire effort was multidisciplinary—drawing on a number of fields outside of forestry, including pulp and paper science, genetics, botany, statistics, soil science, plant breeding, and plant pathology.[137]

As noted, the major operational objective of the cooperative was to provide commercial quantities of improved seed to meet the annual planting needs of members (approximately 400,000 acres or 300 million seedlings in the early 1970s). At the outset, the tree improvement cooperatives promised members a 5 percent gain in volume from improved seed. Member firms would select seeds from superior trees from their own lands and exchange them with the cooperative. These "superior trees" (approximately three thousand for each cooperative) provided the genetic base from which gains could be realized in both the long run (through advanced generation breeding) and the short run (through intensive selection). Based on selected trees, the cooperatives established breeding or research orchards to maintain diversity and support long-run breeding efforts as well as first-generation commercial seed orchards to begin producing improved seed.[138] In the process, researchers performed progeny testing to establish pedigreed lines of improved trees, which in turn became the genetic foundation for industrial forestry in the South.

Given the turnover times associated with trees, however, applying the principles of quantitative genetics to select for and produce commercial quantities of improved seed was a long and laborious process. Even though the southern tree improvement cooperatives began operating in the 1950s, it was not until the early 1970s that commercial quantities of improved seed became available. By 1973, the North Carolina State cooperative was only producing about half the planting stock needed by its members. Not until the end of the decade were all members' needs met. For the region as a whole, the proportion of improved seedlings produced in southern nurseries (public and private) increased from about one in four in 1976 to more than 90 percent in 1986 (out of a total 1.6 billion seedlings).[139] By this time, North Carolina State cooperative members had established some 4,000 acres of seed orchards, which yielded some 630 million seedlings per year (almost 40 percent of the regional total)—enough planting stock to regenerate 900,000 acres annually.[140]

As for the actual gains from the program, the first generation of improved trees developed through the North Carolina State cooperative showed an average increase of 7 percent in height growth, 12 percent in stem volume, and 32 percent in harvest value. Real after-tax returns from the total investment on tree improvement were estimated to be between 17 percent and 19 percent—quite healthy by any standard. By the mid-1990s, the North Carolina State cooperative was moving into its third generation of selection and breeding. In roughly twenty-five years of seed production, the member organizations harvested sufficient seed to plant more than 13 billion genetically improved loblolly pines—enough to cover 19 million acres.[141] Biological intensification had become the driving force of industrial forestry in the region.[142]

The system of tree improvement cooperatives, however, was not the only game in town. The federal government was also an active player. The Southern and Southeastern Forest Experiment Stations of the U.S. Forest Service, for example, undertook research on forest disease and insect problems.[143] The Southern Institute of Forest Genetics, established by the Forest Service in 1954 at Gulfport, Mississippi, also developed a long-term project to investigate "the fundamental principles of forest tree inheritance."[144] In addition, several university departments of forestry carried out research on various issues associated with tree improvement.[145] And, of course, major firms in the industry developed their own tree improvement research programs. International Paper ran a research program and experimental forest at Bainbridge, Georgia. Union Camp operated forestry research programs in Bellville, Georgia, and in Princeton, New Jersey. Weyerhaeuser initiated a program in eastern North Carolina, and Westvaco ran a research facility in Summerville, South Carolina. In the 1980s and 1990s, some of these firms began experimenting with techniques derived from molecular biology. As these "new" biotechnologies are employed in forest tree breeding, proprietary issues will very likely affect the nature of cooperative research in the industry. Indeed, though wide-scale use of recombinant DNA and other techniques derived from molecular biology is still in the future as far as industrial forestry is concerned, there is ample reason to suspect that as particular processes or products (for example, new genetically engineered seeds) become strategic resources and subject to the laws governing intellectual property, the cooperative arrangement that has worked so well in the past may undergo substantial change.

For the time being, however, the cooperative system continues to provide much of the foundation for tree improvement efforts in the South. Looking back over the last half century, one is struck not only by the remarkable success of these efforts in transforming large acreages of the South into highly productive industrial timber plantations but also by the hybrid public-private character of the enterprise and, perhaps most surprising of all, by the extensive cooperation between firms that competed against one another. Part of this may stem from what some have identified as the cooperative culture of the forestry profession in the South during the middle decades of the twentieth century. A more important factor has surely been the complexity and long-term nature of the enterprise, which militated against any single firm embarking unilaterally on tree improvement.[146]

THE FOREST IS THE FUTURE

> To meet permanently the increasing requirements for pulpwood will necessitate placing our forests upon a systematic basis of management for the production of wood as a crop. Only by so doing can manufacturers be assured of supplies within reasonable distances of their mills. Under such conditions the future growth of the industry must necessarily take place *in those regions in which pulpwood can be grown in short rotation with a high rate of growth.*
>
> —JOHN D. RUE, "The Development of Pulp and Paper-Making in the South," 1924[147]

> Today the South has come to count the meaning of the pulp and paper industry as something more than jobs in its towns and money in its woods. The greatest significance of this industry, which cannot move its multimillion-dollar plants like "peckerwood" sawmills, but which provides a market for trees a man can grow and sell in his own years, is already evident. It has made creative forest management in the South not only possible but imperative.
>
> —JONATHAN DANIELS, *The Forest Is the Future*, 1957[148]

In the thirty-odd years separating John Rue's assessment of the challenges facing the development of a pulp and paper industry in the South from North Carolina newspaperman Jonathan Daniels's retrospective, the southern forest underwent a profound transformation. By the late 1950s, when Daniels penned his celebratory account of the forestry revolution transpiring in the South, the region had emerged as the center of the U.S. pulp and paper industry. Given its favorable climate, the vast acreages available for growing trees, and the relatively short turnover times associated with southern pine, it seems quite plausible (even logical) in hindsight that the South was destined to become a major national and international force in the production of pulp and paper. When Rue issued his assessment in the 1920s, however, such an outcome was hardly assured. Throughout the 1910s and 1920s and well into the 1930s, members of the forestry community voiced grave concerns over the future of the southern forest resource and its capacity to support a large forest products industry.

In essence, for a large-scale timber products industry to develop, a new regime of forest management would have to be inscribed on the southern landscape—a big part of which involved subordinating timberlands to the dictates of continuous-flow industrial production. At the most basic level, this involved shifting from the earlier logic of extraction to a logic of intensive cultivation, which treated timber as an industrial crop. Such a transition, driven in part by economic imperatives, required new institutional arrangements to deal with the enormous challenges of making timberlands amenable to rational economic calculation, regenerating cut-over and marginal agricultural lands, and developing and producing improved genetic stock. In all of these areas, extensive cooperation would be required—between government agencies, private landowners and private industry; between universities and firms; and between competing companies within the industry. Through a process of regional collective learning, all of these actors played vital roles in constructing a highly competitive industrial system.[149]

As for the southern timberlands, they underwent a profound ecological transformation—part of a larger agrarian transition initiated by the New Deal that radically altered southern land use patterns. In effect, the southern forest was made over into a highly managed ecosystem more closely akin to a crop monoculture than a biologically diverse forest. Through a process of ecological simplification, timber plantations came to provide an increasing part of the biological foundation for a massive and highly successful industry. Between 1940 and 1990, more than 38 million acres of land were artificially regenerated in the South. During that time, southern nurseries produced over 23 *billion* tree seedlings, the majority of which, since the 1980s, have been genetically improved. As land values have risen in the region, the premium placed on intensive management has also increased significantly. Through biotechnology (old and new) timber plantations are now being subjected to a sort of biological time-space compression.[150] Nature is being (re)made to work harder, faster, better.

Despite such remarkable success, however, new challenges have emerged in the last two decades. The spread of intensively managed pine monocultures throughout the South carries with it the potential for increased vulnerability to a variety of forest pathogens. The loss of species diversity and habitat associated with the ongoing transformation of mixed forests to plantation monocultures has also raised concerns among environmental groups, transforming southern timberlands into a political battleground. Finally, the spread of short-rotation pulpwood plantations in the southern hemisphere combined with persistent overcapacity in the global pulp and paper industry has undermined the profitability of southern producers and raised questions about the long-term viability of the industry in the region.

For now, however, the American South continues to dominate both domestic and global pulp and paper production. In the United States, the region currently accounts for roughly three-fourths of total pulpwood production, more than two-thirds of wood pulp capacity, and over half of paper and paperboard production. In a global context, the southern pulp and paper industry is larger than that of all other countries and is exceeded only by the total production from Asia and Europe.[151] In terms of industrial timber plantations, the South currently accounts for a third or more of the world's total acreage, despite containing less than 3 percent of the world's forest area.[152] In short, the South has emerged as a global leader in industrial forestry and the production of forest products on the basis of a distinctive set of institutional arrangements that have facilitated the intensive cultivation of timber as a crop. Whether or not the region will be able to meet current challenges and remain competitive will depend fundamentally on how effective these institutional arrangements are in adapting the existing industrial forest to the demands of the future.

NOTES

Much of the research upon which this paper is based is part of a larger dissertation project, which has been generously supported by the U.S. Environmental Protection Agency and the MacArthur Foundation. Annalee Saxenian, Michael Watts, and Gavin Wright have provided much-needed assistance and guidance since the beginning of the project. Rachel Schurman and Scott Prudham have also offered valuable assistance along the way. As part of the Second Wave conference, Philip Scranton and Steven Vallas both offered a number of very helpful comments. Fred Cubbage was kind enough to read the entire draft and offer valuable suggestions. Librarians at the Forest History Society in Durham, North Carolina, the Georgia Historical Society in Savannah, Georgia, and the UC-Berkeley Natural Resources and Biosciences library also provided a great deal of help. Many thanks to all of them and especially to all of those I interviewed during my fieldwork. Of course, all errors of fact and interpretation are mine.

1. Calder's words came from a speech he gave at a dinner in Savannah celebrating the formal opening of Union Bag's Savannah mill. Quoted in "Bright Future for Industry," *Savannah Morning News*, 2 October 1936.

2. Formally known as the "resin barrier," this problem consisted of the conviction that highly resinous young pine trees were unsuitable for paper-making. During the 1910s and 1920s, the success of early kraft (also known as sulfate) mills in the South as well as research at the U.S. Forest Products Laboratory in Madison, Wis., demonstrated that suitable paper could be made from young pine trees using the kraft process. Jack P. Oden, "Origins of the Southern Kraft Paper Industry, 1903–1930," *Mississippi Quarterly* 30 (1977): 573–74. Savannah's own Charles Holmes Herty, though sometimes mistakenly identified as the man who debunked the sap myth, did play a very active role in the 1920s and 1930s in heralding the virtues of southern pine for pulp and paper manufacture. James I. Pikl Jr., *A History of Georgia Forestry*, Research Monograph No. 2 (Athens: University of Georgia Bureau of Business and Economic Research, 1966).

3. Warnings of an impending timber famine had been voiced since just after the Civil War and were issued with increasing frequency during the late nineteenth and early twentieth centuries. Henry Clepper, *Professional Forestry in the United States* (Baltimore: Johns Hopkins University Press, 1971), 136, and William Robbins, *American Forestry: A History of National, State, and Private Cooperation* (Lincoln: University of Nebraska Press, 1985), 89–90. On the specific issue of pulpwood supplies, a U.S. Department of Agriculture report from 1924 pointed to a national sense of urgency regarding domestic supplies in the face of a growing dependence on imports from Canada and elsewhere. U.S. Department of Agriculture, *How the United States Can Meet Its Present and Future Pulpwood Requirements*, Dept. Bulletin No. 1241 (Washington, D.C.: GPO, 1924).

4. The city of Savannah, Ga., for example, paid $325,000 in cash for plant site purchase and improvements when Union Bag decided to locate its new mill in the city. In addition, William Murphy of the C&S Bank provided $1 million from his own bank and $1.5 million from other sources as start-up money for the new Savannah mill. Pikl, *Georgia Forestry*, 31. For a more general treatment of industrial recruitment in the South during this period, see James C. Cobb, *The Selling of the South: The Southern Crusade for Industrial Development, 1936–1990*, 2d ed. (Urbana: University of Illinois Press, 1993).

5. The Southern Pine Association cited figures for the third quarter of 1930 that showed a substantial cost advantage (one-third to one-half the cost) for the delivered mill cost of pulpwood in the South relative to other areas. Southern Pine Association, "Economic Conditions in Southern Pine Industry," 1931, 88. Another report noted that Union Bag expected to save on the order of $20 per ton by producing sulfate pulp in the South instead of importing it. American Institute for Economic Research, "A Report on the Future of the Paper Industry in the Southeastern United States and the Effects on Stumpage Values," AIER, Cambridge, Mass., 1938, 69.

6. Thomas D. Clark, *The Greening of the South: The Recovery of Land and Forest* (Lexington: University Press of Kentucky, 1984), chapter 9.

7. See Jack P. Oden, "Development of the Southern Pulp and Paper Industry, 1900–1970" (Ph.D. diss., Mississippi State University, 1973), and Oden, "Southern Kraft Paper Industry," for a discussion of early kraft pulp manufacture in the South. Oden's dis-

sertation represents the most comprehensive treatment of the southern pulp and paper industry to date. According to Oden, the kraft or sulfate process was invented in Germany at the end of the nineteenth century and employs sodium sulfate in the pulping process. Paper produced by this process was very strong, hence the word "kraft," which is German for strength. Hicks notes that more than $100 million were invested in new pulp and paper mills in the South between 1935 and 1940 and that sulfate pulping capacity more than doubled. William T. Hicks, "Recent Expansion in the Southern Pulp and Paper Industry," *Southern Economic Journal* 6 (1940): 440–43. See also Helen Hunter, "Innovation, Competition, and Locational Changes in the Pulp and Paper Industry: 1880–1950," *Land Economics* 31 (1955): 314–27.

8. The Paper and Allied Products industry (SIC Code 26) contains seventeen distinct industries. The basic organization of the industry can be broken down into three major tiers of activity: woodpulp production; paper and paperboard production; and finished products conversion. Integrated pulp and paper mills, which consist of both large pulp mills and paper/paperboard mills on the same site, allow for production to run continuously from raw materials to bulk paper and paperboard products. Large-scale integrated mills are necessarily located close to the sources of raw materials and represent the foundation of the modern pulp and paper industry. Maureen Smith, *The U.S. Paper Industry and Sustainable Production: An Argument for Restructuring* (Cambridge: MIT Press, 1997), 19–27.

9. Oden notes that the southern kraft mills were able to capitalize on a series of innovations, including the introduction of synchronized electric drives in 1919, which permitted substantial increases in production. See Oden, "Southern Kraft Paper Industry," 583. For a discussion of the relationships between increasing scale and locational change in the industry, see Hunter, "Innovation, Competition, and Locational Changes."

10. Today a 2,000 ton per day capacity mill uses about 1 million cords of wood per year, 14 billion gallons of water per year, and approximately 6 billion kilowatt-hours of energy per year. Input numbers are based on information from *Lockwood-Post's Directory of the Pulp, Paper, and Allied Trades* (San Francisco: Miller-Freeman Publications, 1995).

11. In contrast to the lumber industry, the pulp and paper industry was able to utilize much smaller, and hence younger, timber (i.e., timber with a shorter "rotation age"). In the early years, the typical rotation age for pulpwood was between 15 and 20 years (though it could be shorter or longer depending on management needs, and so forth), whereas the optimal rotation age for sawtimber was at least 35 to 40 years. Given the importance of turnover time, such a rotation age differential made it much easier for the pulp and paper industry (as opposed to the lumber industry) to institute a forest management regime that treated timber as a crop.

12. "New Industrial Epoch Begins," *Savannah Morning News*, 1 October 1936.

13. "Mayor Praises Savannah Spirit," *Savannah Morning News*, 2 October 1936.

14. John Popham, "King Cotton Is Dead in Savannah, the Most Famous of the Old South's Cotton Ports, and the Stately Pine Tree Is the New Ruler," *New York Times*, 1 July 1947. This transition had been predicted for some time. Charles H. Herty, for example, declared in 1933 that "some day, in the not far distant future, King Cotton is going

to be replaced by King Pulp." Quoted in F. Basil Abrams, "Paper from Georgia Pines," *Atlanta Journal*, 12 February 1933.

15. Popham, "King Cotton Is Dead."

16. Clepper cites a 1928 editorial from the *Journal of Forestry*, which defined industrial forestry as "timber growing as a business enterprise"—a concept that, at the time, represented quite a departure from the status quo. Clepper, *Professional Forestry*, 202. The U.S. Forest Service noted that by the mid-1980s, the value of roundwood timber products sold in the South (approximately $6.1 billion in 1984) was twice the value of soybean or cotton production and three times the value of tobacco, wheat, or corn crops (valued at local points of delivery). U.S. Forest Service, *The South's Fourth Forest: Alternatives for the Future*, Forest Resources Report No. 24 (Washington, D.C.: GPO, 1988), 18–19.

17. The term "artificial regeneration," widely used in forestry practice, refers simply to reforestation by direct planting or seeding. In contrast, "natural regeneration" refers to the practice of leaving seed trees standing after harvest in order to allow lands to restock "naturally." Obviously, natural regeneration is very much a product of conscious design and directed action and thus could easily be considered artificial. Without getting into the semantic difficulties of using these two terms, this chapter will simply use them as they apply to forestry practice.

18. Scott actually uses the example of German scientific forestry, which strongly influenced scientific forestry in the United States and elsewhere, to illustrate his point about how the commercial and bureaucratic logics of certain state projects necessarily depend on a radical simplification of the natural (and social) world—a process of imposing legibility and regimentation in order to refashion the forest into a monocropped "one commodity machine." Scott also notes in his introduction that such projects of simplification and legibility are by no means exclusive to states. Large firms and capitalist markets can be powerful agents for simplification and homogenization as well. See James C. Scott, *Seeing Like a State: How Certain Schemes to Improve the Human Condition Have Failed* (New Haven: Yale University Press, 1998), 11–22. For a similar perspective on the role of state projects in "simplifying" nature, see Donald Worster, *Rivers of Empire: Water, Aridity, and the Growth of the American West* (Oxford: Oxford University Press, 1985).

19. The term "industrial system" is from Annalee Saxenian, *Regional Advantage: Culture and Competition in Silicon Valley and Route 128* (Cambridge: Harvard University Press, 1994).

20. Alfred D. Chandler, *Scale and Scope: The Dynamics of Industrial Capitalism* (Cambridge: Harvard University Press, 1990); and Chandler, "Organizational Capabilities and the Economic History of the Industrial Enterprise," *Journal of Economic Perspectives* 6 (1992). For Wright's arguments regarding technological change as a form of collective learning, see Gavin Wright, "Can a Nation Learn? American Technology as a Network Phenomenon," in Naomi Lamoreaux, Daniel Raff, and Peter Temin, eds., *Learning by Doing in Markets, Firms, and Countries* (Chicago: University of Chicago Press, 1999); and Wright, "Towards a More Historical Approach to Technological Change," *Economic Journal* 107 (1997): 1560–66.

21. Gavin Wright, *Old South, New South: Revolutions in the Southern Economy since*

the Civil War (New York: Basic Books, 1986), 172-75. I am indebted to Professor Wright for helping me to see the emergence of industrial forestry in the South as an example of regional collective learning.

22. Following scholars of regional development such as Annalee Saxenian and Gary Herrigel, the analytical perspective taken in this essay is what Herrigel calls "constructivist political economy." In contrast to traditional views of industrialization as a unitary phenomenon unfolding according to a single, over-arching logic, the constructivist perspective views industrialization as a historically specific process that is heterogeneous and contingent. Gary Herrigel, *Industrial Constructions: The Sources of German Industrial Power* (Cambridge: Cambridge University Press, 1996); and Saxenian, *Regional Advantage*. For a similar perspective, see Philip Scranton, *Endless Novelty: Specialty Production and American Industrialization, 1865-1925* (Princeton: Princeton University Press, 1997).

23. R. D. Forbes, "The Passing of the Piney Woods," *American Forestry* 29, no. 351 (1923): 134.

24. Rupert B. Vance, *Human Geography of the South: A Study in Regional Resources and Human Adequacy* (Chapel Hill: University of North Carolina Press, 1935), 124-25. See also George B. Tindall, *The Emergence of the New South, 1913-1945* (Baton Rouge: Louisiana State University Press, 1967), 82. Howard Odum noted in 1936 that "Of the 125 million acres in virgin pine, 100 million have been cut-over, ten and a half million absorbed into agriculture, and 33 million remain without new growth." Howard W. Odum, *Southern Regions of the United States* (Chapel Hill: University of North Carolina Press, 1936), 80, 576.

25. J. F. Duggar, "Areas of Cultivation in the South," in *The South in the Building of the Nation*, vol. 5 (Richmond, Va.: Southern Historical Publication Society, 1910), 17, cited in C. Vann Woodward, *Origins of the New South, 1877-1913* (Baton Rouge: Louisiana State University Press, 1951), 118.

26. Quoted in Joel Williamson, *William Faulkner and Southern History* (New York: Oxford University Press, 1993), 399.

27. Charles S. Sargent, *Report on the Forests of North America* (Washington, D.C.: GPO, 1884).

28. For discussions of the labor situation in the southern lumber and naval stores industries, see Vernon H. Jensen, *Lumber and Labor* (New York: Farrar and Rinehart, 1945); Nollie Hickman, *Mississippi Harvest: Lumbering in the Longleaf Pine Belt* (Oxford: University of Mississippi Press, 1962); Thomas F. Armstrong, "Georgia Lumber Laborers, 1880-1917: The Social Implications of Work," *Georgia Historical Quarterly* 67 (1983): 435-50; and Armstrong, "The Transformation of Work: Turpentine Workers in Coastal Georgia, 1865-1901," *Labor History* 25 (1984): 518-32.

29. See, for example, Overton W. Price, "Saving the Southern Forests," *World's Work* 5 (1903): 3207-22; and Gifford Pinchot, "Southern Forest Products, and Forest Destruction and Conservation since 1865," in *The South in the Building of the Nation*, vol. 6 (Richmond, Va.: Southern Historical Publication Society, 1910).

30. The formal title was U.S. Forest Service, *Timber Depletion, Lumber Prices, Lumber Exports, and Concentration of Timber Ownership*, Report of Senate Resolution 311 (Washington, D.C.: GPO, 1920).

31. Ibid., 66–69.

32. Ibid., 20–21.

33. George P. Ahern, *Deforested America: Statement of the Present Forest Situation in the United States*, S. Doc. 216, 70th Cong., 2d sess. (Washington, D.C.: GPO, 1929), 3.

34. Pinchot, "Southern Forest Products," 154–55.

35. As Paul David and Gavin Wright point out in the case of U.S. minerals development, the construction of what they call a "public knowledge infrastructure" (referring to the early geological surveys) was a critical first step in resource discovery and exploitation. Paul David and Gavin Wright, "Increasing Returns and the Genesis of American Resource Abundance," *Industrial and Corporate Change* 6 (1997): 203–45. The early forest surveys played a somewhat similar role in the transition to industrial forestry and the growth of the modern forest products industry in the South. Because most of the timberland in the South was (and is) privately owned, however, the "public infrastructure of knowledge" established through the forest surveys was of primary benefit to private timberland owners.

36. U.S. Department of Agriculture, *Forest Resources of South Georgia*, USDA Misc. Pub. 390 (Washington, D.C.: GPO, 1941), ii; Inman F. Eldredge, "The Forest Survey in the South," Occasional Paper No. 31 (New Orleans: Southern Forest Experiment Station, 1934).

37. The original director of the southern forest survey was G. H. Lentz. Yet, Inman F. "Cap" Eldredge, who succeeded Lentz, was primarily responsible for the effort. See U.S. Forest Service, *A History of Forestry Research in the Southern United States*, Misc. Pub. No. 1462 (Washington, D.C.: GPO, 1989), 40–42. Since the initial surveys of the 1930s, updates have been issued roughly every ten years.

38. E. L. Demmon, "Economics for Our Southern Forests," Occasional Paper No. 59 (New Orleans: Southern Forest Experiment Station, 1937).

39. See, for example, U.S. Department of Agriculture, *Georgia Forest Resources and Industries*, USDA Misc. Pub. No. 501 (Washington, D.C.: GPO, 1943), 2, 17, 19, 20.

40. Ninety-eight percent of the fire damage occurred on nonprotected lands. At the time, some two-thirds of south Georgia timberlands had no fire protection. Ibid., 8–9, 36.

41. Stephen J. Pyne, *Fire in America: A Cultural History of Wildland and Rural Fire* (Seattle: University of Washington Press, 1997), 143.

42. Regional Committee on Southern Forest Resources, *The Southern Forests* (Atlanta: National Resources Planning Board Field Office, 1940), 13.

43. W. W. Ashe, "Forest Conditions in the Southern States and Recommended Forest Policy," *South Atlantic Quarterly* 22 (1925): 299.

44. Pyne, *Fire in America*, 152.

45. Ibid., 155; U.S. Forest Service, *South's Fourth Forest*, 38–41, 43, 287–88 table 2.10; Robbins, *American Forestry*, chs. 4–5. See also Samuel P. Hays, *Conservation and the Gospel of Efficiency: The Progressive Conservation Movement, 1890–1920* (Cambridge: Harvard University Press, 1959); and Michael Williams, *Americans and Their Forests: A Historical Geography* (Cambridge: Cambridge University Press, 1989).

46. U.S. Department of Agriculture, *Woods Burning in the South*, Leaflet No. 40 (Washington: GPO, 1940), 2–3.

47. Ibid., 3.

48. Pikl notes that in 1935, the Georgia Forestry Association passed a resolution urging judges of the Superior court to tighten up on woods-burning. In the fiscal year 1941–42, forty-seven cases were brought against arsons in the state. In 1956, the Georgia legislature passed the Notification of Intention to Burn Law, requiring that citizens notify state officials before engaging in the practice of woods-burning. Pikl, *Georgia Forestry*, 31, 51.

49. Southern Forestry Educational Project, *Second Annual Report* (n.p.: American Forestry Association, 1930); William F. Jacobs, "The Dixie Crusade," *American Forests* (December 1978): 18–21, 38–46; and James E. Mixon, "Progress of Protection from Forest Fires in the South," *Journal of Forestry* 54 (1956): 650–51. Mixon was the state forester of Louisiana.

50. Compounding economic depression, fires ravaged much of the upcountry South during the drought years of 1930–31. The following year, Georgia and Florida both sustained heavy losses. Pyne, *Fire in America*, 156.

51. At the height of CCC activity, there were some 311 forestry camps spread throughout the South—125 on national forest land and 186 operating primarily on private lands. U.S. Forest Service, *South's Fourth Forest*, 46; and Mixon, "Forest Fires in South," 650.

52. Pyne, *Fire in America*, 156.

53. H. H. Chapman, "Forest Fires and Forestry in the Southern States," *American Forestry* 18 (1912): 510–17.

54. H. H. Chapman, "Factors Determining Natural Reproduction of Longleaf Pine on Cut-over Lands in Lasalle Parish, Louisiana," *Yale University School of Forestry Bulletin 16*, New Haven, 1926. For another early statement on the importance of fire in longleaf pine forests and the need for controlled burning in the southern woods, see W. G. Wahlenberg, "Fire in Longleaf Pine Forests," Occasional Papers No. 40 (New Orleans: Southern Forest Experiment Station, 1935). For brief historical overviews of the changing views of fire in the southern forest, see E. V. Komarek Sr., "The Use of Fire: An Historical Background," and Roland M. Harper, "Historical Notes on the Relation of Fire to Forests," in *Proceedings of the First Annual Tall Timbers Fire Ecology Conference* (Tallahassee: Florida State University, 1962).

55. A. B. Crow, *Fire Ecology and Fire Use in the Pine Forest of the South* (Baton Rouge: Louisiana State University School of Forestry and Wildlife Management, 1982).

56. In a national context, the southern forestry community became the first to adopt prescribed burning as a positive tool of forest management—more than a decade before the rest of the country. Williams, *Americans and Their Forests*, 485–87.

57. Pyne, *Fire in America*, 158; U.S. Forest Service, *South's Fourth Forest*, 47.

58. Crow, *Fire Ecology and Fire Use*, 14.

59. As Stephen Pyne has noted, part of this was due to the long and important history of fire in the South and, because of the specific ecology of the southern pine forest, the fact that fire was necessary for industrial forestry to proceed. In his assessment: "Wildland fire . . . [was] . . . progressively removed from the hands of folk practitioners and placed in the grasp of professional foresters. . . . Forestry in the South would have been impossible if promiscuous and malicious woodsburning had continued. But equally, it

would have been impossible if conducted on a dogmatic policy of fire exclusion." Pyne, *Fire in America*, 144–45.

60. Virginia, North Carolina, South Carolina, Georgia, Florida, Alabama, Mississippi, Tennessee, Arkansas, Louisiana, Oklahoma, and Texas.

61. Pikl, *Georgia Forestry*, 50–51; Robbins, *American Forestry*, 208.

62. The success of fire protection efforts in Georgia, for example, was indicated by the fact that in 1957, for the first time in the United States, the privately organized Forest Insurance Company announced that it would accept applications for timber insurance, with coverage up to $50 per acre, on timberlands in counties protected through the Georgia Forestry Commission. Pikl, *Georgia Forestry*, 51.

63. Regional Committee on Southern Forest Resources, *Southern Forests*, 13. In July 1998, however, more than half a million acres of timberland burned in Florida alone—serving as a reminder of just how powerful fire can be in the South, despite extensive fire protection and control.

64. L. W. Orr and R. J. Kowal, "Progress in Forest Entomology in the South," *Journal of Forestry* 54 (1956): 653–56; George H. Hepting, "Forest Disease Research in the South," *Journal of Forestry* 54 (1956): 656–60; and Robbins, *American Forestry*, 206, 215, 220–21.

65. U.S. Department of Agriculture, *Georgia Forest Resources*, 37.

66. Regional Committee on Southern Forest Resources, *Southern Forests*, 17; Resources for the Future, *Forest Credit in the United States: A Survey of Needs and Facilities* (Washington, D.C.: Resources for the Future, 1958). The distinction between industrial owners and small nonindustrial owners is important here. Clearly, access to credit was not a problem for large firms that could borrow in national capital markets.

67. Up until this time, forest land had been considered unimproved property and hence not acceptable as collateral by national banks. The amendment to section 24 of the Federal Reserve Act was sponsored primarily by Pacific Northwest banking and timber interests. It authorized national banks to make mortgage loans secured by first liens on forest tracts that were "properly managed in all respects." Resources for the Future, *Forest Credit*, 53.

68. Ibid., ch. 6. In the early 1950s, the Travelers Insurance Company made its first timberland loans in the South. By 1966, G. A. Fletcher, senior vice president of Travelers, estimated that the insurance industry as a whole had well over $100 million invested in loans on timberlands. G. A. Fletcher, "Timberlands as Long-Term Loan Investments for Insurance Companies," *Forest Farmer* 26 (1967): 15. As for southern banks, the C&S Bank of Georgia was one of the first and most active banks to get involved in timberland loans, often teaming up with life insurance companies such as Travelers. C. M. Chapman, "A Private Banker Looks at Timber Loans," *Forest Farmer* 26 (1967): 16. For smaller timberland owners, the federal land bank and the Farmer's Home Administration were the primary sources of long-term credit. See "Trends in Land Bank Credit for Forest Owners," *Forest Farmer* 26 (1967): 17, 35; "Farmers Home Administration Loans for Forestry Purposes," *Forest Farmer* 26 (1967): 18; and Albert Ernest, "Financing the South's Forest Development," *Forest Farmer* 41 (1982): 6–7, 32.

69. Vance, *Human Geography*, 132.

70. Ibid.

71. "Forest Taxes and Conservation," *Harvard Law Review* 53 (1940): 1018–24; Samuel Trask Dana and Sally K. Fairfax, *Forest and Range Policy: Its Development in the United States*, 2d ed. (New York: McGraw Hill, 1980), 286–87.

72. Ronald B. Craig, an economist with the Southern Forest Experiment Station, researched the issue of tax delinquency extensively during the 1930s. In a 1934 study, he found that 31 million acres of rural land (approximately 14 percent of the gross land area) in eight southern states had been in tax default for more than three years. Some two-thirds of all tax delinquent land that reverted back to public ownership was forest land. Ronald B. Craig, "Reversion of Forest Land for Taxes Increasing in the South," Occasional Paper No. 32 (New Orleans: Southern Forest Experiment Station, 1934), and "The Extent of Tax Default in the Gulf States," Occasional Paper No. 49 (New Orleans: Southern Forest Experiment Station, 1935). Later in 1939, Craig estimated that 22 million acres of rural land (roughly 10 percent of gross land area) in these eight states had been in default for two or more years, and that between 13 and 15 million acres of this was forest land. Ronald B. Craig, "The Forest Tax Delinquency Problem in the South," *Southern Economic Journal* 6, no. 2 (1939): 145–64. Clearly, the Depression had exacerbated the problem of tax delinquency in the region. For Craig, however, the primary reason why such a large percentage of forest lands was in default had to do with the nature of the tax system: "There can be no doubt of the fact of overassessment of forest land in the South.... This is one, if not the chief, reason why forest land forms such a high percentage of the total tax-forfeited area of the South." Craig, "Forest Tax Delinquency," 152.

73. The issue had actually been on the public policy agenda in various guises since the early twentieth century.

74. U.S. Forest Service, *Timber Depletion*, 70–71.

75. Section 3, Clarke-McNary Act (43 Stat 653).

76. Fred R. Fairchild, *Forest Taxation in the United States*, USDA Misc. Publication No. 218 (Washington, D.C.: GPO, 1935), 5–6. Fairchild had previously reported on forest taxation issues in 1909.

77. Ibid., 636.

78. Ibid., 8.

79. Ibid., 525, 533, 537–39. "It is this uncertainty that more than anything else makes the property tax a menace to forestry" (537).

80. Ibid., 636. Still, the report was quite clear in its advocacy for tax reform, though it did not provide a ringing endorsement of the much-heralded severance or yield tax. For not only did the yield tax present considerable complications for local finance, it was also very difficult to administer. Fairchild pointed out, moreover, that there was little evidence to support such a tax scheme: "The fact that after twenty years of experiment no State has yet succeeded in setting up a satisfactory yield tax of broad application is evidence of the difficulties involved." Instead, the report argued for reform of the operation of the property tax system through better assessment, improved collection and enforcement, and more efficient administration. Fairchild also outlined three proposals for correcting some of the inherent defects of the property tax system as applied to timberlands:

an adjusted property tax; a deferred timber tax; and a differential timber tax. Ibid., 637–40.

81. R. Clifford Hall, "The Rise of Realism in Forest Taxation," *Journal of Forestry* 36 (1938): 903.

82. Four basic kinds of special timber tax laws have been developed in southern states: exemptions, modified assessments, yield taxes, and severance taxes. U.S. Forest Service, *South's Fourth Forest*, 65–66, and Margaret P. Hamel, ed., *Forest Taxation: Adapting in an Era of Change* (Madison, Wis.: Forest Products Research Society, 1988).

83. While property tax reform waned as an issue in the 1950s, it has resurfaced frequently ever since and still remains one of the more contentious local issues associated with the forest products industry. During the 1940s, forest taxation under the federal income tax emerged as a prominent source of concern for timberland owners, particularly for corporations. As in the debates over the property tax, the basic argument concerning the federal income tax focused on discriminatory taxation and perverse incentives. For a discussion, see U.S. Forest Service, *South's Fourth Forest*, 65; Charles W. Briggs and William K. Condrell, *Tax Treatment of Timber* (Washington, D.C.: Forest Industries Committee on Timber Valuation and Taxation, 1978), 3–7; U.S. Forest Service, *Impacts of Forestry Associations on Forest Productivity in the South*, Misc. Publication 1458 (Washington, D.C.: GPO, 1988), 13–14; and Hamel, *Forest Taxation*.

84. One historian remarked that by this time forest taxation was a "dead issue." Williams, *Americans and Their Forests*, 456.

85. Henry C. Wallace, "Forestry and Our Land Problem," *American Forestry* 29, no. 349 (1923): 15–16.

86. Price, "Saving the Southern Forests"; Pinchot, "Southern Forest Products"; Forbes, "Passing of the Piney Woods."

87. See, for example, J. W. Toumey, "The Regeneration of Southern Forests," in *Proceedings of the Southern Forestry Congress*, Asheville, N.C., 11–15 July 1916, 144–53.

88. Southern Cut-Over Land Association, *The Dawn of the New Constructive Era*, Report of the Cut-Over Land Conference of the South (New Orleans: Southern Cut-Over Land Association, 1917). See also Frank Heyward, "History of Industrial Forestry in the South," *The Colonel William B. Greeley Lectures in Industrial Forestry* (Seattle: University of Washington College of Forestry, 1958), 16, and Clark, *Greening of the South*, 30.

89. See note 17 for discussion of the terms "natural" and "artificial" regeneration. For early statements by Hardtner, see Henry Hardtner, "A Practical Example of Forest Management in Southern Yellow Pine," in *Proceedings of the Southern Forestry Congress*, Asheville, N.C., 11–15 July 1916, 71–80, and "President's Address," in *Proceedings of the Third Southern Forestry Congress*, Atlanta, Ga., 20–22 July 1921, 11–15. Clepper refers to the Urania lumber company as "the true innovator in practical forestry in the South." Clepper, *Professional Forestry*, 236–37.

90. For an early discussion of the importance of artificial reforestation in the South, see Philip C. Wakeley, *Artificial Reforestation in the Southern Pine Region*, USDA Technical Bulletin No. 492 (Washington, D.C.: GPO, 1935). See also Philip C. Wakeley, "The South's First Big Plantation," *Forests and People* 23, no. 2 (1973): 26–31, and Heyward, "History of Industrial Forestry."

91. U.S. Forest Service, *South's Fourth Forest*, 41, 48.

92. The whole debate was kicked off in 1919 by Pinchot's Society of American Foresters' report, which predicted an imminent timber shortage and called for regulatory controls over private forest practices. As noted previously, this led to the so-called Capper report of 1920. Senator Capper, however, was not content with the rather weak proposals contained in the report that bore his name, and introduced a series of bills calling for direct regulation of cutting on privately owned timberlands. Due to significant opposition, no hearings were ever held on any of Capper's bills. Meanwhile, Senator Bertrand Snell of New York introduced several of his own bills, which reflected the position of Forest Service chief William B. Greeley and others who favored the cooperative approach (federal encouragement of state legislation). The Snell legislation was also blocked, this time by Pinchot's allies, who feared that state legislation would be ineffective because of the influence of industry interests in state governments. In 1924, Senator McNary and Representative Clarke introduced bills in their respective chambers that contained many of the cooperative programs, particularly in fire control, of the earlier Capper report and the Snell bills. The result was the Clarke-McNary Act of June 1924, which laid the foundation for federal-state cooperation in forest protection and management. For analyses of the debate leading up to Clarke-McNary and the impact of the final legislation, see Dana and Fairfax, *Forest and Range Policy*, 126–27; Clepper, *Professional Forestry*, 164; and Robbins, *American Forestry*, 85–99.

93. This was particularly evident in the emerging discourse over the South's underdevelopment. Witness the famous 1938 *Report on Economic Conditions of the South*, which, at least in Roosevelt's view, identified the region as the nation's number one economic problem, and pointed to the waste of natural resources, particularly soils, minerals, and forests, as both cause and effect of underdevelopment: "The paradox of the South is that while it is blessed by Nature with immense wealth, its people as a whole are the poorest in the country. Lacking industries of its own, the South has been forced to trade the richness of its soil, its minerals and its forests, and the labor of its people for goods manufactured elsewhere. If the South received such goods in sufficient quantity to meet its needs, it might consider itself adequately paid." National Emergency Council, *Report on Economic Conditions of the South* (Washington, D.C.: GPO, 1938), 8. The report has sometimes been seen as an example of the colonial economy thesis that shaped much of the thinking during the 1930s and 1940s on southern economic development: that absentee ownership and the South's dependent status were responsible for the region's underdevelopment. As Gavin Wright has argued, however, the colonial economy thesis confuses symptoms with causes and does not explain adequately the underlying reasons for the persistence of southern economic "backwardness." Gavin Wright, *Old South*.

94. Dana and Fairfax, *Forest and Range Policy*, 169; and Clepper, *Professional Forestry*, 146.

95. Heyward, *History of Industrial Forestry*, 32–33; Clepper, *Professional Forestry*, 147–49; Dana and Fairfax, *Forest and Range Policy*, 169–70.

96. U.S. Forest Service, *A Statistical History of Tree Planting in the South, 1925–1985*, Misc. Report SA-MR 8 (Washington, D.C.: GPO, 1986), 19.

97. F. A. Silcox, *Report of the Chief of the Forest Service, 1937* (Washington, D.C.: GPO, 1937), 13. A dedicated New Dealer, Silcox stepped up Forest Service proposals for public regulation of private forest practices and provoked considerable hostility among industry leaders, particularly in the South. Though Silcox concurred with the view that the primary objective of forest policy was to keep forest land continuously productive, he believed that regulation, in addition to cooperation, was necessary to achieve such a goal. Clepper, *Professional Forestry*, 149; and Robbins, *American Forestry*, 131–33.

98. Franklin D. Roosevelt, *Message from the President of the United States Transmitting a Recommendation for the Immediate Study of the National Forest Problem*, U.S. House of Representatives, 75th Congress, 3rd Session, Document No. 539, March 14, 1938 (Washington, D.C.: GPO, 1938), 1–4.

99. The final report of the committee, *Forest Lands of the United States*, was submitted to Congress in March of 1941 and constituted a major disappointment for the proponents of regulation. Of the fifteen recommendations, only one dealt explicitly with regulation. Though the issue persisted in one form or another until the early years of the Truman administration, the Joint Committee's report effectively marked the end of the push for federal regulation. Dana and Fairfax, *Forest and Range Policy*, 171–72; Robbins, *American Forestry*, 131; and Clepper, *Professional Forestry*, 152–53, 162–63.

100. E. H. Wilson, *Savannah Woodlands Operations and Contract System of Wood Procurement as It Affects the Farmers and Landowners* (Savannah, Ga.: Union Bag and Paper Corporation, 1938), 12. The policy also called for selective cutting on noncompany lands in order to promote natural regeneration.

101. T. W. Earle, "Southern Pulpwood Conservation Association at Work for Fifteen Years," Address to the Southern Pulpwood Conservation Association, Atlanta, 19 January 1955, 8–9, 12; Heyward, "History of Industrial Forestry," 39; Clepper, *Professional Forestry*, 251; and U.S. Forest Service, *Impacts of Forestry Associations*, 10–11.

102. Key policies included the Agricultural Adjustment Acts of 1933 and 1938 and the Soil Conservation and Domestic Allotment Act of 1936. For general discussions of this transformation, see Wright, *Old South*, and Bruce D. Schulman, *From Cotton Belt to Sunbelt: Federal Policy, Economic Development, and the Transformation of the South, 1938–1980* (New York: Oxford University Press, 1991). For the South as a whole, tenancy declined by 25 percent between 1935 and 1940 while the rural wage labor population increased by some 14 percent. Schulman, *Cotton Belt to Sunbelt*, 19–20.

103. Gilbert C. Fite, *Cotton Fields No More: Southern Agriculture 1865–1980* (Lexington: University Press of Kentucky, 1984).

104. Clepper, *Professional Forestry*, 14. By 1990, according to one source, 38,000 industry-supported tree farmers actively managed 54 million acres of southern timberlands—60 percent of the U.S. total. See D. L. Knight, "Southern Forest Industry: Shaping a Better Life for Southerners," *Forest Farmer* 50 (1990): 7.

105. In Georgia, for example, the first state nursery was established at Athens in 1929. J. T. May, "Reflections on Southern Forest Tree Nurseries," in *Proceedings of the Annual Meeting of the Southern Forest Nursery Association*, Charleston, S.C., 25–28 July 1988. In 1950, Georgia nurseries produced a record 46 million seedlings—putting the state at the

forefront of southern regeneration efforts. Seedling production by Georgia state nurseries skyrocketed during the 1950s—more than doubling to 95 million seedlings in 1954 and then climbing to an astonishing 305 million in 1959, the peak year for forest regeneration under the Soil Bank program. Pikl, *Georgia Forestry,* 49, 52, 70.

106. For southern farmers, such payments typically ranged between $8 and $10 per acre per year. W. S. Swingler, "Forestry in the Soil Bank," *Journal of Forestry* 54 (1956): 747–49; Larry Lee, "Soil Bank Lands: A Survey of ASCS Directors," *Forest Farmer* 26 (1967): 10–11, 36; L. F. Kalmar, "Soil Bank Lands as Industry Views the Situation," *Forest Farmer* 26 (1967): 12, 39–40; D. A. Craig, "Soil Bank Lands: The Federal Government's Point of View," *Forest Farmer* 27 (1967): 13, 38–39; Jack Cantrell, "Industry's Stake in Soil Bank Plantations," *Forest Farmer* 27 (1968): 10–12; and R. J. Alig, T. J. Mills, and R. L. Shackelford, "Survey of Soil Bank Plantations Shows Very High Retention Rate," *Forest Farmer* 39 (1980): 8–9, 13–14.

107. Georgia led the South and the nation in forest regeneration during these years. Between 1956 and 1961, almost 1.3 million acres were planted/seeded in the state—two-thirds of which were on nonindustrial private land. U.S. Forest Service, *A Statistical History.*

108. Nursery production peaked in the South during the CRP program of the late 1980s at more than 2 billion seedlings per year—approximately 82 percent of total seedling production in the entire United States. Clark W. Lantz, "Role of State Nurseries in Southern Reforestation—An Historical Perspective," in *National Proceedings: Forest and Conservation Nursery Associations—1996,* U.S. Department of Agriculture Gen. Tech. Rep. PNW-GTR-389 (Portland, Ore.: USDA, 1997), 50.

109. Alig et al., "Survey of Soil Bank Plantations."

110. For a critical discussion of the effect of the Soil Bank program on small southern farmers, see Pete Daniel, "The Legal Basis of Agrarian Capitalism: The South since 1933," in Melvyn Stokes and Rick Halpern, eds., *Race and Class in the American South since 1890* (Oxford, U.K.: Berg, 1994).

111. Cantrell, "Industry's Stake."

112. This de facto "securitization" of timberland received a major boost in the 1980s as institutional investors began buying huge acreages of timberland in the South. C. S. Binkley, C. F. Raper, and C. L. Washburn, "Institutional Ownership of U.S. Timberland: History, Rationale, and Implications for Forest Management," *Journal of Forestry* 94, no. 9 (1996): 21–28.

113. According to Lantz, planting on company land peaked in 1986 at 1.2 million acres per year. During this year, industry nurseries in the South were producing over 1 billion seedlings per year. Lantz, "Overview," 5, and Lantz, "Role of State Nurseries," 49.

114. Lloyd Austin, "A New Enterprise in Forest Tree Breeding," *Journal of Forestry* 25 (1927): 928.

115. Scott S. Pauley, "The Scope of Forest Genetics," *Journal of Forestry* 52 (1954): 644.

116. Bruce J. Zobel, "Forest Tree Improvement—Past and Present," in P. K. Khosla, ed., *Advances in Forest Genetics* (New Delhi: Ambika Publications, 1981), 13.

117. Aldo Leopold, "Some Thoughts on Forest Genetics," *Journal of Forestry* 27 (1929): 710.

118. Leopold, "Forest Genetics," 710.

119. Lloyd Austin, "A New Enterprise in Forest Tree Breeding," *Journal of Forestry* 25 (1927): 928.

120. According to Bruce Zobel, tree improvement involves the combination of genetic selection and improved silvicultural practices to increase the productivity of forest trees. Major objectives include adaptability, resistance to pests and diseases, growth rate, tree form and quality, and wood qualities. Bruce J. Zobel, "Increasing Productivity of Forest Lands through Better Trees," *The S.J. Hall Lectureship in Industrial Forestry*, 18 April 1974 (Berkeley: University of California, Berkeley School of Forestry and Conservation, 1974), 4–5.

121. G. Muller-Starck and H. R. Gregorius, "Analysis of Mating Systems in Forest Trees," and J. P. van Buijtenen, "Quantitative Genetics in Forestry," in B. S. Weir, E. J. Eisen, M. M. Goodman, and G. Namkoong, eds., *Proceedings of the Second International Conference on Quantitative Genetics* (Sunderland, Mass.: Sinauer Associates, Inc., 1988), 573–74; C. Gaston, S. Globerman, and I. Vertinsky, "Biotechnology in Forestry: Technological and Economic Perspectives," *Technological Forecasting and Social Change* 50 (1995): 80; and Bruce J. Zobel and Jerry R. Sprague, *A Forestry Revolution: The History of Tree Improvement in the Southern United States* (Durham: Carolina Academic Press, 1993), 24–29.

122. Tree breeders often have to wait as long as twenty to thirty years (depending on the species) before mature traits can be evaluated. William L. Olsen, "Molecular Biology in Forestry Research: A Review," in Frederick A. Valentine, ed., *Forest and Crop Biotechnology: Progress and Prospects* (New York: Springer-Verlag, 1988), 315–16.

123. S. E. McKeand and R. J. Weir, "Economic Benefits of an Aggressive Breeding Program," *Proceedings of the Seventeenth Southern Forest Tree Improvement Conference*, Athens, Ga., 6–9 June 1983, 100.

124. The Eddy station was established in 1925, and was reorganized as the Institute for Forest Genetics in 1932. In 1935, the Institute was donated to the government, to be operated by the U.S. Forest Service. Austin, "New Enterprise"; and Ryookiti Toda, "An Outline of the History of Forest Genetics," in Khosla, *Advances in Forest Genetics*.

125. Toda notes that Swedish researchers working in the 1930s and 1940s had developed a program for selecting superior trees and establishing seed orchards with the grafted ramets of these selected trees. It was not until 1950, however, that Sweden initiated a nationwide program of tree improvement based on a system of elite clonal seed orchards. Similar tree improvement programs were established in other countries in the 1950s, particularly in Germany, Great Britain, Australia, Japan, Hungary, and the United States. Toda, "History of Forest Genetics," 8.

126. For more details on the committee's early efforts, see U.S. Forest Service, *Report of the First Southern Conference on Forest Tree Improvement*, 9–10 January 1951 (Atlanta: USFS, 1951); U.S. Forest Service, *Report of the Second Southern Conference on Forest Tree Improvement*, 6–7 January 1953 (Atlanta: USFS, 1953); and U.S. Forest Service, *Proceed-*

ings of the Third Southern Conference on Forest Tree Improvement, 5-6 January 1955 (New Orleans: USFS, 1955). The 24th Southern Forest Tree Improvement Conference was held in 1997.

127. Zobel and Sprague, *Forestry Revolution*, 59–61. See also Jonathan W. Wright, "The Role of Provenance Testing in Tree Improvement," in Khosla, *Advances in Forest Genetics;* and Philip C. Wakeley, "The Relation of Geographic Race to Forest Tree Improvement," *Journal of Forestry* 52 (1954): 653.

128. Zobel and Sprague, *Forestry Revolution*, 4. In 1981, Zobel estimated "that over 30 percent of all tree improvement programs have been failures or have been only marginally successful because geographic variability within the species was ignored." Zobel, *Forest Tree Improvement*, 16. See also Bruce J. Zobel and John Talbert, *Applied Forest Tree Improvement* (New York: John Wiley and Sons, 1984), 75–93.

129. Provenance or seed source studies focused on determining the genetic variation of trees due to their geographic origins. Provenance tests thus involved planting trees of the same species but from different geographic regions side by side to determine the existence and extent of "racial" differences. Early provenance tests were conducted in Europe on Scotts pine in the late nineteenth century. In the United States, the earliest provenance tests were conducted during the 1910s on Ponderosa pine and Douglas fir in the West and on loblolly pine in Louisiana. Wright, "Provenance Testing," 103; Philip C. Wakeley, "Importance of Geographic Strains," in *Report of the First Southern Conference on Forest Tree Improvement*, 1–9; and Henry I. Baldwin, "Seed Certification and Forest Genetics," *Journal of Forestry* 52 (1954): 654–55. Wakeley's study involved collecting seeds from each of the four southern species in various areas of their natural range. A dozen or so plantations were then established in these areas to test for "racial" differences in survival, growth rate, and disease resistance within each species. E. L. Demmon and P. A. Briegleb, "Progress in Forest and Related Research in the South," *Journal of Forestry* 54 (1956): 674–82, 687–92.

130. Baldwin, "Seed Certification," 655; J. W. Duffield, "The Importance of Species Hybridization and Polyploidy in Forest Tree Improvement," *Journal of Forestry* 52 (1954): 645.

131. Wakeley, "Geographic Race," 653.

132. The West Virginia Pulp and Paper Company developed the first industry seed selection program in 1949. By 1956, the company was planting all seedlings from selected stock. L. T. Easley, "Loblolly Pine Seed Production Areas," *Journal of Forestry* 52 (1954): 672–73; and Zobel and Sprague, *Forestry Revolution*, 84.

133. Clemens M. Kaufman, "Extensive Application of Genetics by the Silviculturist," *Journal of Forestry* 52 (1954): 647–48.

134. Zobel and Sprague, *Forestry Revolution*, 17–21.

135. Thomas O. Perry, "The Cooperative Genetics Program at the University of Florida," in *Proceedings of the Third Southern Conference on Forest Tree Improvement*. Originally, the NC State cooperative had twelve charter members. In 1966 it was divided into two programs, one focusing on hardwood and the other on loblolly pine, with the pine program receiving the bulk of the attention and financial support. Zobel, "Increasing Productivity," 17. In addition, a host of other cooperatives focusing on various aspects of

industrial forestry have been established in the South and, more recently, in other parts of the country.

136. Zobel, "Increasing Productivity," 4.

137. The university served as the headquarters and provided facilities, some operating funds, and salaries for staff members, including university faculty, technicians, and support staff. Cooperative members covered major operational expenses. See ibid., 17–18.

138. Ibid., 17; and Zobel and Sprague, *Forestry Revolution*, 50–55.

139. One hundred percent of the seedlings produced in Georgia, Alabama, and Louisiana in 1986 were genetically improved. Lantz, "Overview," 5; and Lantz, "Role of State Nurseries."

140. This was roughly double the output of the other two tree improvement cooperatives. A. E. Squillace, "Tree Improvement Accomplishments in the South," in *Proceedings of the Twentieth Southern Forest Tree Improvement Conference*, Charleston, N.C., 26–30 June 1989, 10.

141. Gains from the second and third generations are expected to exceed those of the first. J. B. Jett, "Thirty-five Years Later: An Overview of Tree Improvement in the Southeastern United States," in *Proceedings of the Annual Meeting of the Southern Forest Nursery Association* (1988); and Steve McKeand and Jan Svensson, "Loblolly Pine: Sustainable Management of Genetic Resources," *Journal of Forestry* 95, no. 3 (1997): 5, 8–9.

142. The flip side of this transition to intensive forest breeding and management, of course, is the increased risk and vulnerability that accompanies any crop monoculture. Though loblolly pine has been growing in parts of the South in even-aged stands for centuries, the program of intensive selection and breeding undertaken in the South since the 1950s combined with the extensive practice of artificial regeneration in the region has rendered southern timberlands more vulnerable to various insect and disease problems. As with high-input monocrop agriculture, maintaining high productivity on intensively managed timberlands requires increased applications of chemicals to combat pathogens, control competing vegetation, and make up for nutritional deficiencies. For discussions of some of the risks and vulnerabilities associated with forest tree improvement and the spread of pine monocultures in the South, see the collection of articles in Duke University School of Forestry, "Topic 1: Possible Consequences of Southern Pine Monocultures," *Proceedings of the Fourth Conference on Southern Industrial Forest Management* (Durham: Duke University, 1960). For a more general discussion, see John W. Duffield, "Forest Tree Improvement: Old Techniques and the New Science of Genetics," *H. R. MacMillan Lectureship Address* (Vancouver: University of British Columbia, 1960). See also Scott, *Seeing Like a State*, 11–22.

143. See L. W. Orr and R. J. Kowal, "Progress in Forest Entomology in the South," *Journal of Forestry* 54 (1956): 653–56; George H. Hepting, "Forest Disease Research in the South," *Journal of Forestry* 54 (1956): 656–60; and A. J. Riker, "Opportunities in Disease and Insect Control through Genetics," *Journal of Forestry* 52 (1954): 651–52.

144. Demmon and Briegleb, "Progress in Forest Research."

145. H. R. Josephson, *A History of Forestry Research in the Southern United States*, USDA Forest Service Misc. Pub. No. 1462 (Washington, D.C.: GPO, 1989).

146. In the words of Bruce Zobel: "The genetic improvement of forest trees is a long-

term, expensive undertaking. It can be done best through Cooperative efforts because most organizations cannot afford a team of highly trained specialists. In a Cooperative, one trained man can oversee a great deal of research. The need to keep the genetic base sufficiently broad is almost impossible for a single organization but is easily achieved in a cooperative effort. The funds and manpower required for a tree-improvement program for each member is minimal in a cooperative, yet enables maximum genetic gains. Plant materials, methods, equipment and even manpower are exchanged amongst members to the benefit of all. In my view, naturally biased, it would seem wasteful and even foolish for each organization to strike out on its own with an expensive, inadequate, and inefficient program when faster and greater gains are assured through joint action. The Florida, Texas, and North Carolina Cooperatives are convincing demonstrations of how well combined action has succeeded." Zobel, "Increasing Productivity," 4.

147. John D. Rue, "The Development of Pulp and Paper-Making in the South," *Southern Lumberman* (20 December 1924): 143 (emphasis in original).

148. Jonathan Daniels, *The Forest is the Future* (New York: International Paper Company, 1957), 8.

149. The term is adapted from Wright, "Can a Nation Learn."

150. This notion of biological time-space compression is adapted from David Harvey, *The Condition of Postmodernity* (Oxford: Blackwell, 1990).

151. *Pulp and Paper North American Factbook* (San Francisco: Miller-Freeman Publications, 1996), 5.

152. Cubbage et al. offer what they call a "conservative" estimate (relative to U.S. Forest Service estimates) for industrial timber plantation area in the South of 11.2 million hectares, out of a total for the United States of 12 million hectares. Based on a review of estimates of industrial timber plantation areas from around the world, they conclude that "the U.S. industrial plantation area is the largest in the world, with most of it in the U.S. South. In fact, the U.S. industrial wood plantations would just about equal that of all of the countries in the southern hemisphere." Frederick W. Cubbage, Robert C. Abt, William S. Dvorak, and Gerardo Pacheco, "World Timber Supply and Prospects: Models, Projections, Plantations, and Implications," paper prepared for the annual meeting of the Central America and Mexico Coniferous Resource, October 1996, 30.

Greenfields in the Heart of Dixie

How the American Auto Industry Discovered the South

KARSTEN HÜLSEMANN

"Imagine," *Automotive News* enticed its readers in the March 9, 1998 issue, "a place where Japanese, American and German automakers are investing heavily to produce more engines and vehicles for both exports and an extraordinarily strong domestic market. The workers are flexible and educated. And the political and financial stability are, well, world-class."[1] The region this trademark automotive industry journal alluded to is not some hot new market in the fast-developing economies of Southeast Asia or Latin America. No, *Automotive News* was referring to the American southeast, a region hardly known for automotive production in the not so distant past.

A 1961 study of the American auto industry with regard to its locational patterns and spatial distribution conceded a "relative absence of manufacturing centers in the southeast."[2] As recently as the late 1970s, there had been little change. Accounts of the U.S. auto industry continued to make little (if any) reference to the South, whereas studies on the economic history and industrialization of the South hardly mentioned an automotive industry.[3] Yet since the early 1980s, the region has increasingly moved into the national and international limelight. For auto production, the southeast has now become "a regional manufacturing center tied to a global industry"—such, at least, was the theme of the first *Automotive News Southeast Conference*, held at Nashville in late April 1998. The list of speakers gathering in the plush Renaissance Hotel to discuss these developments, and later taking special tours of the Nissan and Saturn facilities located just south of the Tennessee capital, reads like a "who's who" of the new automotive businesses in the southern states. Besides Nissan and Saturn, executives hailed from BMW, Mercedes-Benz, Toyota, and Honda, with dozens of supplier firms sending representatives to attend (and to develop business, of course).[4]

The exact boundaries of the recently developed regional agglomeration are difficult to draw. *Automotive News* has avoided the term "southern." Instead, its definition of "southeast" includes southern Indiana and Ohio, as well as West Virginia. Given the new Toyota truck assembly plant in Indiana and the smaller SIA facility in the same state,[5] Honda's sprawling central Ohio manufacturing complex, and Toyota's new West Virginia engine plant (in addition to its already operating assembly complex in Kentucky), to name just the large automakers' plants, there is good reason to do so. For a full picture of the industry, these border states would surely have to be taken into account. When the focus shifts to the industrialization of the South, as in this chapter, obviously the automotive establishments in the truly southern states are of greater interest.

What, then, is the South?[6] Following Rupert Vance, who argued that history, not geography, made the South, the region here is defined as encompassing the states of the former Confederacy, plus Oklahoma (far from statehood at the time of the Civil War) and Kentucky, "an essentially rural border state with a strong Southern tilt."[7] This makes it the thirteen-state region covered by the famous 1938 "Report on Economic Conditions of the South" (which provided the basis for Roosevelt's characterization of the South as "the nation's no. 1 economic problem").[8]

The relatively new and important role the South has come to play for the American automotive industry—and vice versa—is our central focus. This chapter addresses the underlying shift in locational patterns, as well as the entry of new competitors into an industry which repeatedly has been written off as an old, "sunset" sector, but which has restructured and remodeled itself, has shifted its spatial configuration, and now continues to flourish. To this end, the following pages trace the historic origins of auto production in the South prior to World War II, then briefly sketch developments in the first three postwar decades. The 1980 decision by Nissan to build its first U.S. auto plant in the South accelerated—if not triggered—a "Southern drift," the scope of which few observers would have deemed possible. General Motors also choosing a Tennessee location for its Saturn plant (and Toyota's selection of Kentucky soon after) basically set the course for a success story that has now lasted for more than fifteen years. The influx of auto plants into southern states is explained by two core factors: first, the emergence of a "new American auto industry," carried mainly by foreign companies, and second, a new paradigm of the relationship between automakers and suppliers. This "just-in-time" system of parts supply requires geographical closeness of parts makers to final assembly plants, ideally creating a network of related firms, which is a far cry from the isolated, stand-alone assembly plants of previous times. Finally, the place of the automotive and parts manufacturing industry in the economy of the southern states is discussed, leading to the conclusion that even (or especially) in an age of increasing auto industry globalization, the region appears set to be "thriving locally in the global economy."[9]

THE ORIGINS OF AUTO PRODUCTION IN THE SOUTH

It has been noted that "in their haste to understand slavery, politics, blacks, sharecropping, the Civil War, and Reconstruction, students of the South have overlooked an important factor—the automobile—that has influenced all of Southern life and played a leading role in producing the modern South."[10] Writing in 1979, Preston was not referring to the manufacturing side of the automotive industry, but to its product, the automobile. Here, however, "discovery" of the South by the auto industry is primarily understood not as the marketing and selling of cars, but as the development of the region as an automotive *production base*. Still, the development of a southern *market* for automobiles was an important first step for automakers.

In the industry's formative years, passenger cars were a luxury good, handcrafted and expensive. Per capita income in the South, on the other hand, was very low, and most American automakers could hardly envision the South as a marketplace. In addition, the region was hampered by its poorly developed road system, an impediment to growth against which its "Good Roads" movement had not been able to rally successfully. One breakthrough event was the 1909 "Automotive Week," taking place in Atlanta. This first national auto show held in the South generated a significant boost for the regional market. Thereafter, Atlanta in particular "emerged as an automobile business and distribution center for the southeastern United States."[11]

In the early days of the auto industry, manufacturers of "horseless carriages" were scattered throughout the more industrialized states of the United States. Yet by 1909, the American auto industry had already shifted significantly to the Great Lakes area, where most American automakers concentrated.[12] Still, there were occasional manufacturers far outside that emerging center of auto production, as the example of Nashville's Marathon Motor Works shows.

Between 1910 and 1914, Marathon manufactured passenger cars in Nashville. The company that built them had begun as the Southern Engine and Boiler Works in Jackson, Tennessee, making steam and gasoline engines. By 1906, the firm had put together its first car, sold under the Marathon nameplate. Eventually, a group of Nashville businessmen developed an interest in the venture, led by banker Augustus H. Robinson, who had acquired an empty 1881 Victorian brick factory building in Nashville and was looking to use it profitably. Robinson proposed buying the Jackson company and moving the enterprise into his empty site, along with all its equipment and the workforce to operate it. In 1910, the complete equipment, including some heavy machinery, was shipped to Nashville from Jackson, a relocation of some 120 miles. Soon after, Southern Motor Works, as the only large southern automaker of its time was then aptly named, began making cars in the Tennessee capital. By 1911, at which time Nashville boasted at least sixteen official auto dealerships for cars built in other parts of the country, the company had been renamed Marathon Motor Works. Employing some 400 people, it was quickly adding new models, ultimately building cars in twelve different body styles, fitted with three different engines, and placed on four different chassis types. This diversity, in conjunction with mismanagement resulting in faulty cars, eventually led to the demise of Nashville's first and only automaker.[13] Marathon was taken over by a company from Indianapolis, which chose to terminate car production shortly afterwards; in roughly four years, Marathon had turned out an estimated 3,000 to 6,000 units.[14] The plant itself remained open for three more years, making automobile parts.[15]

Like Marathon Motor Works, few car builders outside Michigan survived. By the time Marathon stopped production, some 80 percent of U.S. motor vehicle production was concentrated in the southeastern part of Michigan.[16] Concentration had also occurred on another scale: The number of firms building automobiles had dwindled drastically, Ford and General Motors had become the two major players, and the balance of power within the industry had shifted markedly from parts makers to final assemblers.

A few days after the 1909 auto show, *Atlanta Journal* editor James R. Gray turned to auto executives and suggested "that it would be advisable for automobile manufacturers to establish branch factories in the South."[17] In time, both Ford and General Motors did. At Ford, the idea of branch plants was born out of a desire to save on freight costs.[18] Initially developed from Ford branch agencies that were sales points rather than final assembly plants, the concept was quickly pushed further, soon leading to a network of plants across the country. Branch assembly plants saved the automaker significantly in freight costs for parts as opposed to completed cars. Railroads, the customary means of transportation for finished vehicles to the dealers, charged automakers dearly. Ford found it could ship twenty-six completely knocked-down cars (all the parts needed to assemble each automobile) in a box car that would hold no more than seven or eight fully built-up vehicles, and at significantly lower freight rates than charged for the assembled product.[19] Thus, between 1909 and 1914, Ford built regional assembly plants in fourteen American cities. By 1917, there were twenty-nine, seven of them in southern cities (Houston, Dallas, Oklahoma City, Memphis, Atlanta, Charlotte, and Louisville). Over the next two decades, various new Ford plants were opened, closed, and reopened.[20] General Motors, Ford's principal rival, was the only other automaker to adopt the idea of branch assembly sites on a large scale, soon building sixteen plants (Atlanta Lakewood being the only southern one), all of which had higher capacity than Ford branches.[21]

In stark contrast to the decentralized system of assembly plants, both Ford and General Motors kept most of their components plants in Michigan and the Great Lakes region. While the patterns diverged because Ford typically constructed new plants whereas General Motors usually acquired existing facilities or formerly independent suppliers, the making of components remained highly clustered in north central states, and parts plants in the South (like Ford's body plant at Nashville and General Motors' at Memphis) were exceptions to the rule.[22] Thus, even though there were southern assembly plants, most remained isolated, receiving all their parts by rail from components plants located in the North.

NOT MUCH CHANGE: THE AUTO INDUSTRY IN THE SOUTH, 1945-1980

For the Southern economy, World War II was an important takeoff point.[23] The war and its aftermath meant, among other things, growing investments due to large federal programs that brought the defense industry and new military bases to the South. Although such federal programs certainly contributed significantly and in certain states clearly shaped the course of industrial development, private businesses in labor-intensive industries actually ushered in the second wave of southern industrialization.[24] Southern states heavily recruited plants and capital from of out-of-state investors.

The roots of active and explicit industrial recruitment in the South reach back to the 1930s. The state of Mississippi's Balance Agriculture with Industry (BAWI) program, first enacted in 1936 and later reenacted because of its perceived success and subsequent public pressure, is usually referenced as the first deliberate policy attempt of this kind.[25] The idea behind BAWI soon became fashionable with Mississippi's neighbors and spread to other states, primarily but not only in the South. The "selling of the South" had begun.[26]

Efforts to build southern growth from within also surfaced. In the immediate postwar years, some southern businessmen and state government leaders had actually sought to create a "homemade modern South, with internally generated capital and local ownership."[27] The proponents of these ideas were motivated as much by the idea of shaking off the image of a colonial economy as they were by the very obvious promise of higher wage and education levels. However, this approach, though championed by some prominent officeholders, never could gather majority support among those who shaped the course of economic development. Thus, the dominant recipe for industrial growth in the South remained to lure industry from the North by the promise of cheap land and labor, low tax rates, lax environmental rules, and other incentives. Additionally, starting in the 1950s, southern states began to significantly reduce corporate income taxes. Whereas at midcentury, the South's median corporate tax rate was 85 percent above the non-South level, by 1978 this figure had dropped to 13 percent *below* it.[28] Other typical incentives offered to new industry included tax abatements or land rented at minimal rates. Yet the most important advantage the South offered new industry was the promise of cheap, non-union labor: "Not only was southern labor cheap, it was 'native born,' a description apparently intended to capitalize on a prevailing stereotype of immigrant workers as particularly susceptible to overtures of union organizers."[29] Paying tribute to a widespread mood that labor had become too powerful in the wake of the Wagner Act, and reinforced by a strengthened conservative coalition after the 1946 elections, the U.S. Congress (in 1947) passed the Taft-Hartley Act over President Truman's veto. Among other provisions that marked a significant setback for the labor movement, the bill gave states the right to bypass federal legislation (which had already tied a whole new set of conditions to closed shops) and rule out closed or union shops altogether. By the end of the year, seven southern states enacted open-shop legislation in the form of so-called right-to-work laws.[30]

Low wage rates and thin unionization in the South carried implications for unions in the better-organized northern states, too. The American labor movement felt a strong need to bring the South into line with the rest of the country. Thus, in 1946, the CIO started "Operation Dixie," a massive campaign to organize workers in the American South. Having established a Southern Organizing Committee in Atlanta, the unions' first targets were large textile firms. Within a relatively short time, the unions lost several key elections, and it became clear that the South could not be organized, at least not according to the CIO's approaches established in the North. "Operation Dixie" collapsed.[31] A strong anti-union sentiment had prevailed in the South, and "by the end of the 1970s, anti-unionism had practically replaced racism as the South's signature prejudice."[32]

James Cobb, one of the most knowledgeable scholars on the subject, has maintained that the "use of subsidies to lure out-of-state industry tightened rather than loosened the grip of traditional New South industries on the region's economy." Even as southern states diligently sought automotive investment, serious resistance arose to new auto plants from the local business communities. "Emphasis on cheap labor undermined efforts to recruit better-paying industries that would not only bid up wages but enhance the prospects for unionizing southern workers. Employers who had been lured to the South by pledges of protection from unions often forced local chambers of commerce and other booster organizations to turn a cold shoulder to firms that might infect the community with unions and/or higher wages."[33]

The case of Mazda's site search for a U.S. assembly plant in 1984 presents a fine example. Among the potential locations the Japanese automaker reportedly considered was a site in South Carolina's Greenville-Spartanburg area. The founder and chairman of a local textile company, a large employer in the area, turned to Mazda, specifically asking the Japanese automaker not to locate there because an auto assembly plant would interfere with the (low) level of local wages. While the attempt to fend off the auto industry's entry to the area seems somewhat desperate, this basic sentiment was echoed officially. In an article titled "Saved from Mazda" [!], the *Greenville News* quoted the local economic development agency's "view that the Mazda plant would have had a long-term chilling effect on Spartanburg's orderly industrial growth. An auto plant, employing over 3,000 card-carrying, hymn-singing members of the UAW would, in our opinion, bring to an abrupt halt future desirable [sic] industrial prospects."[34] Mazda eventually decided to go directly into the auto-industrial heartland, selecting Flat Rock, Michigan, for its plant.[35] South Carolina's industrial developers, though, probably did not know just how right they had been about Mazda's arrival "halt[ing] future desirable industrial prospects." It can be taken as certain that, searching for a U.S. assembly plant site in 1992, BMW would *not* have chosen the Greenville-Spartanburg area had Mazda already set up a plant there.[36]

Long before Mazda or BMW showed up on the scene, though, the large U.S. automakers extended their prewar system of regional branch assembly plants. The South's booming market prompted such expansions, and both Ford and GM continued to see Atlanta as an excellent location.[37] General Motors had its prewar Lakewood, Georgia, plant, which made Chevrolet full-size cars, and opened a second plant in the Atlanta vicinity, at Doraville.[38] Ford, which had sold its old Atlanta plant to the government during the war, began construction of a new Atlanta plant in late 1945. Ford added a second newly built southern factory in Louisville, Kentucky, replacing its prewar assembly plant on the same location. With the opening of a new Chevrolet plant by GM in Arlington, Texas, the first postwar set of southern facilities in Ford's and GM's system of branch assembly was complete.[39]

For a short time after 1945, as new firms entered the industry, it even looked as if the South might once again host an automaker of its own. Lured by the Birmingham Chamber of Commerce, in 1946 an upstart auto company by the name of Bobbi-Kar relocated from San Diego, California, to Huntsville, Alabama, moving into the defunct facilities (the Huntsville Arsenal) of World War II aircraft maker Bechtel-McCone.[40] Renamed Bobbi-Kar of Alabama, the new company planned to begin production of a car smaller than anything the Detroit companies offered. After some changes in management, the newly founded Dixie Motor Car Corporation took over Bobbi-Kar's assets, only to go bankrupt shortly after (before making even a single vehicle). Saved by yet another investor, the company reappeared as Keller Motors Corporation. Keller went out of business early in 1950, never having gotten beyond making the prototypes shown to prospective dealers.

With the benefit of hindsight, it is easy to characterize Keller Motors as a mere footnote in automotive history, and the endeavor a lost cause from the start. But at a time in which demand for new cars could barely be met by the large Detroit firms, smaller automakers had at least a reasonable chance to flourish.[41] In context, the episode is most instructive on two points. Keller, the only southern-based (would-be) automaker at the time, was not truly indigenous to the South. The region apparently had not accumulated the managerial, technical, and design capabilities key to launching a freestanding auto corporation. More important, even tiny Keller Motors of Alabama, during the few years of its existence, opened a Detroit office so as to be closer to established Michigan supplier firms. Without these suppliers, apparently making the smallest of cars, even in a limited production run planned for 16,000 units annually, was not deemed possible in the South. Indeed, although Ford and GM assembly plants operated in the South, most auto parts production, by the Big Three and independent parts makers alike, remained solidly centered in Michigan and adjacent states.

Into the 1960s, the basic locational pattern of the U.S. auto industry remained relatively stable. By the late 1960s, General Motors had opened several new parts plants in the South. Located in Georgia, Alabama, Mississippi, and Louisiana, they chiefly made electrical components, requiring rather low-skilled labor.[42] The UAW was carefully monitoring this more or less cautious move South, and in 1970 chose to target General Motors for negotiations over the next national contract, for the first time in fifteen years.[43] GM's "Southern strategy" became an issue for the UAW because the union had found it hard to organize existing southern plants and was understandably concerned about the two large southern assembly complexes GM was building. In August 1973, General Motors announced Oklahoma City as the site for a new passenger car assembly plant. Reportedly, the company had considered four other possible sites for the facility, three southern (Tulsa, Oklahoma; Tuscaloosa, Alabama; Waco, Texas) as well as one non-southern (Wichita, Kansas). Construction began quickly but, following the first oil crisis and a downturn in demand, was suspended for three years (1974 to 1977) with only a fraction of the works completed. The first car rolled off the Oklahoma City line in April, 1979.[44] General Motors' other new Southern facility in the 1970s was a light truck assembly plant built in Shreveport, Louisiana. Announced in fall 1977, the plant's opening was also somewhat delayed (adjusting to changing model specifications and imperiled by softening demand in the market). The only other location considered for this plant (besides two adjacent sites also in Shreveport) was Tulsa, Oklahoma,[45] about a hundred miles from GM's Oklahoma City plant. "Following" General Motors south, according to a count from the first years, were a mere four independent suppliers to the Oklahoma

City plant (two each in Oklahoma and Texas), with parts makers being even more cautious regarding the Shreveport plant.[46]

The last auto assembly plant General Motors opened in the South prior to Saturn was at Bowling Green, Kentucky. However, this did not involve a full-scale site search as in the Oklahoma City and Shreveport cases. For "the world's only Corvette plant," the automaker refrained from seeking a greenfield site.[47] Rather, GM took over a Chrysler facility built in the early 1960s to make air conditioners, retooled it, and in 1981 moved production of its Corvette there from St. Louis. As the Corvette is a niche product, output has remained rather small-scale. Bowling Green's capacity of 25,000 units annually is about a tenth of the standard output of a regular auto assembly plant.[48] This has made the operation too small to justify suppliers opening dedicated new parts factories in the region.

By the late 1970s, the second wave of industrialization had washed ashore some noticeable but modest automotive investment on southern "beaches." Yet although the American automakers had neglected the South as a production base, a new American auto industry was visible on the horizon. During the 1970s, imports had begun to capture a sizable share of the American car market. In the early 1970s, Germany's Volkswagen was the largest exporter of cars to the United States, soon passed by several Japanese makers whose compact models enjoyed growing popularity after the 1973 oil crisis. By the mid-1970s, both German and Japanese companies pondered plans for U.S. assembly plants.[49]

The first foreign automaker to build a U.S. auto plant was not Japanese, but German. Volkswagen in 1976 announced it was looking for a U.S. site, thereby launching the decade's most publicized case of industrial recruitment. Volkswagen had weighed building its plant on a greenfield site but ended up buying a "semi-brownfield" at rural East Huntington in the southwestern corner of Pennsylvania. State agencies put together a substantial incentive package, as they expected some 20,000 spin-off jobs.[50] The fate of this endeavor is now well known. After less than ten years, Volkswagen closed its Pennsylvania manufacturing operations in mid-1988. Thus ended the first full-scale "transplant" operation in the U.S. auto industry.[51]

What makes the case interesting in this essay's context is the fact that Volkswagen had also considered putting the plant in the South, and several southern states had competed for it. In contrast to other states, which chased it alone, Tennessee, Arkansas, and Mississippi formed a consortium based on the "innovative idea that the winning state would encourage suppliers for VW to locate in the two losers."[52] Still, when various Japanese companies announced they were searching for assembly plant locations in the 1980s, this three-state consortium was as dead as the idea behind it. In the bidding war for the VW plant, none of the southern contenders received the desired prize. It would take a Japanese company to change that.

LEADING THE WAY: HOW NISSAN AND SATURN CAME TO TENNESSEE

On 17 April 1980, Nissan president Takashi Ishihara officially announced that his firm had decided to build an assembly plant in the United States. While it was also disclosed that, at least initially, pickup trucks, not cars, would be produced,[53] Nissan officials would not indicate *where* the assembly site would be. The site search thus opened. However, Nissan was not the first Japanese automaker to locate an assembly plant in the United States. In 1979, Honda had announced that it would do so. Starting out with less investment-sensitive motorcycle production (to test the waters), Honda avoided the auto industry's heartland and selected a site in southwestern Ohio. Analysts speculated that "Honda wanted a site far enough south to be out of union country, yet far enough north to be out of the South. German-Americans in Ohio were thought to be better workers than the Scots-Irish in Tennessee (or Kentucky)," Honda's backup choices.[54]

Nissan made it clear from the beginning that, unlike Volkswagen, it was not interested in recycling an already-used site. Rather, Nissan sought a greenfield site, imitating Honda's approach and being consistent with the general pattern of Japanese companies setting up shop abroad.[55] More strongly than Honda, Nissan sought a location distant enough from the established centers of American auto production (and the UAW) to allow it to create its own company-specific production system and workforce environment. At the same time, a site too far away from the U.S. parts supplier base was not desirable, either. Even though Nissan initially would import most parts from Japan,[56] the corporation regarded having regionally near suppliers as advantageous should it begin looking for more U.S. content.

Unlike Volkswagen or Honda, Nissan focused on sites in southern states from the start.[57] The final contenders, apart from the Smyrna, Tennessee, site selected, were two Georgia locations, McDonough and Cartersville, each about 20 miles from Atlanta. Nissan admired the southern work ethic, which it deemed useful in re-creating (transplanting) its production system on American soil.[58] Like other Japanese firms before and after, Nissan preferred to hire people without automotive, often without any industrial background.[59] Also, Nissan considered the homogeneity of the region's people an advantage.[60] They were "native born" and highly skeptical toward organized labor.

From its beginnings, Nissan and its new head of U.S. manufacturing, Marvin T. Runyon, a charismatic former Ford executive, made it clear that they did not want a union in the plant. Tennessee had passed a right-to-work law in February 1947, a mere four weeks after the Taft-Hartley Act had opened the door for states to rule out union shop agreements.[61] In 1978, union membership in Tennessee was below the national average, but not dramatically (17.7 vs. 23.5 percent of nonfarm employment).[62] The important union issue related, however, to the fact that no *large* auto industry employers operated in the state. Thus, the UAW, the union that would eventually attempt to organize the Nissan workforce, had no sizable local organizations in Tennessee (as it did in Georgia with the Ford and GM plants). For constructing its plant, Nissan had hired a non-union company. This, along with Nissan's (perceived or real) stance on unions in general, caused Tennessee union locals to stage a protest at Nissan's groundbreaking ceremonies in February 1981. This incident, which Lamar Alexander would later call his "most embarrassing moment as governor,"[63] triggered a joint resolution by the Tennessee legislature the next day. It condemned the protest and aimed to assure Nissan it *was* welcome in the state. In one assessment, the event "discredited trade unionism in middle Tennessee for years to come."[64]

When Nissan decided to build its U.S. plant in 1980, the UAW had organized virtually 100 percent of auto workers in both the United States and Canada, with workers at a few parts firms being the only exceptions. Thus, for the UAW, organizing the Nissan plant soon became a vital issue. "Cracking" the staunchest anti-union company represented the stepping stone to organizing the other Japanese auto transplants, too.[65] The UAW saw its chances rise as some labor trouble over work injuries started to build up after Nissan's "honeymoon."[66] Following a long organizing drive and a heated campaign on both sides, in 1989 the UAW finally called for an election. The outcome was devastating to the union's hopes of bringing the Japanese auto plants into a bargaining framework. Some 71 percent of the Smyrna workforce voted against UAW representation. Since this bitter defeat, the UAW has not again seriously attempted to organize the workforce at any of the large Japanese-owned assembly plants in the country.[67] Meanwhile Nissan, twice making it into the "100 Best Companies to Work For in America" and seizing the title of the most efficient American auto plant in the renowned Harbour Report (for five consecutive years), has remained an attractive employer in the region. Swedish researchers on a field trip to several transplant facilities recited a comment by their cab driver from Nashville to the Smyrna plant that "people could kill to get a job there."[68]

In retrospect, the significance of Nissan for the state can hardly be overestimated: "The Nissan project was the largest manufacturing investment ever made by a Japanese company in the U.S. or anywhere else outside of Japan, and the largest by any new industry in Tennessee history."[69] Lamar Alexander, governor at the time, as well as when the Saturn decision ensued five years later, has called Nissan's decision to locate its U.S. plant in Tennessee a "watershed," pointing out that the "largest overseas Japanese investment ever was to be made in a state that had never had an automobile plant."[70] Nissan's selection of Tennessee triggered what scholars at the University of Michigan's Center for Japanese Studies have termed a "southern drift" of the American auto industry.[71]

If Nissan's arrival generated fanfares, that furor was nothing in comparison to

Saturn. GM's nationwide search for a plant, conducted in spring and summer 1985, prompted "the largest site selection bidding war of all time."[72] "Saturn mania" swept the country, and thirty-eight states and dozens of communities expressed their interest in hosting the plant.[73] Spring Hill, the Tennessee hamlet that eventually landed the prize, was not one of them. Ultimately, the deal was struck at the state level. Governor Alexander had proposed to GM the notion of Tennessee's "level playing field," which would allow GM's Saturn to go head to head with the largest Japanese-owned plant. Competing directly with the Japanese exactly matched GM's conception of Saturn. This newly founded "independent subsidiary" was the world's largest automaker's attempt to build a quality small car in America, using U.S. workers and as many U.S. parts as possible. At $5 billion, it represented the largest site-specific investment in the history of American industry. Some 7,000 jobs would be created through Saturn, with another 20,000 in related industries, as Saturn was to fully employ a just-in-time system of parts supply.

For both Nissan and Saturn, Tennessee had put together incentive packages that entailed the usual mix of infrastructure improvements, tax abatements, and so on. When Saturn opted for the Spring Hill site, its management officially named freight costs as the single most important consideration.[74] The population shift of the postwar decades had clearly enhanced Tennessee's central location with regard to national markets. The state found itself at the right place on the map, with an infrastructure including several major interstate highways, rail lines, airports, and waterways, ensuring that Tennessee could promote itself as the state that reached more than 70 percent of the American population within a 500-mile radius, the critical limit given for one-day truck delivery without costly overnight stops.

Ever since Saturn's formation, public attention has focused on its special system of shop floor management and the unique relationship between Saturn management and the UAW.[75] Due to a unique accord with the UAW (which Saturn management recognized as a full partner from the beginning), GM employees from other plants could secure Saturn jobs. Bringing in its entire workforce from outside the state, Saturn received anything but a warm welcome locally.[76] Disappointment (both within and outside the plant) grew further after GM repeatedly postponed "Module II," the proposed second plant on the same site.[77] Eventually, the phrase was dropped, and it became clear that GM would not build a second plant at Spring Hill. Rather, additional capacity for a second model (the midsize model range, code-named Project Innovate) now comes from a refurbished GM plant in Wilmington, Delaware. In its advertising, Saturn has extensively and very effectively used the rural down-home southern theme to convey its official line, "A Different Kind of Company. A Different Kind of Car." It remains to be seen how the image and self-perception of Saturn as a different southern automaker will evolve in the long run.

THE "HUB OF THE SOUTHERN WHEEL"

When in 1977 Nissan site search teams reportedly first explored Tennessee as a potential location for a U.S. plant, 49 auto parts manufacturers operated in the state.[78] As of late 1997, almost 500 auto-related businesses were active, employing about 100,000 Tennesseans.[79] Precise figures are hard to come by and estimates by local papers, industry associations, and state government vary widely. Even if the available figures are inconsistent, the general message is clear, the overall trend indisputable: Tennessee has seen a remarkable growth of auto-related investment and employment in the years since Nissan announced it was going to build its plant there. The state's auto industry has become an established force. By 1986 the Tennessee Automotive Manufacturers Association (TAMA) coalesced, accepting as full members all manufacturers of autos and auto parts with facilities in the state.

Within a decade (1984–1994), Tennessee shot up to third place in the production of passenger cars, with only Michigan and Ohio boasting a higher share of U.S. auto output. Tennessee's 10 percent share may still seem minor when compared to Michigan's whopping 33 percent. Yet given the fact that there was *no* production of passenger cars at all in Tennessee as recently as 1984, the state has made a remarkable leap into the premier league of U.S. auto-producer states. In total auto-related production, Tennessee in 1997 ranked fourth (behind Michigan, Ohio, and California).[80]

In the growth of the state's supplier industry, Nissan and Saturn played very different roles. In contrast to the established American automakers, Nissan obviously did not have in place a U.S. supplier network when it started making cars in Smyrna. Thus "Nissan could establish a classic 'greenfield' plant . . . because it could induce its suppliers to follow it."[81] Indeed, within a short time, suppliers actually did begin following Nissan into Tennessee. In the first decade after Nissan's announcement, the Tennessee Department of Economic and Community Development counted more than a hundred new auto parts production facilities in the state.

Over the years, the Nissan plant experienced several rounds of expansion, most significantly through the addition of a second passenger car line, announced in 1989, effectively doubling plant size and employment. With every expansion and model changeover, local content (the share of parts made in America) increased. Likewise, the number of Nissan's U.S. suppliers grew. The plant currently has some 260 U.S. parts suppliers, 40 in Tennessee. Once Nissan's Smyrna plant had fully come on stream, Tennessee economic developers wanted to believe that the story with regard to suppliers would repeat itself, possibly on a greater scale, as Saturn shaped up for production in 1990. They were wrong.

To begin with, the Saturn plant is a substantially more highly integrated manufacturing complex than Nissan's. It represents the most highly integrated assembly plant now in the United States, meaning that most of the parts used are actually made on site: "It's almost self-contained over there [at Saturn] whereas many suppliers for Nissan are scattered all around."[82] Next, the role of the UAW at Saturn extends into the selection of suppliers. Where possible, the union naturally urged Saturn to source parts from existing GM-owned, UAW-organized suppliers. While Saturn could have relied more strongly on a local supplier base that had grown because of business from Nissan or other Japanese-affiliated automakers (like the Toyota assembly plant in Georgetown, Kentucky), in many cases it ended up contracting with suppliers from GM's parts plants network. Thus, Saturn's supply lines are much longer than those of Nissan, with many of its supplier partners (as they are called in Saturn-speak) located in the Midwest and Great Lakes area rather than the South. In order to run a system of just-in-time production reliably, however, the company employs what is probably the auto industry's most sophisticated system of supplier and parts management.[83]

In effect, then, the impacts of Nissan and Saturn on the state proved dissimilar. While Nissan has benefited Tennessee in that it really did serve as a magnet to suppliers, Saturn's effects are somewhat less tangible. Although Saturn has also drawn a number of new suppliers to Tennessee through direct business dealings, it has mainly served to lure new auto-related investments by its mere presence in the state, by the image boost it bestowed on Tennessee. Still, Saturn has attracted more suppliers to its host region than any of the auto plants built in the 1970s. This is not a negligible outcome, though it somewhat pales in contrast to Nissan's effect.

These two automakers have contributed to the growth of the state's economy in many ways. Not only has the number of direct auto-related jobs increased significantly, a sizable spin-off from the auto industry in terms of jobs in other industries has occurred. Based on calculations from the U.S. Chambers of Commerce, the state's Department of Economic and Community Development has maintained that for every 100 jobs in the state's auto industry, another 247 jobs are created, among them 31 in manufacturing, 12 in transportation, communications, and utilities, 38 in wholesale and retail, 9 in finance, insurance, and real estate, and 52 in services and government.[84] Significantly, for years now, transportation equipment, as classified in SIC 37, has led the list of Tennessee's exports.[85]

THE AUTO INDUSTRY IN THE OTHER SOUTHERN STATES

Beginning in the 1980s, southern auto and parts plants were no longer sparse, but had become a common feature of regional economies. One key influence that helped bring the auto industry to the South was a shift of paradigms in automobile production. With the success of Japanese automakers, attention soon shifted to the much-touted Japanese system of production, which gained prominence under the label of "lean production."[86] According to its proponents, one of its essential features is the just-in-time delivery of parts, also referred to as the "pull principle" (in contrast to the "push principle" of mass production). Large inventories are now considered wasteful, as they tend to cover up faults in production instead of addressing them. Japanese firms were the first to abolish large inventory spaces and to rely on steady, short-notice supplies of key parts to keep their factories running. This, of course, necessitated a cooperative relationship with external suppliers. During the 1980s, almost every automaker worldwide shifted to some form of JIT production, making supplier relations and supplier *location* very important. Component manufacturers realized that, to supply parts on a JIT basis, they had to be within easy reach of their customers, thus parts plants concentrated near assembly plants.

As Bingham and Sunmonu have found, the historically strong tendencies of U.S. auto suppliers to locate in the same *county* as their main customer remain strong but are declining. This has resulted in "a distinct and novel geographic pattern of production: regional-scale concentration and local-scale dispersal,"[87] a pattern that has also been observed by a Japanese analyst: "It appears that Japanese parts suppliers have located their plants in villages that are about one hour's car ride apart, lest workers of neighboring plants should bid up their wages."[88] The first Japanese auto suppliers to open new plants in the United States stayed with that pattern. Yet as more and more Japanese-affiliated auto supply plants opened over the 1980s and 1990s, plant dispersal became increasingly difficult.

While Japanese suppliers may seem to be scattered throughout the South, they are rarely located in *really* rural areas. In an analysis of regional growth patterns in the United States, Nelson has identified "exurban" areas as those exhibiting the strongest growth. According to his definition, "exurban areas are tied to urban areas, although they may appear rural in many respects. They are within about an hour's commute . . . [and] within trucking range to urban markets. In contrast, truly rural areas are well beyond reasonable commuting and trucking range to urban areas."[89] This divergence in the pattern of economic development by rural and urban/suburban/exurban areas of the South has been found in several other studies.[90]

Much as the concept of just-in-time delivery may have driven auto-industrial

Greenfields in the Heart of Dixie

growth in the South, it was the entry of new competitors (mainly from Japan) that pushed this development. The new plants opened over the past two decades are no longer mainly operated by the Big Three. Chrysler's newest facility is the Detroit (Jefferson North) plant, where the Grand Cherokee is assembled, which replaced an old plant in the same location. After opening several new assembly sites in the 1980s and Saturn in 1990, General Motors has not built further in the United States. Ford has not dedicated a new American auto assembly plant since 1974. Thus the hope for new assembly plants, usually the most desired prize sought by industrial developers, came to rest with foreign automakers.

After the Japanese invasion ebbed a little, the next wave of foreign investment set in. At its center were two German automakers, BMW and Mercedes-Benz. BMW decided in 1992 to build a U.S. assembly plant, its first full-scale operation outside Germany. The company quickly narrowed its choices to Omaha, Nebraska, and the Greenville-Spartanburg area of South Carolina, the location dismissed by Mazda some years earlier. The most recent auto assembly complex built in the South is the Mercedes-Benz facility in Vance-Tuscaloosa, Alabama. It is important to note that none of the Japanese automakers had located in the Deep South, nor had most of the Japanese-affiliated suppliers. For its part, BMW, while choosing a more southern location than either Nissan or Saturn, lodged its plant where a sizable amount of auto-related industry already existed. Indeed, in contrast to Japanese suppliers following their customers in the 1980s, "BMW has essentially followed its suppliers to America,"[91] for German and other European parts makers already had plants in South Carolina, as did U.S.-based firms supplying BMW's German plants.

Ultimately, a German automaker gave the Deep South its first new auto assembly operation: Mercedes, in the fall of 1993, dared locating its first overseas passenger vehicle assembly plant in the heart of Dixie. A company once hesitant about building cars in northern Germany boldly went where no automaker had gone before, taking industry observers by great surprise: "There it is, smack in the heart of deepest Dixie—a Mercedes factory. . . . It's about the last place you'd expect to find the buttoned-down German automaker."[92] The plant has already drawn nine new supplier facilities to Alabama, thus replicating the pattern set by the other new assembly plants. ZF, one of the German parts makers that chose to build new plants there specifically to supply Mercedes, purposefully selected a site at some distance from Tuscaloosa. One of its reasons was the risk of unionization in the Tuscaloosa area. According to a ZF spokesman, "the more companies are concentrated in one region the more active the unions become. Out here, they leave us alone."[93]

THE "NEW AMERICAN AUTOMOBILE INDUSTRY"

If from an industrial location perspective the question regarding the emergence of a new auto and auto-related industry sketched out above was "Why Tennessee?" or "Why the South?" one could ask from another perspective, "Why the Japanese?" or "Why foreign automakers first?" In fact, the two perspectives are closely interrelated. In an insightful industrial ethnography of Japanese industry in the South, Kim argues that "in contrast to common belief, the Japanese are not the ones who discovered the South and the southerners. Instead, the southern political apparatuses—aggressive governors, supportive state legislatures, and business circles equipped with attractive incentive packages—discovered the Japanese industrialists in Tokyo."[94] Indeed, proactive industrial recruitment has played a major role in bringing the Japanese auto industry to the South.

Yet specific (and successful) targeting of Japanese industry is only one strand of explanation. Building on Markusen's influential profit-cycle theory and applying it to the American automobile industry,[95] Bingham and Sunmonu arrived at the conclusion that by the early 1990s, there were "actually two motor vehicle sectors in the USA characterized by very different modes of behavior, very different locational patterns, and likely to have very different futures. The 'old' motor vehicle sector is characterized by the U.S. 'Fordist' production style whereas the 'new' sector is characterized by the Japanese mode of production." They continue to argue that "these two systems are at different phases of the profit cycle but exist in one country simultaneously and produce the same product. [They] currently exist side by side."[96]

A not always peaceful coexistence of these two industrial systems has characterized the American auto industry for the last fifteen years, though generalizations like this almost always fail to accommodate every detail. It seems to be oversimplifying to put American automakers in one camp. The same holds true if one compares the success stories of Honda and Toyota to the smaller Japanese transplants. Yet by and large, this model offers an interesting and helpful interpretation that differentiates between complementary developments. A history of auto plant closings in the Great Lakes region (but also in the coastal states) has been accompanied by a history of new plant openings in some midwestern states and in the South.

This pattern of industrial and territorial development is, historically speaking, not unusual. In a valuable study of industrialization and territory, Storper and Walker have shown how such "new or radically restructured industries, with distinctive lines and production methods, usually take up new locations, often outside previously industrialized regions."[97] This has happened in the case of the Japanese- or German-affiliated new American auto industry, which differs from the traditional American auto industry in a number of respects, ranging from a more cooperative approach and teamwork on the shop floor to supplier relations.

Still, one might ask why U.S. firms have been comparatively slower at moving into the South, for it was the new American auto industry that first located there. Yet in the only case to date where the old American auto industry explicitly started with a blank sheet approach and chose to develop an all-new auto assembly plant on U.S. soil (this case being Saturn), it too chose a southern location. Perhaps the old American auto industry, in restructuring and remodeling itself, has increasingly come to appreciate the characteristics commonly associated with the South (paternalistic structures, anti-union sentiment). In fact, U.S. firms have begun emulating Japanese automakers with regard to utilizing these characteristics, as Yanarella critically noted in a comparative analysis of worker training measures at Saturn and Toyota (Kentucky).[98]

Interestingly, the domestic American auto industry is involved in a lively discussion about how it is going to rearrange itself politically. The American Automobile Manufacturers Association (AAMA) has long represented the old American auto industry (the Big Three), whereas America's new automakers, having been refused entry to the AAMA, formed AIAM, the Association of International Automobile Manufacturers.[99] Now, as Chrysler has merged with Daimler-Benz, the lines between the two associations and the companies and industries they represent are becoming blurred, and AAMA is considering opening up to all automakers with U.S. production facilities.

CONCLUSION: FROM DIXIE TO THE WORLD MARKETS?

Clearly, despite a very slow postwar start, a tremendous growth of auto-related investment and employment in the southern states has taken place over the past two decades. But growth is not evenly distributed among the southern states. While figures in table 1 show that a sizable number of southerners now work in auto-related jobs, the overall total is still relatively small when compared to Michigan, the industry's single most important state. The share of national automotive employment in the southern economy remains significantly below that of the nation's premier automaking state. Moreover, although the South has more than three times as many auto and auto parts plants as Michigan, total employment (by AAMA standards) at these plants is still less than in Michigan alone, indicating that many of the southern auto parts plants are relatively modest ventures, more often than not located in small, non-urban communities.

Among the southern states, Tennessee now has the highest share of auto-related employment (with Kentucky in second place). This indicates that seizing the two large assembly plants has paid off for the state, yielding more auto in-

Table 1: Motor Vehicle and Equipment Manufacturing in the Southern States and in Michigan (1995)

	AUTO AND PARTS MANUFACTURING PLANTS	NUMBER OF EMPLOYEES	PER 10,000 STATE RESIDENTS
Alabama	76	11,240	27
Arkansas	54	6,306	25
Florida	173	7,512	5
Georgia	129	13,574	19
Kentucky	N/A	22,560	58
Louisiana	24	N/A	N/A
Mississippi	52	N/A	N/A
North Carolina	134	19,275	27
Oklahoma	90	9,194	28
South Carolina	49	7,016	19
Tennessee	142	35,691	68
Texas	268	13,837	7
Virginia	59	10,076	15
South-total	1,518[1]	156,281[2]	--
Michigan	508	182,466	191

[1] without figures for Kentucky.
[2] without figures for Louisiana and Mississippi.

Source: American Automobile Manufacturers Association (AAMA)

See <http://www.aama.org/economic/states.html>, accessed 3 April 1998, for the most recent set of data available from that source. Apparently there is a mismatch between the figures provided by AAMA and those provided by other sources (see section on Tennessee), indicating AAMA is using a different formula to compile them. Yet AAMA provides a publicly accessible set of data for all fifty states. Thus, even if AAMA figures were not appropriate with regard to absolute numbers, it is reasonable to assume that the same formula was applied for every state, allowing cross-state comparisons on the *relative* significance of the industry.

vestment and employment than its neighbors secured. Automotive capital is still pouring into the region, and states, counties, and localities continue to seek new auto-related enterprises. Even as further assembly plants seem unlikely to develop in the face of an already sizable overcapacity, the supplier industry has shown continuing expansion. Also, growth at the German assembly plants now operating is not yet over. Daimler-Benz recently announced that it would boost capacity at its U.S. plant,[100] and BMW then added production of a new SUV to its American facility, entailing further expansion. Its investment of $600 million will bring another 1,000 jobs to South Carolina. State officials expect five more suppliers to appear, investing another $75 million and providing another 500 auto jobs. This surge is happening in a region that has seen auto-related employment skyrocket over the past decade, growing a full ten times faster than the national average. Given that the area already boasts a record low rate of unemployment (below 2 percent in Spartanburg County, and 1.1 percent in Greenville County), the new employees are likely to hail from adjacent counties.[101] Finally, Porsche has moved its North American headquarters from Reno, Nevada, to Atlanta. While Porsche still declines to comment, there have been rumors of a U.S. assembly plant, to be located in the Atlanta area, making a Porsche SUV mainly for the American market.[102] Overall, then, the "rapid increase in the auto manufacturing sector in the Southeast suggests that the region is experiencing a 'second wave' of industrialization."[103]

So how close has the relationship between southern economies and the new auto industry become? For some observers, the answer is quite simple: "[N]o longer can Smyrna, LaVergne [where Bridgestone has its American HQ and a large tire plant], and Spring Hill be identified as little farming towns in Tennessee. Rather they are identified now as huge manufacturing towns and auto and electric capitals of America and the world."[104] While interpreting Tennessee towns as the incarnation of the American automotive industry, as Kim has done, is a bit far-fetched (as of now, at least), there is indeed a growing relationship between the industry and the region that has come to host many of its new operations. Already the Tennessee economy is beginning to experience the auto industry's cyclical changes, though the state has largely been able to ride out business cycles in the 1980s and 1990s. With Nissan depending on the products of its only U.S. plant, and Saturn sourcing 100 percent of its products from the Tennessee plant, both facilities have been running at high capacity. It seemed safe to suppose they were giving the state "an auto industry that is as bulletproof as it gets in the car business."[105] But in late 1997, the first bullets hit. With U.S. sales rising for light trucks and sport utilities but rapidly slipping for compact and subcompact cars, both Nissan and Saturn found themselves unable to sell all their output. If anything, this confirms that "product mix is everything for an auto plant. Regardless of overall conditions in the national economy, an auto plant will prosper if the models it produces are in demand."[106] Over the past year, they were not, and the consequences for the local economy became visible.

Although 1997 saw the rate of economic growth in Middle Tennessee fall below the national average for the first time in six years,[107] this does not necessarily mean that dark clouds lie on the economic horizon. Yet any economy is more volatile if tied to the success of a single industry, company, or even plant. Already, *Automotive News* has detected "new factory towns in Tennessee and Kentucky,"[108] not a connotation that evokes fond memories among state and local economic developers. Too well do many southerners recall the case of the textile industry, which carried southern industrialization in earlier decades but eventually moved on to overseas locations with even lower wages. Changing from one dependency to the next can hardly be the goal of responsible industrial development. Not to "put all the eggs in one basket" has proven to be sound policy advice.

Whereas textile manufacturers could (and did) shut down their operations literally overnight, put the entire equipment on trucks, and ship it to another location, auto assembly plants cannot so easily be moved. With several hundred million dollars of investment in machinery, most of which represents fixed capital, these plants are not prone to be closed down lightly. Yet this judgment should not lead to the conclusion that auto plants will remain forever. General Motors' history of American plant closings puts Saturn's commitment to being a "one hundred year company" in perspective. Equally troubling, Nissan did the unthinkable when it closed its Zama, Japan, assembly plant in 1995, becoming the first Japanese automaker ever to do so. Likewise, Nissan has shuttered its Australian assembly plant, and the financially troubled automaker has scheduled its smaller-scale New Zealand plant to be closed in the near future as well.

Today, many quality automotive products may be made in the South, but decisions relating to the automotive industry are still mostly made elsewhere. In that regard, little has changed for the South. Obviously, none of the large international automakers is indigenous to the South. But even in the supplier industry, the picture is not much different. A list of the top 150 (OEM) parts suppliers to North American auto assembly plants for 1997 shows that, the growth of auto parts plants in the South notwithstanding, there are still very few significant auto parts suppliers actually *based* in the South. Only 15 of the top 150 are headquartered in a southern state, with seven of these in Kentucky alone. On scale terms, the first southern auto supplier comes in at rank 24 (the first Tennessee-based supplier at rank 39). In comparison, Michigan alone still accounts for more than half (77) of the top 150 suppliers (with 6 of the top 10, 14 of the top 25).[109] Clearly enough, then, the auto parts industry is not an indigenous industry for the South. Even when foreign firms build parts plants in the South, they are unlikely to put their North American headquarters in a southern state.

For many years, observers have noted that the American South long resembled a colonial economy. Yet by the mid-1980s, the argument goes, the South no longer was "a colony to any other geographic entity, but to placeless global organizations and markets." Regrettable as this may seem, this shift has at least put the South in the same boat with other regions in the United States and elsewhere, which now also begin to "resemble the economy of the antebellum South."[110] Thus, in the face of increasing global competition, the nationalization of the southern economy has led to a "decided Southernization of the nation's economy."[111] In a recent book, Peter Applebome, a northern journalist, has maintained that economic and population shifts have made the entire United States more like the South.[112] Along the same vein, one could argue that the U.S. auto industry is on its way to becoming southernized. Yet while in politics the South has come to largely dominate the national arena, the strings of the region's major automotive companies are still pulled elsewhere, more often than not outside

Greenfields in the Heart of Dixie

the United States. In Tennessee, for example, where almost one-half of all foreign investment is from Japan, "Japanese investments were critical in establishing the state's automotive industry, now one of the most important and vital parts of the Tennessee economy. [However, one] can plausibly assert that Japanese investment decisions of the past decades have as much impact on the state economy as any decision made inside this state."[113]

Rosabeth Moss Kanter has suggested that regions and localities have taken different paths to make the global economy work and spatially distinguishes "thinker" clusters from those of "makers" and "traders."[114] Kanter predicts that a "maker" region can do well in the global economy if it perfects its competitive advantages in manufacturing. If so, the South is poised to prosper from the new auto industry it has attracted over the past decades. The individual auto manufacturing businesses in the South will increasingly find themselves tied into the emergent global strategies of their corporate parents on the one hand, while trying to retain their recently earned regional or local embeddedness on the other. This need not necessarily be a conflict, as the concept of a "regional manufacturing base in a global industry," noted at this chapter's beginning, indicates.

EPILOGUE (SUMMER 1999)

"What a difference a year makes," *Ward's Automotive Reports* opened a June 1999 story of the "Nissan turnaround."[115] What a difference a year makes, indeed. This, at least, is the message for students of the automotive industry in the American South. In contrast to many other stories in southern industrialization, that of the automotive industry has yet to be told in full. This, by the way, could hold an important lesson for any scholar: Beware of doing research on a moving target. And the automotive industry is a fast-moving target these days. Barely a week passes by without an announcement of a merger, an acquisition, a new product, or a plant opening (or eventually closing). Yet looking at the automotive industry in the American South, one finds that the current developments are generally along the predicted growth trajectory.

By summer 1999, the automotive conference cited in the beginning of this essay is on track to becoming a regular event. May 1999 saw Nashville host *Automotive News*'s second "New American Manufacturing Conference." As in 1998, the program included tours of the Nissan and Saturn facilities. The conference will take place in Birmingham, Alabama, in 2000, but will be back at Nashville the year after. Tennessee, the state that undoubtedly led the way for the automotive industry in the American South, appears to be on a path to further auto-industry related growth. Despite the 1998 downturn, neither Nissan nor Saturn has laid off any people. To the contrary, Tennessee's total employment in the automotive and supplier industry has passed the 100,000 mark, meaning about one in five manufacturing jobs in the state is now auto-related, as are more than 800 companies according to ECD's count.[116] Last year, Tennessee's two volume automakers suffered mainly from the same cause—a slump in demand for the kind of small cars made at their Tennessee plants. Even with Nissan and Saturn using relatively flexible production systems, there is still a significant lead time for the manufacture of new vehicles. Where a company does not *define* the market, or at least a large enough segment (as GM did in the immediate postwar period), it is forced to play catch-up with the market (a game at which some, like Honda or Toyota, seem better than others). Tennessee's Nissan and Saturn each requested, and eventually obtained, new product from their corporate parents. So both have shifted their strategy and now appear on the rebound, albeit in different ways.

In March 1999, the last Sentra compact rolled off the line at Nissan's Smyrna plant, thus ending the fourteen-year production run of Tennessee's first mass-produced passenger car. With Sentra production shifting to Nissan's plant in Aguascalientes, Mexico, Smyrna began production of a new SUV (named Xterra) a month later. Thanks to positive market response to the Xterra and a new four-door compact truck, the rate of cars assembled is going up again. More new product will be added at Smyrna: a sports utility truck (SUT) off the Frontier platform. Also, Nissan announced it will build its Maxima flagship sedan at Smyrna in the years to come. All this should give the facility the kind of product that is likely to bring back success in the marketplace and a better use of existing capacity—thus significantly improving the outlook for Smyrna and Nissan suppliers scattered throughout the state.

The most significant event to affect Nissan's U.S. operations in future, though, is its new alliance with French automaker Renault. For years, Nissan in America had been characterized by a paradox: While Smyrna, its only U.S. assembly plant, routinely finished ahead of everybody else in surveys of plant management and efficiency, the company's overall U.S. operations showed losses and contributed significantly to the severe financial troubles building up at its corporate parent. In fact, Nissan lost money in six out of the past seven business years. In May 1999, then, Renault and Nissan announced the French automaker would come to Nissan's rescue and take a controlling 36.8 percent stake in Nissan. The effects of this new global alliance on Nissan's operations in Tennessee and its suppliers in the South still remain to be seen, especially as purchasing will be a key area in which savings are targeted, and many established Nissan suppliers will face a review. But rumor also has it that the Xterra could be exported to Europe (and sold under the Renault nameplate there), which would make it the first Tennessee-built vehicle to be officially exported to the Old World.[117]

On Saturn's side, a range of all-new midsize cars launched in summer 1999 was generally expected to offset the slump in the company's small car sales. But the LS series is built at a GM plant in Wilmington, Delaware, and will do relatively little to ease the situation at Spring Hill. While Saturn's home plant makes some plastic panels for the LS, most of the components come from elsewhere.[118] It thus came as a great relief to Saturn people at Spring Hill when in May 1999, GM's board finally approved funding for the long-awaited Saturn SUV. Production of a small, car-based vehicle is scheduled to begin in 2001.[119] With this move, capacity at Spring Hill may be raised to 500,000 units per year—the volume originally planned for the compact car series alone when Saturn was conceived back in 1984. And if Saturn's UAW Local 1853 succeeds in keeping as much component production for the next-generation small car series as possible at Spring Hill, the plant might add up to 1,000 new manufacturing jobs.

Further growth related to the auto industry is not, however, limited to Tennessee. The states that had won new assembly plants in the 1980s and early 1990s fared best. South Carolina, for example, where BMW is kicking off production of its x5 luxury SUV at the Spartanburg plant, has continued to add many auto jobs. But the biggest recent winner could be Alabama. Often derided for having paid more than $250 million in site development, tax breaks, and worker training for the Mercedes plant, the state now appears to be raking in the benefits. To date, nine suppliers to the Mercedes plant have located facilities in the state, creating a total of 3,700 new jobs. Current demand for the M-Class luxury SUV, the Alabama plant's only product, is beyond expectations. Having already boosted capacity at Tuscaloosa by 20 percent (to 80,000 units a year), DaimlerChrysler searched for additional capacity, which it found in Graz, Austria.[120] But Alabama also profits from M-Class production in Europe: The Mercedes-Benz Consolidation Center America (MBCCA), opened right off the assembly plant in Bessemer, handles the parts supply to Graz for all American-made parts and modules, accounting for some 300 jobs. And while current European demand is met from Graz, DaimlerChrysler has already hinted that it plans to source the next-generation M-Class entirely from Alabama—which should translate into yet another round of expansion and more auto jobs in the state. Already, the state's economic development agency touts automotive as the first of the state's key industries.[121]

Alabama, meanwhile, no longer has to rely on Mercedes for future auto-related growth: In April 1999, heavy truck maker Navistar International announced that it would to open a plant at Huntsville, Alabama, to build diesel engines, creating some 600 direct jobs. And at a time of global overcapacity, when few expected announcements for new assembly plants, Honda decided to add further assembly capacity in North America. In early May, the Japanese automaker announced it would build an assembly facility at Lincoln, Alabama. When the plant reaches full capacity in 2003, it will build 120,000 vehicles (Honda has yet to decide whether they will be minivans and/or SUVs) and make 120,000 engines. About 1,500 new jobs—not counting spin-off effects once suppliers set up new facilities in its vicinity—are expected. Honda officials quoted the state's favorable business atmosphere, its climate, and the availability of a workforce as the reasons for choosing Alabama.[122]

Honda's selection of an Alabama site for its fifth assembly plant in North America is only the latest, but probably not the last big event in the development of the southern automotive industry. Toyota, too, has announced it might build another manufacturing facility in North America. A decision is due by the end of 1999. Given that a site search and plant construction at an all-new site would take at least two years, there is a good chance that Toyota will decide to build this factory next to its newest (truck) assembly plant at Princeton, Indiana. It is safe to assume that this would lead to more business for Toyota's established supplier network in Kentucky and other southern states.

Yet Honda's selection of a site in northern Alabama is also noteworthy in other ways: Rather than going into Mississippi or Arkansas, Honda chose an Alabama site despite the established presence of Mercedes-Benz in the state—a move that breaks with the existing pattern. Saturn's selection in 1985 of a Tennessee site was, among other things, a deliberate attempt to go head to head with a major Japanese competitor in the same state. But Japanese and German automakers have generally avoided settling in competitive territory, that is, a state that was already taken by another automaker.[123] Honda's most recent site selection now indicates that this may no longer be the case as parts of the South are becoming crowded with automotive industry, even though there still may not be direct competition in terms of local labor supply.

These developments might also make it necessary to look at the South in a more differentiated manner. First, with regard to the auto industry it is worth looking at the individual states that make up the American South because they have not prospered equally from and with the automotive industry. There are states that historically have had at least some automotive production (such as Georgia, particularly the Atlanta area); states that have prospered by being in the first round of new manufacturing sites set up by foreign automakers in the 1980s (such as Kentucky and certainly Tennessee); states that came into the game somewhat belatedly, but apparently not too late (such as South Carolina or Alabama); and those that will likely continue to be passed by (such as Arkansas and Mississippi). Second, even within the same state, growth is not evenly spread: Tennessee's Western Division has not seen very much of the state's auto-related growth.

Finally, one has to keep in mind that for an industry often considered "sunset," the automotive and its supplier industries have become quite dynamic and are rapidly globalizing. No longer are there national auto industries as we knew them from not all that long ago. Talk of Japanese and German transplants, for example, has given way to the more respectful reference to the new domestic manufacturers.[124] Changing to the market side, the auto industry has historically been characterized by marked cyclical changes. When the overall pie does not get bigger (and sooner or later the North American auto market will hit another ceiling, despite a series of records), it depends on how you slice it. At present, the southern-based automakers and their suppliers appear well prepared, as do the states that host the plants along with them. Fortunes in the automotive industry can change, though, and it is dangerous to sit back and follow developments from a distance. Where the current system seems to favor regional embeddedness (increasing the cost of simply pulling out), new methods of automobile production in the years to come may not. Consider the fate of Flint, Michigan, hometown of GM's Buick division and in a sense the birthplace of General Motors. At its peak, the city had some 28,000 auto workers. In summer 1999, as the Tennessee automakers appear to be back on a growth path, Flint's 93-year history of automaking came to an end as GM permanently shut down operations there. The industry's southward drift continues.

NOTES

I would like to thank Jens Borchert for the encouragement to write the proposal that led to this chapter, as well as friends and former colleagues at Göttingen University's Center for European and North American Studies for their willingness to comment on the draft version. I am also indebted to Steve Vallas, whose helpful, critical comments reshaped the flow of the argument, and to Phil Scranton, who contributed significantly to making this a more comprehensive and readable text. Research that led to this chapter was done in the context of my Ph.D. project ("Global Strategies and Regional Economies in the Automotive Industry: Nissan and Saturn in Tennessee"). Conduct of the study, in particular on location in Tennessee, would not have been possible without a grant provided by the German Marshall Fund (Grant No. A-0172-12) and a fellowship by the German State of Lower Saxony (Niedersachsen).

1. Peter Brown, "Leaders to Examine Southeast Auto Role," *Automotive News* (9 March 1998): 14.

2. Charles W. Boas, "Locational Patterns of American Automobile Assembly Plants, 1895-1958," *Economic Geography* 37 (July 1961): 218-30 (quote from 220).

3. See, for example, John B. Rae, *The American Automobile Industry* (Boston: Twayne, 1984), or Brock Yates, *The Decline and Fall of the American Automobile Industry* (New York: Empire Books, 1983). See, among many others, James Cobb, *Industrialization and Southern Society, 1877-1984* (Lexington: University Press of Kentucky, 1984), or Gavin Wright, *Old South, New South: Revolutions in the Southern Economy since the Civil War* (New York: Basic Books, 1986). This is true as well for more recent textbooks on the South,

for example, John B. Boles, *The South through Time: A History of an American Region* (Englewood Cliffs, N.J.: Prentice Hall, 1995).

4. In a corporate reorganization in 1996, Mercedes-Benz was merged into its corporate parent, Daimler-Benz. In the biggest merger in automotive history, Daimler-Benz and Chrysler announced in early May 1998 that they had agreed to combine their operations and form a new company, DaimlerChrysler. Throughout this chapter, the name Mercedes-Benz will be used to refer to the Daimler-Benz automotive division.

According to sources at *Automotive News*, the success of the conference may well make it a regular event in the future. In August 1998, Nashville also hosted an even larger event, the *Southern Automotive Manufacturing Technology Conference*, organized by the Society of Automotive Engineers.

5. SIA is a joint venture of two smaller Japanese automakers, Subaru and Isuzu, who have joined forces for a U.S. plant located at Lafayette, Indiana.

6. This is by no means a trivial question. The eleven states that made up the old Confederacy are usually counted as southern, with Texas and Florida at times considered somewhat detached from the rest of the region. As for other states, it depends on whatever standards are applied. See, for example, the various indicators probed by John Shelton Reed, *My Tears Spoiled My Aim and Other Reflections on Southern Culture* (Columbia: University of Missouri Press, 1993).

7. Vance quoted by Bruce J. Schulman, *From Cotton Belt to Sunbelt: Federal Policy, Economic Development, and the Transformation of the South, 1938–1980* (New York: Oxford University Press, 1991), xi. The second quote is from John Calhoun Wells, "The Kentucky Experience: State Government as a Partner in Labor-Management Relations," *State Government* 60, no. 1 (January–February 1987), 44–53 (quote from 44).

8. In fact, this has become a fairly common definition used by several scholars of the South. It is also used "not because this collection of states satisfies any precise criterion regarding economy, polity, or climate, but because New Deal–era policymakers generally did so." Schulman, *From Cotton Belt to Sunbelt*, x.

9. Rosabeth Moss Kanter, *World Class: Thriving Locally in the Global Economy* (New York: Simon and Schuster, 1995).

10. Howard L. Preston, *Automobile Age Atlanta: The Making of a Southern Metropolis, 1900–1935* (Athens: University of Georgia Press, 1979), xv.

11. Preston, *Automobile Age Atlanta*, 19, 78.

12. Boas, "Locational Patterns," 222–23. On the beginnings of the American automobile industry and the emergence of Michigan as the center of automotive production in general, see John B. Rae, "Why Michigan?" in *The Automobile and American Culture*, ed. David D. Lewis and Laurence Goldstein (Ann Arbor, Mich.: University of Michigan Press, 1983), 1–9; James M. Rubenstein, *The Changing U.S. Auto Industry: A Geographical Analysis* (London and New York: Routledge, 1992), 25–40.

13. There had been an earlier venture to build cars in Nashville, which is, however, little more than a footnote in the history of the industry and the city. The first car in Nashville was built by Preston Dorris, who fabricated a prototype in his brother's bicycle shop in downtown Nashville in 1897. Dorris eventually decided to go into production, but because of family connections of his companion, they left their hometown of Nashville for

Missouri. There, the St. Louis Motor Carriage Co. made several lines of cars until it dropped out of the market in 1926 and resorted to making auto parts. See Louise Davis, "When Autos Were Made in Nashville," *The Tennessean*, 4 April 1992, 1–F, 2–F.

14. Louise Davis, "Nashville-Made Autos Left a Trail of Highways," *The Tennessean*, 30 May 1992, 1–F, 2–F.

15. Shifting to the production of auto parts was not unusual for automakers dropping out of the market in those years. Boas has observed this pattern for many former automakers from the early years of the automotive industry, so that a "residual industry is known to exist in many former centers of automobile manufacture in the form of automotive parts and equipment manufacturers." Boas, *Locational Patterns*, 230.

16. Rubenstein, *The Changing U.S. Auto Industry*, 46.

17. Preston, *Automobile Age Atlanta*, 29.

18. This section is building on the detailed account of Ford's development of branch assembly plants by Rubenstein, *The Changing U.S. Auto Industry*, 47–77.

19. On the issue of freight rates, see also Neil Hurley, "The Automotive Industry: A Study in Industrial Location," *Land Economics* 35 (February 1959): 1–14.

20. As these were pure assembly sites, there was relatively little investment in physical facilities that would be lost over a closing.

21. Due to its corporate history and more complex divisional structure, GM built plants separately for Chevrolet on one hand and its upscale divisions on the other. See Rubenstein, *The Changing U.S. Auto Industry*, 72–84.

22. For a precise account of locational differences by firm on one hand and components group on the other, see Rubenstein, *The Changing U.S. Auto Industry*, 99–119.

23. Wright, *Old South*, 455.

24. The notion of a "second wave" in this context must not be confused with the "second wave" efforts of industrial development as understood by several scholars on the issue. To them, the term "second wave" refers to a discernible shift in the practice of state industrial development efforts much later. According to this concept, "first wave" efforts focused on smokestack chasing, that is, recruiting industry from out of state, and were the strategy of industrial development preferred during the postwar decades. First wave efforts were employed heavily by southern states in the 1950s and 1960s; other American regions and states had also gotten into the game by the 1970s. As the effectiveness of this strategy became increasingly questionable and its shortcomings more and more visible, many states shifted to new ways of fostering economic growth. Replacing their strategies, or at least complementing them, they developed "second wave" efforts to strengthen their economies from within, centering on homegrown industries, technology, and labor skills, rather than luring outside investment. See Peter K. Eisinger, *The Rise of the Entrepreneurial State: State and Local Economic Development Policy in the United States* (Madison: University of Wisconsin Press, 1988); R. Scott Fosler, ed., *The New Economic Role of American States: Strategies in a Competitive World Economy* (New York and Oxford: Oxford University Press, 1988); David Osborne, *Laboratories of Democracy: A New Breed of Governors Creates Models for National Growth*, 2d ed. (Boston: Harvard Business School Press, 1990). By the late 1980s, as these strategies began to show their limits, some states

shifted to another approach that scholars have labeled "third wave." For a description of these concepts, which have been strongly promoted by the Corporation for Enterprise Development, a Washington-based think tank, see Daniel E. Pilcher, "The Third Wave of Economic Development," *State Legislatures* (November 1991): 34–37; Doug Ross and Robert E. Friedman, "The Emerging Third Wave: New Economic Development Strategies," in *Local Economic Development. Strategies for a Changing Economy*, ed. R. Scott Fosler (Washington, D.C.: International City Management Association, 1999), 125–37. Building on existing industry and resources, of course, is a viable option only for a state that has such resources in the first place. In contrast to the more industrially developed states in the North, many southern states had rather little to build upon in those terms.

25. See Cobb, *Industrialization and Southern Society*, 38–39, for a brief but detailed account of the origins of BAWI.

26. James C. Cobb, *The Selling of the South: The Southern Crusade for Industrial Development, 1936–1990*, 2d ed. (Urbana: University of Illinois Press, 1993).

27. Numan V. Bartley, *The New South, 1945–1980* (Baton Rouge: Louisiana State University Press, 1995), 19.

28. See Wright, *Old South*, 259.

29. Cobb, *Industrialization and Southern Society*, 49.

30. In the following years, all remaining states in the South but Kentucky and Oklahoma followed suit, as did nine states outside the South (mainly in the West). Today, the southern states make up the largest contingent area with right-to-work laws in the United States.

31. In the four years following the start of "Operation Dixie," the rate of certification elections won by unions actually receded, with the "no union" vote going from 20 to 35 percent. Schulman, *From Cotton Belt to Sunbelt*, 80.

For the most detailed account of the campaign and an analysis of its failure, see Barbara S. Griffith, *The Crisis of American Labor: Operation Dixie and the Defeat of the CIO* (Philadelphia: Temple University Press, 1988).

32. Quoted by Schulman, *From Cotton Belt to Sunbelt*, 162.

33. Cobb, *Industrialization and Southern Society*, 43 and 137. Cobb reports that in 1969, three Mississippi bishops joined the state in the attempt to get General Motors to build a plant in Jackson. See Cobb, *The Selling of the South*, 79.

34. Thomas A. Lyson, *Two Sides to the Sunbelt: The Growing Divergence between the Rural and Urban South* (New York: Praeger, 1989), 6.

35. Ford, which since 1979 has held a 25 percent share in Mazda (increased to 33.4 percent in summer 1996), can be assumed to have exercised some pressure on the Japanese automaker. This seems all the more likely as Mazda deviated from the pattern of the other Japanese automakers in at least two important dimensions: From the start, the company recognized the union as a bargaining partner. Also, Mazda did not go for a true greenfield as it built its plant on a site that had housed a Ford casting plant, closed in 1981. See Lynn W. Bachelor, "Flat Rock, Michigan, Trades a Ford for a Mazda: State Policy and the Evaluation of Plant Location Incentives," in *The Politics of Industrial Recruitment: Japanese Automobile Investment and Economic Development in the American States*, ed. Ernest J.

Yanarella and William C. Green (New York: Greenwood Press, 1990), 87–102 (quote from 89); Joseph and Suzy Fucini, *Working for the Japanese: Inside Mazda's American Auto Plant* (New York: Free Press, 1990), 9.

36. Interestingly, in its negotiations with South Carolina state officials in 1992, the German automaker actually "promised to discourage union activity." *Automotive News*, (1 February 1993): 45.

37. Chrysler, as the smallest of the Big Three, simply lacked the volume to build regional assembly plants all over the country. In addition, Chrysler did not own many parts plants whereas both Ford and General Motors each commanded a vast empire of parts plants.

38. The Lakewood plant was permanently closed in summer 1990. While Lakewood initially made Chevrolets, the Doraville plant was built to make Pontiac, Buick, and Oldsmobile cars. Doraville, in 1996, converted from cars to minivans, as the Shreveport, Louisiana, plant was shifting to the production of compact SUVs, and is now making GM's minivans.

39. For a detailed analysis, see Rubenstein, *The Changing U.S. Auto Industry*, 87–97.

40. The following section is based on Ken Gross and Rich Taylor, "America's Most Needed Car: 1948 Keller Super Chief," *Special Interest Autos* (September–October 1975): 31–40, 59, reprinted, <http://www.redstone.army.mil/history/auto/welcome.html>, accessed 10 February 1998.

41. Other new, independent entrants into the industry, such as Henry J. Kaiser, showed that it was possible to break into the ranks of the established automakers for a limited time. Yet even well-financed startups such as Kaiser-Frazer eventually bowed to the market power of the established automakers.

42. See Rubenstein, *The Changing U.S. Auto Industry*, 119–25.

43. For setting the typical three-year national contract covering the industry, the UAW used to alternate among the Big Three automakers but had long chosen to escape a showdown with deep-pocketed GM, which would generally accept the conditions the union had negotiated with either Ford or Chrysler. See Rubenstein, *The Changing U.S. Auto Industry*, 241.

44. Ricardo C. Springs, *Pilot Case Study: The Decision by Nissan Motor Manufacturing Corporation U.S.A. to Build a Light Truck Assembly Plant in Smyrna, Tennessee*, vol. 2 (Washington, D.C.: U.S. Department of Transportation, DOT-P-10–81–89, April 1981), 2–3.

45. Springs, *Pilot Case Study*, pp. 6–7.

46. Springs, *Pilot Case Study*, pp. 3, 7.

47. A greenfield plant or site is one that literally is set up on a green field, where no industrial activity has happened before. These sites have to be developed in terms of infrastructure (such as roads, sewage, electricity), and the physical facilities are built from scratch. Brownfield sites, on the other hand, are sites that are already developed in terms of infrastructure, with a given set of facilities. Semi-brownfields, then, are sites that fall in between—sites that have been developed but where the facilities have not yet been put to use.

48. For a long time, standard wisdom in the auto industry has held 240,000 to 250,000 cars per year to be the capacity to justify the investment in an assembly line. Only specialty vehicles have seen separate lines or even plants going up with significantly lower capacity.

49. It has often been argued, particularly with regard to the rise of Japanese auto plants in the United States over the 1980s, that the decision to build cars in the United States was mainly caused by pending import restraints. Yet by setting up plants in America, Japanese companies were following a pattern that has characterized the industry for a long time. Writing almost seven decades ago, and eyeing the strategy of U.S. automakers in Europe, Phelps considered the establishment of production sites abroad "the natural outgrowth of an orderly course of development in dealing with the foreign market which can be divided into three phases: that of complete unit export, that of foreign assembly, and finally actual production in those markets which had previously been handled in other ways." Dudley M. Phelps, "Effect of the Foreign Market on the Growth and Stability of the American Automobile Industry," *Michigan Business Studies* 3 (October 1931): 553–728 (quote from 556).

50. The site was an assembly plant built by Chrysler in the 1960s that the financially troubled U.S. automaker had abandoned half-finished. In the case of Volkswagen, the high hopes the Pennsylvania state government had pinned to it as a magnet for supplier firms never materialized. A nearby industrial park set up for Volkswagen suppliers remained vacant. See Robert Goodman, *The Last Entrepreneurs: America's Regional Wars for Jobs and Dollars* (New York: Simon and Schuster, 1979), 8.

51. See William Beaver, "Volkswagen's American Assembly Plant: *Fahrvergnugen* Was Not Enough," *Business Horizons* 35 (November–December 1992): 19–26.

52. Goodman, *The Last Entrepreneurs*, 8.

53. For this decision, Nissan provided three reasons: Trucks have longer model runs than passenger cars, thus the new overseas facility would not face a model changeover too soon after beginning operation; the Big Three were gearing up for production of small cars again, and Nissan feared their huge production scale would give them a competitive advantage there; and the market segment for pickup trucks was expected to grow steadily. Other aspects probably entered into the equation but were not explicitly mentioned by Nissan. With trucks, "fits and finishes" have been somewhat less crucial than with cars, and Nissan was skeptical about any American workforce's capability to meet Nissan's quality standards. Finally, there were no significant tariffs on imported passenger vehicles, but there was a stiff 25 percent tariff on trucks imported from Japan.

54. David Gelsanliter, *Jump Start: Japan Comes to the Heartland* (New York: Farrar, Straus, and Giroux, 1990), 21.

55. See Mamoru Yoshida, *Japanese Direct Manufacturing Investment in the United States* (New York: Praeger, 1987).

56. The Nissan plant is located within a Foreign Trade Zone (FTZ). The existent FTZ was extended to encompass the Smyrna plant. Created by Congress in 1933 and administered by the U.S. Customs Office, FTZs have grown in large numbers around the United States. Initially intended as an industrial development tool, they have become so commonplace that almost every auto assembly in the country today is in one. Location in an FTZ gives manufacturers major financial benefits in the form of discounts on import duties. The duties are only levied on final goods actually bound for the American market, whereas parts imported and processed are basically duty-free.

57. For an exhaustive account of the site search, Nissan's site criteria, and its decision,

see Springs, *Pilot Case Study*. For a different perspective, with the usual bias of official company histories, see John Egerton, *Nissan in Tennessee* (Smyrna, Tenn.: Nissan Motor Manufacturing Corporation, 1983). It certainly helped that Marvin T. Runyon, a former Ford executive, whom Nissan wanted to run their U.S. manufacturing operations, had made it clear that he was looking to work in the South, and the South only. The degree to which Runyon's personal preferences actually tilted the site decision is unclear, but Halberstam who recounts this episode lends it some significance. See David Halberstam, *The Reckoning* (New York: William Morrow, 1986), 619.

58. The southern work ethic is still officially touted as one of the region's strong incentives for manufacturers, as can be seen from the Tennessee Valley Authority director's reference to the region's "dependable, good people who work hard for a modest living." See Johnny Hayes, "The Just-in-Time Workforce," *Economic Edge* 2 (Spring 1997): 10–12.

59. Second-generation farmers, for example, were seen as "accustomed to working sixteen-hour days." This has been openly expressed by Nissan top management, "[W]hen they come to a place that says we are only going to make you work for eight hours they think that it is half a job." NMMC's current president Jerry Benefield, quoted by Judith A. Lilleston, "Japanese Management in the United States Auto Industry: Can It Be Transported? Nissan: A Case Study" (Ph.D. diss., City University of New York, September 1993), 59.

60. A contemporary article in the *Cleveland Plain Dealer*, exploring Tennessee's success in industrial recruitment, defined homogeneous workforce as "one in which the people are the same race and have similar values and backgrounds." Quoted by John Russo, "Saturn's Rings: What GM's Saturn Project is Really About," *Labor Research Review* 9 (Fall 1986): 67–77 (quote from 76).

61. It has been suggested that Nissan simply went down South on the map from Michigan till it came to the first right-to-work state. UAW organizer, interview with author, Smyrna, Tenn., July 1994.

62. Springs, *Pilot Case Study*, 20.

63. Lamar Alexander, *Steps along the Way: A Governor's Scrapbook* (Nashville: Thomas Nelson Publishers, 1986), 57.

64. Gelsanliter, *Jump Start*, 58.

65. Nissan's anti-union image goes back to the company's crushing of the independent auto union in Japan in 1953 and replacing it with a docile company union. In retrospect, it is hard to understand why the UAW picked Nissan as its target. Honda, with a no less outspoken yet less militant anti-union stance, well established in Ohio, a state without a right-to-work law, would have made a more obvious first target in an effort to organize the Japanese-affiliated auto industry in the United States, but the UAW called off its campaign on the eve of the election there. In that sense, the UAW very much fell along its traditional lines of organizing. The failure of Operation Dixie, the CIO's attempt to organize workers in (mainly textile industry) southern plants right after World War II, is also largely attributed to the fact that the unions stubbornly tried to crack the most powerful firms first—which was too large a job to accomplish. See Griffith, *The Crisis of American Labor*, 10–11, 175.

66. See John Junkerman, "Nissan, Tennessee: It Ain't What It's Cracked Up to Be," *The Progressive* (June 1987): 16–20.

67. In late 1997, the UAW had started a second attempt to organize Nissan workers, this time pointing to the higher annual bonuses paid at Nissan's unionized neighbor and rival, Saturn, and involving Saturn workers in the effort. As of mid-1998, that campaign has again been called off due to lack of support.

68. Christian Berggren, Torsten Björkman, and Ernst Hollander, *Are They Unbeatable? Report from a Field Trip to Study Transplants, the Japanese Owned Auto Plants in North America* (Stockholm: Royal Institute of Technology, 1991), 23.

69. Egerton, *Nissan in Tennessee*, 31.

70. Alexander, *Steps along the Way*, 129.

71. Quoted by David I. Verway, "Impact of the Transplants," Peter J. Arnesen [Ed.], *The Auto Industry Ahead: Who's Driving?* (Ann Arbor, Mich.: Center for Japanese Studies, University of Michigan, 1989), Michigan Papers in Japanese Studies, no. 18, 37–42 (quote from 39).

72. Shelley O. Metzenbaum, "Making the Most of Interstate Bidding Wars for Business" (Ph.D. diss., Harvard University, 1992), 84. Metzenbaum's is the most detailed analysis. As the most publicized in American history, Saturn's site search is also well documented elsewhere. See, among others, Timothy J. Bartik, Charles Becker, Steve Lake, and John Bush, "Saturn and State Economic Development," *Forum for Applied Research and Public Policy* 2 (Spring 1987): 29–40; William F. Fox and Warren Neel, "Saturn: The Tennessee Lessons," *Forum for Applied Research and Public Policy* 2 (Spring 1987): 7–16; David R. Riesland, "Factors and Decisions Involved in the Eventual Location of the Saturn Plant in Tennessee," *Tennessee Business and Economic Review* 15 (Fall 1988): 1–5; Rubenstein, *The Changing U.S. Auto Industry*, 137–41; Stuart C. Gilbert, "Observations on the Saturn Project: Site Selection, Financial Incentives, and Impact," *Economic Development Review* 12 (Fall 1994), 35–44. For the fascinating journalistic account, see Joe Sherman, *In the Rings of Saturn* (New York and Oxford: Oxford University Press, 1994), 97–166. For an example of contemporary fiction picking up the topic, see Tom T. Hall, *Spring Hill, Tennessee: A Novel* (Marietta, Ga.: Longstreet Press, 1990).

73. Russo, *Saturn's Rings*, 68. Notwithstanding the high level of publicity, Saturn's site search became increasingly secretive the closer it moved to the actual decision.

74. See Metzenbaum, *Interstate Bidding Wars*, 181; Rubenstein, *The Changing U.S. Auto Industry*, 137–41.

75. For an insider perspective of the system from a UAW representative, see Jack O'Toole, *Forming the Future: Lessons from the Saturn Corporation* (Cambridge, Mass.: Blackwell Publishers, 1996). For the most profound analysis to date, see Saul A. Rubinstein, "Saturn, the GM/UAW Partnership: The Impact of Co-Management and Joint Governance on Firm and Local Union Performance," (Ph.D. diss., MIT, Alfred P. Sloan School of Management, June 1996).

76. Sherman, *In the Rings of Saturn*, 288–96. A study on citizen perceptions of Saturn, commissioned and funded by the company and conducted by University of Tennessee scholars, showed divergent opinions between residents of Maury County (where

Saturn is sited) and more affluent neighboring Williamson County. While the latter showed favorable views regarding Saturn's impact, the former were much more skeptical. See David H. Folz, Linda Gaddis, William Lyons, and John M. Scheb, "Saturn Comes to Tennessee: Citizen Perceptions of Project Impacts," *Social Science Quarterly* 74 (December 1993), 793–803. The authors were later prohibited from passing on primary data, and a follow-up study (interesting as it would have been) was not commissioned.

77. Greg Keller, *Saturn Corporation's Module II Decision*, Harvard Business School case study paper, HBS 9–795–011 (August 1994).

78. Robert Perrucci, *Japanese Auto Transplants in the Heartland: Corporatism and Community* (New York: Aldine de Gruyter, 1994), 55. The term "Hub of the Southern Wheel" is promoted in the official Tennessee Economic Development Guide 1997–98, 34.

79. "State's Rank Goes from 49th to 4th in Auto Industry," *Nashville Banner*, 10 November 1997, <http://www.nashvillebanner.com/search/digest/forum11101997 .html>, accessed 15 February 1998.

80. Ibid. The ranking of Tennessee as 49th in auto-related production as late as 1987, though, seems wrong in the face of the auto industry that had emerged in the state by the mid-1980s.

81. Erica Schoenberger, "Technological and Organizational Change in Automobile Production: Spatial Implications," *Regional Studies* 21 (1987): 199–214 (quote from 208).

82. Official from Tennessee Department of Economic and Community Development, interview with author, May 1994.

83. For an account of the uniqueness of Saturn's system of parts supply and supplier management, see Karsten Hülsemann, "Der Trick von Saturn: Neue Wege in der Teile-Logistik," *Automobil-Produktion* (June 1996): 80–84.

84. See Gina Finn, "Auto Industry Helps Steer State Economy," <http://www .nashvillebanner.com/search/digest/auto10311997.html>, accessed 10 February 1998. However, these numbers do not nearly add up to 247.

85. Department of Economic and Community Development, <http://www.state .tn.us/ecd/extopsic.htm>, accessed February 2, 1998.

86. For an idealistic description (actually: *prescription*) of "lean production," see what has became known as "the MIT study," James P. Womack, Daniel T. Jones, and Daniel Roos, *The Machine That Changed the World* (New York: Rawson, 1990).

87. Richard D. Bingham and Kola K. Sunmonu, "The Restructuring of the Automobile Industry in the USA," *Environment and Planning A* 24 (June 1992), 833–52 (quote from 834).

88. Arnesen, quoted by Verway, "Impact of the Transplants," 41.

89. Arthur C. Nelson, "Regional Patterns of Exurban Industrialization: Results of a Preliminary Investigation," *Economic Development Quarterly* 4 (November 1990), 320–33 (quote from 322). Interestingly, between 1965 and 1985, generally considered the two decades of strongest economic growth in the South, this trend has been less pronounced than in other regions of the United States. Yet as the total volume of exurban job growth in the South exceeds that of others, this can be considered a sign of Southern urbanization in general (ibid., 328).

90. See, for example, Lyson, who argues that "the disparity between the haves and the

have-nots has a geographic focus. People living in rural and black belt areas of the South have seen their living standards and economic opportunities steadily deteriorate." Lyson, *Two Sides to the Sunbelt*, 118.

91. *Automotive News* (29 June 1992): 40.

92. Justin Martin, "Mercedes: Made in Alabama," *Fortune* (7 July 1997), <http.pathfinder.com/.../fortune/1997/970707/bnb.html>, accessed 8 July 1997. When the company acquired a plant in Bremen in the 1970s, there was a good deal of discussion within Mercedes whether cars could actually be made under the same quality standards as in its Swabian home region in southwest Germany.

93. Quoted in *Automobile Management International* (January 1998): 55.

94. Choong Soon Kim, *Japanese Industry in the American South* (New York and London: Routledge, 1995), 166.

For a diverse and balanced perspective on Japanese auto investment in the United States, see Ernest J. Yanarella and William C. Green, eds., *The Politics of Industrial Recruitment: Japanese Automobile Investment and Economic Development in the American States* (New York: Greenwood Press, 1990). Also, see Perrucci, *Japanese Auto Transplants*.

95. Ann R. Markusen, *Profit Cycles, Oligopoly, and Regional Development* (Cambridge, Mass.: MIT Press, 1985). See also Markusen's *Regions: The Economics and Politics of Territory*, (Totowa, N.J.: Rowman and Littlefield, 1987), and Doreen Massey, *Spatial Division of Labour: Social Structure and the Geography of Production* (London: Macmillan, 1984).

96. Richard D. Bingham and Kola K. Sunmonu, "The Restructuring of the Automobile Industry in the USA," *Environment and Planning A* 24 (June 1992), 833–52 (quotes from 845 and 850). Note that their study preceded the announcements of BMW and Mercedes-Benz, thus they focus only on Japanese automakers.

97. Michael Storper and Richard Walker, *The Capitalist Imperative: Territory, Technology, and Industrial Growth* (Oxford: Basil Blackwell), 1989.

98. Ideological hegemony (in a Gramscian sense), Yanarella argues, is achieved in a very similar fashion. Ernest J. Yanarella, "Worker Training at Toyota and Saturn: Hegemony Begins in the Training Center Classroom," in *North American Auto Unions in Crisis: Lean Production as Contested Terrain*, ed. William C. Green and Ernest J. Yanarella (Albany: State University of New York Press, 1996), 125–57.

99. AIAM members include international automakers that have only sales or marketing arms in the United States. Members with production facilities, in AIAM-speak, are referred to as the "new American manufacturers."

100. *Automotive News* (19 January 1998): 6.

101. "BMW plans sport-utility at U.S. plant" <http://www.auto.com/autowire/qbmw13.html>, accessed 13 May 1998.

102. *Automotive News* (10 November 1997): 26.

103. David Mayes and Matthew N. Murray, "The Automobile Industry and the Economic Development of Tennessee and the Southeast: New Investment Has Increased Production Capacity," *Survey of Business* 30 (Winter 1995): 41–52 (quote from 42).

104. Kim, *Japanese Industry in the American South*, 151.

105. Lindsay Chappell, "State's Auto Industry Charges Ahead," <http://jnlco.com/tedg/article12.html>, accessed 4 February 1997.

106. *Mid State Economic Indicators* 8 (Spring 1998): 2.

107. *Mid State Economic Indicators* 7 (Fall 1997).

108. *Automotive News*, editorial (4 May 1998), <http://aida.org/automnews/autonews.htm>, accessed 11 May 1998.

109. *Automotive News* (30 March 1998), 1, 18–26. Note that in many cases the headquarters listed are those of the North American subsidiaries of non-U.S. companies, not those of worldwide operations.

110. Wright, *Old South*, 273.

111. Cobb, *Selling of the South*, 281.

112. Peter Applebome, *Dixie Rising: How the South Is Shaping American Values, Politics and Culture* (New York: Times Books, 1996). The basic argument can be traced back to a book by southern historian John Egerton, aptly titled *The Americanization of Dixie: The Southernization of America* (New York: Harper's Magazine Press, 1974).

113. Steven G. Livingston, "Foreign Direct Investment in Tennessee," <http://www.mtsu.edu/~berc/gc1-2/fdi.html>, accessed 7 November 1996.

114. Kanter, *World Class*, 201–326. Her case study of a "maker" region, by the way, is South Carolina, and the BMW plant and auto suppliers play a key role in her argument.

115. See <http://www.wardsauto.com/asia/990611nissan.htm>, accessed 11 June 1999.

116. See <http://www.tennessean.com/sii/99/05/23/autoconf23.htm>, accessed 11 June 1999.

117. Saturn already sells cars in Taiwan and Japan, but since GM is covering the European market through its Opel and Vauxhall subsidiaries, there is unlikely to be a role for Saturn in the European market.

118. Where the original Saturn, the S-series, has boasted a domestic content of 95 percent, the L-series shows 85 percent.

119. Visitors to the second "Saturn Homecoming," held at the Spring Hill site in July 1999, were shown the factory space being prepared for SUV production.

120. The Graz assembly plant is owned and operated by Steyr-Daimler-Puch (SDP), an Austrian group well known for its capacities in the development of 4WD systems and niche vehicle assembly. In summer 1998, SDP was acquired by Magna International, the Canadian-based supplier of automotive parts and systems.

121. See <http://www.edpa.org/keyindustries.html>, accessed 8 May 1999.

122. See <http://167.8.29.16/money/consumer/autos/mauto562.htm>, accessed 8 May 1999.

123. Toyota's location in Indiana is the exception, because SIA already had a—rather small-scale—operation going at the time Toyota decided to build its truck assembly plant in that state.

124. The AAMA, which had long fought off its new competitors, no longer exists. The merger of Daimler-Benz and Chrysler (now DaimlerChrysler) helped usher in its dissolution. A successor organization, the Alliance of Automobile Manufacturers, was formed in January 1999. The lines between this organization and the Association of International Automobile Manufacturers (AIAM) still remain blurred.

Guns and Butter, North and South

The Federal Contribution to Manufacturing Growth, 1940–1990

GREGORY HOOKS

This chapter examines the role played by federal installations in the growth of manufacturing in the United States, with an emphasis on the southern region, since 1940. This research addresses this issue from a unique vantage point because it is based on a comprehensive accounting of the federal presence in each American county. Drawing on a number of sources, including recently declassified reports, data have been collected on each industrial investment made by the federal government during World War II and each property in possession of the federal government in the post–World War II period. For the postwar period, data on federal property ownership have been compiled for 1953, 1960, 1970, 1980, and 1990.[1] The unique strength of these data sheds light on southern economic development by comparing the influence of federal installations over time, across local areas of the southern United States, and between the South and other regions of the United States. In addition this research design allows an examination of the variation among types of facilities and agencies controlling them.

Prominent theories, including the neoclassical tradition in economics and social ecology in sociology, discount the government's ability to influence regional economic development. These intellectual frameworks view local economic development as a "natural" process and the state's interventions as unnatural.[2] However, this chapter draws on (and seeks to contribute to) a growing literature that documents the manner in which the federal government, especially the defense program, *has* influenced economic development.[3] Specific to the southern United States, there are at least two reasons to believe that the federal role has been decisive. First, due to the seniority of southern legislators and the pattern of federal patronage during the middle decades of this century, one could reasonably believe that southern states absorbed a disproportionate share of federal investments. Second, because the southern region of the United States had relatively little manufacturing activity and its associated infrastructure was underdeveloped prior to World War II, federal investment and ongoing activity may have had a substantial impact on the emergence and strong growth of manufacturing over subsequent decades. While this view of manufacturing growth is compelling and several studies provide suggestive evidence consistent with this line of thinking, the federal role in southern manufacturing growth still has not been examined in a systematic manner.

In examining the federal contribution to southern industrialization, the study focuses on the growth in manufacturing employment as reported in the Census of Population, employing a panel design to identify the determinant of growth in manufacturing for each decade from 1940 to 1990 (details on measurement and analytic strategy are provided in the appendix). To provide a point of comparison, these analyses are conducted for counties in the South (defined as the states that seceded to form the Confederate States of America) and all other counties in the contiguous forty-eight states. The findings contradict the assertion that southern states received a disproportionate share of federal investments. Nevertheless, the federal government made an important contribution to southern industrialization. The concluding discussion explores the implications of these findings for contemporary developments and reconsideration of the recent past.

THE FEDERAL ROLE IN LOCAL ECONOMIC DEVELOPMENT

To my knowledge, there has been no systematic examination of the federal contribution to southern industrialization. However, a number of studies have highlighted the relationship between federal programs (especially national security) and local economic growth, suggesting that federal activity in southern states may have played a central role in promoting manufacturing growth since World War II. For instance, when examining the rise of the Sunbelt, the role of the federal contribution is frequently emphasized.[4] In addition to the southern states that are the focus of this study, the Sunbelt also includes the Southwest and California. Specific to defense production, researchers have called attention to disproportionate federal investments in southern and western areas—and away from the traditional manufacturing zones in the North and East.[5]

Mollenkopf contends that the government steered World War II expenditures away from the liberal cities of the North and West to discipline working-class political coalitions and reform-minded politicians.[6] When examining the 1940s and 1950s, Hooks found that because southern legislators were members of the majority party and virtually certain of reelection for decades, seniority and committee rules worked to their advantage. "Deep South constituencies were overrepresented within the Democratic party and even more concentrated in the higher seniority ranks of the separate committees."[7] The deflection of federal spending toward the South loomed large because government-financed construction projects had long been among the most important nonagricultural employment alternatives in the South and were central to the patronage system operating there.[8] In his examination of Houston's rapid growth, Feagin emphasized the federal role and the politics of steering federal spending toward this city.[9] To adopt language typical of the legal system, there is reason to believe that southern legislators had a motive and an opportunity to steer a disproportionate share of federal investments to their own districts during and after World War II.

While the thesis that the South received a disproportionate share of federal outlays is plausible, there is reason to view this claim with some skepticism. Federal investment decisions are also constrained by commercial, logistical, and (in the case of the military) strategic considerations.[10] Moreover, legislators from each state have an interest in securing their district's "fair share" of federal outlays.[11] Hence, while southern politicians may have influenced federal investment and site selection processes at the margins, significant obstacles worked against a wildly disproportionate share of federal outlays flowing to the South.[12] In fact, because World War II was mass industrial war and the South was relatively less industrialized, southern counties may have absorbed relatively fewer investments during this period.

Studies of governmental influence on local economic development typically make a distinction between military and civilian programs, with most ignoring the role played by civilian programs.[13] The emphasis on national security facilities is understandable given that defense spending has surpassed civilian outlays by a large margin. Yet examining the possibility that civilian installations and activities have contributed to local economic development makes possible a more comprehensive analysis. One distinction that has been recognized conceptually but rarely developed empirically is the difference between the roles played by large offices and administrative facilities (including military bases) and those installations concerned with science and industrial policy.[14] As they assemble a labor force, military bases and civilian offices exert a direct influence on the federal payroll but are unlikely to have a profound impact on manufacturing activity.

In contrast to military bases and civilian offices, installations involved in the nation's de facto industrial and technology policies have stimulated local manufacturing growth—not through the federal payroll, but through procurement and related spin-off activities. During the Cold War, the federal government identified important missions and built institutions to develop and produce the technologies needed to accomplish them. National security missions were the most prominent in terms of budgetary commitments and technological development. To maintain technological superiority over rival military powers, especially the Soviet Union, the United States invested heavily over a number of years in aeronautics and nuclear weaponry.[15] A large and steady stream of funds flowed to military agencies charged with developing, producing, testing, and maintaining state-of-the-art planes, missiles, and armaments. The Department of Energy (DOE) oversaw research and development of nuclear arms and the manufacture of nuclear bombs. Whether controlled by the military or by DOE, national security labs and factories placed a premium on performance characteristics and less emphasis on cost control. They recruited a highly educated and well-paid labor force and aggressively pursued technological innovation.[16] Military research generated spin-off technologies that were eventually adapted to commercial purposes. Because these installations concentrated a well-paid labor force and contributed to the growth of high-tech industries, it is anticipated that growth in private sector economic activity was higher in regions housing these installations.[17]

National security programs have dominated federal science and technology initiatives. Nevertheless, there have been comparable civilian efforts. Most important, the National Aeronautics and Space Administration (NASA) has pursued space explorations and National Institutes of Health (NIH) has supported biomedical research and development. Because these civilian programs also attract and sustain a highly skilled labor force and give rise to spin-off businesses and technologies, it is expected that such programs have made contributions to local manufacturing growth that are roughly comparable to the stimulus provided by national security facilities.

Drawing on the research summarized above, this chapter explores two key questions.

Did southern states receive a disproportionate share of federal wartime and postwar investments? This study examines this question empirically, anticipating that southern counties did *not* absorb a disproportionate share.

Have federal investments and activities influenced manufacturing growth in the South? Even if southern counties absorbed similar or fewer federal investments than counties in the North and West, these investments may have had a relatively larger impact in the South. Because southern counties were relatively less industrialized prior to World War II, it is expected that federal investments and ongoing activities at federal installations played a profound role in southern industrialization.

The discussion now turns to the data on federal property ownership and the methods employed to address these questions.

FEDERAL PROPERTY OWNERSHIP IN U.S. COUNTIES

Due to a lack of alternative data, previous research into the federal contribution to regional growth has concentrated on military activity and has typically relied on state-level procurement summaries provided by the Department of Defense. Only in the 1970s, with the emergence of the controversy over the rise of the Sunbelt, did the federal government begin to provide more complete information concerning its outlays. Prior to the late 1980s, the available data are spotty and misleading. At best, federal reports on defense contracts identify where the payment was received, but they do not disclose where the funds were actually spent.[18] This problem is compounded because defense outlay data only report on prime contracts and do not indicate where subcontracting occurs.[19] For this research, I adopt a different strategy to measure federal involvement in local economies. Instead of focusing on procurement, I examine federal investments and property ownership. These measures tap into the federal government's long-term presence in local areas. Such a strategy sacrifices information on current spending but provides unprecedented detail on the specific activities undertaken in federal installations.

The World War II economic mobilization was unique. The federal government made unparalleled industrial investments and owned over 40 percent of all industrial assets by the war's end.[20] After the war, these federally owned factories were closed, sold to private firms, or transferred to the military.[21] Especially in less industrialized areas such as the South, these World War II investments may have provided a decisive spark. In 1953, the government began compiling a comprehensive report on the properties in its possession.[22] Because these reports provided information on the location and activities conducted at each installation, they remained classified throughout most of the Cold War. In the wake of recent declassification, I acquired and encoded these reports for several reporting years (1953, 1960, 1970, 1980, and 1990). These data furnish information on the location and activities conducted at each federal facility (except the Central Intelligence Agency) throughout the last half century.

World War II Investments

Comprehensive reports on investments greater than $25,000 made by the federal government from 1939 to 1944 contain information on the location of the facility and the product manufactured during the war.[23] Each investment was converted to constant 1972 dollars and linked to the four-digit Standard Industrial Classification (SIC) code describing the economic activity occurring in the facility. Several industrial sectors were identified: airframe (SIC 3721), shipbuilding and repair (SIC 3731), ordnance (SIC 3482–3489), aircraft parts (SIC 3724 and 3728), petroleum (SIC 2892, 3795, 3792, 3481, and 3490), and miscellaneous civilian (not elsewhere classified). The miscellaneous civilian category includes mining, metal fabrication, chemicals, and various other civilian manufacturing industries.[24]

A significant portion of investments in the defense industries (ordnance, airframe, and shipbuilding) was deliberately directed away from established manufacturing centers in the North and East. Strategic planning called for locating new factories in the less industrialized interior of the nation (at least 200 miles from the nation's borders and away from major manufacturing centers) in order to reduce vulnerability to enemy attacks.[25] As the defense industries were being expanded several times over, dispersion away from prewar manufacturing centers was also a consequence of a spillover from centers operating at peak capacity to less industrialized centers.[26] However, the South was not the prime beneficiary of this dispersion. As a result of the "opening of the Pacific Front in World War II, a tremendous number of civilian and military personnel were transferred to the West coast, and an industrial complex that included shipyards, steel mills, machining factories, and electronics were underwritten by the federal government."[27] One of the research questions posed is whether or not the South absorbed a disproportionate share of federal wartime investments. When compared to counties in the North and West, the evidence presented in table 1 suggests that southern counties absorbed relatively *fewer, not more*, federal investments during World War II. Only twenty-two southern counties received federal shipbuilding investments, compared to sixty-seven nonsouthern counties. Moreover, the total investment and investment per employed person was larger in the nonsouthern counties. Although the overall trend suggests the South received less, it should be noted that Norfolk (Virginia), Charleston (South Carolina), and Mobile (Alabama) were among the ten leading shipbuilding centers. A portion of wartime ordnance investments was made outside prewar manufacturing centers, but as was the case with shipbuilding, southern states were not the leading beneficiaries of this dispersion. Still several southern cities did receive sizable investments: Huntsville (Madison, Alabama), Talladega County (Alabama), Pine Bluff (Jefferson, Arkansas) and Johnson City (Hawkins, Tennessee). The distribution of airframe manufacture is of special importance because this industry was at the center of the military-industrial complex and grew rapidly after the war.[28] In this sector, only nine southern counties absorbed wartime investments and the dollars invested per employed person were higher outside the South. While the larger comparison offers a reminder that the southern region did *not* attract a disproportionate share, Dallas (Texas) drew the highest level of investments of any county, and nearby Fort Worth (Tarrant County) also received a sizable wartime infusion. The federal government also built aircraft factories in Birmingham (Jefferson County), New Orleans (Orleans Parish) and near Atlanta (Cobb County).

The expansion of aircraft parts facilities reinforced established production

Table 1: Distribution of World War II Federal Investments among Southern and Nonsouthern Counties (3,107 counties in the contiguous 48 states)

Type of investment	SOUTHERN COUNTIES (n=1,144)			NONSOUTHERN COUNTIES (n=1,963)		
	Number of counties	Dollars (in thousands) (FY 1972)	Dollars per employed person in 1940	Number of counties	Dollars (in thousands) (FY 1972)	Dollars per employed person in 1940
World War II industrial						
Ordnance	57	1,791,229	$168.95	273	6,302,445	$182.12
Petroleum	14	1,030,740	96.64	36	926,629	26.78
Airframe	9	447,326	41.94	48	1,631,908	47.16
Aircraft parts	13	57,931	5.43	131	4,365,414	126.15
Shipbuilding	22	675,873	63.37	67	2,542,010	73.46
Miscellaneous civilian	108	1,588,825	148.97	463	7,889,413	227.98
World War II military base construction	247	4,299,841	322.85	378	6,325,970	182.80

centers because many of these plants produced automobile parts before the war and were reconverted to civilian production at the war's end.[29] Table 1 clearly reflects this trend. Whereas the federal government expanded aircraft parts production in 131 nonsouthern counties, it did so in only 13 southern counties. Moreover, the investment per employed person in southern counties ($5.43) was much lower than elsewhere in the nation ($126.15). Among southern cities, the federal government chose Houston (Harris, Texas), Memphis (Shelby, Tennessee), and Dallas (Texas) as sites for aircraft parts facilities. Wartime investments in miscellaneous civilian industries (e.g., mining, metal fabrication) also focused on established manufacturing centers outside the South. Although nonsouthern counties were more likely to receive miscellaneous civilian investments, a relatively high number of southern counties (108, or nearly 10 percent) also received these investments. The larger cities dominate the list of southern investment locations. Table 1 also summarizes the World War II investments in military bases (data taken from County and City Data File, measured in 1972 dollars). On this score, the regional comparison indicates that military base construction was widespread and extensive, and the South received the larger share ($322.85 per employed person versus $182.80 in the North and West).

The petroleum industry was the one industrial sector in which the Southeast, especially the Texas and Louisiana coast, was the focus of federal investment. In fact, Pittsburgh and Los Angeles are the only nonsouthern cities to be among the top ten centers of petroleum investments. The wartime expansion of this industry had enduring consequences. Without "the rapid infusion of federal capital assistance during the World War II period . . . , U.S. oil and petrochemical industries would not have grown as rapidly as they did."[30] Furthermore, without the expansion of this industry, Houston and other southern cities reliant upon the petroleum industry would not have grown so quickly after the war.

Due to the extraordinary level of wartime investment, it is estimated that the federal government owned approximately 40 percent of all capital assets by 1945.[31] Many of these facilities, especially in the defense industries, were absorbed into the inventory of federal properties. World War II shipbuilding facilities are included among the navy's postwar industrial and miscellaneous properties. In similar fashion, the army's industrial properties include facilities in which ordnance investments were made during the war, and the postwar air force and navy industrial properties include many of the facilities in which the federal government made airframe investments. Most federally owned petroleum, aircraft parts, and miscellaneous civilian facilities were returned to the private sector at the war's end and are, therefore, not included among federal properties after World War II. The examination of postwar manufacturing growth will consider the contribution of these wartime civilian investments.[32]

Federal Property Ownership after World War II

This research takes advantage of reports that detail the government's real estate holdings. The General Services Administration (GSA) has maintained records on all federal property and has produced *The Detailed Listing of Real Property Owned by the United States*.[33] Reports on military properties have only been declassified with the end of the Cold War. The GSA made the 1990 data file available on floppy diskettes, data for 1970 and 1980 has been encoded under the author's supervision. For each federal installation, the GSA reports the agency, location, function performed, and floor space (U.S. General Services Administration 1983a, p. vii). Table 2 distinguishes between southern and nonsouthern counties (in the contiguous forty-eight states) and summarizes the distribution of federal installations in 1980.

Miscellaneous civilian (all office and miscellaneous space controlled by civilian agencies except NIH, NASA, and DOE) includes post offices, federal courts, and a diverse set of agencies and functions. In both the South and elsewhere in the country, approximately 80 percent of all counties house at least one of these miscellaneous civilian facilities. However, when expressed as the ratio between square footage and employed persons in 1980, the southern counties house a relatively smaller share of civilian installations. Military bases (the miscellaneous

Table 2: Distribution of Federal Facilities among Southern and Nonsouthern Counties, 1980 (3,107 counties in the contiguous 48 states)

Type of facility	SOUTHERN COUNTIES (n=1,144)			NONSOUTHERN COUNTIES (n=1,963)		
	Number of counties	Total square feet in region	Square feet per employed person in 1980	Number of counties	Total square feet in region	Square feet per employed person in 1980
Military bases						
Air Force	96	154,296,078	5.98	262	315,568,165	4.43
Army	185	146,923,194	5.69	430	276,954,352	3.89
Navy	100	160,833,570	6.23	209	245,186,741	3.44
Military R&D facilities						
Air Force	11	4,577,699	0.18	37	12,326,271	0.17
Army	17	2,696,536	0.10	43	19,315,502	0.13
Navy	17	1,908,966	0.07	58	8,965,833	0.27
Military industrial facilities						
Air Force	5	8,482,292	0.33	21	10,172,723	0.14
Army	16	4,843,189	0.19	43	31,995,510	0.45
Navy	17	4,862,583	0.19	44	11,623,613	0.16
NASA (all functions)	11	19,996,234	0.77	12	12,373,457	0.17
Department of Energy, nuclear weapon laboratories	1	56,600	0.00	7	24,071,243	0.34
National Institute of Health, R&D	4	847,294	0.03	8	6,609,704	0.09
Miscellaneous civilian	864	126,990,004	4.92	1,616	434,659,401	6.10

and office space controlled by the military) are also widely distributed. While most of these installations are active bases, recruitment offices and other smaller facilities are also included in this measure. Although more nonsouthern counties contain a military base or office, the square footage per employed person is larger in the South for each branch of the armed services. The army is present in over 185 southern counties and 430 nonsouthern counties. Comparable navy measures are 100 and 209 counties. Finally only 96 southern counties contain air force facilities, compared to 262 nonsouthern counties.

R&D and manufacturing facilities are expected to influence growth in manufacturing, but these facilities are located in only a handful of counties (table 2). For each branch of the armed services, fewer than 20 southern counties house military R&D facilities. For nonsouthern counties the range is from 37 (air force) to 58 (navy) counties with R&D facilities. When considering the air force and army R&D facilities, table 2 does not demonstrate a sharp discrepancy in the square footage per employed person. However, the navy's R&D facilities are much more prominent outside the South. The military's industrial facilities are also scattered thinly across the nation. For the air force and navy's industrial facilities, the ratio between square footage and employed persons is significantly higher in southern states, while the army's industrial facilities are more concentrated in the North and West. No branch of the military maintained more than 20 facilities in the South, whereas the army and navy each operated over 40 comparable facilities outside the South. The distribution of air force factories is especially noteworthy. There are only five air force plants in the South: Marietta (Cobb, Georgia [in the Atlanta metropolitan area]), Fort Worth (Tarrant, Texas), San Antonio (Bexar, Texas), Pensacola (Okaloosa, Florida), and Coffee County (Tennessee).

The Department of Energy (DOE) controls the facilities that develop and manufacture nuclear weapons. The DOE's nine multipurpose laboratories (Los Alamos, Lawrence-Livermore, Sandia, Idaho National, Pacific Northwest, Lawrence-Berkeley, Brookhaven, Argonne, and Oak Ridge) house the vast majority of the nation's nuclear weapon development and production capabilities.[34] As Lawrence-Livermore and Lawrence-Berkeley are in the same county, these nine laboratories are located in only eight counties. Only one of these facilities (Oak Ridge, near Knoxville, Tennessee) is in the South. By all measures (number of counties, total square footage, and square feet per employed person), the North and West house a disproportionate share of nuclear weapons laboratories. NASA has contributed to the development of the aerospace industries. NASA installations are found in 23 counties (11 in the South and 12 in nonsouthern locations), and in the majority of these installations both R&D and manufacturing activity take place. With major facilities in Florida and Texas, a disproportionate share of NASA's facilities and the ratio between building space and employed persons points toward a concentration in the South. NIH plays a prominent role in health and biomedical industries, especially the War on Cancer and Human Genome Project. Four NIH facilities are located in southern counties. However, a much larger concentration of NIH facilities are located in other regions.

This overview of World War II investments and postwar property ownership calls into question the assumption that the South houses a disproportionate share of federal installations. During World War II (table 1), the South surpassed the rest of the nation in only two measures: petroleum and military base construction. In all other dimensions of the wartime mobilization, the North and West received a relatively larger infusion of federal funds. The postwar comparison (table 2) displays a more mixed pattern, with the South housing a higher concentration of military bases, NASA facilities, and industrial facilities (air force and navy). Otherwise, when expressed in terms of the ratio between square feet and employed persons, federal facilities are spread evenly or a disproportionate share are located in the North and West (NIH, nuclear weapons laboratories, army industrial, and miscellaneous civilian facilities). This is not to suggest that the southern region has been cheated but to contradict the view that the South received a disproportionate share of federal largesse and to provide guidance for the ensuing analyses. In other words, federal investments and activity have had a relatively greater influence over the economic development of southern counties; this influence, however, is due to differences in the impact of the activities and does not derive from a disproportionate concentration of federal facilities in the South.

THE FEDERAL CONTRIBUTION TO LOCAL ECONOMIC GROWTH

Many of the contributors to this book provide a detailed narrative of one or two localities. In contrast, this chapter provides a quantitative and statistical analysis of economic growth in each county. Although the details of specific cases are lost in this quantitative analysis, this approach offers several advantages. By considering trends in each county, this type of analysis can identify general trends that influenced economic growth across the nation. Specific to the research at hand, the statistical techniques employed for this research (see appendix for details) make it possible to isolate the effects of federal facilities on local economic growth while holding constant a host of factors that also contribute to economic growth and decline. Together, the quantitative methodology that serves as the foundation of this chapter and the historical case studies that have been provided by the other contributors to this volume offer complementary insights into southern industrialization. A quantitative approach can specify the general context in which the industrialization of the South occurred, while case studies can shed light on experiences of specific places and the choices made by historical actors.[35]

The ensuing paragraphs present findings concerning the factors that contributed to the growth in manufacturing from 1940 to 1950 (table 3) and 1950 to 1990 (table 4). The goal is to distinguish between the influence of theoretically important factors (i.e., the various measures of federal investment and property ownership) while holding constant a number of other factors that influence economic growth. For this reason, these analyses include a number of control variables: prior manufacturing employment, prewar manufacturing capacity, population density, population change, infrastructure development (as measured by commercial aircraft activity), levels of taxation, hazardous waste sites in the local area, and manufacturing growth in nearby counties (Land-Deane spatial effects term). When examining the preliminary findings, it was determined that including Los Angeles County (California) and the core counties of the Dallas–Fort Worth metropolitan area (Dallas and Tarrant) lowered confidence in the overall analysis. For this reason, these three counties are not included in the findings presented in tables 3 and 4. In the text, I present the results of the statistical analyses with few technical details. Details on measurement, the justification for including control variables, data sources, analytic strategy, and diagnostic procedures are provided in the appendix.

For each variable included in the analysis, tables 3 and 4 report the unstandardized regression coefficient and the standard error (in parentheses). One asterisk or more indicates that the variable is statistically significant. A positive and statistically significant coefficient suggests that the independent variable contributed to the growth in manufacturing. Conversely, a negative coefficient indicates that the presence of this variable impeded local economic growth. The absence of an asterisk indicates this independent variable *did not* make a significant contribution to economic growth.

The Growth of Manufacturing Employment, 1940–50

Table 3 summarizes the analysis of growth in manufacturing over the 1940–50 period. The control variables included in this estimation provide few surprises. As anticipated, manufacturing employment in 1940, bank deposits in 1944, and manufacturing establishments in 1939 are predictive of growth over the ensuing decade. Population density in 1940 is associated with growth in the nonsouthern counties but not in the South. Only in southern counties did population growth between 1930 and 1940 predict manufacturing growth in the 1940s.

After controlling for the influence of a number of variables, these analyses provide evidence that although federal investments played an important role for both southern and nonsouthern counties, wartime investments made greater contributions to nonsouthern counties. Ordnance and military base construction are positively associated with manufacturing growth only outside the South. Recall that the major centers of airframe investment were dropped from these analyses due to their undue influence on the estimation (Dallas and Tarrant Counties from the southern model and Los Angeles County from the nonsouthern model). Among the counties retained for analysis, airframe investments are associated with manufacturing growth outside the South, but are negatively related to growth among southern counties. The finding that airframe investments impeded manufacturing growth in the South should be interpreted with great caution. Recall that only nine southern counties received airframe investments (see table 1), and the two most important counties have been dropped. The remaining counties had a small prewar manufacturing capacity and absorbed relatively few

Table 3: Determinants of Growth in Manufacturing Employment 1940–1950, by Region (2 stage least squares[a])

	SOUTHERN COUNTIES (n=1,111)[b]		NONSOUTHERN COUNTIES (n=1,953)[c]	
	Regression Coefficient	Standard Error	Regression Coefficient	Standard Error
Land-Deane spatial effects term	0.18	(0.23)	0.01	(0.02)
Manufacturing employment, 1940	0.16**	(0.02)	0.17**	(0.00)
World War II federal industrial investments				
Ordnance	0.00	(0.00)	0.01**	(0.00)
Airframe	-0.05**	(0.01)	0.08**	(0.01)
Aircraft parts	0.33**	(0.06)	0.06**	(0.00)
Shipbuilding	-0.02**	(0.00)	-0.04**	(0.00)
Petroleum	0.02**	(0.00)	0.02*	(0.01)
Miscellaneous civilian	0.01**	(0.00)	0.03**	(0.00)
World War II military base construction	3.81	(19.10)	28.73*	(14.15)
Population density, 1940	-0.09	(0.29)	1.20**	(0.20)
Population change, 1930–1940	2.60*	(1.23)	4.13	(2.65)
Bank deposits, 1944	0.01**	(0.00)	0.00**	(0.00)
Manufacturing establishments, 1939	62.71*	(29.65)	291.04**	(44.56)
Constant	-246.35	(302.80)	-593.17**	(117.96)
Adjusted r-square	0.74		0.91	

[a] A dummy variable coded 1 if the state experienced the first Industrial Revolution, coded 0 otherwise (Wheat 1986), and the average age of residential housing stock in 1950 were used as instrumental variables for these analyses.
[b] The two counties at the center of the Dallas-Ft. Worth metropolitan area (Dallas and Tarrant) were identified to be influential cases and are not included in these estimations (see text for details).
[c] Los Angeles County was identified to be an influential case and is not included in these estimations (see text for details).

federal investments. The impacts of shipbuilding (negative), petroleum (positive), and miscellaneous civilian (positive) were similar among southern and nonsouthern counties. The implications of these findings will be discussed in greater detail later in this chapter. For now, the most important point to emphasize is that when the focus is specific to the 1940–50 decade, nonsouthern counties appear to have received the strongest boost from the wartime mobilization.

The Growth of Manufacturing Employment, 1950–90

Table 4 provides evidence that the federal government influenced southern and nonsouthern counties. The role played by the military's industrial properties

Table 4: Determinants of Growth in Manufacturing Employment 1950–90, by Region (2 stage least squares[a])

	SOUTHERN COUNTIES (n=1,111)[b]		NONSOUTHERN COUNTIES (n=1,953)[c]	
	Regression Coefficient	Standard Error	Regression Coefficient	Standard Error
Land-Deane spatial effects term	0.45	(0.61)	0.33*	(0.17)
Manufacturing employment, 1950	0.10	(0.09)	-0.50**	(0.02)
Manufacturing establishments, 1939	479.91	(329.01)	903.78**	(318.64)
Property owned by federal government, 1953				
Military industrial				
Air Force	6,716.55	(6,766.46)	10,924.25**	(2,851.54)
Navy	-2,522.38	(2,081.55)	1,870.68	(1,769.55)
Army	-3,202.59	(3,248.83)	-4,017.93*	(1,884.02)
Nuclear weapons laboratories (Department of Energy)	-9,179.30	(6,999.53)	16,368.25**	(4,651.50)
Miscellaneous civilian	15.13	(49.21)	-170.86*	(69.33)
Military bases				
Air Force	182.51*	(81.53)	42.79	(103.12)
Navy	-40.15	(156.80)	485.62**	(99.06)
Army	-137.66	(119.75)	71.41	(91.14)
Military research & development				
Air Force	10,283.70**	(2,629.77)	-1,397.41	(1,873.82)
Navy	5,224.79**	(1,473.72)	3,908.27*	(1,708.03)
Army	12,206.90	(6,362.22)	-468.71	(2,036.83)
National Aeronautics and Space Administration	6,445.90**	(1,887.07)	41,949.70**	(3,339.80)
National Institute of Health	7,733.17*	(3,493.10)	15,070.87**	(3,927.74)
Population density, 1950	-0.16	(1.45)	-0.57**	(0.16)
Population change, 1940–50	39.91	(27.43)	57.02**	(13.73)
World War II federal industrial investments				
Miscellaneous civilian	0.08**	(0.02)	0.01	(0.01)
Petroleum	0.05*	(0.02)	-0.07	(0.04)
Commercial aircraft activity, 1966	1,891.52**	(473.13)	1,981.42**	(400.01)
Per capita property tax, 1962	1,402.87	(3,216.57)	4,222.26	(7,232.62)
National Priority List toxic waste sites	980.96	(829.29)	2,944.38**	(432.67)
Constant	-3,102.71	(3,929.56)	-3,681.60**	(1,372.33)
Adjusted r-square	0.27		0.60	

[a] A dummy variable coded 1 if the state experienced the first Industrial Revolution, coded 0 otherwise (Wheat 1986), and the median education in 1960 were used as instrumental variables for these analyses.

[b] The two counties at the center of the Dallas-Ft. Worth metropolitan area (Dallas and Tarrant) were identified to be influential cases and are not included in these estimations (see text for details).

[c] Los Angeles County was identified to be an influential case and is not included in these estimations (see text for details).

reflects the shift away from mass industrial war. Among southern counties, industrial properties owned by the armed services did not significantly influence manufacturing growth. Among nonsouthern counties, air force factories contributed to growth while comparable army facilities were negatively related to manufacturing growth.[36] Military bases exerted a weak and uneven influence over manufacturing growth. Air force bases played a positive role in the South, while navy bases had a comparable impact among nonsouthern counties. The Department of Energy's weapons laboratories contributed to manufacturing growth outside the South, but this relationship is not statistically significant for southern counties. It should be borne in mind that only one southern county (Anderson, Tennessee, in which the Oak Ridge Laboratory is located) contains a weapons laboratory. This finding indicates that Anderson County did not experience significantly more manufacturing growth than other southern counties.

There were several notable differences between southern and nonsouthern counties. Miscellaneous civilian facilities are negatively related to manufacturing growth in nonsouthern counties but not in the South. Two civilian agencies—NASA and NIH—contributed to manufacturing growth in both southern and nonsouthern counties. However, the coefficients for both measures for nonsouthern counties are larger than the comparable coefficients among southern counties. World War II era investments—both miscellaneous civilian and petroleum investments—contributed to manufacturing growth in the South but not in other regions of the country. Among nonsouthern counties, only the navy's R&D facilities are associated with growth in manufacturing. However, in the South, air force and navy R&D facilities are associated with growth.

DISCUSSION

The results presented in tables 3 and 4 provide evidence that federal installations influenced economic growth in both the southern and nonsouthern counties. At the same time, there appear to be important differences in the way that federal facilities influenced growth in the southern and nonsouthern regions of the country. Additional statistical tests were undertaken to determine whether these differences are statistically significant (see appendix for details).

The results presented in table 5 show a very different pattern during World War II and the postwar period. Over the 1940–50 period, federal investments were more likely to benefit counties outside the South. That is, southern counties received a significantly smaller boost in manufacturing employment from federal investments in ordnance, airframe, and miscellaneous civilian industries. Please bear in mind that the centers of airframe production among nonsouthern counties (Los Angeles) and southern counties (Dallas and Tarrant Counties)

Table 5: Tests of Significant Differences between the Determinants of Manufacturing Growth in Southern and Nonsouthern Counties between 1940 and 1950 and over the 1950–90 Period (Wald Tests)

	1940–1950	1950–1990
Growth in manufacturing employment 1940–50 (see table 3)		
World War II federal industrial investments		
Ordnance	⇓	—
Airframe	⇓	—
Aircraft parts	⇑	—
Shipbuilding	⇑	—
Petroleum	...	—
Miscellaneous civilian	⇓	—
World War II military base construction	...	—
Growth in manufacturing employment 1950–90 (see table 4)		
Federal property		
National security		
Industrial		
Air Force	—	⇓
Army	—	...
Navy	—	...
R&D		
Air Force	—	⇑
Army	—	⇑
Navy	—	...
Military bases		
Air Force	—	...
Army	—	↑
Navy	—	⇑
DOE weapons laboratories	—	...
National Institute of Health, R&D	—	...
National Aeronautics and Space Administration	—	⇓
Miscellaneous civilian facilities	—	⇑
World War II federal industrial investments		
Petroleum	—	⇑
Miscellaneous civilian	—	⇑

⇑ coefficient for southern counties is *greater* and the difference is significant at 0.05 level.
↑ coefficient for southern counties is *greater* and the difference is significant at 0.10 level.
⇓ coefficient for southern counties is *smaller* and the difference is significant at 0.05 level.
↓ coefficient for southern counties is *smaller* and the difference is significant at 0.10 level.
... difference between coefficients for southern and nonsouthern counties are *not* significantly different.
— not applicable, variable does not appear in the model.

were dropped (see appendix for details). The coefficient for aircraft parts and shipbuilding was significantly greater for southern counties. However, only 13 southern counties (versus 131 nonsouthern counties) absorbed aircraft parts investments, and the coefficient for shipbuilding is negative in both regions.

These findings reinforce the trends revealed in tables 1 and 2. On the whole, the southern region received a smaller share of wartime investments (table 1), and these investments were less likely to induce strong manufacturing growth in the South. This should come as no surprise. World War II was a mass industrial mobilization.[37] The United States, as was the case with other belligerents, invested in manufacturing to produce munitions as quickly as possible. In contrast to the highly specialized weaponry currently employed, World War II munitions were not dramatically different from commercial goods. For this reason, the United States converted a number of existing factories to war production—and many of these plants returned to civilian production at the war's end.[38] As the existing industrial base was concentrated in the North, the vast majority of federal investments were directed toward this region of the nation. Moreover, to the extent that strategic and logistic imperatives required the creation of a new industrial infrastructure, the western states—not southern states—were the prime beneficiaries.

These findings do not suggest that politics are unimportant, but they do offer a reminder of the limitations of political influence. It appears that logistical and strategic considerations were the overriding concerns—and these concerns ensured that nonsouthern counties received the highest level of investment and, in turn, enjoyed the largest benefits during the 1940s. However, within these constraints, political influence may well have played an important role. Dallas–Fort Worth provides one of the most compelling examples. Given its meager prewar manufacturing base, it is surprising that the Dallas–Fort Worth area absorbed the highest level of wartime airframe investments—a level that even exceeded Los Angeles. To reduce exposure to enemy attack, wartime planners gave priority to locating new airframe manufacturing facilities in the interior of the nation and between the Appalachian and Rocky Mountains. While Dallas–Fort Worth met this broad strategic criterion, so did a great many other cities. During World War II, the Speaker of the House (Sam Rayburn) represented the Dallas–Fort Worth area in Congress. It is quite likely that the power of the Speaker did influence the flow of federal investments toward this region. In fact, if this is true, his unique political intervention may have contributed to these counties being exceptional cases (and ultimately dropped from the analysis for statistical reasons).

By the same token, petroleum was the one industrial sector in which the majority of wartime investments flowed toward the South (table 1). Prior to World War II, this industry was already concentrated along the Texas-Louisiana coast.

However, a leading Houston businessman, Jesse Jones, played a pivotal role in guiding wartime investment policies. Before the war, he served as the director of the Reconstruction Finance Corporation (the organization that made most of the petroleum investments) and retained direct control of this agency when promoted to secretary of commerce in the early 1940s.[39] Jesse Jones's track record of steering federal investments toward Texas, especially Houston, was so impressive that Drew Pearson and Robert Allen referred to Jones as "Texas' last great unexploited resource."[40] Even if one accepts the thesis that both Dallas and Houston benefited from the interventions of powerful and well-placed politicians, the research reported here indicates that these interventions did not represent a complete redirection of federal investments to the benefit of the South as a whole.

If examination of the 1940–50 panel suggests that the South received fewer benefits from the wartime mobilization, an examination of the postwar panel suggests that southern counties were then more likely to benefit from federal activity. In general, coefficients are larger among southern counties (the arrow points up in table 5). The two exceptions are air force industrial facilities and NASA. As both types of installations are heavily involved in the aerospace sector and the most important centers of aircraft manufacture (among southern and nonsouthern counties) have been dropped, this finding should be interpreted with some caution. Southern counties received relatively greater stimulus from federal installations, including army bases, navy bases, and miscellaneous civilian facilities. It is likely that the significant regional difference in the role played by civilian facilities is due to the location of many civilian facilities in densely populated urban centers located in the North. In the era of deindustrialization, many urban counties in the North and West experienced sharp declines in manufacturing employment. It is also notable that the postwar stimulus of World War II federal investments (both petroleum and miscellaneous sectors) was significantly larger among southern counties. This difference may also be related to deindustrialization. Whereas World War II investments in northern manufacturing centers had the unanticipated consequence of reinforcing the concentration of mature industries in such cities, comparable investments in the less industrialized South may have contributed to the creation of a manufacturing base and industrial infrastructure.[41]

Table 5 reveals a notable difference in the role played by military R&D facilities. The army's and the air force's R&D facilities provided a significantly larger boost in manufacturing employment among southern counties. As noted earlier, one plausible explanation centers on the difference in levels of industrial development at the beginning of the period. Because southern counties had relatively less manufacturing in 1940, federal investments and activities may have played an important role in sparking and guiding industrial development. The positive role played by the federal government's World War II investments among southern counties is consistent with this thesis. However, it may also be the case that federal activities are different in the North and South. The positive role played by military R&D facilities in the South and the larger coefficients for NASA facilities in nonsouthern counties raise the possibility that the federal agencies may be undertaking substantially different activities in the southern and nonsouthern facilities. More detailed information concerning specific installations and local economic areas is needed to fully understand these dynamics.

CONCLUSION

At the most general level, these findings run counter to theoretical traditions that doubt the state's investments and priorities can influence regional growth. Social ecology (in the sociological literature) and neoclassical economics tend to assume that the state merely reinforces rational economic processes already underway in the private sector or that the state's efforts to pursue noneconomic goals have only a small and temporary impact.[42] Thus, when reviewing 25 years of studies, Stevens is not surprised that past studies have yielded mixed evidence concerning the effects of tax inducements and other governmental efforts to influence the "business climate" because these interventions exert "a relatively minor influence on location decisions."[43] However, this study—in concert with a growing literature—has documented that federal activity has influenced regional growth in both the North and the South. Many of the federal government's investments were made to secure and maintain a position of global military leadership.[44] However, as we enter the post–Cold War period and can anticipate relatively lower levels of defense spending, it is notable that NASA and NIH facilities have also contributed to growth. Although proposals to promote federal influence over science, technology, and industrial development are controversial—especially in civilian sectors—the evidence presented in this study suggests that these interventions have spurred and continue to contribute to local economic growth.

When examining the role of defense activity in regional economic growth, Crump proposed a model of cumulative causation.[45] Applying this reasoning to the present study, the original siting of a facility in a region gave that region a decided advantage in securing subsequent defense contracts, attracting new employers, and thereby exerting an influence on manufacturing beyond the activities specific to the installation. This research has identified the cumulative effects of federal installations during and after World War II for both southern and nonsouthern regions. Although southern counties received relatively fewer World War II investments and experienced less manufacturing growth during the 1940s, it appears that the cumulative effects of federal activity are greater among southern counties. Over the 1950–90 period, many (but not all) types of federal facilities—including World War II industrial investments—were significantly more likely to spur manufacturing growth in the South than comparable facilities in nonsouthern counties (see especially table 5).

While the answers provided by this study are useful, the questions posed by these findings may be more interesting still. First, these quantitative analyses must be complemented by more detailed studies of individual counties and facilities.[46] A quantitative analysis can highlight the shared characteristics of a large group of cases. However, several of the most interesting federal facilities are located in only a handful of counties (e.g., NASA, DOE nuclear weapons laboratories). To understand the role these facilities have played, it is necessary to examine the specific activities undertaken in a given facility and its ties to businesses and other governmental organizations in the area. Second, these findings suggest that despite lower levels of federal investment during World War II, wartime investments and the presence of federal facilities after the war provided relatively greater stimulus to manufacturing growth in southern counties. I have argued that this greater stimulus is due to the fact that southern counties had a smaller industrial and economic base at the beginning of the period. At present, the differences between the South and other regions of the country are modest. As such, there may be a convergence of the role played by federal facilities in southern and nonsouthern counties. Finally, this study has documented the role played by the federal government over the past fifty years. Future research is required to determine if the recent past is an exceptional period or if the government will continue to influence economic growth in future decades.

APPENDIX

In the text, I summarized the analysis of manufacturing growth while minimizing technical details. This appendix provides detail on these technical issues. All references to tables in the ensuing paragraphs refer to the five tables presented in the text. The analyses are based on a panel design that focuses on the factors that contributed to growth in manufacturing employment during World War II and in the postwar era. The World War II period is examined separately because this wartime mobilization was unique in its magnitude and, for many counties, significantly altered the path of economic development.[47] Due to severe problems with missing data in Alaska and Hawaii (especially in the years before 1960), the sample is restricted to the counties in the contiguous forty-eight states.[48] To highlight the experiences of the South, these panels distinguish between southern and nonsouthern counties.

Measurement Strategy

The ensuing paragraphs describe the measurement strategy employed for federal property ownership (independent measures), change in manufacturing employment (the dependent measure), and control variables.

Measures of Federal Property Ownership This study documented the uneven distribution of federal property (see tables 1 and 2). Federal R&D and manufacturing facilities are located in only a few counties. When expressed as the building space (square feet) controlled by a given agency, over 90 percent of all counties have a value of 0, while several counties have very large values. Preliminary analyses confirmed that severe problems resulted from this highly skewed distribution. Whether the raw value or one of several transformations (natural log or one of several power transformations) was employed, collinearity remained prevalent. For example, because the air force's large industrial facilities often contain a small R&D capability, it was impossible to distinguish the effects of air force R&D and industrial facilities when examining economic growth. Problems of this nature proved pervasive. For instance, both the navy and NIH have their largest R&D facility in suburban Washington, D.C. (Montgomery County, Maryland). The raw (and transformed) measures of NIH and navy R&D are highly correlated. In addition to collinearity, standard diagnostic statistics (Cook's D and dfbeta) provided compelling evidence that when employing the raw or transformed values, several cases exerted undue influence on the estimates (preliminary results are available upon request). To overcome the difficulties posed by this highly skewed distribution, dummy variables were created to identify the presence of each type of federal manufacturing and R&D facility (coded 1 if present, 0 otherwise). This measurement preserved detail on the agencies and functions in each county while avoiding the problems of collinearity and influential cases. Although miscellaneous civilian and military bases are widely distributed, there are several counties with a very high concentration (i.e., the distribution is skewed to the right). To reduce the risks of heteroscedastic disturbances and influential cases, a log transformation of each of these measures has been undertaken.

Dependent Measure: Growth in Manufacturing Employment The dependent measure is growth in manufacturing employment (data taken from the Census of Population). This source provides valid data for each local area in 1940, 1950, and 1990. The choice of dependent measure is based upon the availability and continuity in measurement over the 1940–1990 period.[49] For each panel (1940–50 and 1950–90), the dependent measure is a simple change score, manufacturing employment at the end of the period minus manufacturing employment at the beginning of the period. A common strategy for analyzing change employs two-stage least squares analysis and regresses the dependent measure at time 1 on the dependent measure at time 2. The simple change score employed in this analysis is algebraically equivalent to a model with a lagged endogenous variable, but the change score on the left side of the equation includes the dependent measure at time 1 with the implicit coefficient of 1.[50] A change score is used instead of a lagged endogenous variable because the Land-Deane/Anselin correction for spatial autocorrelation (see below) requires the use of two-stage least squares and does not allow for a second endogenous variable in the equation.[51]

Control Measures Reflecting the variety of explanations put forward in the literature on regional growth, a number of factors that may influence regional growth have been considered. Due to space limitations, only an abbreviated discussion of control variables is provided.[52]

1. Agglomeration. Throughout the period under investigation, economic activity has been concentrated in urban areas. A set of positive externalities (i.e., agglomeration) contributes to this concentration, including "the operation of scale factors . . . , the spatial clustering of innovations, and the nature of industrial decision-making."[53] The *population density* (persons per square mile) in a county has been included to control for agglomeration.[54] The growth in population is likely to add additional momentum to agglomeration tendencies. For this reason, *the change in population during the preceding decade* is also included as a control measure.

2. Quality of infrastructure. Air transportation became increasingly important in the latter half of the period under consideration. Previous studies suggest that counties in which an airport is located have grown more quickly than counties lacking an airport.[55] The natural log of *total commercial aircraft operations* provides a measure of infrastructural development.[56] Commercial banking resources constitute an important infrastructural resource that facilitates local growth. *Total bank deposits* in a county have been included in these estimations, with the expectation that this variable is positively associated with growth.[57]

3. Deindustrialization. Bluestone and Harrison called attention to the decline of traditional manufacturing industries, and with this deindustrialization—the decline of regions in which mature industries had concentrated. Moriarity provides evidence that, since 1970, local areas containing older manufacturing facilities more often experienced deindustrialization.[58] To identify regions housing mature industries, the *natural log of manufacturing establishments in 1939* has been included.[59] It is anticipated that this measure is positively associated with manufacturing growth in the earlier panels and negatively associated with growth in manufacturing after 1970.

4. *Local government fiscal structure.* A number of researchers suggest that employers are sensitive to the tax rate.[60] To control for the effects of local taxation, *per capita property taxes* have been included among the independent variables.[61]

5. *Environmental side effects of growth.* Citizens and policymakers have become increasingly concerned with environmental damage. These concerns were pronounced over nuclear weapons production facilities and military installations.[62] The Environmental Protection Agency (EPA) has been charged with identifying uncontrolled hazardous waste sites. Based upon the toxicity of the materials, the likelihood that these materials will be released into the environment, and the danger to humans and ecosystems should a release occur, hazardous sites are considered for the National Priorities List.[63] This list includes "Superfund" sites (sites for which no private firm is responsible or capable of conducting the cleanup) as well as hazardous waste sites for which a firm or government agency bears responsibility for abating or controlling hazardous wastes. Over 38,000 sites have been nominated for inclusion on the National Priorities List; of these proposed sites approximately 1,800 reached the final list. A dummy variable identifying counties containing *National Priorities List final sites* has been included in the latter panels to control for environmental side effects (coded 1 if present, 0 otherwise).

6. *Land-Deane spatial effects term.* It is likely that manufacturing growth or decline in one county influences economic processes in nearby counties (e.g., commuting to work across county boundaries and expansion or contraction of service industries to support economic activity in nearby counties). If a spatial process is unmeasured, there is a possibility that the results will be biased. For these reasons, these analyses also address the problem of spatial autocorrelation.[64] Diagnostic and corrective procedures that rely on maximum likelihood estimates have been available for some time. However, due to the extraordinary computational requirements needed for maximum likelihood estimation, it has been impossible to control for spatial autocorrelation when the sample size is large. Land and Deane developed a two-stage least squares estimator that efficiently computes and produces results similar to maximum likelihood estimates. To calculate the spatial effects term, "each place is treated successively as the point of reference, and the sum of quotients of the [dependent measure] of every other place divided by its distance from the reference point is computed."[65] As the spatial effects are determined simultaneously with the dependent variable, ordinary least squares estimates are likely to be biased. Therefore, following

Land and Deane's recommendation, two-stage least squares are employed for these analyses.

Influential Cases

A number of diagnostic procedures were undertaken to gain greater confidence in the results, including the examination of residual plots and the search for influential cases that distort findings.[66] The concern over influential cases is not that the estimation is inaccurate concerning these cases (though it often is). The larger concern is that by including influential cases, the overall estimation is distorted. The diagnostic procedure (examination of residual plots, Cook's D, dfbetas, and comparison of the standard errors of the estimates with and without the influential cases) provided evidence that Los Angeles County, California, the central county in the Los Angeles economic area, should be omitted. Los Angeles County experienced the fastest growth in manufacturing of any county in the nation during the World War II and postwar periods. Moreover, this county absorbed a very high level of World War II federal investments, and the federal government—especially national security agencies—maintained an exceptionally large number of industrial and R&D facilities there after the war. The preeminence of the Los Angeles area was especially pronounced in the aerospace sector, which grew at a spectacular rate over the period under investigation and was heavily dependent on the government.

Diagnostic procedures also revealed that the core counties of the Dallas–Fort Worth metropolitan area (Dallas and Tarrant) exerted undue influence on the analysis of growth among southern counties. When the focus is restricted to the South, Dallas County displayed the second fastest growth during World War II and third during the postwar period, while Tarrant County was fourth and fifth respectively. Moreover, these counties attracted a surprisingly high level of federal wartime investments. In fact, during World War II, the federal government invested more in the aviation industry in the Dallas–Fort Worth area than in any other area (including Los Angeles).[67]

Comparing Differences among Coefficients

The results presented in tables 3 and 4 provide evidence that federal installations influenced economic growth, but there were differences in the way that federal facilities influenced growth in the southern and nonsouthern regions of the country. However, it is impossible to determine whether these differences are significant simply by inspecting the coefficients presented in separate tables. To address these issues, southern and nonsouthern counties were examined simultaneously (see table 5). The reasoning behind the comparison is summarized below.

$$\begin{bmatrix} Y_{north} \\ Y_{south} \end{bmatrix} = \begin{bmatrix} V_{north} & 0 \\ 0 & V_{south} \end{bmatrix} \begin{bmatrix} \beta_{Vnorth} \\ \beta_{Vsouth} \end{bmatrix} + \begin{bmatrix} X_{north} & 0 \\ 0 & X_{south} \end{bmatrix} \begin{bmatrix} \beta_{Xnorth} \\ \beta_{Xsouth} \end{bmatrix} + \begin{bmatrix} E_{north} \\ E_{south} \end{bmatrix}$$

where

Y_R = average change in nonfederal earnings in region R (north or south)
V_R = variable of interest in region R
β_{VR} = coefficient for variable V in region R
X_R = all other independent measures region R
β_{XR} = coefficients for all other variables in region R
E_R = error term in region R

For these analyses the influential cases (Los Angeles, Dallas, and Tarrant Counties) were dropped. With the remaining southern and nonsouthern counties, 3,064 cases are included. An F test is employed to test "the hypothesis that some or all the regression coefficients are different" between the two regions. More specifically, because the variance is different in the two periods, the Wald statistic is employed to test for significant differences.[68]

Table 5 (see text) compares the difference in coefficients between southern and nonsouthern counties. For instance, when considering the stimulus attributable to the air force's R&D facilities, separate measures for this variable in southern and nonsouthern counties were included and the data for all counties then analyzed in a single calculation. The coefficient for the air force's R&D facilities in southern counties was compared to the comparable measure for nonsouthern counties. The Wald statistic provides the means to determine if difference between the two regions achieves statistical significance.

NOTES

This research was supported by the National Science Foundation (SBR-9320043). I would like to acknowledge the cooperation of the General Service Administration in making information available for this research. Nathan Fahrer, Jennifer Vickers, Annie Mtika, and Vicki Getz played an important role in the collection and management of data. I am indebted to Mike Allen and Tom Rotolo for valuable advice. Direct correspondence to Gregory Hooks, Department of Sociology, Washington State University, Pullman, Washington 99164-4020; ghooks@wsu.edu.

1. U.S. General Services Administration, *Detailed Listing of Real Property Owned by the United States and Used by Civil Agencies* (Washington, D.C.: GPO, 1954, 1961, 1973, 1983. The General Services Administration made available the 1990 data on diskette.

2. For a summary, see Gregory Hooks, "Regional Processes in the Hegemonic Nation: The Determinants and Consequences of World War II Commercial and Military Investments," *American Sociological Review* 59 (1994): 746–73.

3. Jeffrey Crump, "The Spatial Distribution of Military Spending in the United States, 1941–1985," *Growth and Change* 20 (1989), 50–62; Ann Markusen, Peter Hall, Scott Campbell, and Sabina Deitrick, *The Rise of the Gunbelt: The Military Remapping of Industrial America* (New York: Oxford University Press, 1991).

4. Kirkpatrick Sale, *Power Shift: The Rise of the Southern Rim and Its Challenge to the Eastern Establishment* (New York: Random House, 1975).

5. Roger Bolton, *Defense Purchases and Regional Growth* (Washington, D.C.: Brookings Institute, 1966); Robert Parker and Joe Feagin, "Military Spending in Free Enterprise Cities: The Military-Industrial Complex in Houston and Las Vegas," in *The Pentagon and the Cities*, ed. A. Kirby (Newbury Park, Calif.: Sage, 1992), 100–125; Gregory Hooks and Leonard Bloomquist, "The Legacy of World War II for Regional Growth and Decline: The Cumulative Effects of Wartime Investments on U.S. Manufacturing, 1947–1972," *Social Forces* 71 (1992): 303–37; Andrew Kirby, "The Pentagon Versus the Cities?" in *The Pentagon and the Cities*, 1–22; John Lovering, "Fordism's Unknown Successor: A Comment on Scott's Theory of Flexible Accumulation and the Re-Emergence of Regional Economics," *International Journal of Urban and Regional Research* 14 (1990): 159–74; Edward Malecki, "Federal R&D Spending in the United States of America: Some Impacts on Metropolitan Economies," *Regional Studies* 16 (1982): 19–35; Ann Markusen, "Defense Spending and the Geography of High Tech Industries," in *Technology, Regions and Policy*, ed. John Rees (New York: Praeger, 1986), 94–119; Markusen et al., *The Rise of the Gunbelt*.

6. John Mollenkopf, *The Contested City* (Princeton, N.J.: Princeton University, 1983).

7. Richard Bensel, *Sectionalism and American Political Development 1880–1980* (Madison: University of Wisconsin Press, 1984), 241.

8. Arthur Maass, *Muddy Waters: The Army Engineers and the Nation's Rivers* (Cambridge, Mass.: Harvard University, 1951); Francis Butler Simkins, *The South Old and New: A History, 1820–1947* (New York: Alfred A. Knopf, 1947).

9. Joe Feagin, "The Global Context of Metropolitan Growth: Houston and the Oil Industry," *American Journal of Sociology* 90 (1985): 1204–30.

10. Kenneth Mayer, "Patterns of Congressional Influence in Defense Contracting," in *Arms, Politics, and the Economy*, ed. Robert Hicks (New York: Holmes and Meier, 1990), 202–35.

11. Markusen et al., *The Rise of the Gunbelt*.

12. Hooks, "Regional Processes in the Hegemonic Nation."

13. Bolton, *Defense Purchases and Regional Growth;* Hooks, "Regional Processes in the Hegemonic Nation"; Kirby, "The Pentagon Versus the Cities?"; Markusen et al., *The Rise of the Gunbelt*.

14. Gregory Hooks and Vicki Getz, "Federal Investments and Economic Stimulus at the End of the Cold War: The Influence of Federal Installations on Employment Growth, 1970–1990," *Environment and Planning-A* 30 (1998): 1695–1704; Ann Markusen, Peter

Hall, and Amy Glassier, *High Tech America: The What, How, Where, and Why of the Sunrise Industries* (Boston: Allen and Unwin, 1986); John Rees and Howard Stafford, "Theories of Regional Growth and Industrial Location: Their Relevance for Understanding High-Technology Complexes," in *Technology, Regions and Policy*, ed. Rees, 23-50.

15. Lewis Branscomb, "The National Technology Debate," in *Empowering Technology: Implementing a U.S. Strategy*, ed. L. Branscomb (Cambridge, Mass.: MIT Press, 1993), 1-35.

16. Ann Markusen and Joel Yudken, *Dismantling the Cold War Economy* (New York: Basic Books, 1992).

17. Manuel Castells, "High Technology, Economic Restructuring and Urban-Regional Process in the United States," in *High Technology, Space, and Society*, ed. M. Castells (Beverly Hills, Calif.: Sage, 1985), 11-40; Markusen et al., *High Tech America*.

18. Clyde Browning, "Federal Outlays and Regional Development," in *Federalism and Regional Development: Case Studies on the Experience in the United States and the Federal Republic of Germany*, ed. G. Hoffman (Austin: University of Texas Press, 1981), 123-53; John Rees, "The Impact of Defense Spending on Regional Industrial Change in the United States," in ibid., 193-222.

19. John Rees, "The Impact of Defense Spending."

20. Gregory Hooks, *Forging the Military-Industrial Complex: World War II's Battle of the Potomac* (Champaign: University of Illinois Press, 1991); Hooks, "Regional Processes in the Hegemonic Nation."

21. Hooks and Bloomquist, "The Legacy of World War II."

22. U.S. General Services Administration, *Detailed Listing of Real Property Owned by the United States Used by Civil Agencies* (see note 1); U.S. General Services Administration, *Detailed Listing of Real Property Owned by the United States and Used by the Department of Defense for Military Functions* (Washington, D.C.: GPO), various dates.

23. U.S. War Production Board, *War Manufacturing Facilities Financed with Public Funds through June 30, 1944* (Washington, D.C.: GPO, 1944); U.S. War Production Board, *War Manufacturing Facilities Authorized through December 1944, by State and County* (Washington, D.C.: GPO, 1944).

24. For additional information on measurement and related analyses, see Hooks and Bloomquist, "The Legacy of World War II."

25. Elbertson R. Smith, *The Army and Economic Mobilization* (Washington, D.C.: GPO, 1959).

26. George Q. Flynn, *The Mess in Washington: Manpower Mobilization in World War II* (Westport, Conn.: Greenwood Press, 1979).

27. Markusen, "Defense Spending and the Geography of High Tech Industries," 25.

28. Gregory Hooks, "The Rise of the Pentagon & U.S. State-Building: The Defense Program as Industrial Policy," *American Journal of Sociology* 96 (1990): 358-404; Markusen et al., *The Rise of the Gunbelt*.

29. Hooks, *Forging the Military-Industrial Complex;* U.S. Small War Plants Corporation, *Economic Concentration and World War II* (Washington, D.C.: GPO, 1946).

30. Joe Feagin, *Free Enterprise City: Houston in Political-Economic Perspective* (New Brunswick, N.J.: Rutgers University Press, 1988), 68.

31. Hooks, *Forging the Military-Industrial Complex;* Hooks, "Regional Processes in the Hegemonic Nation."

32. For additional detail on the postwar transfer and use of these wartime facilities, see Jacques Gansler, *Defense Industry* (Cambridge, Mass.: MIT Press, 1980); Hooks, *Forging the Military-Industrial Complex;* and Hooks, "Regional Processes in the Hegemonic Nation."

33. Top secret national security installations and the properties controlled by the Central Intelligence Agency were not included in these reports. It is unlikely that these secret installations constitute a significant portion of all federal properties, and for the present examination of regional economic growth, it is unlikely that these secret properties substantially alter the findings reported.

34. U.S. Office of Technology Assessment, *Defense Conversion: Redirecting R&D* (Washington, D.C.: GPO, 1993), 14.

35. For a comparable effort to integrate quantitative and historical methods, see Gregory Hooks and William Luchansky, "Warmaking and the Accommodation of Leading Firms," *Political Power and Social Theory* 10 (1996): 3–37.

36. Comparable analyses were conducted for each decade over the 1950–90 period. For the earlier decades (1950s and 1960s), the military's industrial facilities did contribute to growth among northern counties; in the latter panels the relationship was less likely to be statistically significant—or in the case of the army the coefficient turned negative. Results available upon request.

37. Alan Milward, *War, Economy, and Society* (Berkeley: University of California Press, 1977).

38. Hooks, *Forging the Military-Industrial Complex.*

39. Joe Feagin, "The Global Context of Metropolitan Growth: Houston and the Oil Industry"; Gerald White, *Billions for Defense: Government Financing by the Defense Plant Corporation* (University, Ala.: University of Alabama Press), 1980.

40. White, *Billions for Defense* 127.

41. Hooks and Bloomquist, "The Legacy of World War II."

42. Henry Herzog Jr. and Alan Schlottmann, "Introduction," in *Industry Location and Public Policy*, ed. H. Herzog and A. Schlottmann (Knoxville, Tenn.: University of Tennessee Press, 1991), 1–22.

43. Benjamin Stevens, "Location of Economic Activities: The JRS contribution to the Research Literature," *Journal of Regional Science* 25 (1985): 663–85, quote from 674.

44. Castells, "High Technology"; Kirby, *The Pentagon and the Cities;* Ann Markusen et al., *High Tech America.*

45. Crump, "The Spatial Distribution of Military Spending in the United States."

46. Hooks and Luchansky, "Warmaking and the Accommodation of Leading Firms."

47. In the analyses reported here, only one panel examines the postwar period, and this panel spans the 1950–90 period. I have also examined each decade over this period of time (1950–60, 1960–70, 1970–80, and 1980–90). Due to space limitations these results are not presented in this chapter. These more detailed analyses are consistent with the findings reported in this chapter, but highlight the ups and downs of military and civilian spending over the postwar period (results available upon request). For additional

discussion of the regional consequences of the trade-off between military and civilian spending, see Hooks, *Forging the Military-Industrial Complex;* Hooks, "Regional Processes in the Hegemonic Nation"; and Hooks and Getz, "Federal Investments and Economic Stimulus at the End of the Cold War."

48. In the postwar period, Virginia made extensive changes to the boundaries of counties. Most important, several cities were identified as an independent county and the surrounding area as a second county. As this study covers the period before and after this change, a number of variables lack valid data for these counties. The decision was made to drop these counties (although future efforts will be made to impute valid data). The loss of these cases is unfortunate because much of Virginia's manufacturing activity occurs in the counties that have been dropped from this sample. The reader—especially readers primarily concerned with dynamics in Virginia—should interpret the findings with caution.

49. The federal government publishes a number of alternative measures of economic activity at the county level. However, many of these alternatives were not available until well after World War II. For example the *Regional Economic Information System, 1969–94* (Washington, D.C.: U.S. Department of Commerce, 1996), provides information for each county on an annual basis, but this data series only begins in 1969. Several measures included in the Economic Census (for example value added in manufacture) can also be used to measure industrial activity. However, the federal methodology changed dramatically between the pre–World War II and postwar periods. Moreover, the Economic Census is based on information provided by business establishments. To protect the anonymity of respondents, information for a county is suppressed if it is possible to identify characteristics of individual firms based on county summaries. In panels covering the 1940–1990 period, over one-third of all counties lack data on measures taken from the Economic Census (see Hooks and Bloomquist, "The Legacy of World War II for Regional Growth and Decline"). When compared to alternatives, the information on manufacturing employment supplied in the Census of Population provided the best source of information over the period under investigation.

50. Robert Jackman, "A Note on the Measurement of Growth Rates in Cross-National Research," *American Journal of Sociology* 86 (1980): 604–17.

51. Kenneth Land and Glenn Deane, "On the Large-Sample Estimation of Regression Models with Spatial- or Network-Effects Terms: A Two-Stage Least Squares Approach," in *Sociological Methodology,* ed. Peter Marsden (Cambridge, Mass.: Blackwell Publishers, 1992), 221–48.

52. For additional information on measurement and justification of control variables, see the following related works: Hooks, "Regional Processes in the Hegemonic Nation"; and Hooks and Getz, "Federal Investments and Economic Stimulus at the End of the Cold War."

53. Rees and Stafford, "Theories of Regional Growth and Industrial Location." For an examination of contemporary agglomeration with consideration of federal influences, see Allen J. Scott, *Technopolis: High Technology Industry and Regional Development in Southern California* (Berkeley: University of California Press, 1993).

54. U.S. Department of Commerce, Bureau of the Census, *USA Counties 1994 on CD-ROM* (Washington, D.C.: U.S. Department of Commerce, 1995).

55. Michael Irwin and John Kasarda, "Air Passenger Linkages and Employment Growth in U.S. Metropolitan Areas," *American Sociological Review* 56 (1991): 524–37.

56. U.S. Federal Aviation Administration, *Air Traffic Activity* (Washington, D.C.: GPO), published annually since 1967.

57. U.S. Department of Commerce, Bureau of the Census, USA *Counties 1994 on* CD-ROM.

58. Barry Bluestone and Bennett Harrison, *The Deindustrialization of America* (New York: Basic Books, 1982); Barry Moriarity, "Productivity, Industrial Restructuring, and the Deglomeration of American Manufacturing," in *Technology, Regions and Policy*, ed. Rees, 141–70.

59. U.S. Department of Commerce, *County and City Data Book, Consolidated File, County Data 1947–1977* (Ann Arbor, Mich.: Inter-University Consortium for Political and Social Research, 1981).

60. Bluestone and Harrison, *The Deindustrialization of America;* Moriarity, "Productivity, Industrial Restructuring, and the Deglomeration of American Manufacturing"; W. Parker Frisbie and John D. Kasarda, "Spatial Processes," in *Handbook of Sociology*, ed. N. J. Smelser (Beverly Hills, Calif.: Sage, 1988); Robert Newman, "Industry Migration and Growth in the South," *Review of Economics and Statistics* 65 (1983): 76–86; Thomas Plaut and Joseph Pluta, "Business Climate, Taxes and Expenditures, and State Industrial Growth in the United States," *Southern Economic Journal* 50 (1983): 99–119.

61. U.S. Department of Commerce, Bureau of the Census, USA *Counties 1994 on* CD-ROM. The Census Bureau assigned the sum of New York City tax data to one county (New York) and assigned a missing value to the remaining four counties comprising New York City (Queens, Kings, Richmond, and Bronx). To retain these counties in the analysis, valid tax data have been imputed for each of these five counties.

62. Gerald Jacob, "The Legacy of the Pentagon: The Myth of the Peace Dividend," in *The Pentagon and the Cities*, ed. Kirby, 154–70; Seth Shulman, *The Threat at Home: Confronting the Toxic Legacy of the U.S. Military* (Boston, Mass.: Beacon Press, 1992).

63. U.S. Environmental Protection Agency, *The Revised Hazard Ranking System: Background Information* (Publication 9320.7–03FS) (Washington, D.C.: Environmental Protection Agency, 1990); idem, *Supplementary Materials: National Priorities List, Proposed Rule* (Publication 9320.7–051) (Washington, D.C.: Environmental Protection Agency, 1994).

64. Land and Deane, "On the Large-Sample Estimation of Regression Models"; John Odland, *Spatial Autocorrelation* (Newbury Park, Calif.: Sage, 1988).

65. Land and Deane, "On the Large-Sample Estimation of Regression Models." Distances have been computed using the standard trigonometric function and the latitude and longitude coordinates of each county (details available on request).

66. David Belsey, Edwin Kuh, and Roy Welsch, *Regression Diagnostics: Identifying Influential Data and Sources of Collinearity* (New York: John Wiley, 1980); Kenneth Bollen and Robert Jackman, "Regression Diagnostics: An Expository Treatment of Outliers and Influential Cases," *Sociological Methods and Research* 13 (1985): 510–42.

67. Hooks, "Regional Processes in the Hegemonic Nation." Several statistics (for example, Cook's D and dfbeta) have been developed to highlight suspicious cases and the

variables most sensitive to the inclusion of an influential case. There is not, however, a specific value established to determine automatically that a case is overly influential. When judging whether or not to drop an influential case, the impact on the standard error of the estimates was the deciding factor. All else being equal, it is expected that dropping a case will result in a modest increase in the standard error of the estimates. However, when Los Angeles County was dropped from the sample of nonsouthern counties, the standard error of the estimates increased systematically and significantly. A comparable improvement in the standard error of the estimates was noted when Dallas and Tarrant County were dropped from the sample of southern counties.

68. William Greene, *Econometric Analysis* (New York: Macmillan, 1990), 223.

Afterword

GAVIN WRIGHT

It is a common observation that the more recent the events, the harder it is to write about them as history. To write history with conviction, one must have some sense of how the story ends: Are we talking about a success story, or a failure? A wave of the future, or another lost cause? The problem is especially acute in economic life, where the outcomes of one decade may be reversed in the next, and historical discussion often spills over into our own uncertainties about where the world is headed. Thus the Civil Rights Revolution of the 1960s has now passed safely into history, because we can be confident that the core of its legacy is no longer reversible. Economic historians, however, have not yet come to terms with the post–World War II era. A central reason is that we do not really know why the success story of rapid economic growth between 1945 and 1973 gave way to the disappointing sluggishness of the last quarter century.

These apprehensions are all the more severe when a region long known for its distinctive economy and politics claims to have thrown off this history and started afresh. Skepticism is surely in order in such a case, and many southerners have indeed been skeptical about the reality and the legitimacy of the South's newfound postwar prosperity. Much of what has been written about the New South economy reflects this rhetorical debate between boosterism on the one hand and social protest on the other. How can we as historians escape the terms of this essentially political exchange?

Because this challenge has proven so daunting, I applaud the organizers of the Second Wave conference at Georgia Tech, for their efforts to bring the postwar economy of the South into the realm of true historical scholarship. Their energies have been amply justified by the fine set of studies presented in the present volume. The coverage of topics is by no means comprehensive, but these chapters represent an essential beginning, one that future work will want to build on

Fig. 1. Per Capita Income of Southern Regions as Percentage of U.S. Average, 1880–1995

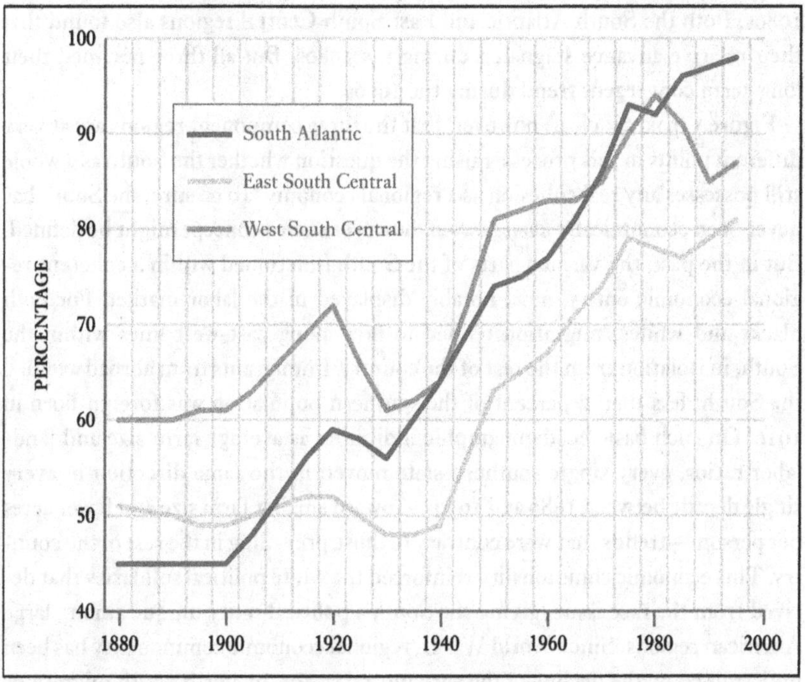

Source: U.S. Bureau of the Census, *Historical Statistics of the United States*, Series F287, R292, F293, F294 (with adjustments); *Statistical Abstract of the United States 1997*, No. 706.

and emulate. It would surely be premature at this stage to try to aggregate these industry-level case studies into a new regional synthesis. But perhaps it would be appropriate for me to devote these concluding comments to placing these chapters into a larger regional and national context, as a way of reflecting on their nascent implications and suggesting directions for future research.

THE DISAPPEARING SOUTHERN ECONOMY?

From today's fin de siècle vantage point, it now seems safe to declare that the economic revolution of the postwar South is also irreversible. Figure 1 displays the course of per capita income since 1880 relative to the national average, in the three census regions of the South. Whereas earlier cotton-based gains were reversed in the 1920s, the takeoff that began with World War II has been maintained and extended over the subsequent half century. The pace has not been altogether uniform. The West South Central region converged "prematurely" on the na-

Afterword

tional average during the energy boom of the 1970s, and then slipped back in the 1980s. Both the South Atlantic and East South Central regions also found that their relative advance stagnated during the 1980s. But all three resumed their long-term convergent trend during the 1990s.

Figure 1 makes it clear, however, that the three component regions are at very different points in this process, raising the question whether the South as a whole still possesses any real cohesion as a regional economy. To be sure, the South has never been economically *homogeneous*, however such a concept might be defined. But in the past, the various parts of the South functioned within a coherent regional economic entity, most notably displayed in the labor market. For both blacks and whites, migration tended to flow along east-west lines within the South, in isolation from the rest of the country. Immigrants from abroad avoided the South; less than 2 percent of the southern population was foreign-born in 1910. On such basic ecodemographic indicators as average farm size and land-labor ratios, every single southern state moved in the same direction in every single decade between 1880 and 1930—toward smaller farm size and fewer acres per person—trends that were contrary to those prevailing in the rest of the country. This economic commonality reinforced the white political solidarity that derived from the race issue, giving the South a political unity unique among large American regions. Since World War II, regional economic commonality has been undermined by the decline of the agricultural sector, by north-south migrations (in both directions), by the federalization of labor standards, and by the Civil Rights Movement and associated changes in racial attitudes and policies. Toby Moore's chapter on the dismantling of the cotton mill village is a fitting epitaph for that particular institutional manifestation of the old low-wage southern economy.[1]

Indeed, when we look beneath the surface of the regional aggregates to distinguish trends in urban versus rural areas of the South, the effect is to diminish even the limited sense of regional commonality conveyed by figure 1. Per capita income in southern cities was more than 90 percent of the national average by the 1960s if not earlier, and by the 1990s no urban regional income gap remained. But in the nonmetropolitan areas, despite continuing outmigration over many decades, per capita income is barely 70 percent of the national average, showing little relative progress since the 1960s. In many southern states, one or two metropolitan areas account for the great bulk of the state's entire job growth. Atlanta, for example, with less than half the population of Georgia, accounted for 68 percent of the state's net new jobs between 1979 and 1993.[2] It has often been said in recent years that in reality there are two Souths, one urban and one rural. But because these rural areas are poorly integrated with each other as well as with the rest of the nation, it might be truer to say that there are many Souths, a metropolitan core and a large number of poor and declining remnants of former times.

Despite this diversity within the South in economic conditions, the region has retained a distinctiveness in politics and in what one might call "political economy." Don't worry, I am not going to join the parade of pundits making pronouncements about subjective feelings of regional identity. But when I published *Old South, New South* in 1986, it seemed intuitively obvious that ongoing economic integration would tend to homogenize the country culturally and politically, slowly perhaps, but surely. Mancur Olson concluded his 1982 presidential address to the Southern Economic Association on this note:

> Thus the South will eventually lose its position as a leader in American economic growth. In that sense, the South will fall again. In another sense, it will not only fall, but even fall out of sight. With a per capita income similar to the rest of the country, with institutional arrangements and racial policies much the same as those in the nation as a whole, and with rapid and inexpensive transportation linking it with the rest of the country, the South is losing its regional peculiarities. Southerners, like people elsewhere, will no doubt continue to have special attachments to their communities, perhaps even to their states. But the South as an utterly distinctive region with its own sense of nationhood—the South of the old evils and the old romance— is already disappearing, and becoming one with the nation as a whole.[3]

Again with the aid of additional hindsight, we can see how wrong this forecast was. Today the South appears more distinctive than ever. On a wide range of attitudinal indicators, southerners are consistently more conservative and more religiously oriented than residents of any other region. The South has been an outlier in presidential elections for decades, so much so that many observers feel that the regional agenda has exerted disproportionate political influence on the politics of the entire nation, rather than the other way around.[4]

This evidence of social and political persistence might not matter for present purposes, except that southern politics has a profound effect on economic life. Because Craig Colten's essay provides a vivid account of the emergence of "modern environmental issues" in Texas in the 1940s, consider the evidence on the "Green Index" of conditions and policies as of 1991 (table 1). The rankings summarize 179 indicators of environmental conditions and 77 indicators of environmental policies. The validity of any such measures can be debated, but the position of the South near the bottom is clear enough to be beyond debate.

Poor environmental ratings are closely linked to the postwar South's persistent political drive to attract outside investment. The states listed in table 1 held down nine of the top fifteen places in a 1986 ranking of "business climate." Southern

Table 1: Green Index Rankings for Southern States, 1991

STATE	GREEN CONDITIONS	GREEN POLICIES	FINAL GREEN INDEX
Florida	30	13	18
North Carolina	37	18	23
Virginia	36	22	32
South Carolina	35	32	36
Georgia	38	29	39
Tennessee	45	40	45
Texas	48	35	46
Mississippi	44	46	47
Arkansas	40	50	48
Louisiana	50	34	49
Alabama	47	49	50

Source: Bob Hall and Mary Lee Kerr, *1991–92 Green Index* (Washington, D.C.: Island Press, 1991).

corporate tax rates have consistently been the lowest in the nation, while the region has been a leader in promotional advertising and in the use of bond subsidies and tax instruments for industrial recruitment.[5] Is it surprising that critics refer to the region as the home of "look-the-other-way policies and giveaway tax breaks"?[6]

How can we explain this persistent regionalism, in defiance of the logic of convergence that seemed so persuasive only a decade or two ago? The explanation cannot be a simple matter of cultural inertia, because as many of the contributions to this volume make clear, the political posture of aggressive industrial recruitment was a *change* from the old isolationist regime, a part of the Second Wave now under scrutiny. What seems to have occurred, in the wake of the Civil Rights Revolution and the demise of segregation, is that in each of the southern states a new political equilibrium has been established in support of this brand of political economy. Of course this political leadership has historical links to the older, prewar South. But its manifestation as the distinctive *regional* economic tendency is the outcome of a complex political selection process, rather than a simple expression of exogenously defined regional economic interests. It is as though the South now derives its economic interests from its politics, whereas formerly it was the other way around. The result has been a region peculiarly open to the global economic forces of the late twentieth century, markedly polarized in its economic conditions.

This reemergent southernization of political economy has been described, and often deplored, many times. Explaining it in refined historical terms, however, should be a central part of the research agenda coming out of the Second Wave conference and volume.

SECOND WAVE SOUTHERN INDUSTRY AND NATIONAL ECONOMIC TRENDS

In pursuing this agenda, it will be important to place the southern industrial story in historical context, not just of regional politics but of deep national and global trends in technology and economic geography. During the long era of southern backwardness, the dominant national technologies featured giant investments in tangible forms of fixed capital; combined with mass production methods and heavy resource requirements, these technologies displayed a powerful tendency toward geographic concentration. The century-long dominance of the northeast-midwest "manufacturing belt" created high "barriers to entry" for the peripheral regions trying to break into the national market—barriers that were as real for the high-wage West as they were for the low-wage South. Under the umbrella of this geographic persistence, even the smaller-scale and more flexible forms of manufacturing, which Phil Scranton has analyzed, tended to locate in the northeastern quadrant of the country. Indices of regional and industrial concentration show a rising trend through the nineteenth century, peaking during the interwar era. Since World War II, as transportation costs have fallen and the range of technological choices has widened, these same indicators show a steady trend toward geographic dispersion.[7]

One important aspect of this new trend is that science-based technologies have relaxed many of the constraints that implicitly limited the geographic spread of modern practices to the temperate zone. With the aid of hindsight, perhaps we can begin to comprehend the more purely geographic dimensions of historic southern backwardness more clearly and objectively than earlier generations could. This notion does not necessarily imply that the environment of the South was intrinsically harsher and more intractable than that of the northern states. But the technologies emerging from the burgeoning inventive networks of the northern states had a "northern bias"—not from a conspiracy to subjugate the South, but because their problem-solving environment reflected northern conditions. The labor-saving character of American technology, for example, reflected the needs of northern rather than southern employers. More broadly, the distinctive climate, soil, and disease environment that southern farmers had to confront—to say nothing of the *human* disease environment—was not the first priority of the firms and agencies generating useful knowledge in the northern states. The technologies of the twentieth century have made great strides in diminishing this geographic differential.

These generalizations are strikingly portrayed in the chapter on southern forestry by William Boyd. But the complex blend of motives and influences that he describes is a far richer story than would be implied by the top-down conception that "modern science" figured out how to cultivate southern forests successfully on a sustained basis. External advances in tree biology and forest genetics do play an important enabling or background role in Boyd's account. But the science-based breakthroughs were not more essential to the process than the institutional and political restructuring that reduced the frequency of forest fires to a small fraction of its historic levels—an essential precondition for profitable investments with an extended time horizon. Most notably for present purposes, Boyd shows that the implication of advanced scientific knowledge was not to *diminish* the relevance of region-specific knowledge but to *enhance* its relevance and potential return. Thus, contrary to Mancur Olson's prediction, the course of the twentieth century has seen the *rise* of a host of regionally organized institutions to develop and disseminate such useful knowledge, from the Southern Pulpwood Conservation Association of 1939 to the Southern Forest Tree Improvement Committee of 1951, and from university-industry to U.S. Forest Service cooperative structures. According to Boyd, this process of "regional collective learning" has put the South on the path to becoming the "wood basket of the world."

When we turn to manufacturing, it is perhaps surprising that one of the first of the Second Wave industries to break out of this regional pattern was aircraft. Although the airplane was in many respects a successor to the automobile from a technological standpoint, the two industries were distinguished by the fact that aircraft never became a true mass production commodity. (The one period when aircraft might be placed in that category came during the all-out production of bombers during World War II, at the Willow Run plant in Michigan.) Because the location of production was not dictated by economies of scale and transport, the door was open for choices to be influenced by the accidents of personalities and politics, as in the Marietta story recounted by Thomas A. Scott. Accounts of industry development on the West Coast are remarkably similar. In both cases, World War II is commonly identified as the takeoff date; but again in both places, on closer scrutiny the Korean War stands out as the point at which the locational choice was consolidated for the indefinite future. West Coast operations had a certain advantage in technology over those of the South, because of the industry's association with aeronautical research centers at such institutions as Cal Tech, the University of Washington, and Stanford University. As described by Richard S. Combes, however, the institutional infrastructure for aircraft manufacturing in Georgia has become increasingly more elaborate and advanced. The transfer of Lockheed's Aircraft Division Headquarters to Georgia in 1995 stands as a culmination of this long-term locational evolution.[8]

No matter where located, aircraft manufacture is big business, dependent for its success not just on technology but on large-scale purchasing decisions by government agencies and by major airlines. In many ways that type of industry is less the wave of the future in the American economy than the decentralized, entrepreneurial industrial district of northwest Georgia described in Randall Patton's essay. That story is a welcome contrast to the reports of impending death for southern textiles that have appeared so often in recent decades. Patton draws a sharp contrast between the traditional cotton textile industry as represented by the Crown Cotton Mill of Dalton, Georgia—which really did die in 1984—and the rise of the more flexible and innovative tufted carpet mills in the same area. Several features of the case strike the general reader as noteworthy. The first is that, as with aircraft, the location of carpet manufacture was not tightly dictated by natural resources and transportation costs; in principle, it could have been almost anywhere. Once underway, however, such industries display powerful tendencies toward geographic persistence, sustained not by fixed investments in tangible capital, but by the infrastructure of "network externalities" found in suppliers, technical knowledge, skills, and access to fast-changing information. Indeed, Paul Krugman uses precisely the case of Dalton, Georgia, to illustrate models emphasizing the role of historical accident in industrial location. Drawing on local lore, Krugman traces the industry's origins back to a bedspread prepared as a wedding gift by the teenaged Catherine Evans in 1895—tufted, of course.[9] Whether this tale is the literal truth, I cannot say. But for an industrial district selected to represent the newest version of the New South, it is striking that Dalton's local expertise in tufted fabrics goes back to the early twentieth century, if not farther.

Although Patton wisely does not press the analogy excessively, the obvious parallel is to the Silicon Valley phenomenon, in which network economies external to the firm but internal to the district substitute for the coordination benefits of vertical integration. Such districts are especially strong in entrepreneurial energy and rapid response to change. Their potential weakness is in their capacity to sustain the long time horizons necessary for generating advanced forms of technological change. In Silicon Valley, that type of technological infrastructure has been supplied by research universities, or financed by the Defense Department. In the carpet industry of north Georgia, it appears that crucial thresholds were crossed more than once, when the scale of the district became large enough to support private-sector investments in new technologies. The first of these occurred with the rise of an indigenous regional machine-building industry for carpet manufacture, beginning with the Cobble Brothers in the 1940s. A second milestone was in the late 1950s, when DuPont found it worthwhile to engage in intensive research over several years on an all-nylon tufted carpet. These high-tech breakthroughs revolutionized the carpet industry, opening opportunities for large numbers of enterprises whose individual expertise lay in style and marketing. This is a very modern pattern indeed, certainly one with promise for the rural South. But such local cultures develop historically, and even in the modern age, they are difficult to create from whole cloth. Even when successful, life in an industrial district is likely to be turbulent and uncertain.

Much the same can be said of the envisioned southern auto corridor described in the essay by Karsten Hülsemann. The spread of auto assembly plants and their suppliers in the South refutes the notion that the region can only attract firms and industries offering low-paying, dead-end unskilled types of jobs. To be sure, as Hülsemann tells it, the attraction of "greenfields"—open space, a fresh workforce, preferably nonunion—have played a considerable role in attracting foreign firms. To some degree, these features may continue to define the geography of the southern economy, whose outlines on the map bear a remarkable resemblance to those of the old regional economy. But the account also stresses that these locational decisions are interdependent, a function of the requirement for geographic closeness in modern "just-in-time" systems. The implication is that the corridor should not be seen as a reflection of the infinite malleability of corporate investment decisions in the modern global economy. Instead, the emerging regional economy still appears to have a material reality and a geographic shape. Understanding the bases for, and limits of, these apparent network externalities over a broad geographic area stands as a challenge to economists and economic historians, and not just those who specialize in the South.

PRODUCTIVITY AND INEQUALITY IN THE SOUTH AND IN THE NATION

The other prominent feature of postwar American economic history is not a trend, but a bipartite division of the era into two roughly equal subperiods. The first, from the end of the war to the collapse of the Bretton Woods system of exchange rates in 1971–73, was characterized by productivity growth at 3 percent per year, and low levels of inequality. The second, from the early 1970s to the present, has featured 1 percent productivity growth and rising inequality. Comprehending these two phases and the transition between them should be a top-priority agenda item for both economics and economic history. It is certainly not my intention to lay out a new interpretation here and now—not that I possess one in any case. But an account of Second Wave southern industrialization will not be complete until it is satisfactorily placed into this broader national context. For that matter, no national history of these phenomena will be complete until it comes to terms with the South, specifically including the race issue and the Civil Rights Revolution.

Only one of the essays in the volume takes up this challenge explicitly, the fine chapter by Karen Ferguson on the politics of exclusion of black workers from job opportunities in wartime Atlanta. Her account is both affecting and cogent, but its long-term significance is not necessarily self-evident. On the one hand, we get a vivid foretaste of the issues and tactics of the Civil Rights Movement, another demonstration that black political mobilization of the 1950s drew upon a rich body of prior experience. The policy of reserving industrial and government work for whites only—which Ferguson calls an "irrational pattern of exclusion"—was already well entrenched in 1940, and remained so with few exceptions until the 1960s. On the other hand, the terms of black political engagement were distinctly limited, if measured by latter-day standards. This is one of Ferguson's main points. The Atlanta Urban League, though tireless in its advocacy role, clearly pictured well-behaved, middle-class blacks as its prime constituency. According to Ferguson, the top priority for the AUL was gaining entry for blacks into training programs that would qualify them for skilled jobs at the Bell Aircraft Plant, and before referring applicants, the AUL screened out all but the most educated, respectable, and responsible of Atlanta's black labor force. As a result, the largest number of black workers had no lasting foothold in the urban labor market when the wartime boom ended.

This indictment is perhaps somewhat harsh in historical context. Admonitions to act as a "credit to the race" were part of the discourse of the times, full of implicit prejudice to be sure, but not necessarily within the power of any one local organization to change. Further, the range of strategic choices open to groups like the Atlanta Urban League was constrained, not just by prevailing racial attitudes but by conditions in the broader labor market that were far beyond local influence. From this standpoint, a striking part of Ferguson's study is the discussion of obstacles to black participation in training programs at Bell and other defense plants. Potential applicants were discouraged by sixth-grade educational prerequisites, by the absence of any real assurance of employment at the end of the three-week session, and by an inability or unwillingness to self-finance three weeks without pay. This last factor was especially acute during wartime conditions, when the "opportunity cost" of training for an uncertain skilled job was three weeks of definitely lost wages at the relatively well-paying unskilled jobs that were then available in the Atlanta area. This was a lot to ask as an individual contribution to advancement of the race. Of course, the tight labor market conditions did not survive the war, but then neither did the skilled jobs at the Bell Plant. Faced with discouraging prospects at both ends of the labor market, the AUL dissolved its industrial department in 1946; again, it is not clear that they had much choice. But as Ferguson notes, the wartime experience had a lasting impact on at least a significant minority of Atlanta's black population, a legacy that very likely had long-term consequences for the city's political and economic history.

Studies that trace the linkages among industrialization, politics and race should be a core part of the Second Wave research agenda. There is now a well developed and sophisticated historical literature on the Civil Rights Movement, but its economic dimensions have been strangely neglected. Standard histories focus on the South through the turbulence of the early 1960s, culminating in the dramatic legislative victories of 1964 and 1965, but then their attention shifts, along with that of the national media, to the late 1960s violence in northern cities, often described as a reaction to disillusionment over the limited and largely symbolic gains of the movement itself. Statistical evidence for this impression is more often than not confined to national aggregates. If we follow through on the aftermath of the Civil Rights Revolution in the South, I believe we will find that such an impression is mistaken.

Central to any such research is recognition that the high-growth postwar golden age took place under a labor market framework descended from the New Deal. It might be called the progressive or high wage economic strategy, featuring strict social and regulatory limits on "substandard" wage levels; a strong role for organized labor; and extensive social investments in education to facilitate the upgrading of labor standards and the advance of technology. For the country as a whole, this regime worked remarkably well in its time. But for the South, the implication was that wages were forced above market-clearing levels, creating a chronic labor surplus environment and a scarcity of jobs. Indeed, slowing down the rise of low-wage southern competition was part of the political logic for this program in the first place. Under these conditions, southern employers could afford to be highly selective in their employment decisions, and in that historical era, the obvious basis for selection was race. Sometimes racial exclusion was implemented by union rules and seniority ladders; sometimes merely by company personnel systems and job assignment policies. Either way, the first generation of Second Wave industrial jobs were reserved almost exclusively for whites. An illustrative example is the Paper and Allied Products Industry, whose racial employment structure for South Carolina is graphed in figure 2. The pattern could hardly be clearer.

This policy of racial exclusion may have been irrational at its core, but I am not convinced that the rigidities of segregation hindered the rise of Second Wave industry in any direct economic way. One might suppose that enlightened southern businessmen should have led the way in breaking down racial barriers, but the evidence suggests that most were extremely reluctant to do so. In city after city, business leaders chimed in on the side of compromise only after political turbulence reached the point where it threatened the flow of investment capital. For their part, employers had no strong economic motives for challenging racial norms, since low-end wages were governed by federal law, and few blacks were qualified by education or experience for high-end jobs. This perverse regional equilibrium might have survived indefinitely on purely economic grounds. But ultimately the irresistible force of the Second Wave came into collision with the immovable object of Jim Crow. Understanding how and why this occurred is a prime topic for future research.

One strong candidate for closer study is the role of the Department of De-

Fig. 2. Nonsalaried Workers in South Carolina Paper and Allied Products Industry, 1940–80

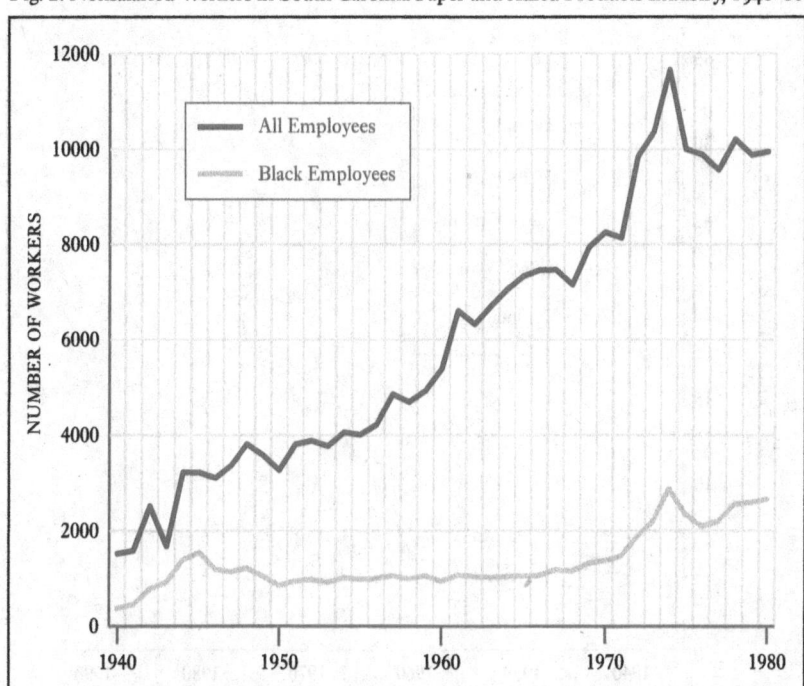

Source: South Carolina Department of Labor, *Annual Reports.*

fense; or perhaps more to the point, the DOD and its budget. As the evidence presented by Gregory Hooks suggests, defense spending was only one of several stimuli to accelerated economic growth in the South, by no means the prime or exclusive mover. But whatever its overall economic impact, defense in the South was undeniably large. The South's share of prime military contract awards steadily increased, from less than 10 percent in 1951 to 25 percent in 1970; in many southern states, defense became the largest single employer, outpacing agriculture, textiles, lumber, and all the others. After Truman's integration order of 1948, military bases represented a large, disturbing integrated presence in the heart of the Deep South, generating jobs for black workers that paid far better than other regional opportunities. In itself, this visible demonstration of the viability of desegregation might have had little impact. Its potential for economic leverage, however, was very great. In response to political pressure from northern states, military and defense contract policies began to exert active pressure toward equal opportunity employment goals by the 1960s.[10]

Federal pressures played at least a modest role in the single most dramatic la-

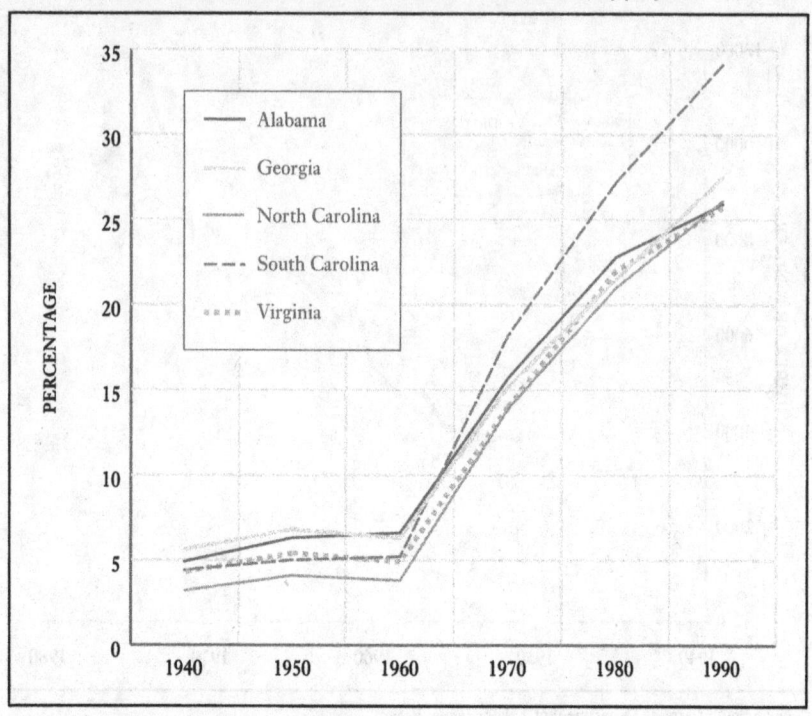

Fig. 3. Percentage of Southern Textile Workers Who Are Black, 1940–90

Source: U.S. Bureau of the Census, Decennial Volumes.

bor market innovation of the Civil Rights Revolution, integration of the textile industry, long the most lily-white in the region.[11] Though rarely covered in standard Civil Rights histories, this was an authentic revolution, reversing a pattern of racial exclusivity that had been maintained for a century. Facilitated by tight labor market conditions of the 1960s, the breakthrough was almost concurrent with passage of the Civil Rights Act. Since then, the percentage of black employment in the industry has increased steadily in all the major textile states (figure 3). In the leading economic study of this phenomenon, Heckman and Payner reject the interpretation that textile integration was merely the result of tight labor market conditions, as well as the claim that the change can be directly attributed to black educational gains. Instead, it was a combination of tight labor markets, federal pressure, and assertive black job-seeking in the wake of the Civil Rights Act of 1964. Although textiles may not qualify as a Second Wave industry, for blacks these were "good jobs" compared to alternatives, accounting for a significant upward jump in relative black incomes in the South. In oral history evidence from the 1970s, blacks in textile areas referred to integration as

"The Change," and believed that it accounted for the reversal of migration flows *into* the South between the 1960s and 1970s.[12]

If the economic gains from the Civil Rights Revolution were so clear and so widespread among ordinary people, why then do so many people believe that little of substance really changed? There may be many reasons, but surely one major factor is the change in the underlying macroeconomic climate of the nation. The strong growth of labor demand and productivity did not survive the stagflation decade of the 1970s. Integration was not reversed, and African Americans entered higher education and middle-class occupations in growing numbers; but over the same quarter century, average real wages for unskilled labor have stagnated or declined, and income inequality has steadily increased—among blacks as well as whites, in the North as well as the South, for the population as a whole and within every sizable demographic subgroup. These trends are national or global in character, beyond the control of southern state politics with or without the Voting Rights Act. But they have hit the South with unusual force, and they have coincided historically with the retreat or demise of New Deal labor market institutions and policies. Any analysis of post–Second Wave southern economic life will have to be placed within this broader context.

Economists are not agreed on the reasons for this sea change in the national economy, nor even on whether there is any linkage between its two components, productivity and inequality. Some emphasize the role of growing international trade and immigration in putting downward pressure on unskilled wages. Others point to the effects of skill-biased technological change. Still others argue that the bias of technological change is inextricably linked to globalization and to changes in the institutions that generate new technologies in the global economy. We cannot hope to sort out these disputes here. But it appears that these phenomena are deep and global in character, not readily subject to deflection by regional business and political choices.

But this does not mean that regional choices and regional history are of no consequence and have no effect. The emerging global economy offers vast new opportunities as well as new risks and pressures. But only in retrospect does it seem obvious that the New South would participate in this new adventure so wholeheartedly. Not all countries and regions of the world have done so. The South might have followed the example of Quebec, choosing isolation over economic progress. Or it might have gone the way of Northern Ireland: two hostile peoples occupying the same geographic space, so suspicious of each other that compromise arrangements are painfully difficult to negotiate and even more difficult to maintain. Instead, the South has followed the American road of boosterism and inclusion, and on the whole we can be thankful for that.

NOTES

1. I develop this interpretation in *Old South, New South: Revolutions in the Southern Economy since the Civil War* (New York: Basic Books, 1986; reprint, Baton Rouge: Louisiana State University Press, 1996).
2. The biennial *State of the South* reports of MDC, Inc., a research organization in Chapel Hill, N.C., are a good source of regional economic data. See <http://www.mdcinc.org/>.
3. Mancur Olson, "The South Will Fall Again," *Southern Economic Journal* 49 (1983): 932.
4. Regional distinctiveness in presidential elections is shown in Earl Black and Merle Black, *The Vital South: How Presidents Are Elected* (Cambridge: Harvard University Press, 1992). Political and ideological regionalism is documented in Robert P. Steed, Laurence W. Moreland, and Tod A. Baker, eds., *The Disappearing South* (Tuscaloosa: University of Alabama Press, 1990). See particularly the foreword by John Shelton Reed, the eminent sociologist of southern regionalism, who notes that his favorite statistic in the volume demonstrates that born-again Yankees strongly resemble native-born southerners (p. x).
5. James C. Cobb, *The Selling of the South: The Southern Crusade for Industrial Development, 1936–1990*, 2d ed. (Urbana: University of Illinois Press, 1993), 91, 263, 272.
6. Donald Schueler, "Southern Exposure," *Sierra* 77 (November–December 1992), quoted in Robert D. Bullard, *Dumping in Dixie* (Boulder, Colo.: Westview Press), 1994.
7. Sukkoo Kim, "Expansion of Markets and the Geographic Distribution of Economic Activities," *Quarterly Journal of Economics* 110 (November 1995). On the American "manufacturing belt," see Paul Krugman, *Geography and Trade* (Cambridge, Mass.: MIT Press, 1991).
8. This paragraph draws on Paul Rhode, "Technology, Markets and the Dynamics of Business Location: The Pacific Coast Aircraft Industry," presented to the All-UC Group in Economic History, Santa Clara University, 1998.
9. Krugman, *Geography and Trade*.
10. Bruce J. Schulman, *From Cotton Belt to Sunbelt: Federal Policy, Economic Development, and the Transformation of the South, 1938–1980* (New York: Oxford University Press, 1991), chapter 6.
11. The following paragraphs draw upon Gavin Wright, "The Civil Rights Revolution as Economic History," *Journal of Economic History* 59 (June 1999): 267–89.
12. James J. Heckman and Bruce Payner, "The Impact of the Economy and the State on the Economic Status of Blacks: A Study of South Carolina," *American Economic Review* 79 (March 1989): 138–77; Mary Fredrickson, "Four Decades of Change: Black Workers in Southern Textiles, 1941–1981," *Radical America* 16 (November–December 1982), especially 74–75. Recent research by Timothy Minchin emphasizes the role of federal government pressures, and the continuing difficulties black textile applicants faced, even after initial integration. See *Hiring the Black Worker: The Racial Integration of the Southern Textiles Industry, 1960–1980* (Chapel Hill: University of North Carolina Press, 1999).

The Contributors

WILLIAM BOYD is a doctoral candidate in the University of California, Berkeley's Energy and Resources Group, and a law student at Stanford University.

CRAIG E. COLTEN is associate professor in the Department of Geography and Anthropology at Louisiana State University. His work has focused on human impacts to the environment, and he is currently working on an environmental history of New Orleans.

RICHARD S. COMBES is Senior Research Engineer at the Georgia Tech Research Institute and a doctoral candidate in history, technology, and society at the Georgia Institute of Technology.

KAREN FERGUSON is assistant professor of history at Simon Fraser University, British Columbia, Canada.

GREGORY HOOKS is associate professor of sociology at Washington State University, Pullman.

KARSTEN HÜLSEMANN is market research analyst at the European headquarters of a Canadian automotive supplier and a doctoral candidate in social sciences at the Center of European and North American Studies, University of Göttingen (Germany).

TOBY MOORE completed his doctoral dissertation in geography on the dissolution of southern cotton mill villages at the University of Iowa in 1999. Presently, he is an analyst for the Voting Section of the Civil Rights Division, U.S. Department of Justice.

RANDALL PATTON is associate professor of history at Kennesaw State University in Georgia. The University of Georgia Press published his monograph, *Carpet Capital*, in 1999. He is currently working on a study of Shaw Industries, a key enterprise in North Georgia's economic development.

THOMAS A. SCOTT is professor of history at Kennesaw State University in Georgia.

PHILIP SCRANTON is professor of the history of industry and technology at Rutgers University, director of the Center for the History of Business, Technology, and Society at the Hagley Museum and Library, and co-editor of the University of Georgia Press series Economy and Society in the Modern South.

GAVIN WRIGHT is William Robertson Coe Professor of American Economic History at Stanford University. His studies of the South's economic development from the antebellum era to World War II and after have crucially influenced a generation of research in southern history.

Index

advertising, 93–94, 99; and brand names, 95–96
African Americans, x, 31, 131–33, 139, 193; in Atlanta, 48, 72; in Cobb County, Ga., 3–4; and wartime racial conflicts, 51–54, 56–57. *See also* elite, African American
air conditioning, 29
aircraft: Airacobra, 8, 29; B-17, 25; B-29, 12–14, 16, 24, 29, 32, 34; B-47, 16, 33, 36; C-5, 34, 35, 36, 37; C-130, 16, 33, 35, 36; C-141, 34, 35; DC-3, 93; F-22, 34
aircraft industry, 15, 58, 148, 260, 266, 269, 271, 292. *See also entries for specific manufacturers*
airports, 4–5, 7–12, 19 (n. 16), 27
Alester G. Furman Co., 124–28
Alexander, Lamar, 229, 230
Alexander Smith and Sons, 86, 94
Allen, Ivan, Sr., 5, 9, 28
American Airlines, 37
American Automobile Manufacturers Association, 236, 254 (n. 124)
American Carpet Institute, 93–94, 95, 96
American Cyanamid, 161
American Federation of Labor, 50
American Forestry Association, 180
Andrews, Mildred Gwin, 116
Applebome, Peter, 239
Applied Technical Services, Inc., 35
Arlington, Tex., 225
Arnall, Gov. Ellis, 16, 22 (n. 48), 110 (n. 9)
Ashe, W. W., 178
Association of International Automobile Manufacturers, 236

Atlanta Chamber of Commerce, 5, 9, 10, 27, 28
Atlanta Federation of Trades, 50
Atlanta University, 46, 54, 56
Atlanta Urban League (AUL), 46, 61, 63, 64, 65, 66, 295; All-Citizens Registration Committee, 70–71; Council of Defense Training, 62, 63, 73; and worker placement, 67–68
Atomic Energy Commission, 37
Austin, Lloyd, 193, 194
automobile industry, 219–44 *passim*, 294; parts suppliers, 231–33, 239. *See also entries for specific manufacturers*
automobiles, 118, 221, 292

Balance Agriculture With Industry (BAWI), 81, 86, 223
Bankhead, Sen. John H., 189
Banks, William, 137
Bartley, Numan V., 85
Barwick, Eugene T., 92, 93
Barwick Mills, 84, 99
baseball, industrial, 120, 134, 135–36
Bateman, F. O., 186
Bavarian Motor Works (BMW), 234, 242
Beasley, Max, 88
bedspread industry, 31, 87
Bell, Lawrence, 8–9, 13–15, 58, 65
Bell, William, 62
Bell Aircraft Corporation, xi, 1, 11, 13, 14–15, 25, 32, 47–48, 50, 58, 72, 295; Marietta workforce of, 29–30, 61–68; worker benefits at, 30, 32
Bemis Corp., 133

Bentley, Sr., Fred, 3, 14
Bibb Manufacturing Co., 127
Bigelow Carpets, 94, 95
Bingham, Richard D., 233, 235
biotechnology, 201
Birmingham, Ala., 52, 63, 240, 260
Blair, Leon M., 1, 4–5, 7–17 *passim*, 28
Blease, Gov. Cole, 122
BMW, 234, 242
Boeing, 9, 25–34 *passim*, 37, 39
Booker T. Washington High School (BTWHS, Atlanta), 63, 64, 65, 66
boosterism, xii, 24, 27, 28, 38, 101, 223, 286, 299
Borders, William Holmes, 71
Bowling Green, Ky., 227
branch plants, x, xiii, 24, 222–23; GM-Lakewood (Atlanta), 223, 225
Buffalo, N.Y., 2, 8, 14, 26, 29, 32, 33
Burbank, Calif., 25, 33
Burlington Mills/Industries, 82, 116, 128
Bynum, N.C., 124

Cabin Crafts, 84, 87, 88, 91
Calder, Alexander, 168, 169
California Institute of Technology, 292
Candler, Asa, 27
Cannon Mills, 114, 117, 133, 139
Canton Mills, 128, 134
Capper, Sen. Arthur, 174, 184, 187
Card, Lewis, 88, 96
Carlton, David, 85, 122, 138
Carmichael, James V., 1, 6–17 *passim*, 27, 28, 33, 36
Central Intelligence Agency, 259
Chandler, Alfred, 172
Chapman, H. H., 180
Charleston, S.C., 260
Charlotte, N.C., ix, 121
Chattanooga, Tenn., 82, 88
chenille bedspread industry, 31, 87
Chicopee Manufacturing Co., 116
Chivers, Walter, 49
Chrysler Corp., 227, 234, 236

Chupka, John, 101
citizenship, 44, 45, 46, 51, 54, 61, 73, 74, 117, 299
Civil Aeronautics Administration, 4, 5–7, 10
Civilian Conservation Corps (CCC), 30, 180, 188
civil rights, 43, 45, 72–74, 286, 288, 290, 294, 295, 296, 298
Civil War, 2–3, 84; legacy of, 17, 72
Clarke-McNary Act, 179, 180, 181, 184, 186–87, 191
Clay, Lucius D., 1, 4, 5, 7–8, 10, 15
Cobb, James, xiii, 81, 224
Cobb County, Ga., 1, 2, 27, 35, 39, 58, 260; government in, 6, 9–10, 30; nativism, 28; population, 14
Cobble Brothers, 88, 89, 91, 96, 293
Collins, Capt. Harry E., 13
Collins and Aikman, 105
Community Chest (Atlanta), 71
Cone, Caesar, 123
Congress of Industrial Organizations, 43, 50, 224
Connolly, Donald H., 4
Conservation Reserve Program, 192
Constangy, Frank, 101, 103–4
construction, factory, 28–29, 231, 248 (n. 47), 294
consumption, 49, 83, 106, 140
Cover, Carl, 13, 22 (n. 39), 32
Crown Cotton Mills, 81, 128, 293
Crump, Jeffrey, 273
culture, southern, xii, 31, 67, 118, 120, 137, 179–80, 221, 289–90
Curry, Margaret, 56

Daimler-Benz, 236, 237
DaimlerChrysler, 242
Dallas, Tex., 260, 261, 266, 269, 278
Dalton, Ga., xii, 81–106 *passim*, 128, 293; Dalton Utilities, 91; Water, Light, and Sinking Fund, 90–91
Daniels, Jonathan, 200, 201

Dan River Mills, 123, 124
Defense Plant Corporation, 9
deindustrialization, 272, 276–77
Detroit, Mich., 64, 226
Dixie Belle Mills, 102–6
Dixie Highway, 6–7
Dixie Motor Car Corp. (Bobbi-Kar), 225–26
Dodge, Witherspoon, 13
Doraville, Ga., 225
Douglas, Donald A., 8
Duke, James Buchanan, 85
DuPont Corp., 92, 93, 97–99, 156–57, 158, 159, 293
Durham, N.C., 130, 133

E&B Carpets, 93
Eastern Airlines, 7, 27
East Texas Salt Water Disposal Co., 153
economics, 255, 273, 286, 299
Eisenhower, Dwight D., 15, 38
elite, African American, 43, 46, 54, 56, 58, 66, 73–74; and ideology of racial uplift, 54–55
Emory University, 6, 16, 32
engineering, 33–36, 116
entrepreneurship, 82, 84, 85, 87, 93, 106, 292
environment, industry's impact upon, xi, xiii, 107–8, 146–62, 277, 289–90
Environmental Protection Agency (EPA), 107–8, 277

Fairchild, Fred Rogers, 184, 185, 210 (n. 80)
Fair Employment Practices Commission (FEPC), 13, 51, 61, 62, 64, 65, 68
Fair Labor Standards Act, 120
Farmer's Home Administration (FHA), 125, 126, 133, 183
farming, ix, 2, 4, 171, 191–92, 193, 250 (n. 59), 288
Faulkner, William, 174
Feagin, Joe, 257

Federal Bureau of Investigation, 52
federal contracts, 37, 49, 61–64, 292; cost plus fixed fee (CPFF), 25–26, 36; program evaluation and review technique (PERT), 37; total package procurement system (TPPS), 37
federal investment, x, xi, xiii, 12, 256–79 *passim*; in government-owned, contractor-operated (GOCO) plants, 26, 37–39
federal regulation, 189
Fieldcrest Mills, 120
Firestone Tire Co., 48, 64, 72
Flamming, Douglas, xi, 81, 115
Fordism, 115, 138, 140, 235
Ford Motor Co., 9, 222, 223, 225, 226, 234
forest depletion, 173–75, 203 (n. 3)
Forest Farmers Association, 191
forest fires, 175–79
Forest Pest Control Act, 181
forestry research, 176–78, 181, 194–99, 291
Fort Worth, Tex., 27, 34, 38, 260, 264
Fulton Bag Co., 128
Furman, Alester G., Jr., 124–28
Furman, Alester G., III, 124–25

Gainesville, Ga., 116
Galaxy Mills, 93
Gamble, Thomas, 169
Gastonia, N.C., 131
gender, 54, 56, 133–34, 136
General Dynamics Corp., 34
General Motors Corp. (GM), 9, 15, 26, 29, 64, 222, 234, 238, 244; Southern strategy, 226–27. *See also under* branch plants; Saturn
General Services Administration, 262
geography, 134, 139–40, 196, 291, 292–94
George, Senator Walter, 10, 11, 28, 36, 39
Georgetown, Ky., 232

Georgia Institute of Technology, 6, 30, 35, 47
Georgia Power Co., 9–10, 23 (n. 51), 91
Georgia Rug Mills, 84
GI Bill, 72
Glenn L. Martin Co., 8, 26, 29
globalization, xi, 221, 240
Grady, Henry, 81, 169
Graniteville, S.C., 128, 131
Grantham, Dewey, 24
Gray, James R., 222
Great Depression, 3, 8, 84, 96, 116, 118, 138, 168, 187
Great Migration, x, 4, 48
Greeley, William B., 187
Greenville, Miss., 86
Greenville, S.C, 114, 118, 124, 129, 132, 137, 225, 238

Hall, R. Clifford, 184
Hamilton, R. E., 103
Hardtner, Henry, 186
Harrigan, Lt. Com. D. Ward, 10, 11
Harris County (Tex.) Health Department, 159
Hartsfield, William B., 5
Haughton, Dan, 16, 36
Hays, Samuel, 147
Henderson, Jacob, 62, 65, 66
Herod, Henrietta, 56–57,
Herring, Harriet, 114, 116, 117
Higginbotham, Evelyn Brooks, 54
highways, 15, 30, 124; Dixie Highway, 6–7
Hills, James, 35
Hirschman, Albert O., x
Hobsbawm, Eric, 95
Holt, Donald S., 133
home ownership, 117–18, 129
Honda, 220, 228, 235, 242–43
Hopkins, Harry, 4
Houston, Tex., 261
Humble Oil Co., 158, 159
Huntsville, Ala., 225, 242, 260

International Association of Machinists, 50
International Paper Corp., 199
Ishihara, Takashi, 228

Jackson, Maynard, 74
Jackson, Tenn., 133, 221, 222
James Lees and Sons, 99
Janiewski, Dolores, 115
Jay, Herbert, 94
Jefferson Chemical Corp., 159
Jim Crow, 43, 47, 48, 49, 52, 53, 57, 58, 61, 66, 137, 296
Joanna Mills, 126
Johnson, Lyndon B., 36
Jones, Jesse, 4, 272
J. P. Stevens Co., 119
Judson Mill, 129

Kansas City, Mo., 27, 37
Kanter, Rosabeth Moss, 240
Kaufman, Clemens, 197
Kelley, Robin, 52
Kennedy, John F., 36
Kim, Choong Soon, 235
King, Martin Luther, Sr., 71
Korean War, xii, 16, 25, 33, 83, 292
Krugman, Paul, 108, 293
Ku Klux Klan, 5

labor markets, xi, 27–28, 49, 100–101, 288, 298; family system, 118–19
labor turnover, 122
labor unions, 31, 45, 49, 86, 228–29, 230; organizing, 50, 100–105, 120, 224. *See also entries for specific unions*
LeCraw, Roy, 11, 28, 40 (n. 17)
Leopold, Aldo, 194
Light, Frances, 31–32
Lindbergh, Charles, 25, 168
Lockheed Aircraft Co., xi, 16, 24–25, 292; Georgia Division, 33–38
Los Angeles, Calif., 266, 278
Louisville, Ky., 225

Love, Spencer, 82, 116
Lowenstein and Sons, M., 130

Macon, Ga., 127, 181
management, factory, 13–14, 29–30, 32, 33, 61–63, 103, 129, 220, 233; scientific, 116
management, forest, 171–72
Mankin, Helen, 70
Manufacturing Chemists' Association, 158
manufacturing practices, 31, 83, 110 (n. 15)
Marathon Motor Works, 221–22
Marietta, Ga., xii, 2, 11, 16, 35
Markusen, Ann, 24, 38, 235
Marshall, George C., 7
Marx, Karl, 140
Mazda, 224–25
McCarty, Frank, 92, 93
McGill, Ralph, 12
McMillan, George H., 6, 7, 11, 12, 28
McNamara, Robert, 37
McSweeny-McNary Forest Research Act, 176
Memphis, Tenn., 223, 261
Mercedes-Benz, 81, 234, 242
migration, x, xi, 39, 45, 55, 67
military bases, 257, 264, 269, 272, 297
mill villages, textile, xii, 30, 114–40 *passim*, 288; and African Americans, 131–33; house sales in, 125–126, 127, 143 (n. 30); schools in, 136–37
Minchin, Timothy, 105, 115, 124
Mitchell, Broadus, 121
M. Lowenstein and Sons, 130
Mobile, Ala., 64, 260
Mohasco, 94
Mollenkopf, John, 256
Monsanto Corp., 157
mortgages, 115, 124, 139

Nashville, Tenn., 219, 221, 222, 223, 240, 245 (n. 13)

National Aeronautics and Space Administration (NASA), 258, 262, 264, 265, 274
National Association for the Advancement of Colored People (NAACP), 43, 71
National Defense Advisory Commission, 26
National Institutes of Health (NIH), 258, 262, 264, 265
National Labor Relations Board, 102
National Urban League, 63, 64
National Recovery Administration, 119, 187
National Youth Administration, 5, 30
Navistar International, 242
Nelson, Bruce, 47
New Deal, ix, x, 2, 15–16, 24, 38, 46, 119, 171–72, 188, 190, 299
Nissan, 219, 220, 228–29, 232, 238, 239, 240, 241, 249 (n. 53), 250 (n. 55)
Nixon, Richard, 17
Norfolk, Va., 260
North Carolina State University, 197–99
Northcutt, Guy, 11
Norton, Donald, 15
nuclear weapons, 265, 273; Manhattan Project, 26
nylon, 92, 97–100

O'Connor, William J., 9, 11
O'Daniel, Lee, 150
Oklahoma City, Okla., 226, 227
Olson, Mancur, 289, 292
Opelika, Ala., 115
Open Housing Bill, 132–33

Pacific Mills, 115, 125
Painter, Mose, 88
papermaking industry, 168–71, 204 (n. 8), 296
Parrott, V. D., 90–91
paternalism, 48, 50, 61, 74, 114, 115–16, 118
Pauley, Scott S., 193, 195
Pepperell Corp., 115

petrochemical industry, ix, xii, 146–62 *passim*; production in Texas, 149–50
petroleum refining, Gulf Coast, 150–51, 261–62, 266, 271
Pinchot, Gifford, 174, 176, 178, 187, 212 (n. 92)
place, sense of, 134–37, 140
plants, branch. *See* branch plants
politics, national/congressional, x, 36, 188–89, 224, 256–57, 289; state (Georgia), 6, 70–71
pollution, industrial, 146–62 *passim*; laws relating to, 147–48; research on, 156–57. *See also* environment, industry's impact upon
Pope, Liston, 121, 131
Porsche, 238
Pratt, Joseph, 149
Preston, Howard, 221
productivity, southern industrial, 294–99
Proxmire, Sen. William, 36
public transportation, Atlanta, 52–53, 55

Quebedeaux, Walter, 160

race, 115, 288, 294. *See also* African Americans; citizenship; civil rights; Jim Crow; segregation
railroads, 1, 2; Southern Railway, 11
Rainey, Glenn, 47, 49, 51
Ramspeck, Rep. Robert, 11, 70
Rayburn, Sam, 4, 271
recession, economic, 107
Reconstruction Finance Corp., 272
regional advantage, 82, 108, 173, 292
regional political economy, 289–91
Reid, Ira DeA., 68
Renault, 241
research and development, 34, 100, 263–64, 269, 272–73, 275
retailing, 87, 135, 139; G. Fox and Co., 92, 99; John Wanamaker, 87; Marshall Field and Co., 116, 130; Sears, Roebuck and Co., 92, 95; Wal-Mart, 135

Reynolds, William, 95, 96
Rhodes, John, 108
Rhyne, Jennings J., 121
Rickenbacker, Eddie, 7, 27, 28, 30
Rickenbacker Aircraft Training School, 12–13, 30
Rickenbacker Field (Cobb County, Ga.), 7, 10, 11, 27, 40 (n. 18)
Rieve, Emil, 119
Rivers, Gov. E. D., 27
Roach, Raymond, 105
Robert and Co., 12, 28
Robinette, J. M., 121
Robinson, Augustus, 221
Rockingham, N.C., 130
Roessner, David, 24, 38
Roosevelt, Franklin D., 2, 26, 38, 188, 220
Rue, John D., 200, 201
Runyon, Marvin D., 228
Russell, Sen. Richard, 11, 36, 39

San Antonio, Tex., 264
Sargent, Charles, 174
Saturn, 219, 220, 230, 232, 236, 238, 241
Savannah, Ga., 34, 169
Saxenian, Annalee, 108
Schulman, Bruce, 1, 24
Scott, C. A., 62
Scott, James, 172, 205 (n. 18)
Scranton, Philip, 82–83, 96
Scripto, Inc., 16, 32
segregation, 1, 13, 27, 36–37, 45, 131–33, 137, 296; and job opportunities, 47–48, 49, 66, 79 (n. 49), 297. *See also* Jim Crow
Shaw, Frank, 27–28
Shaw, J. C., 89
Shaw, Robert, 89
shipbuilding, 148, 149, 260, 262, 266
Shreveport, La., 226, 227
Silcox, F. A., 188
Silicon Valley, 109, 293
Smith, Joel, 66
Smyrna, Tenn., 228, 229, 231, 238, 241

Society of American Foresters, 174, 212 (n. 92)
sociology, 255
Soil Bank Act, 191–93
Southern Conference on Human Welfare, 43
Southern Fire Lab, 181
Southern Forest Disease and Insect Research Council, 182
Southern Forest Experiment Station, 176, 180, 210 (n. 72)
Southern Forest Tree Improvement Committee, 195–96, 292
Southern Forestry Congress, 186
Southern Homestead Act, 174
Southern Institute of Forest Genetics, 199
Southern Natural Gas Co., 91
Southern Pine Association, 186, 203 (n. 5)
Southern Pulpwood Conservation Association, 190, 292
Southern Technical Institute, 35
Spartanburg, S.C., 114, 122, 225, 234, 238, 242
Spelman College, 56
Spring Hill, Tenn., 230, 238, 242
Stanford University, 292
Star Finishing, 89–90
Stevens, Benjamin, 273
Storper, Michael, 235
subcontracting, 9, 37, 39
Sunmonu, Kola K., 233, 235
Swaity, Paul, 102

Taft-Hartley Act, 224, 228
Tall Timbers Research Station, 181
Talmadge, Gov. Eugene, 2, 16, 17, 27
Tarver, Rep. Malcolm, 11, 28
taxes, timberland, 175, 183–85, 210 (n. 72, 80)
technological change, 82, 87–89, 96, 98–99, 173, 190, 257–58, 291, 293
Tennessee Automobile Manufacturers Association, 231

Texas A&M University, 157, 197
Texas Department of Health, 155
Texas Game, Fish and Oyster Commission, 146, 147, 152, 153, 155–57, 159, 161
Texas Industrial Commission, 150
Texas Water Pollution Advisory Council, 147
Textile Girls Baseball League, 136
textile industry, x, 81–108 *passim*, 239, 298–99; chenille bedspread industry, 31, 87; post–World War II changes, 120–21. *See also entries for specific mills*
Textile Workers Union of America (TWUA), 86, 101–5, 120, 130
Towers, Adm. John H., 11
Toyota, 220, 232, 235, 236, 241
Truitt, Herman Newton, 135
Tufted Textile Manufacturers Association (TTMA), 100–105
Tulsa, Okla., 27, 37, 226
Tuscaloosa, Ala., 226, 234, 242

unemployment, 107, 237
Union Bag and Paper Corp., 168, 169, 171, 189
Union Carbide, 158
Union Camp, 199
unions. *See* labor unions
United Auto Workers (UAW), 29, 64, 226, 228, 229, 230, 232, 242
United Merchants and Manufacturers Corp., 128
U.S. Air Force, 25
U.S. Army Air Corps, 9, 25
U.S. Army Corps of Engineers, 4, 11, 26, 29
U.S. Bureau of Labor Statistics, 117
U.S. Census of Population, 256, 275
U.S. Chambers of Commerce, 232
U.S. Department of Defense, 37, 293, 296
U.S. Department of Energy, 37, 258, 262, 264, 273
U.S. Department of Justice, 133

U.S. Department of War, 7, 11, 26, 52
U.S. Employment Service, 62, 63, 64, 65
U.S. Federal Reserve Board, 183
U.S. Forest Service, 175, 180, 181, 195, 199, 292
U.S. Public Health Service, 154, 157
U.S. Supreme Court, 70, 132
University of Florida, 197
University of Michigan, 229
University of North Carolina, 93
University of Washington, 292

Vance, Rupert, 183, 220
Veterans Administration, 133
Vinson, Rep. Carl, 11, 36, 39
Volkswagen, 227
Voting Rights Act, 299

wages: Atlanta-area, 9; in carpet industry, 97, 102, 105–6; in textile industry, 119, 123–24, 130
Wagner Act, 224
Wakely, Philip, 196
Walker, Richard, 235
Wallace, Henry, 22 (n. 48), 185
War Labor Board, 50
War Manpower Commission, 47, 62, 63
Washington, Forrester B., 46, 54
Washington High School. *See* Booker T. Washington High School
water supplies, 90–91, 107
Watts, Lyle, 180

Weeks Act, 179, 186
West, Don, 101
Weyerhauser Corp., 199
White, Milton, 66
Whitener, Katherine Evans, 87, 108
Whiting, Margaret, 56
Wichita, Kans., 37, 39, 226
Wilkerson, William H., 84, 85
Wilmington, Del., 230, 242
Wilson, Mack, 3
Wiscassett Mills, 129
Wolfe, Gen. Kenneth, 36
Woodson, Omer L., 13, 32
Woodward, C. Vann, 47
worker housing, 29–30, 117. *See also* mill villages, textile
workers: African American, 31, 43; —, and racial conflicts, 51–54, 68; automobile, 236–38, 241; domestic, 47, 49, 72, 73; handicapped, 13, 31; laundry, 50–51; women, 31–32
worker training, xi, 9, 12–13, 30, 34–35, 39, 62–66, 295
Works Progress Administration, 4, 5
Wright, Annette C., 82
Wright, Gavin, 122, 172
Wynne, Edward, 102

Yanarella, Ernest J., 236

Zobel, Bruce, 197–98, 215 (n. 120), 217 (n. 146)

www.ingramcontent.com/pod-product-compliance
Lightning Source LLC
Chambersburg PA
CBHW011753220426
43672CB00017B/2943